RESTORATION STUDIES V

RESTORATION STUDIES V

A Collection of Essays about the
History, Beliefs, and Practices
of the
Reorganized Church of Jesus Christ of
Latter Day Saints

Paul M. Edwards
Series Editor

Darlene Caswell
Editor

Graduate School of Religion
Park College

Herald Publishing House
Independence, Missouri

Copyright © 1993
Herald Publishing House
Independence, Missouri

Library of Congress Cataloging-in-Publication Data
(Revised for vol. 5)

Restoration Studies.

   Vol. 3: Debra Combs, assistant editor.
   Vol. 4: Marjorie B. Troeh, editor; Eileen M. Terril, assistant editor.
   Vol. 5: Darlene Caswell, editor.
   Includes bibliographies.
   1. Reorganized Church of Jesus Christ of Latter Day Saints. 2. Mormon Church.
I. Draper, Maurice L. II. Lindgren, A. Bruce. III. Combs, Debra, 1952–
BX8674.R46   1983   289.3'33   83–23375
ISBN 0-8309-0650-9

Printed in the United States of America

96 95 94 93   1 2 3 4   12–0561–7

Board of Editorial Advisers

Articles included in this fifth volume of *Restoration Studies* cover a wide range of subject matter and viewpoints. They are commended to the reader to encourage exploration and dialogue on subjects of interest to members of the Reorganized Church of Jesus Christ of Latter Day Saints. They come from both members and friends of the church who are living in several countries. Members of the Board of Editorial Advisers are especially thanked for their review and comments on numerous manuscripts that were circulated anonymously. Just as the Board of Editorial Advisers found their evaluation of articles were different, readers will both agree and disagree with authors' viewpoints. Hopefully, these articles will challenge thinking, encourage further research, and stimulate dialogue on issues that concern our faith.

Darlene Caswell, editor
February 1993

Contents

I
THE PURSUIT OF PEACE

II
THEOLOGICAL PERSPECTIVES

III
IDENTITY AND MISSION

IV
SCRIPTURE STUDIES

V
BIOGRAPHICAL REFLECTIONS

Preface

Education and religion share a common experience in that believers need to constantly confront the growing edge of their understanding. For religious conversion is not a one-time event and, like being educationally contemporary, requires constant participation and study and, as well, occasional risk. With the publication of this fifth volume of *Restoration Studies*, concerned readers are called to look more deeply, understand more broadly, and invest more personally in their participation with, and in, the Reorganized Church of Jesus Christ of Latter Day Saints.

This volume's editor, Darlene Caswell and the Board of Editorial Advisers, as well as the Temple School Center staff—Charlotte Faris, Joni Wilson, and Ruth Ann Wood—have done an excellent job in bringing together a great variety of essays. Many of these are on widely diverse subjects, a good number by authors new to *Restoration Studies*, and all worthy of your time and effort.

The essays in this volume stand on their own merit, representing the views of the authors, and are presented for the purpose of exchange among those interested in the Restoration community. There is no intention, implied or otherwise, to suggest the ideas expressed here represent an official position of the Reorganized Church of Jesus Christ of Latter Day Saints.

So deep is our belief in the need for a volume of scholarly dialogue that even as this volume goes to press we are in the process of collecting materials for *Restoration Studies VI*. Interested authors should contact the Temple School Center if they have manuscripts for consideration.

This fifth volume of *Restoration Studies* is published by Herald House in conjunction with the Graduate School of Religion at Park College. We hope you find the collection interesting and insightful.

Paul M. Edwards, dean
Graduate School of Religion
Park College

I
Pursuit of Peace

I

THE PURSUIT OF PEACE

Editor's Note

With the Temple focus on the pursuit of peace and the dedicatory events of 1993, few topics have been researched, studied, conceptualized, and programmed into action as much as that of peace. Most studies reveal its multifaceted nature and reliance on the righteousness that comes from God as the foundation.

Andrew Bolton explores one of the major peace movements: Anabaptism. He gives a historical summary with a review of its place in Christianity, draws parallels with the Restoration movement, and suggests that there might be benefits from dialogue between the two groups. In a violent world with economic and social injustices, might there be strength in sharing among those who hold a common dream?

To build the kingdom of God on earth has been the motivation of many groups of people with vastly differing results. This desire was part of the dream that gathered the early Saints to Missouri. What follows is a sad chapter in the story of the Restoration. Ron Romig and John Siebert deal with some of the actions of the Saints when they felt other resources were exhausted and how the Reorganization reacted to this chapter of history. What is there to be learned from this experience that informs today's commitment to the pursuit of peace?

Rick Sarre, from an international perspective, suggests that there needs to be more research on the links between violence and religion—especially the violence perpetrated by religious groups in the furtherance of their own ends. He makes suggestions for those who seek to mediate such violence. Rather than treating violent episodes as being politically motivated, there needs to be a dialogue between the religious faiths, the communities of which they form a part, and the governmental agencies that seek to control the disorder.

Learning from Anabaptism:
A Major Peace Tradition
Andrew Bolton

Introduction

Since 1984 the peace mission of the Reorganized Church of Jesus Christ of Latter Day Saints has begun to be more clearly focused through the temple project in Independence, Missouri.[1] The building of the kingdom of God on earth, Zion, had been the clear call to people like Oliver Cowdery, Hyrum Smith, and others a year or more before the church was officially organized on April 6, 1830.[2] Zion in the Book of Mormon, published in 1830, is inseparably linked with peace.[3] The church seal of the Reorganization has visually kept peace before us in the Isaiah 11 depiction of a lion lying down with a lamb and a little child leading them. The call to build a temple "dedicated to the pursuit of peace"[4] some would argue is simply a heightening of our traditional peace concern.

Reorganized Latter Day Saints have also taken seriously the task of being open to learn from others. This openness is mandated in the earliest years of our movement: "...obtain a knowledge of history, and of countries, and of kingdoms, of laws of God and man, and all this for the salvation of Zion."[5] We have been willing to learn in recent years from Christian scholars, particularly Protestant. I personally have benefited from this. However, I want to suggest in this paper that exploring historical and contemporary Anabaptism would be particularly fruitful and enriching. As a Christ-centered, historic peace movement more than 450 years old with a very strong tradition of economic sharing, we have much to learn from it.

In this paper I want to give a historical summary of Anabaptism, review its place in Christianity, look at some parallels with Latter Day Saintism, review the cause of these parallels, and then conclude with some assessment of the benefits to be gained from dialoguing with Anabaptism.

A Historical Summary[6]

The Protestant movement began in 1517 when Martin Luther fastened to the door of the Wittenberg Castle church in Germany his objections to the abuses of the medieval church. Other centers of "protest" began elsewhere, including Zurich in Switzerland. Here the Reformation, beginning in 1522, was led by Huldreich Zwingli. In one of Zwingli's Bible study groups were a number of people who left eventually to begin the *Anabaptist* movement. This Anabaptist movement was led in these early days in Switzerland by Conrad Grebel, George Blaurock, and others. These Anabaptists were more radical and "left wing" than either Luther or Zwingli.

The Anabaptists believed along with other reformers that the medieval church was fallen from the original teachings of Jesus. The Anabaptists went further than other Reformers in:

- abandoning infant baptism. They believed only baptizing adults—hence Anabaptist, which means second baptism;
- being a gathered church, a voluntary brotherhood of committed believers rather than a parish church which included everybody living there, many of

whom would be Christian in name only; the Anabaptists were committed to a disciplined life, centering in Jesus and especially his teachings in the Sermon on the Mount (Matthew, chapters 5–7);

- attempting to restore the true nature of the church along New Testament lines;
- stressing equality, which was expressed by believing everyone was a priest ("priesthood of all believers") and in economic sharing and mutual help; and
- refusing to fight in war or participate in use of the courts. They were thus pacifists who would have nothing to do with violence or force. Law and government were necessary for unbelievers in the world, but the Anabaptists lived by a higher voluntary ethic. They would abide by the law insomuch as it did not conflict with the law of Christ. They believed in the separation of church from state and believed that a particular church being enforced on everyone by the law was wrong.

The Anabaptists thus appeared to be very different from both Catholics and Protestants. The degree of difference will be explored further in the next section. It is sufficient to say here that Anabaptists were cruelly and violently persecuted, first by Protestants and then by Catholics.

Present-day Anabaptists can be traced to three distinctive streams. Another stream, the revolutionary Münster Anabaptists, more Old Testament than New Testament, were brutally wiped out in 1535.

These Anabaptistic streams from the sixteenth century are as follows:

1. **The Swiss Brethren** from Switzerland and South Germany began the Anabaptist movement in 1525 when the first adult baptism was done. George Blaurock made a profession of faith and was baptized by Conrad Grebel.

2. **The Hutterites**, the communal Anabaptist group, began in South Germany and Austria. This group, also pacifists, began in 1529 and was shaped into an effective and continuing movement by Jacob Hutter in 1533–1535. His leadership only lasted two years, then he was captured and in 1536 was cruelly tortured and martyred. Yet in those two years of leadership Jacob Hutter enabled solid foundations for pacifist community living to be established that have endured for more than 450 years. The Hutterites are perhaps the most successful community group in European and North American history. A new Hutterite movement began in Germany after World War I under the leadership of Eberhard Arnold. Expelled from Nazi Germany in 1937, it now has communities in England, the eastern United States, and recently has returned to Germany and made a beginning in Nigeria and Japan.

Another communal Anabaptist group was the very different Anabaptists at Münster, in Germany.

3. **The Münster Anabaptists**. At the end of 1533 an Anabaptist group at Münster in Westphalia, Germany, under the leadership of Bernard Rothmann, took control of the city council. Early in 1534 a Dutch prophet and former innkeeper called John of Leyden appeared in Münster believing he was called to make the city the new Jerusalem. His group seized the city hall. By March 2 all who refused to be baptized were banished and Münster was proclaimed a city of refuge for the oppressed.

The Catholic Bishop of Münster collected an army and began a siege of the city. An attempted coup within the city was brutally suppressed by the Anabaptists. In August, John of Leyden was proclaimed "King of New Zion." Laws were decreed to establish community of goods, and polygamy also began to be practiced. In June 1535 the Münster Anabaptists were betrayed by some men within the city opening the gates to let the bishop's army enter. The Anabaptists there were brutally executed.

Münster Anabaptists, although believing in common property, were Old Testament rather than New Testament, believing in armed violence, polygamy, and a crowned king. The pattern was more King David than Jesus. The Münster Anabaptists caused persecution to increase against the pacifist Anabaptists who were thought to be as dangerous as the Münster ones. The persecution was to last for more than a hundred years.

4. *The Mennonites*. This group of pacifist Anabaptists was led by Menno Simons in northern Germany and Holland after the events of Münster. Today the Swiss Brethren are also called Mennonites. This group believed in mutual help and economic sharing but do not live communally. It is reported that,

Direct descendants of Anabaptists today number 730,000 in 57 countries, with the largest numbers in North America, Zaire, Indonesia, and the USSR. Over half live in third world countries. There are *21 distinct groups, among them Mennonites, Amish, Hutterites, Mennonite Brethren, and Brethren in Christ*.[7]

A Comparison of Catholicism, Protestantism, and Anabaptism

Was early Anabaptism (up until 1561) essentially Roman Catholic, Protestant, or a distinctive third alternative?

Davis[8] sees the origins of Anabaptism in the *Devotio Moderna* as an expression of Erasmian and Catholic ascetic influences. However, Davis admits there are no direct institutional links and only tenuous literary links. However, Snyder[9] appears to argue successfully for the intellectual taproot of Swiss Anabaptism lying firmly in Benedictine monasticism.

Williams[10] places general Anabaptism with revolutionary Anabaptism as part of the left wing or radical reformation. Bender and Blanke also agree and say:

Anabaptism is the culmination of the Reformation, the fulfillment of the original vision of Luther and Zwingli, and thus makes it a consistent evangelical Protestantism seeking to recreate without compromise the original New Testament church, the vision of Christ and the Apostles.[11]

Anabaptism sprang from the soil of the Reformation; it is a child, though an unsubmissive child, of the Reformation. The first congregations are found where the Reformation had already begun.[12]

Other scholars argue that Anabaptism occupies a place on its own, distinct from both Catholicism and Lutheran or Calvinistic Protestantism. I find these arguments quite persuasive and their evidence quite revealing; I have made a summary of these arguments in a longer paper.[13] It has been said that the Anabaptists were as different as oil from water as Zwingli's own testimony indicates: "They went out from us, but they were not of us."[14] Emphasizing the distinctiveness of Anabaptism, Walter Klaassen has written a book with the title *Anabaptism: Neither Catholic nor Protestant*.[15] The Latter Day Saint movement has also made the claim that it is neither Catholic nor Protestant. Are there any other parallels between Anabaptism and Latter Day Saintism?

Parallels between Anabaptism and Latter Day Saintism?

There are some interesting parallels between Anabaptism in the sixteenth century and Latter Day Saintism in the nineteenth century even though there are 300 years of history and the Atlantic Ocean lying between the two.

Both are restitution or restoration movements, aiming to restore the New Testament Church in spirit and practice; both claimed that reform was not enough. The Latter Day Saints called their movement just that in order to identify with the early, "Former Day" New Testament Saints. Anabaptism generally looked for restoration authority in the Bible, although some looked beyond the

Bible to the authority of the Holy Spirit. Latter Day Saintism began with the Bible, but more important was revelation from the Holy Spirit through Joseph Smith, Jr.

For most Anabaptists the canon is within the four Gospels and within them the Sermon on the Mount. In the climax of the Book of Mormon, Jesus is described teaching the Sermon on the Mount in an almost identical form to Matthew, chapters 5–7. Nevertheless, the characteristic emphasis of Latter Day Saintism has tended to be Old Testament in some respects, violence being a notable example. However, Rothman's restitutionism [restorationism] in Münster, as Williams[16] points out, was also distinctly Old Testament.

In fact, one of the closest historical parallels between Latter Day Saintism and Anabaptism lies with the events in Zion or the New Jerusalem at Münster, Westphalia (1534–1535), and Nauvoo, Illinois (1839–1844). Persecution combined with apocalypticism and charismatic leadership that became, in both Smith and John of Leyden, increasingly authoritarian. In the siege mentality that resulted, we see in both Nauvoo and Münster the development of Old Testament kingship, polygamy, and "holy" violence ending in defeat.

In the wreckage following Münster and Nauvoo, the pastoral ministries of Menno Simons returning to New Testament restorationism are paralleled by Joseph Smith III in the Reorganization. The extension of Nauvoo Mormonism through Brigham Young to Utah has no Münster parallel; if there had been a wilderness to escape to, there was no mercy (or divine provision) in the sixteenth century to permit such an exodus.

Baptism as an adult commitment to Christ is foundational in both movements and was an essential act of returning to early Christianity. Although in Latter Day Saintism it had been baptism by immersion (instead of pouring), the seriousness of the commitment and the psychological and spiritual impact of the act was just as dramatic in both movements. In both cases it was a commitment not only to Christ, but just as importantly a commitment to brothers and sisters in the fellowship of the church. In both movements salvation is seen as more social than individual.

Friedman's[17] description of Anabaptist theology matches remarkably with many aspects of early Latter Day Saint theology as well as Reorganization theology. For both movements it was an implicit theology, what Friedman calls existential and realized Christianity, where Christ is genuinely encountered directly. Theology for both movements especially emphasizes the kingdom of God, where there is no basic split between faith and life—all of life is sacred. There is a distinct theology of holiness enabled by the close community support and often disciplined rigorously by the ban in Anabaptism and excommunication in early Latter Day Saintism.

Both movements were critical of forensic justification by faith.[18] That was not enough. Both stressed that through grace salvation is realized by a balance of faith and works. Both movements argued strongly that grace from Christ's atonement was unlimited and available for all, especially little children. There is a strong belief in human perfectionism in both movements linked with a common theology of holiness.[19] Both movements had strong impulses to "baptize economics" and bring money, production, and consumption of goods under the Lordship of Christ. Early Latter Day Saintism attempted to be communitarian as the Hutterites did, although the Hutterites were much more successful. The success of the Hutterites is something this paper will return to.

Both Latter Day Saintism and early Anabaptism were international missionary movements and yet insisted on withdrawing from the world to create an alternative society reflecting the kingdom of God. Both were persecuted violently by other Christians, in part because of their fearless missionary testimony and subversive separation from the world. Both the Reorganization and later, Anabaptism, in response to a hostile world, became quiet and subdued in the land. Utah Mormonism has, in comparison, remained an aggressive missionary movement.

Both movements were lay movements hostile to any idea of a professional clergy; however, the Latter Day Saint movement tended to be more authoritarian and hierarchical.

Here, in summary, are some impressive parallels between early Latter Saintism and Anabaptism. The closest parallel is between Latter Day Saintism and the Revolutionary Münster Anabaptists, rather than with the New Testament-based, Sermon on the Mount-inspired, evangelical Anabaptists. The Reorganization, whilst showing some tendencies to more nearly correspond to evangelical Anabaptism, is still "Nauvoo-ish" in its highly centralized and hierarchical organization. Furthermore, whilst "peace" is in the logo, the Reorganization has dutifully supported its young men to come to the aid of their country in all the major wars of this century. Its theology, like the Book of Mormon's and the Old Testament, is predominantly "just war" rather than pacificist. However, as the Reorganization begins to think more about peace, it's possible our "just war" beliefs will change. Dialogue with Anabaptism may help us become more clear and self-critical about our position.

Why the parallels between Anabaptism and Latter Day Saintism?

At this point, having described some of the significant parallels and differences between Latter Day Saintism and Anabaptism, I want to ask what is the explanation, if any, for them?

There is, first, the simple faith answer that suggests that God is attempting with various degrees of success to work with responding humans to bring to pass the kingdom. I personally believe this and believe that what God has been doing among the Anabaptism movement, and especially the Hutterites, is something we should hear and be helped by as Latter Day Saints.

Second, I want to explore the possibility of a historical connection between the two movements. However, when one reads a history of American Christianity like Ahlstrom's,[20] it is apparent that there is little or no genetic link between the Baptist movements in America and Anabaptism. Much less likely, therefore, is any descent or connection between sixteenth-century Anabaptism and nineteenth-century Mormonism.

So what then is the explanation of Latter Day Saint and Anabaptist parallels? Junke[21] suggests that while there are distinct differences between sixteenth-century Europe and nineteenth-century America, both were marked by major social upheaval and religious revival. In other words, both were ages and religious cultures in periods of major transition. Anabaptism arose on the left wing of Protestantism; America was soaked in Puritanism more thoroughly almost than any European country. Whilst there is no link with original Anabaptism, it is not surprising to find "Anabaptist themes," especially restorationism, thrown up time and time again during 200 years of American religious history. In nineteenth-century America when separation of church and state was an accomplished fact, when restorationism was a major religious issue as in the Campbellites (and from whom came a number of early Latter Day Saints, including the communitarian-minded Sidney Rigdon), it is not perhaps surprising that a charismatic young man like Joseph Smith, Jr., with a New England Puritan heritage, should catch up, rework, and bring together a latter-day American Anabaptist movement. However, Puritanism had a "just war" or "just revolution" Old Testament theology that gave holy sanction to violence. Hence it is no surprise that the Mormon latter-day Anabaptism was more like Münster Anabaptism than the New Testament evangelical Anabaptism with its emphasis on the Sermon on the Mount.

Paul M. Edwards[22] among others suggests that the parallel between Anabaptism and Latter Day Saintism is that both were mystical antinominalist responses to their day. Mormonism in its early days was specifically a response against the materialism and individualism of Jacksonian democracy and a return to the values of social solidarity of Puritan New England.

It appears the parallels between the two movements may possibly be explained by a similar mode of response by earnest religious people to an age of rapid change. That is to say earnest devout people, on the left wing of Protestantism with a Restoration vision, were responding to an anomie experience in ages of major transition by recapturing community in the company of the committed.

In our own time, with many rapid changes, we perhaps all face anomie. Is it time to renew the quest of restoration by dialoguing with others who have attempted this also?

Benefits from dialoguing with Anabaptism

It is quite amazing to me that we have been willing to dialogue with mainline Protestantism and yet have almost ignored dialogue with the Anabaptist tradition. Perhaps part of the reason is geographical. The concentration of Mennonites in North America is not where RLDS have perceived a call to gather. Goshen College in Indiana is some distance from Graceland College, Iowa. In comparison, Saint Paul School of Theology or Park College are just down the road from the RLDS Church's headquarters in Independence, Missouri. Another reason, perhaps, is that Anabaptists were not respectable like Barth, Niebuhr, Bonhoeffer, and Tillich. Trends to denominationalize the RLDS Church from an originally disreputable, if not radical, sect has seen us perhaps look more for the respectable than for the radically faithful.

There are two groups of contemporary Anabaptists with whom we can begin dialoguing. The first are the Mennonites who, like us, are a congregation-oriented church. They have their own colleges and an increasing number of serious scholars for us to read and meet. John Howard Yoder, working in a number of ecumenical contexts, is perhaps one of the most notable, but there are a number of significant others. The second group are the communal Anabaptists, the Hutterites. Among the Hutterites the group sometimes called the New Hutterites are of particular interest. They began in 1920 in the aftermath of World War I under the leadership of Eberhard Arnold in Germany. They are much more active in relating with others outside their communities and run their own publishing house and have a magazine called *The Plough*.[23]

What are the potential gains from dialoguing with the Anabaptists?

1. *Taking the principle of Restoration seriously*. The Anabaptist movement and the Latter Day Saint movement believe in restoration, not simply reformation. Restoration is more radical and thorough than reformation. It is an attempt to return to the old Jerusalem gospel and at the same time encounter the contemporary Je-

sus. This is the theme in Joseph Smith's first vision: "This is my beloved Son, hear him," not hear the accumulated doctrines of men.[24] It is the theme of every Communion service when we promise "to take upon [us] the name of [Jesus], and always remember him and keep his commandments."[25] Anabaptists see Jesus and his teaching as normative for discipleship in a way that we would understand and yet which Catholics and mainline Protestants do not.[26] How much Jesus is seen as normative determines not only our faithfulness but whether cultures subvert the gospel or the gospel transforms cultures. This is true particularly in relationship to attitudes to violence and property.

It has become unfashionable to talk about the apostasy, partly because of the way we did it. However, contemporary Anabaptist scholars continue to take apostasy, including the Constantinian shift in the fourth century, very seriously. As Yoder, for instance shows, it has serious implications for a peace theology.[27] If we want to continue to be serious about being a restoration church, especially if we are interested in peace, we need also to return to asking what the apostasy means. Anabaptists, ancient and modern, can help us return to taking apostasy seriously and perhaps more responsibly and fruitfully than in the past.

2. **The nature of the church and discipleship**. Anabaptism is not only Christ-centered, it is also church-centered. We RLDS understand that, although recently we have become self-critical of being so church-centered and have attempted to become more Christ-centered. We can be helped here, I think, by the clearer vision of Anabaptists. To be the true church for Anabaptists is to follow Jesus *and* to be committed to other disciples. It is not Jesus or the church, it is both. This commitment includes church discipline. Yoder, for instance, points out that "binding and loosing" in the context of discipline are the only places in the Gospels where Jesus uses the word *church*.[28] For us, the true church may have become a superficial understanding of faith, repentance, and baptisms and having a restored structure of apostles, prophets, etc., rather than living a transformed life together as Jesus' disciples. We have also become more permissive of a lower standard of discipleship among the membership of the church in perhaps the mistaken belief that we are more aware of the importance of grace. This is not always how we have seen it. For instance, Elbert A. Smith said:

...you are admonished that you be not unduly concerned because you are few in number as compared with the world. That is not your concern, but be concerned only that your righteousness shall be very great. For a few righteous men can accomplish very much, and a little leaven leaveneth a great lump.[29]

Perhaps Anabaptism can help us catch again in practice the gracious reconciling intent of church discipline.

3. **Creating a canon of scripture within the canon**. Because Jesus is normative for Anabaptists in all aspects of life, the Gospels and the life of the early Christian Church assume more importance than the Old Testament. In particular, the Sermon on the Mount becomes central. So what Jesus says about loving enemies is of greater authority than what Moses, Joshua, and David said about smiting them. When Jesus tells Peter to put away the sword at his arrest, he thereby disarms every would-be disciple after him. Instead of taking up the sword and inflicting suffering, the admonition is to take up the cross of persecution and endure suffering with Christ.

If we are to be serious as a peace church, do we need to do the same? We have ignored the significance of the passage in the Book of Mormon in which Jesus is portrayed giving the Sermon on the Mount, which is a higher view of conflict resolution than the "just war" theory justified elsewhere in the Book of Mormon,[30] as well as by Joseph Smith in the early years of our church.[31]

If the Anabaptist movement is serious about nonresistance with just the Matthew account of the Sermon on the Mount, how much more serious should we be because we have Jesus repeating the Sermon on the Mount in the III Nephi account? At this point some readers may be thinking that I have a naive view of the historicity of the Book of Mormon. I do not want to enter into the debate here of whether the Book of Mormon is inspired history or inspired fiction/parable. Whatever its origins, it exists as part of our story and as part of our scripture. For me its authority is demonstrated by the fact that some passages in particular minister to many people, including myself. I would argue that we should take it seriously as part of our story. Stanley Hauerwas, for instance, has argued cogently in recent years for taking narrative seriously for doing Christian ethics.[32] I am also arguing we need to take our Restoration story seriously but in a new way for working out our peace ethics and theology. I am saying we need to sort out a new canon within a canon in order to highlight what is really true and faithful to the life, teaching, and crucifixion of Jesus. In particular, I am also suggesting we should let the Sermon on the Mount stand out both in the New Testament and in the Book of Mormon.

Not only is our theology of peace and war going to be affected by what we choose as a canon within the canon, but so will our theology of Zionic community.

4. *Recovering living in community*. If you ask people today in the RLDS Church what is meant by community, the answer would be it is the people, neighborhood, and institutions outside the church that we are called to help make better for everyone concerned. However, our original thrust modeled on Acts 2 and 4 is for the church to *be* the community of sharing and caring disciples living all things in common, that is living in "common-unity" as disciples of Jesus. It was to witness as a "city set on a hill" of the divine possibility for all humans.

There is a great deal of discussion as to whether the Acts 2 description of community of goods is normative for Christians. Trevor Saxby,[33] for one, argues yes it is. Luke Johnson,[34] an ex-monk, argues, for example, it is not. This debate needs to be continued and developed further for us.

We attempted in the 1830s to live out a modified form of all things common. Not only did we have the Acts Jerusalem model but also IV Nephi and the people of Enoch:

And the Lord called his people Zion, because they were of one heart and one mind, and dwelt in righteousness; and there was no poor among them....[35]

as well as other contemporary revelation.[36]

Are Acts and IV Nephi still within our present canon of canons? In theory yes, in practice no. Communitarianism did not last very long in the 1830s for us. All the various communitarian groups in North America in the nineteenth century have perished—except for one. With this track record, communitarianism looks impossibly Utopian, except for the fact that the one solitary exception is very significant. It is Anabaptist Hutterianism that goes back in its tradition for not just 100 years but for more than 450 years. Elsewhere I have written of my own encounters with the Hutterite tradition.[37] It is sufficient to say here that I believe they challenge us to look again very seriously about living in community. Further reading on their history and recent sociology is suggested in an endnote.[38]

The demonstration of the Hutterites living together in Christian community is empirical: people can verify it as possible for themselves. As Philip said to Nathanael, "Come and see."[39] The Hutterites do not talk about a Zionic way of life, they live it. They do not teach courses, they create in their life together a tangible learning experience for anyone who visits. It is not a head trip, it's a life pilgrimage—together—visible for all to see. This human need for personal verification was recognized as important by Jesus long before the twentieth-century philosophy of logical positivism made "sense evidence" the criteria for all truth.[40]

Jesus said at the beginning of the Sermon on the Mount:

You are the light of the world. A city set on a hill cannot be hid.[41]

"Cannot be hid," to me, means a public demonstration, a public verification of the kingdom in the way disciples are called to live out the gospel together. And at the end of Jesus' teachings in the Sermon on the Mount he says: "You will know them by their fruits."[42] Jesus' word is not just about ideas, it has to become flesh, fruit, lived out, making an observable difference.

And after washing the feet of his disciples at the Last Supper Jesus said:

By this all men will know that you are my disciples, if you have love for one another.[43]

The presence of God may be ambiguous in the world, but it should not be so in the life of the church. Anabaptist scholar Walter Klaassen writes:

Truth is therefore not abstract and ideological but existential in nature. It is not resident in ideas but living. It is not discovered in Paris, the chief seat of medieval Catholic learning, nor in Wittenberg, the new Lutheran seat of learning. Rather it is discovered in the footsteps of Christ in everyday life.[44]

For the RLDS, Joseph Luff said it simply in his hymn: "...And by deeds your purpose show."[45]

Anabaptists are committed, as we have been, to living out the gospel, making the word flesh, incarnation as the theologians

say. The Hutterites, particularly the New Hutterites, extend that possibility further for us. Their witness is one of both nonviolence as well as living all things in common. They challenge us to remember that just sharing and peace go together. How many conflicts are problems arising out of covetousness, out of arguments over property or territory or resources like oil? The Hebrew word for peace, *shalom*, includes the idea of justice. Peace and just sharing should not be separated. Similarly, peace focused through the Temple should not be divorced from justice issues. There is something odd about endowment funds invested for profit in capitalism. I question how nonviolent the capitalist world economy is on the poor in First, Second, and Third Worlds.[46]

So, do the New Hutterites in particular challenge us to develop "temple communities" living all things common? Could such "temple communities" of committed, volunteer Saints in different parts of the world (as well as Independence, Missouri) relate to the international RLDS Church as a branch but modeling the possibilities of communitarianism rather than congregationalism? Both communitarianism and congregationalism are present in the New Testament, in the Book of Mormon, in Anabaptism, and in early Latter Day Saint history. Do we not need both in dynamic and creative tension in the present-day RLDS Church? Are we still not called to build the peace and justice of Zion? Are not Zionic communities a step in the direction of global Zion?

Conclusion

The above is just one beginning agenda for dialogue between Anabaptism and the RLDS Church. It is important that we learn how to live in peace. It is our call to demonstrate that it is possible. Anabaptism is a tradition to help us, for it points very clearly to the Prince of Peace, Jesus, who rules not from a palace defended by tanks but from a cross.

We live in a violent world that needs our witness that peace, including economic justice, is possible. Between 1700-1987 more than 471 wars were fought. During this time at least 100 million people were killed, half of whom were civilians. Disturbingly, 90 percent have been killed in the twentieth century.[47] However, unjust economics is a quieter but more diabolically effective cause of human carnage. About 15 million children, for instance, die every year of entirely preventable diseases and malnutrition.[48] In just ten years this is 150 million children, one and a half times greater than those killed during nearly 300 years of war since 1700. This is just the first tenth of human suffering. There is more through men oppressing women, whites oppressing blacks, and so on. There is the violence of abortion also. The world's victims and those that mourn them cry out for the witness of Zion and its peace.

William Juhnke, a Mennonite professor at Graceland College, Iowa, wrote:

As a latter-day Anabaptist, I frequently ask myself: Will it ever be possible for humankind to respond from strength with nonviolent love? Just imagine for a moment: What if the Mormons—with all their visionary leadership, their positive Zion-building energy, their organizational and administrative genius, and their opportunity in a frontier haven—had responded from strength with nonviolent love? Would they have failed miserably, losing their lives and their vision? Or would they have transformed the world?[49]

Now that the RLDS Church is building the Temple in Independence dedicated to the pursuit of peace, it is time for Juhnke's challenge to be heard more widely and for us to take advantage of a second chance. The kingdom of God is still at hand. Jesus still calls us to repentance.

Notes

1. Doctrine and Covenants 156:5a.
2. Doctrine and Covenants 6:3a, 10:3a, 11:3b, 12:3a.
3. For example, I Nephi 3:187–189; IV Nephi 1:1–20.
4. Doctrine and Covenants 156:5a.
5. Doctrine and Covenants 90:12 (May 1833).
6. This historical review is taken from Owen Chadwick, *The Reformation* (Baltimore: Penguin Books, 1964) and "The Radical Reformation: The Anabaptists," *Christian History Magazine* 4, no. 1 (1985).
7. Ibid., vol. 4, no. 1 (1985): 6.
8. Kenneth R. Davis, *Anabaptism and Ascetism: A Study in Intellectual Origins* (Scottdale, Pennsylvania: Herald Press, 1974), 296.
9. Arnold Snyder, "The Monastic Origins of Swiss Anabaptist Sectarianism," *The Mennonite Quarterly Review* (January 1983): 5–26.
10. George H. Williams and Angel M. Mergal, eds., *Spiritual and Anabaptist Writers* vol. 25 *(Philadelphia: Westminister Press, 1957), the introduction.*
11. Harold S. Bender, "The Anabaptism Vision" in *The Recovery of the Anabaptist Vision* ed. Guy F. Hershberger (Scottdale, Pennsylvania: Herald Press, 1957), 36.
12. Fritz Blanke, "Anabaptism and the Reformation" in *The Recovery of the Anabaptist Vision*, ed. Guy F. Hershberger (Scottdale, Pennsylvania: Herald Press, 1957), 66.
13. Andrew Bolton, "Peace—Latter Day Saints Learning from Anabaptists" (unpublished paper, written 1989), pages 11–16; available from the author: 4, Chaucer Street, Leicester, LE2 IHD, England.
14. John Howard Yoder, cited in J. A. Oosterbaan, "The Reformation of the Reformation: Fundamentals of Anabaptist Theology," *The Mennonite Quarterly Review (July 1977): 193.*
15. Walter Klaassen, *Anabaptism: Neither Catholic nor Protestant* (Waterloo, Ontario: Conrad Press, revised edition, 1981).
16. George H. Williams, *The Radical Reformation* (Philadelphia: Westminster Press, 1962), 377.
17. Robert Friedmann, *The Theology of Anabaptism: An Interpretation* (Scottdale, Pennsylvania: Herald Press, 1973).
18. Kenneth R. Davis, 130.
19. Ibid., 129.

20. Sydney E. Ahlstrom, *A Religious History of the American People* (New Haven and London: Yale University Press, 1972).

21. William E. Juhnke, "Anabaptism and Mormonism: A Study in Comparative History," *The John Whitmer Historical Association Journal* 2 (1982): 40.

22. Paul M. Edwards, *Preface to Faith: A Philosophical Inquiry into RLDS Beliefs* (Midvale, Utah: Signature Books, 1984).

23. *The Plough* magazine and catalog can be obtained from: *The Plough*, Hutterian Brethren, Spring Valley, Rt. 2, Box 446, Farmington, PA 15437-9506, USA.

24. *The History of the Reorganized Church of Jesus Christ of Latter Day Saints,* Volume 1 (Herald House: Independence, Missouri, 1951), 9–10. (I am aware of other versions of Joseph Smith's first vision, but this one is the most familiar and part of our present story. I am aware that we have not necessarily seen the radicalness of this part of Smith's testimony.)

25. Doctrine and Covenants 17:22d (slightly edited).

26. See Walter Klaassen, chapter 3; also John H. Yoder, *The Politics of Jesus* (Grand Rapids, Michigan: Eerdmans, 1978). Klaassen is reviewing Jesus as normative on traditional Anabaptist grounds. Yoder, in an influential book, is arguing on the grounds of modern New Testament scholarship that Jesus can be normative for ethics.

27. John H. Yoder, *Christian Attitudes to War, Peace and Revolution—Companion to Bainton* (Goshen Biblical Seminary, 1983), chapter 3.

28. John H. Yoder, "Binding and Loosing," *CONCERN* 14 (FEBRUARY 1967): 14.

29. "Expression…'Evangelists of Love'" given through Brother Elbert A. Smith, Lamoni, Iowa, November 4, 1917, *Saints' Herald* 64, no. 46 (November 14, 1917): 1081.

30. For example, Alma 20:50–52; Mormon 1:76–81.

31. Doctrine and Covenants 95:5a-f.

32. Stanley Hauerwas, *The Peaceable Kingdom: A Primer in Christian Ethics* (Notre Dame, Indiana: University of Notre Dame Press, 1983), chapter 2.

33. Trevor J. Saxby, *Pilgrims of a Common Life—Christian Community of Goods through the Centuries* (Scottdale, Pennsylvania: Herald Press, 1987).

34. Luke T. Johnson, *Sharing Possessions—Mandate and Symbol of Faith* (London: SCM Press, 1986).

35. Doctrine and Covenants 36: 2h-l.

36. For example, Doctrine and Covenants 42 and the earlier version of this revelation in the *Book of Commandments.*

37. Andrew Bolton, "Peace…" and also Andrew Bolton, "The Witness of a Christian Community," *Saints Herald* 139, no. 1 (January 1992): 11–13.

38. Some further reading on the Hutterites is as follows:
a. "Old Hutterites." The Hutterites' own story is told simply and movingly from about 1525–1665 in: *The Chronicle of the Hutterian Brethren Volume 1,* edited and translated by the Hutterian Brethren (Riftin, New York: Plough, 1987); volume 2 is in preparation. An excellent overview of the beginning of Hutterianism and concentrating on their "Golden Years" (1565–1578) is given in: Leonard Gross, *The Golden Years of the Hutterites—The Witness and Thought of the Communal Moravian Anabaptists During the Walpot Era, 1565–1678* (Scottdale, Pennsylvania: Herald Press, 1980). A sociological study of modern Hutterianism in North America with a good overview of their history and beliefs is: John A. Hostetler, *Hutterite Society* (Baltimore: Johns Hopkins University Press, 1974).
b. "New Hutterites." Emmy Arnold, wife of Eberhard Arnold the first leader of the "New Hutterites," tells the story of their beginnings in a testimonial form from 1920 and before, up to their expulsion by the Gestapo from Germany in 1937 in: Emmy Arnold, *Torches Together* (Rifton, New York: Plough, 1984). A friendly outsider's view of their modern life together is given in: Ulrich Eggers, *Community for Life* (Scottdale, Pennsylvania: Herald Press, 1988). A self-critical account of their struggles is found in: Merrill Mow, *Torches Rekindled: The Bruderhof's Struggle for Renewal* (Ulster Park, New York: Plough, 1989). A critical sociological account is given by B. D. Zablocki. "New Hutterites" would argue that their movement is not fully understood or accurately portrayed by a sociological account. However, it is still a useful critical view, whilst bearing the limitations of sociology in mind: B. D. Zablocki, *The Joyful Community; An Account of the Bruderhof, A Communal Movement Now in Its Third Generation* (Baltimore: Penguin, 1971).

39. John 1:46.

40. I am not suggesting that all truth can be tested by the criteria of logical positivists. However, it seems to me that the Christian belief in incarnation suggests that the material can express the spiritual and that experience of Christian fellowship and community can for humans be a confirmation of spiritual reality. Another way of putting it more

simply is to say that the quality of our lives together can witness persuasively of Christ.

41. Matthew 5:14 RSV.
42. Matthew 7:16 RSV.
43. John 13:35 RSV.
44. Walter Klaassen, 19–20.
45. Joseph Luff, "O My People, Saith the Spirit," *Hymns of the Saints* (Independence, Missouri: Herald House, 1981), No. 387, at the end of the first verse.
46. Marx is, of course, the great critic of Victorian capitalism and its impact on the poor. Followers of Marx have been analyzing the impact of economy on the poor ever since. A less ideological approach for those not keen on Marx is to simply ask, What is the effect on children of a particular economic system? One attempt at doing this is by United Nations Children's Fund. For example, see James P. Grant, *The State of the World's Children 1985 Part 1* (New York: Oxford University Press), 18.
47. Ruth Leger Sivard, *World Military and Social Expenditures 1987–88* 12th edition (Washington, D. C.: World Priorities, 1987), 28, 31.
48. See James P. Grant, *The State of the World's Children 1982–83* (New York: UNICEF), 1.
49. William E. Juhnke, 44.

Contours of the Kingdom: An RLDS Perspective on the Legions of Zion

Ronald E. Romig and John H. Siebert

Benjamin F. Johnson retrospectively observed that during Mormonism's early years, "The Prophet Joseph laid the foundation of our Church in a *Military Spirit* and as the Master taught his disciples So he [Joseph] taught Us to 'Sell our Coats and buy Swords.'"[1] Examples of militarism in the early Restoration, such as this, tend to reinforce perceptions that the church was militant, i.e., displaying a predisposition toward violence or aggressive action. Nonetheless, it may be argued that the church was not militant but, rather, assumed a militaristic methodology in response to a succession of inimical encounters for the purpose of attaining envisioned goals. This distinction suggests a rationale, though not justification, for the development of escalating militarism as an element of an agenda tied to the establishment of the kingdom of God and the redemption of Zion.

Theocratic constructs depicting this envisioned kingdom date from the Restoration's earliest days. The Book of Mormon depicts a governmental model uniting military leadership with a significant religious authority role. Replete with examples of justified militaristic violence, the book also portrays the use of nonviolent methods for righteous purposes. However, neither element of this ideological conflict is identified as superior.[2]

Developing church theology relied on terms of divine governance and heavenly militarism, though this was initially little more than millennialistic symbolism. However, as the movement's cultural identity emerged, Joseph Smith, Jr., tried to fashion a modern style of government paralleling conservative Book of Mormon themes. Charged with images of sovereignty, this cultural construct proposed that by living out heavenly patterns, the church could claim the privilege of inaugurating God's kingdom on earth. This theory prompted the idea of "a literal gathering place, or Zion," enjoining human and divine relationships, "best expressed in the phrase kingdom of God."[3] Participants were perceived as adopted members of God's covenant people. And, as Richard Howard has observed, Joseph styled himself a latter-day Moses.[4] Competitive aspects of Joseph Smith, Jr.'s personality engendered a contest of sorts, pitting the movement against all contravening forces.[5] Some suggest that as early as 1830 the church envisioned an assumption of political dominion, not simply religious power. Sidney Rigdon later related, "We began to talk about the kingdom of God as if we had the world at our command. We talked with great confidence, and talked big things."[6]

In keeping with images of a literal city of God, Jackson County, Missouri, was identified as a place of gathering. Joseph, himself reluctant to move to the frontier, disclosed by way of revelation, on 11 September 1831, that the Lord designed to "retain a strong hold in the land of Kirtland," for five years.[7] Nevertheless, key personnel were vanguarded to Jackson County to lay the city's physical foundation. Reflecting gentle civilized qualities of their New England town builder heritage, colonists were more inclined to turn the other cheek than resort to fighting.[8] However, an early revelation characterizing Jackson Countians as enemies became a self-fulfilling prophecy.[9]

On 20 July 1833, nonmembers demolished the church's printing office. Bishop Edward Partridge, tarred and feathered during this outburst, provided disciples with a nonviolent example. He bore this abuse with so much resignation and meekness, "that it appeared to astound the multitude...their sympathies having been touched."[10] The church press concluded, "Having passed through the most aggravated insults and injuries, without making the least resistance, a general inquiry prevailed at this time, throughout the Church, as to the propriety of self defence [sic]."[11] At this pivotal point, members were gradually swayed by more aggressive urgings from Lyman Wight and others.

Initially, Joseph urged members to avert violence, as suggested by a revelation of 6 August 1833, redefining limits of Christian restraint.[12] If three offers of peace were rejected then church members would be "justified in responding in their own defense."[13] This rational and possible advice from Joseph "to stand their own defense" may have influenced members.[14] Former Indian missionary Benton Pixley observed, "the Mormons began to muster, and exhibit military preparations," when the Whitmer settlement was attacked in late October.[15] John Corrill reported, "Having no time to lose we concluded to advise each branch of the church to gather into bodies the best way they could for their own preservation."[16] Eventually men from each side died when the armed groups clashed.[17] After the nonmember militia disarmed the church, members fled "before the merciless mob" as chaff blown before the wind.[18]

In December Joseph received a revelation (Section 98) containing a parable, "concerning the redemption of Zion." From this point the expulsion was blamed upon the "jarrings, and contentions, and envyings, and strifes, and lustful and covetous desires among" the church in Zion.[19] Parley P. Pratt and Lyman Wight's arrival at Kirtland on 22 February 1834 with detailed news of their sufferings, deeply stirred the eastern brethren to devise means for the "redemption of Zion."[20] Oliver Cowdery recorded the prevailing rationale: "It is of little consequence to proclaim the everlasting gospel of men, and warn them to flee to Zion for refuge, when there is no Zion, but that which is in possession of the wicked. Lo, Zion must be redeemed...."[21] Following the reception of a 24 February 1834 revelation, Joseph concluded that the redemption of Zion must come by force, as suggested in the December 1833 parable. Reed Peck observed, "In accordance with the *interpretation* of this parable Joseph Smith called for volunteers collected about 210 'Warriors' and marched to Clay County [Missouri] under arms."[22]

Thus, Joseph embarked on a persistent course designed to redeem Zion but which ultimately became a grand preoccupation assuming proportions of a holy war.[23] In addition, Joseph renewed efforts to clarify his authority.[24] Interestingly, systematic priesthood emerged at about the same point in the life of the church as the inception of militarism.[25]

While negotiating with Missouri Governor Dunklin, Joseph became convinced that should the church send a body of armed men to Missouri, the governor would send state militia to escort them back to Jackson County.[26] Zion's Camp revelation commissioned Pratt and Wight to gather an army to go to Zion "and organize my kingdom upon the consecrated land; and establish the children of Zion, upon the laws and commandments which have been, and which shall be given, unto you."[27] While preparing for the expedition, Smith and Wight visited "Father Bosley's" farm in New York State. Wight claimed, "Here Joseph ordained me to the office of Benamey [sic] in the presence of an angel [to take the lead of Zion's Camp] I shall never forget the conversation held between him and Br. Joseph."[28] Wight asserted that Joseph was denominated Baurak Ale, which "is the officer of the highest rank in the army of the strength of the Lord's hosts and Banemy is an appendage there unto."[29] Wight's statement suggests that these specific pseudonyms were tied to efforts to redeem Zion.[30]

A strong expectation developed regarding participation in the camp.[31] And, upon departure, military attitudes were effected. George A. Smith recalled, Levi W. Hancock "made a fife, from a joint of sweet elder, Sylvester Smith marched his company to the music of that fife. That fife may be considered almost the introduction of martial music among the Mormons."[32] As the camp neared its goal there was great anticipation, Luke Johnson reported,

Having made a declaration before I started that I would go into Jackson co., or die in the attempt, in company with my brother Lyman and others I procured a boat, and rowed over the Mo. river and landed in Jackson co., where we discharged three rounds of our small arms, and immediately got into the boat, and with all our energies rowed back. Meanwhile the mob in Jackson co. lined the shore, and commenced firing upon us.[33]

Exiled members in Clay County were also eager.[34] But as negotiations with the governor and Jackson Countians failed, antichurch forces prepared to repulse the camp.[35] Joseph determined that fighting was unacceptable and disbanded the body on 22 June 1834.[36] The revelation, according to John Whitmer, asserted "that it was not wisdom to go to Jackson county at this time and that the armies of Israel should become very great and terrible first, and the Servants of the Lord be endowed with power from on high previous to the redemption of Zion."[37]

On 22 June 1834, several "first elders"

were selected to "receive their endowment from on high" in Kirtland.[38] These leaders were to gather up the strength of the Lord's house in preparation for another attempt to redeem Zion.[39] Before all left, Joseph organized a high council with David Whitmer as president. While the camp had not successfully effected a physical "establishment of the kingdom," the council was its symbolic realization.[40]

A new effort to redeem Zion designated David Whitmer captain of the Lord's host, with various assistants, and Joseph at the head.[41] This shadowy arrangement was precursor to militaristic developments to follow.

Planning at the highest levels of the church renewed the promise of a forthcoming return to Zion.[42] The intensity of such is reflected in an entry penned in Joseph's own hand into his 1835–1836 sketchbook:

September 24th 1835 This day the High Council met at my house to take into consid[e]ration the redeem[p]tion of Zion. . . . We [should] go next season to live or dy [die] to this end so the dy is cast in Jackson County.

We truly had a good time and Covena[n]ted to strug[g]le for this thing u[n]till death shall desolve [dissolve] this union....This day drew up an Arti/c/le of inrollment for the redem[p]tion of Zion that we may obtain volunteers to go next spring /to M[iss]o[uri]/. I ask God in the name of Jesus that we may obtain Eight hundred men /or one thousand/ well armed [men] and that they may ac[c]omplish this great work.[43]

There were many allusions to Zion's redemption during the Kirtland Temple dedicatory activities.[44] The promised empowerment integrated endowment elements dating from 1831 with the redemption of Zion.[45] On 13 March 1836, Joseph met with the Presidency and some of the apostles and counseled with them on the subject of removing to Zion in the spring. "We conversed freely upon the importance of her redemption and the necessity of the Presidency removing to that place....We finally come to the resolution to emigrate on or before the 15th of May next if kind providence Smiles upon us and opens the way before us."[46]

Joseph's dedicatory prayer upon the temple emphasized the redemption of Jackson County, "...make bare thine arm, O Lord, and redeem that which thou didst appoint a Zion unto thy people."[47] During a 30 March 1836 cleansing ceremony, Joseph instructed, "let the redem[p]tion of Zion be our object, and strive to affect it by sending up all the strength of the Lord's House wherever we find them."[48] Then Joseph led them into a covenant, "that if any more of our brethren are slain or driven from their lands in Missouri by the mob that we will give ourselves no rest until we are avenged of our enemies to the uttermost."[49]

Anticipation soared as September 1836 neared.[50] Corrill wrote, "The church also continued to gather in Clay County, till the appearance was that they [author's note: nonmembers] would sooner or later be overrun by the Mormons." As citizens of Clay began to stir up excitement, "the Mormons began to prepare for self defence [sic]."[51] Members were greatly dismayed when the 11 September 1836 deadline for the return to Jackson County passed without result. In 1836 the Missouri presidency worked to achieve a new county in northern Missouri, known as Caldwell, for the "Mormons."[52] The church agreeably left Clay County for this new land.[53]

After Joseph and Sidney visited Missouri in the summer of 1837, strong opposition emerged against the Missouri presidency. Dissension and legal challenges in Ohio prompted Joseph and Sidney's removal to Far West, where they were given town lots. Meanwhile, the Missouri presidency and Cowdery were made quite unwelcome and forced out.[54] The problem with dissenters and the delay in returning to Jackson County did not slow the gathering to north-

ern Missouri. And, Zion assumed a broader meaning, encompassing regions round about.[55]

A subtle change ensued as the abstraction of the kingdom of God began to evolve a political dimension.[56] Priestly assignments assumed temporal governmental embellishments. Not content with simply driving out dissidents, church leaders took measures to establish the kingdom of God in a more definite form. Phelps indicated that the church's territorial pursuits went so far as to attempt to create a sovereign state within northern Missouri.

Before the 4th day of July last, I heard D. W. Patten say that Rigdon was writing a declaration, to declare the church independent. I remarked to him, I thought such a thing treasonable—to set up a government within a Government. He answered, it would not be treasonable if they would maintain it, or fight till they died.[57]

George Hinkle affirmed that the teachings of the presidency were like the little stone spoken of by Daniel, that the kingdom they were setting up was a *temporal* as well as a spiritual kingdom.[58] Intimations of the kingdom's governmental/military capacity found expression in an organization, since called Danites. Corrill explained the initial purpose was to clean the chaff from within the church. "Afterwards it grew into a system to carry out the designs of the presidency; and if necessary to use physical force to upbuild the kingdom of God; it was to be done by them."[59]

An entry in Joseph's "Scriptory Book," penned by scribe George W. Robinson, dated 27 July 1837, though subsequently crossed out in pencil in the original, seems to confirm this intention.[60] "[W]e have a company of Danites in these times, to put right physically that which is not right, and to cleanse the Church of verry [sic] great evils which hath hitherto existed among us inasmuch as they cannot be put to right by teachings & persuasyons...."

Tensions over political and geographic control of the region escalated, as émigrés secured land beyond Caldwell County.[61] Hostilities started 6 August 1838 at the election in Gallatin.[62] After winning the affray, in which there were many gashes, cuts, and bruises, church men retreated to Adam-ondi-Ahman.

Members from Caldwell responded with almost 150 men under Danite leaders. While church members did not view their actions as aggressive or illegal, Daviess citizens were alarmed, as Missouri law prohibited bodies of armed men from crossing into another county without proper authorization.[63]

Members in Daviess gathered their families to Diahman for protection under Wight's leadership.[64] Believing Mormons were forcing settlers to sell and move out, nonmembers renewed hostilities. Church leaders resolved to defend the church at any cost. Corrill recalled Joseph's public statement: "If the people would let us alone, we would preach the gospel to them in peace; but, if they came on us to molest us, we would establish our religion by the sword; and that he would become to this generation a second Mahomet."[65]

In preparation for hostility, church raiding parties were dispatched throughout Daviess and Clinton counties to gather provisions for the church army. Capturing suspected enemies and driving others from their homes, they returned to Diahman with cattle, hogs, and property. Their belief that they were chosen people, that they were helping to build the kingdom of God, and that they were justified in their retaliation spurred them to acts they would not normally commit.[66]

George Hinkle tried to call up the Caldwell militia.[67] Instead, the church deployed its own "Army of Israel" without legal justification.[68] Their attack on a group of legally constituted militia at Crooked River was seen as mob action against state forces.

Peck wrote, "A few individuals of us were ever after this opposed to the rule of the presidency perceiving that all spiritual and temporal affairs were under their control...."[69] Cast in the role of doves, Hinkle, Corrill, Peck, Phelps, John Cleminson, and others supported church doctrines but apparently tried with little success to redirect the church from its militaristic course.[70] Burr Riggs reported, "Two or three days before the surrender of the Mormons to the militia at Far West, I heard Jos. Smith, jr. say that the sword was now unsheathed, and should not again be sheathed until he could go through these United States, and live in any county he pleased, peaceably."[71]

Hinkle indicated that as the final confrontation neared, "The presidency was to have the supreme rule, and that their war office, or headquarters, was to be at Diahman, where, Joseph Smith, jr., said, they could have all necessary preparation to carry on the war in a warlike manner...."[72] However, units of the state militia surrounded Far West before such arrangements were effected.

The siege of Far West, following the tragedy at Haun's Mill, caused Joseph to realize that the church could not win. Facing utter destruction, according to both Corrill and Peck, Joseph urged them to work out a compromise with the militia and, if necessary, "beg like a dog for peace."[73] Hinkle added that Joseph wished a treaty "on any terms short of a battle."[74]

After this spectacular reverse Joseph assured members, via letter, that he was not responsible for the church's tribulation nor had he committed any crimes. The turn of events was again ascribed to religious persecution.[75] Further, Joseph successfully dissociated himself from the Danites without offending loyal supporters within by laying blame for "many false and pernicious things" on Sampson Avard and church doves.[76]

There are some who wish to admit no involvement by Joseph in the excesses resulting from the operation of the Danites.[77] Knowing who was behind the Danites may be beyond historical proof.[78] But as current researcher Michael Riggs observed, in terms of motivating participation, what members of an organization perceive about the beliefs of their leaders is often more important than what those beliefs or actions are in reality.[79]

Riggs and John Thompson have also called attention to a little-noted affidavit by Justus Morse, which illustrates the perception of a faithful member, associating Joseph with what Leland Gentry identified as the later Danite phase.[80] Research by Thompson tends to bring Joseph and Hyrum's presence at the described Danite meeting into question. But, whether present or not, it was clearly Morse's perception that Joseph was not only involved with but approved of Danite teachings and activities.

While recent scholarly treatments, such as Stephen LeSueur's *The 1838 Mormon War in Missouri* and others, have broadened our understanding of events in northern Missouri, they narrow the ultimate range of responsibility ever nearer to Joseph himself. Early members had initially placed their hopes for theocratic dominion on God's destruction of the wicked rather than anticipating their own assumption of power. But it appears that during the "Mormon War" church members envisioned winning political power by force of arms. This disposition, while disturbing, is a reflection of the kingdom mentality that was an inherent dimension of early Mormonism.

Defeat temporarily dulled the popularity of such ideas. Following their exile, survival itself sublimated marshal dreams. Even Joseph was wary at first, though their experience confirmed the church's identity as a peculiar people. Kenneth Winn observed that church members were no longer willing to invoke passive dependence on God as a means of obtaining redress. They "...became obsessed with the wrongs they had suffered, and in their circumscribed world, their sense of injury remained ever fresh, reverberating from the pulpit to the flock and back again, coloring all of their subsequent thought and action."[81] Christian restraint was further reinterpreted as Joseph advised, "Be not the agaressor [sic] bear untill [[sic] they strike on the one cheek offer the other & they will be sure to strike that, then defend yourselves & God shall bear you off."[82]

Experience persuaded that the U.S. Constitution was an inadequate guarantee of individuals' rights.[83] From this perspective, Joseph nurtured expanded uses of the church's growing political power as a means of accomplishing frustrated, kingdom-related goals. After establishment at Nauvoo, Illinois, on 19 July 1840, Joseph reportedly preached an analogy of the church's future course:

the servants of that Lord shall begin to lay the foundation of a great and high watch Tower [of Zion]....Then the Enemy shall come as a thief in the night....Even this Nation will be on the very verge of crumbling to pieces and tumbling to the ground and when the constitution is upon the brink of ruin this people will be the Staff up[on] which the Nation shall lean.[84]

Apparently Joseph adopted the belief that the redemption of Zion must, in the end, be preceded by the ruin of the federal government.

Efforts aimed at precluding a repetition of their injuries resulted in an unusual amount of governmental autonomy for the Saints at Nauvoo. The Nauvoo Charter and creation of the Nauvoo Legion reflected their continuing apprehension. Practiced and polished, military appellations gained fashion among the Saints, while the Legion attained notoriety throughout the country.[85]

The Council of Fifty was a further attempt to coalesce kingdom themes represented within church priesthood organization.[86] By such means, Joseph proposed to manage the goals of an envisioned political extension of the kingdom of God.[87] For two years Joseph unfolded related temple ordinances designed to confer ultimate priesthood authority with initiates' ordained as kings and priests.[88] Not merely a religious organization, it was devised to restore the Lord's government to the earth. It was apparently believed that after a brief visit upon the advent of the millennium, Christ would depart and earthly rule would fall on their shoulders.[89]

As perceived constitutional deficiencies precluded the successful establishment of the kingdom within the United States, the Council began considering emigration beyond U.S. borders.[90] It was no doubt assumed that the Council's eventual ascendancy would allow the church to one day return to God's designated Zion. Such is hinted at in a proposed placement of Mormon troops throughout the great West. Via proclamation, Joseph proposed that the U.S. government authorize the church to police the regions to the west, thereby protecting citizens, and extending the principles of universal liberty.[91]

Joseph's candidacy for president of the United States was a related effort to realize the kingdom through political power. At a 7 March 1844 general meeting of citizens of Nauvoo, Joseph justified his candidacy saying, "...the world has used the power of government to oppress and persecute us, it is right for us to use it for the protection of our rights. We will whip the mob by getting up a candidate for President."[92] In May 1844 the Council sent missionaries throughout the United States to exhort Joseph's election.[93]

The anticipated kingdom of God was ultimately established with Joseph ordained king.[94] On 3 May 1844 Brigham Young informed Ruben Hedlock in England that "The kingdom is organized; and, although as yet no bigger than a grain of mustard seed, the little plant is in a flourishing condition, and our prospects brighter than ever."[95] Following Joseph's death, Brigham promoted the further development of the kingdom's "Legions of Zion" through the Mormon Battalion and Utah Wars.

When viewed as a whole, examples from various periods of church history appear to delineate an emerging militaristic pattern.[96] Struggling to develop appropriate methodologies and short on resources, Joseph felt justified using all means at his disposal. As inspiration was tested against experience, an emerging identity narrowed the range of available methods. When preferred administrative mechanisms failed, less desirable methods were employed by default. This is no indication of a militant rabble. But rather it is a reflection of the frustration of a movement whose path placed them at an excruciating disadvantage within the larger society. As a result, they gradually turned to militaristic methods to pursue church objectives. While decisions leading to such a posture may not necessarily be justified, they may have appeared expedient.

Despite the nonviolent examples of a number of prominent early church figures, the church was inexorably drawn into a widening militaristic stance to advance the perceived kingdom of God on earth. Joseph's efforts to promote the kingdom were creative and sometimes inconsistent. The church's behavior also echoed these ambiguities.[97]

Just as contradictory paradigms appear in the Book of Mormon, frequent inconsistencies appear between Joseph's private beliefs and the church's public actions. Directing the course of the church, Joseph's conduct somewhat resembled the gambler's bluff. Aggressive language and acts may have been calculated to advance church objectives. But when on the brink of disaster, Joseph typically withdrew. While yielding to the lure of militarism, Joseph's personal reliance on force appears somewhat provisional. Though competitive, Joseph was not self-destructive.

While incongruous to many religionists, militarism in the early church was an ill-fated administrative device that gained ascendancy as a byproduct of their vision of the kingdom and Joseph's deep ambition for the redemption of Zion.

Through the years, the Reorganized Church has retained a commitment to the kingdom of God ideal, yet it has conscientiously disengaged itself from any aggressive posture. Joseph Smith, Jr.'s son, Joseph III, set the tone by admitting his own discomfort with the militaristic strain in early church history. Rather than seeking to justify the early church and his father's involvement in such activities, Joseph III, and consequently the RLDS Church, explicitly repudiated the spirit of militarism that took possession of leading early church authorities. Joseph declared, "Looking back along the pathway I feel it was a pity that such a spirit crept in among them, however, and a still greater one that the leading minds of the church partook of it."[98]

Sad experience often provides the impetus for finding a better way. The church's history has represented, for some, a compelling example of the need for reconciliation and healing in our world.[99] Though the church's response is still very much emerging, from its earliest days to the present the Reorganization appears to have benefited from an important understanding Joseph III brought to his administration, "that the best goals of the gospel could sometimes not be squared with the limiting factors of humanity and society," and that for the sake of the movement, some compromise of the ideal is at times essential.[100] The RLDS movement has not yet fully resolved all such issues encountered by the early Restoration. For the RLDS Church continues to struggle to come to grips with the meaning of the upbuilding of the kingdom of God in today's world. But, happily, among present members, this historic struggle has fostered an RLDS commitment to build the Temple as a worldwide ensign, dedicated to the pursuit of peace.

Notes

1. "An Interesting Letter From Patriarch Benjamin F. Johnson to Elder George S. Gibbs," Special Collections, H. B. Lee Library, Brigham Young University.
2. Book of Mormon (Independence, Missouri: Herald Publishing House, 1955), Alma 14:41, 49–52.
3. Forest Roberts, "The History and Development of the Stewardship Idea," RLDS Senior Religio Study Outline (1923), 13.
4. "By the spring of 1829 then, a particular image of Joseph Smith was emerging for Smith and a few close friends: a modern Moses, one commissioned by the Divine to do a task as vital in the latter days as the ancient work of Moses," Richard P. Howard, "Latter Day Saint Scriptures and the Doctrine of Propositional Revelation," in Dan Vogel, ed., *The Word of God: Essays on Mormon Scripture* (Salt Lake City, Utah: Signature Books, 1990), 3.
5. Early converts equated the presence of gifts and spiritual authority within the movement with an expectation of Christlike behavior. See description of Oliver Cowdery's demeanor, John Murdock Journal, microfilm typescript, RLDS Library-Archives, Journals, Reel #439, 12, 15, 16.
6. B. H. Roberts, *History of the Church of Jesus Christ of Latter-day Saints* 6 (Salt Lake City, Utah: Deseret Book Company, 1946), 289, hereafter cited LDS History; see Kenneth H. Winn, *Exiles in a Land of Liberty: Mormons in America, 1830–1846* (Chapel Hill, North Carolina: University of North Carolina Press, 1989), 79.
7. Doctrine and Covenants 64:4c (Independence,

Missouri: Herald Publishing House, 1962), hereafter cited RLDS D&C.

8. Their perception of a Christlike walk was perhaps guided by scriptural images found in Romans and the Book of Mormon. See King James Version, Romans 12: 17–21; and III Nephi 5:85.

9. RLDS D&C 52:9e (LDS 52:42); also, *Star Extra* (February 1834), reproduced in Peter Crawley, "Two Rare Missouri Documents," *Brigham Young University Studies* 14 (Summer 1974): 502–515. Intrusive values of church members conflicted with the established political culture and personal values of their neighbors.

10. LDS History 1:391. Chapman Duncan recalled, "Bishop Partridge, Chas. Allen, Harvey Allen, and myself, were taken by the mob into town. They tarred Bishop Partridge and Allen's Brother. Olmstead and myself passed through the mob unobserved, as they were gazing intently on the usual proceedings. I saw them about to commence as I was brought into the ring for that purpose, but I escaped unhurt," Chapman Duncan, Ms 6936, LDS Archives; Charles Allen, also tarred and feathered, echoed Partridge's pacific example. His daughter related, "My Father Charles Allen saw a crowd of the mob and went to see what they ware doing they got holt of him and wanted him to say he would give up his faith or leave the country he said he was a free man and he intended to live thare and die thare so they tard and fethered him. When they ware goin to whip him he maid the mason sine of distres the whip was jurked out of the mans hand and as father was the first to bee whipped they did not whip Brother Partridge," Maria Galland, undated statement, RLDS Library-Archives, Accretion Papers, P68, f4.

11. Star Extra (February 1834).

12. RLDS D&C 95:5a–f, 6c, given 6 August 1833 (LDS 98). After repeated [3] provocations the Saints were to "bring their testimonies before the Lord." Joseph anticipated, "the Lord, would give unto them a commandment, and justify them in going out to battle...and...would fight their battles." Further, as a group the Saints were to meet each provocation with an offer of peace, RLDS D&C 95:6c-e. See Graham St. John Stott, "Just War, Holy War, and Joseph Smith, Jr.," *Restoration Studies IV*, Marjorie B. Troeh, ed. (Independence, Missouri: Herald Publishing House, 1988), 139.

13. RLDS D&C 95:6c–d (LDS 98), as discussed in Stott, 139.

14. William E. McLellin claims Joseph sent this message to Jackson County, via Orson Hyde and John Gould in September 1833, McLellin to President Joseph Smith, Independence, Jackson County, Missouri (July 1872), RLDS Library-Archives, P13, f213. After successive attacks upon the Whitmer settlement, church members tried for a peace warrant. "We accordingly went to a magistrate and applied for one...but he disregarded it, and said he cared nothing about it," John Corrill, *The Evening and the Morning Star* (January 1834): 124–126, hereafter cited EMS.

15. William Mulder and A. Russell Mortensen, eds., *Among the Mormons: Historic Accounts by Contemporary Observers* (New York: Alfred Knopf, 1958), 82.

16. Corrill, EMS, 124–126; *The History of the Reorganized Church of Jesus Christ of Latter Day Saints*, Volume 1 (Independence, Missouri: Herald Publishing House, 1969), hereafter cited RLDS History, 342.

17. For details of Whitmer battle (4 November), see Corrill, EMS, 125; also: Ebbie L. V. Richardson, "David Whitmer" (Brigham Young University, thesis, 1952), 15; Henry Alanson Cleveland, LDS Journal History (4 November 1833); Alexander Majors, *Seventy Years on the Frontier* (Rand, McNally and Company, 1893), 46–47; David Whitmer, *Saints' Herald* 28 (1 July 1881): 197, as reprinted from the *Kansas City Journal* (5 June 1881). In a letter to the editors of the *New York Observer* (7 November 1833), Benton Pixley suggests, "The same night the Mormons pretended to have a revelation from heaven...*to arise and peruse and destroy their enemies*," Mulder and Mortensen, 83. Militia, under command of Colonel Pitcher, proceeded to the Temple Lot and stopped in the road opposite Isaac Morley's house. "After considerable consultation back and forth, the mormons at length complied," delivering up forty-nine guns and one pistol. Also see, L. W. Boggs, letter to the *Missouri Republican* (30 November 1833).

18. *Times and Seasons* 6 (15 May 1845): 897.

19. RLDS D&C 98: 3a, 6a (LDS 101:6); also, *Reed Peck Manuscript* (Salt Lake City, Utah: Modern Microfilm), 2, original at H. B. Lee Library, Archives and Manuscripts, Brigham Young University, hereafter cited Peck.

20. RLDS History, 1:435; also, Peck, 2.

21. Cowdery to W. W. Phelps (3 March 1834), quoted in Donna Hill, *Joseph Smith, The First Mormon* (Garden City, New York: Doubleday, 1977), 170.

22. Peck, 3; see RLDS D&C 100:3d (LDS 103).

23. The confrontation became more than a "just war"

in that to them it was no longer simply a contest of human initiative, Stott, 137.

24. At a meeting held 24 April 1834 in Norton, Ohio, Smith "gave a revelation of obtaining and translating the Book of Mormon, the revelation of the Priesthood of Aaron, the organization of the Church in 1830, the revelation of the High Priesthood, and the gift of the Holy Ghost poured out upon the Church..." LDS History 2:52.

25. Authority shifted from a model of charismatic or spiritual power to hierarchical priesthood relationships. Bruce Lindgren has noted that authority in the early Restoration was originally patterned on the Book of Mormon model of charismatic or spiritual power, not on priesthood ordination; Bruce Lindgren, "The Development of the Latter Day Saint Doctrine of Priesthood, 1829–1835," *Courage: A Journal of History, Thought and Action* 2 (Spring 1972): 439–443. Dan Vogel suggests the emergence of assertions of angelic ordination represents an effort to strengthen authority claims and consolidate control by meeting literalistic seekers' expectations of both spiritual endowment and angelic ministry; Dan Vogel, *Religious Seekers and the Advent of Mormonism* (Salt Lake City, Utah: Signature Books, 1988), 120. William McLellin treats the issue of source of authority saying, "There has been no hereditary rights since these 'old [paper-torn laws]' were all done away!! All priestly authority in the gospel age comes by direct faith in God, but not in consequence of pedigree, lineage, or birthright in any sense....All those revelations, and silly items of doctrine were got up after Joseph's fall, hence fictitious & silly"; William E. McLellin to My dear old friends, Independence, Missouri (21 October 1870), RLDS Library-Archives, P13, f198. Vogel further observed, "The emergence of a sophisticated church hierarchy allowed less room for individuality of belief." The swing away from simple spiritual authority to "the introduction of the concept of lineal religious authority made it easier to thwart usurpers and pretenders. The claim of uninterrupted succession of ordinations back to one who had undisputed authority was a stabilizing force."

26. Roger D. Launius, *Zion's Camp: Expedition to Missouri 1834* (Independence, Missouri: Herald House, 1984), 108.

27. Klaus J. Hansen, *Quest for Empire* (Lincoln, Nebraska: University of Nebraska Press, 1974), 48, quoting from RLDS D&C 100:6g (LDS 103:34–35).

28. Lyman Wight, Medina River (July 1855), the *Northern Islander*, published by Cooper and Chidester, St. James, Beaver Island, Michigan, RLDS Library-Archives, Lyman Wight Letterbook 1853–1855, 21–26, P13, f79, RLDS Library-Archives.

29. Ibid.

30. Pseudonyms such as these appear in a number of revelations printed in later versions of the Doctrine and Covenants. Such names are usually associated with church leaders' later desire to conceal the identity of United Firm members, referring to Joseph Smith, Jr., as Gazelam. Whereas, Baurak Ale denotes a military connection.

31. John Murdock described his dilemma: "For the 1st time that I had consented to take fire arms to go into the field of battle for I had never shed the blood of any man, nor with firearms, any animal, save one Dog. But I took my Riffle on my shoulder, my pistol in my pocket, my Dirk by my side.... Being one Hundred twenty in number took up the line of march with our Armour [sic], Tents, Camp equipage and baggage wagons, in martial array. A Camp of Israel by the order of God," John Murdock Journal, 24.

32. Discourse of George D. Watt, *Journal of Discourses by Brigham Yougn, His Two Counselors, the Twelve Apostles, and Others* Volume 11 (Liverpool and London, England: F. D. Richards, 1855), 7.

33. Luke Johnson, Autobiography, *Millennial Star* 26 (1864): 836.

34. John Whitmer wrote, "The Saints here are preparing with all possible speed to arm themselves and otherwise prepare to go to Jackson Co., when the camp arrives, for we have had some hints from Joseph the Seer that this will be our privilege," "Book of John Whitmer," chapter 13, RLDS Library-Archives, hereafter cited John Whitmer History.

35. There was even a petition to the president: Gilbert, Phelps, Partridge, Corrill, John Whitmer, to President of the United States (10 April 1834), John Whitmer History, chapter 11.

36. D. Michael Quinn has remarked that Joseph had no illusions that the kingdom of God would be served by a suicidal confrontation; Quinn, "The Mormon Church and the Spanish-American War: An End to Selective Pacifism," *Dialogue* 17 (Winter 1984): 13.

37. John Whitmer History, chapter 13. The revelation rationalized in part, "Were it not for the transgressions of my people,...they might have been redeemed even now.... Therefore...it is expedient in me that mine elders should wait for a little season

for the redemption of Zion," RLDS D&C 102:2a, 3c (LDS 105).

38. These elders had all lived in Jackson County: Edward Partridge, W. W. Phelps, Isaac Morley, John Corrill, John Whtimer, David Whitmer, Algernon S. Gilbert, Peter Whitmer, Jr., Simeon Carter, Newel Knight, Parley P. Pratt, Christian Whitmer, Solomon Hancock, Thomas B. Marsh, and Lyman Wight; "History of Joseph Smith," *Times and Seasons* 6 (1 February 1846): 1104–1105; read in connection with Fishing River Revelation, RLDS D&C 102 (LDS 105).

39. Launius, 144; *Far West Record* (23 June 1834).

40. The council was to refine and purify those who were in exile, that they might be worthy of returning to Jackson County. They were told they could not reenter Jackson County until this was accomplished. After returning to Ohio, Joseph reminded the Missouri High Council that the first elders were to receive their endowment in Kirtland before the redemption of Zion. "You will recollect that your high council will have power to say who of the first Elders among the Children of Zion are accounted worthy...", Joseph Smith to Lyman Wight, Edward Partrige [sic], John Carrill [sic], Isaac Morley, and Others of the High Council (16 August 1834), in Dean C. Jessee, *The Personal Writings of Joseph Smith* (Salt Lake City, Utah: Deseret Book, 1984), 329. Edward Stevenson, who tarried after Zion's Camp, wrote that Joseph sent the high council a very encouraging letter, dated 16 August 1834, saying: "If the citizens of Clay County do not befriend us, to gather up the little army, and be set over immediately into Jackson County and trust in God, and do the best he can in maintaining the ground. But, in case the excitement continues to be allayed, and peace prevails, use every effort to prevail on the churches to gather to those regions and situate themselves to be in readiness to move into Jackson County, in two years from 11 Sep next [1834] which is the appointed time for the redemption of Zion"; Edward Stevenson, *Autobiography* (1986), cited in Backman, "Writings of Early Latter-day Saints...A Data Base Collection." Another letter by Joseph reveals plans for an additional attempt at restoration employing forceful methods. He told the Missouri High Council to prepare the church and promised a date for a return. "Use every effort to prevail on the churches to gather to those regions and situate themselves to be in readiness to move into Jackson Co. in two years from the Eleventh of September next which is the appointed time for

the redemption of Zion..."; Jessee, *The Personal Writings of Joseph Smith*, 330.

41. Of the effort, John Whitmer observed, "This much for the war department by revelation," John Whitmer History, chapter 17.

42. As part of this effort, kindling hopes for an early regathering, W. W. Phelps wrote letters back to Kirtland describing the Platt region of upper Missouri and encouraging members to continue moving to the state. W. W. Phelps, "Letter No. II," *Messenger and Advocate* 1 (December 1834): 33.

43. Scott H. Faulring, *An American Prophet's Record: The Diaries and Journals of Joseph Smith* (Salt Lake City, Utah: Signature Books, 1989), 34–35.

44. In a 21 January 1836 meeting of the First Presidency and the Twelve, several participants saw magnificent visions during purification rites of washing and anointing. Joseph, who experienced a vision of the celestial kingdom wrote, "My scribe also received his anointing/ with us/ and saw in a vision the armies of heaven protecting the Saints in their return to Zion..."; Faulring, Diaries (21 January 1836), 120.

45. In addition to the redemption of Zion, endowment elements included: a gathering, preparatory ordinances, supernatural manifestations, and empowerment for mission. An earlier endowment experience occurred 4 June 1831 at a Kirtland conference; Corrill, *A Brief History of the Church* (St. Louis: 1839), 18, photomechanical reprint, Modern Microfilm, hereafter cited *A Brief History*. A second endowment-like event is associated with the opening of the School of the Prophets, Kirtland High Council Minutes (23 January 1833). This third endowment experience took place in conjunction with the dedication of the Kirtland Temple; Faulring, Diaries (30 March 1836), 153–155. During this later event, little distinction was made between "First Elders" endowed earlier and those selected later. ALso, see "History of Joseph Smith," *Times and Seasons* 6 (1 February 1846): 1104–1105.

46. Faulring, 1835–1836 Diaries, 140–141, also on 29 March 1836 these elders assembled for the appointed solemn assembly. "At 11 o'clock A.M. Presidents Joseph Smith, Jun[ior], Frederick G. Williams, Sidney Rigdon, Hyrum Smith, and Oliver Cowdery met in the Most Holy Place in the Lord's House and sought for a revelation from Him to teach us concerning our going to Zion and other important matter[s]," Faulring, Diaries (29 March 1836), 152.

47. See dedicatory prayer, Faulring, Diaries, 149.

48. "The brethren began to prophesy upon each other's heads and cursings upon the enemies of Christ who inhabit Jackson County, Missouri," Faulring, Diaries (30 March 1836), 154; see also LDS History, 2:431.

49. LDS History, 2:432; Faulring, 1835–1836 Diaries, 155. "This covenant was sealed unaminously [sic] by a hosanna and Amen. I then observed to the quorums that I had now completed the organization of the Church and we had passed through all the necessary ceremonies. That I had given them all the instruction they needed and that they now were at liberty after obtaining the lisences to go forth and build up the kingdom of God." At this same time, Joseph also reinforced the expectation of the removal of church government to Missouri: "that the time that we were required to tarry in Kirtland to be endued [endowed] would be fulfilled in a few days, and then the Elders would go forth and each must stand for himself, that it was not necessary for them to be sent out two by two as in former times...", Faulring, 154. A further attempt was planned to raise money in an effort to buy out their opponents. Joseph and Cowdery were appointed, "to raise, in righteousness, all the money we could for a season, to send by, or to, certain wise men appointed to purchase lands in Zion in obedience to a revelation or commandment of the Lord, for the mutual benefit of the council," LDS History, 2:434. W. W. Phelps alluded he was among four "appointed in a private meeting in the temple at Kirtland as wise men to purchase all the land in Jackson County and in the regions round a bout for money &c I was ordained president of this new quorum, with Edward Partridge, John Whitmer and John Corril [sic] for my assistant wise men," Phelps, "A Short History of W. W. Phelps' Stay in Missouri," Ms 6019/7, LDS Archives. Phelps left another record of the expectation to return to Jackson County as recorded in his famous song, long associated with the dedication of the Kirtland Temple, "The Spirit of God Like a Fire Is Burning." Lyric references to inheritances, armies of heaven, and restoring of judges earnestly allude to Jackson County and the church's anticipated return.

50. Edmund Flagg, a western traveler, encountered a group of Mormons during the summer of 1836, who explained that they were on their way to Mount Zion and that "...the Saviour was about to descend in Jackson county, Missouri; the millennium was dawning, and that all who were not baptized...and forthwith repaired to Mount Zion...would assuredly be cut off"; Edmund Flagg, The Far West; or, A Tour Beyond the Mountains, 2 vols. (New York: Harper and Brothers, 1838), 2:111. Corrill wrote, "With the exception of some little threatening, the church lived in peace, until the summer of '36; and, not withstanding all these difficulties, it continued to gather in Clay County; and in the adjacent counties, the members hoping that they would get back to Jackson County"; Corrill, A Brief History, 21; see also, Wilford Woodruff's mission to the South, Wilford Woodruff's Journal 1 (Midvale, Utah: Signature Books, 1983), 88, 96–97.

51. Corrill, A Brief History, 26.

52. Corrill, with the help of attorney Alexander Doniphan, worked out an arrangement through the state legislature for the Mormon refuge.

53. Max Parkin suggests that indeed two church settlements were attacked, reminiscent of the experiences in Jackson County; Parkin, Missouri Symposium, Brigham Young University (Provo, Utah: March 30, 1991).

54. David Whitmer wrote, "In the spring of 1838, the heads of the church and many of the members had gone deep into error and blindness. I had been striving with them for a long time to show them the errors into which they were drifting, and for my labors I received only persecutions. In June, 1838, at Far West, Mo., a secret organization was formed, Doctor Avard being put in as the leader of the band; a certain oath was administered to all the brethren to bind them to support the heads of the church in everything they should teach. All who refused to take this oath were considered dissenters from the church, and certain things were to be done concerning these dissenters, by Dr. Avard's secret band"; Whitmer, Address to All Believers in Christ, 27. It has been observed, "That community is already in the process of dissolution where each man begins to eye his neighbor as a possible enemy, where noncomformity with the accepted creed, political as well as religious, is a mark of disaffection; where denunciation, without specification or backing, takes the place of evidence; where orthodoxy chokes freedom of dissent..."; Learned Hand, "Speech, Convocation of the Board of Regents, University of the State of New York" (24 October 1952), as quoted in John Bartlett, Familiar Quotations, thirteenth ed. (Boston: Little, Brown and Company, 1955), 860.

55. But the earlier, precise, and narrow definition of Zion as Jackson County continued to have meaning to individual members. Lumon Shurtliff wrote,

"We stopped in Far West June 2nd 1838 I thought this the most beautiful country I ever saw and I felt to rejoice that I and my family had bin permitted to gather with the Saints in such a good land whare [sic] I expected to live until the Saints went to Jackson County"; Lumon Shurtliff, History 1807–1881, typescript, 89, original in LDS Archives.

56. Joseph appeared to turn, with increasing frequency, to Book of Mormon patterns for solutions to emergencies. See RLDS Book of Mormon, Alma 28:14–19.

57. Senate Document 189, photomechanical reprint (Salt Lake City, Utah: Modern Microfilm), 44.

58. Ibid, 23: Hinkle said, "Until lately, the teachings of the church appeared to be peaceable, and that the kingdom was to be set up peaceably; but lately a different idea has been advanced—that the time had come when this kingdom was to be set up by forcible means, if necessary. It was taught, that the time had come when the riches of the Gentiles were to be consecrated to the true Israel."

59. Corrill, A Brief History, 32; Senate Document 189, 14.

60. Quoted in, "The Last Months of Mormonism in Missouri: The Albert Perry Rockwood Journal," Dean C. Jessee and David J. Whittaker, eds., Brigham Young University Studies 28 (Winter 1988): 14 and 37, n. 24.

61. Church leaders turned toward Daviess County, where in May 1838 they laid out the city of Adam-ondi-Ahman; Joseph Smith and Sidney Rigdon to Stephen Post (17 September 1838), photocopy, LDS Archives.

62. John L. Butler, a large and powerful Mormon, bristled after a speech that advocated restricting Mormon suffrage. "The first thing that came to my mind was the covenants entered into by the Danites...and I hollowed [sic] out to the top of my voice saying 'O yes, you Danites, here is a job for us'.... [wielding a large wooden club from a nearby woodpile] I never struck a man the second time, and while knocking them down, I really felt that they would soon embrace the gospel..."; Journal History (6 August 1838), Butler account.

63. Stephen C. LeSueur, The 1838 Mormon War in Missouri (Columbia, Missouri: University of Missouri Press, 1987), 67.

64. "Impetuous, bold, and fiercely loyal to Joseph Smith, Wight personified the growing militant spirit in Mormonism" (LeSueur, 86–87). See, David Osborn, Autobiography, 31, Brigham Young University, Archives. Local judges issued writs of arrest for Joseph, Lyman, and others in response to their visit to Adam Black's house

(LeSueur, 68). But church men resisted trial by Daviess County citizens. Lyman Wight indicated, "That he owed nothing to the laws—the laws had not protected him..."; William Swartzell, Mormonism Exposed, being a Journal of a residence in Missouri from the 28th of May to the 20th of August, 1838, photomechanical reprint, Pekin, Ohio, 1840 (Salt Lake City, Utah: Utah Lighthouse Ministry), 32. However, the first armed encounter occurred at DeWitt where church families had been sent to establish a church port on the Missouri River, to facilitate the transportation of goods in and out of the Mormon domain. Their makeshift town of tents and wagons overlooked the Missouri River (LeSueur, 102). Carroll Countians, set on removing the Mormons, prepared for an anticipated battle. The arrival of 200 Saints from Canada in late September provoked an attack. George Hinkle, a member who was a colonel in the state militia "declared that he would rather die than be driven from the town" (LeSueur, 102, 109). This caused a dilemma for many DeWitt Saints. "Some of the Mormons, having endured several months of abuse from the Carroll settlers, stood ready to fight eye-for-eye and tooth-for-tooth against the vigilantes. Other Mormons, especially those who had just arrived from Canada and who knew little about the long-developing conflict, were reluctant to turn so quickly to guns and violence" (LeSueur, 104). Zadock Judd reflected the powerful feelings of some at DeWitt: "This state of affairs was very trying to some of our sober, serious Christians that had been taught that it was wicked to fight; it almost rocked their faith in the gospel; to take up arms and try to kill their fellow mortals was a new doctrine that some could hardly endure..."; Zadock Knapp Judd, Autobiography, 8–9, typescript, Brigham Young University, Archives and Manuscripts. See also, Biography of Christopher Merkley (Salt Lake City, Utah: J. H. Parry & Company, 1887), 4. Joseph's arrival, with additional troops, fortified the Missourians determination to force the church from their county. Though the Saints sought to end the crisis peacefully, repeated appeals to civil authorities were fruitless. Church leaders saw the hopelessness of their position and withdrew to Caldwell and Daviess counties.

65. Senate Document 189, testimony of Corrill, 12.

66. LeSueur, 121.

67. Hinkle found militia officers very much disorganized and inquired as to the reason why. "They answered, they cared nothing for their commissions; that the organization of the Danite band had

taken all power out of their hands.... On the day before the battle with Captain Bogart, there was a council held in Far West, in which Patten was appointed commander-in-chief of all the horse[men] he could raise in Caldwell county. I inquired (inasmuch as I commanding colonel of the militia of the county) how this was to be. President Smith told me that, if it reduced my command to ten men, I must be satisfied with it"; *Senate Document 189*, 22–23.

68. LeSueur, 250. The term "Army of Israel" is used by Albert P. Rockwood in his journal, *BYU Studies* 28 (Winter 1988): 19. See also RLDS D&C 102 (LDS 105).

69. Peck, 9.

70. Joseph's 1838 diary reflects his perception of Corrill's dovish role during this period (Faulring, Diaries, 209). Enmeshed in zeal gone astray, John Cleminson indicated he had little choice. "I went in the expedition to Daviess in which Gallatin was burnt, as I felt myself compelled to go from the regulations which had been made. It was generally understood that every movement made in Daviess was under the direction and supervision of the first presidency..." (*Senate Document 189*, 16); also, Phelps wrote, "Finding that I should have to go out, and not wishing to be put in front of the battle, I sought a situation, and went out with my wagon. This was the expedition in which Gallatin and Millport were burnt" (*Senate Document 189*, 45). These dissidents were not cowards nor apostates interested only in working at cross purposes with the majority church members (LeSueur, 251). Though they foresaw church policies reaping disastrous consequences their warnings only brought condemnation from church leaders. Hinkle related, "I spoke to Mr. Smith, jun., in the house, and told him that this course of burning houses and plundering, by the Mormon troops, would ruin us; that it could not be kept hid, and would bring the force of the State upon us; that houses would be searched, and stolen property found. Smith replied to me, in a pretty rough manner to keep still; that I should say nothing about it; that it would discourage the men...." Also, see Hinkle, *Senate Document 189*, 21–22.

71. Senate Document 189, 29–30.

72. Ibid., 25.

73. Corrill, *A Brief History*, 41; Peck, 24.

74. George Hinkle, letter to W. W. Phelps (14 August 1844), reproduced in *Journal of History* 13 (October 1920): 449.

75. Joseph wrote (16 December 1838), "...we stood in our own defense, and we believe that no man of us acted only in a just, a lawful, and a righteous retaliation..."; LDS History, 3:229.

76. LDS History, 3:231–232.

77. Leland Gentry's groundbreaking research has thwarted such claims. Gentry establishes a connection between the society and the accomplishment of church purposes in two early phases of Danite operation. But he disassociates Joseph from a third phase, involving stealing from nonmembers, Leland Gentry, "A History of the Latter-day Saints in Northern Missouri from 1836 to 1839" (Ph.D. dissertation, Brigham Young University, 1965). Historically, Avard has received the major blame for the church's militaristic actions. See also Marvin S. Hill, "The Role of Christian Primitivism," 247; and Kenneth H. Winn, *Exiles in a Land of Liberty: Mormons in America, 1830–1846* (Chapel Hill, North Carolina: The University of North Carolina Press, 1989), 153.

78. Many have wondered, "Did Joseph know about, condone, or ever participate in the Danite organization?" In a recent article in *BYU Studies*, Dean Jessee and David Whittaker effect a reanalysis of the Danite issue. Jessee and Whittaker appear concerned about the appearance of recent works tending to implicate Joseph. Jessee and Whittaker maintain that Avard was guilty of shifting all blame to Joseph and that this action has perpetuated a misunderstanding of Joseph's role. They draw heavily on one source, the letter journal of Albert Perry Rockwood, and further argue that Stephen LeSueur's *The 1838 Mormon War in Missouri* misinterprets Rockwood and ignores Leland Gentry's thesis: That Joseph and Hyrum Smith knew and condoned early stages of Danite activities, including the expulsion of dissenters and a pre-October 1838 defensive function, but that Avard himself initiated later Danite efforts including stealing from nonmembers. Michael S. Riggs makes a relatively fresh observation suggesting that blame was actually shifted both ways. Riggs suggests, in repsonse to Gentry, that Joseph seemed to use Avard as much as Avard used Joseph, "Where Cain Killed Abel: Latter-day Saint Views on the Mormon Surrender of Far West and Their Forced Expulsion From the State of Missouri" (Senior Project, University of San Francisco, 1988), 48. It should be noted that many contemporary journals and reminiscences, including those of faithful members, seem to reinforce the perception that Joseph knew and approved of the Danites and directed plundering and burning of nonmember homes in Daviess County.

79. Riggs, 49.

80. See above note regarding Gentry. Morse contended that he and nine other Danites were taken to a deep, well-guarded ravine near Far West in 1838 and "Was there taught and instructed by Joseph Smith, Sydney Rigdon and Hyrum Smith, that the Church could not advance without means, and we must obtain, must get money and means to carry on the work whether right or wrong honest or dishonest—that the Church should 'suck the milk of the gentiles,' that we had been injured by the mob in Missouri, and to take from the gentiles was no sin"; Justice Morse Affidavit (23 March 1887) in Charles Shook, *The True Origin of Mormon Polygamy* (Cincinnati: Standard Publishing Co., 1914), 167–171.

81. Winn, 156–157.

82. Andrew F. Ehat and Lyndon W. Cook, eds., *The Words of Joseph Smith: The Contemporary Accounts of the Nauvoo Discourses of the Prophet Joseph Smith* (Provo, Utah: Religious Studies Center, Brigham Young University, 1980), 218.

83. Vigorous, though unsuccessful, attempts were made to obtain redress from the U.S. government for church losses and suffering during the Missouri period. States rights precluded federal involvement, even though legal remedies had clearly been denied.

84. Notes of a sermon apparently taken by Martha Jane Knowlton, Dean C. Jessee, "Joseph Smith's 19 July 1840 Discourse," *BYU Studies* 19 (1979): 390–394. Se allso another instance in Orson Pratt to George A. Smith (21 January 1841), LDS Church Historical Archives, cited in Davis Bitton, "Joseph Smith in the Mormon Folk Memory," *Restoration Studies I*, Maurice L. Draper, ed. (Independence, Missouri: Herald House, 1980), 82–83.

85. John Bills, the Nauvoo tailor, became the busiest person in town fashioning uniforms. Paul Bailey, *The Armies of God* (Garden City, New York: Doubleday and Company, Inc., 1968), 16.

86. Andrew F. Ehat, "It Seems Like Heaven Began on Earth: Joseph Smith and the Constitution of the Kingdom of God," *Brigham Young University Studies* 20 (Spring 1980): 254.

87. This dimension of kingdom design is reflected in Smith's revelation (7 April 1842) denominating this endeavor: "The Kingdom of God and His Laws...."

88. See Heber C. Kimball Journal, kept by William Clayton (26 December 1845), LDS Church Historical Archives; Ehat, 257.

89. Winn, 196. John D. Lee added, "This Council aluded too is the Municipal department of the Kingdom of God set up on the Earth, and from which all Law eminates, for the rule, government & control of all Nations Kingdoms & tongues and People under the whole Heavens but not to controle the Priesthood but to council, deliberate & plan for the general good & upbuilding of the Kingdom of God on the Earth"; John Doyle Lee, *A Mormon Chronicle: The Diaries of John D. Lee, 1848–1876*, 2 vols., Robert Cleland and Juanita Brooks, eds. (San Marino, California: Huntington Library, 1955), 1:80.

90. An attempted settlement in Texas was but one of the options explored. The church also sent George J. Adams to Russia, probably with instructions to solicit Russian opinion on the feasibility of founding an independent Mormon state within their borders; Hansen, *Quest for Empire*, 59–60. Also, the Autobiography of Bishop George Miller, typescript, RLDS Library-Archives, 61–62.

91. LDS History, 6:276.

92. Ibid., 6:243.

93. One electioneer, Justus Morse, was "instructed to maintain his [Joseph's] character against all calumnies, which thing I was bound to do under any and all circumstances and to sustain him, because of my oath as a Danite"; Justus Morse Affidavit, Shook, 170.

94. William Marks was witness to the formal inauguration of the kingdom, as envisioned by Joseph. "I was also witness of the introduction (secretly) of a kingly form of government, in which Joseph suffered himself to be ordained a king, to reign over the house of Israel forever..."; William Marks, *Zion's Harbinger and Baneemy's Organ* 3 (St. Louis: July 1853): 53.

95. LDS History, 6:354.

96. As Carmen Hardy recently observed, "Institutions, like men, can only be comprehended when the integrity of their full experience over time is understood"; B. Carmen Hardy, "Mormon Polygamy in Mexico and Canada: A Legal and Historigraphical Review," in *The Mormon Presence in Canada* (Edmonton, Alberta: University of Alberta Press, 1990), 199.

97. Kenneth Winn observed, "At one moment, they strutted like arrogant empire builders, dreaming of theocratic rule over a vice-ridden world. At the next, they proposed to join other well-meaning citizens in reforming the Republic. At still another time, they humbly asked only for their liberties and the opportunity to lead quiet, industrious lives" (Winn, 182).

98. Joseph Smith III, "The Memoirs of President

Joseph Smith, 1832–1914," *Saints' Herald* 81 (25 December 1934): 1638.

99. See Roger D. Launius, *Father Figure: Joseph Smith III and the Creation of the Reorganized Church* (Independence, Missouri: Herald Publishing House, 1990), 40–41, 190, for observations regarding Joseph Smith III's development of a "moderate Mormon stance" in an effort to prevent the Reorganized Church from becoming entrapped by what he perceived as mistakes of the past. Launius posits that Smith was both attracted and repelled by his memories of the Nauvoo experience. And that his reaction to issues, such as the promotion of peace versus the promulgation of the warrior mentality, contributed to the development of his method of presidential leadership and approach to problems.

100. Ibid., 192.

Religious Violence: An International Reflection*

Rick Sarre

Sadly, the world in which we live is dogged by violence. In Latin America, Ireland, southern and northern Africa, the Middle East, parts of southeast Asia, and eastern Europe to name but a few regions, a spiral of political and ethnic violence is commonplace. Violence is now recognised as one of the major public health concerns in the world today.[1] However, those who stand clear of the immediate violence are not immune from its effects. If nothing more, the dignity of the community suffers by its inability to prevent the contraventions of human rights taking place.

It is not the purpose of this paper to discuss the etiology of political violence generally. It has been suggested that factors including class conflict, economic exploitation, and the unequal distribution of resources lay at the heart of the problem. Much of this violence can be linked to activities of the former colonial powers and the de-colonisation policies adopted by them. In many instances, small ruling classes are maintained in power today by the direct assistance of foreign governments. Tribal and ethnic rivalries, intense nationalism, uncompromising political ideologies, and despotism also play a part in fuelling the fires of conflict.

While much has been written on these political, economic, and historical aspects of such violence, there has been little research conducted on the links between violence and religion. Yet as I write, the newspapers in Australia report bomb blasts at Hindu festivals in Uttar Pradesh, riots in northern Nigeria between Muslims and Christians, and the ongoing hostage saga being played out in Lebanon by the various Islamic groups such as Hezbollah (Party of God) and Islamic Jihad. It is important to discuss not only the reasons for such violence but appropriate responses to it. That is made more difficult by the lack of literature on this subject.

It is not difficult to guess why this gap in knowledge exists. Very often, it seems, the religious component in violence is categorised by law enforcement officials as either being irrelevant, inconsequential, or useless. For example, there is a suspicion that many politically motivated violent struggles are dressed in the clothing of "religious" warfare because that avenue is perceived by the violent zealots to have ulterior political advantages. For example,

...the young Sikh radicals...by clothing their actions in the moral garb of religion...have given their actions legitimacy. Because their actions are morally sanctioned by religion, they are fundamentally political actions: they break the state's monopoly on morally-sanctioned killing. By putting the right to kill in their own hands, the perpetrators of religious violence are also making a daring claim of political independence.[2]

It is a theme of this paper, however, that it is too simplistic to dismiss all violence which has a religious component as being "merely" political terrorism by another name. A better response would involve a greater consideration for the religious issues and the extent to which religiously esoteric factors influence the proclivity of adherents

* Reproduced in part from an article in *Criminology Australia* 3, no. 1 (June/July 1991): 22–25. Used by permission. Oxford English has been retained.

to violent conduct and fanaticism, an issue dealt with below. No one religiously motivated violent struggle is going to be identical to another, and law enforcement agencies would be unwise to act as if all religious antagonists were in some way of like mind.

Religious violence can take many forms. It has existed since time immemorial. It should not be forgotten that there is a sorry historical record—worldwide—of official, state-sponsored, and private violence which has been perpetrated for centuries upon many religious organisations and ethnic groups. The religious violence that is the subject of this paper, however, is the violence perpetrated *by* religious groups in the furtherance of their own ends.

All justice agencies will face definitional difficulties which need to be addressed. Where do the boundaries between political, ethnic, and religious violence lie? What historical factors have influenced current tensions? How may the situation differ in which the religion and the state are virtually inseparable (as exists, say, in Islamic fundamentalist countries) or in which there is a strict separation of church and state (for example, in the Soviet Union) or in which lip service is paid to such a separation but the leaders consult with religious principals and make outward displays of religious faith (for example, in the United States)? Is there any difference between the situation in which violence is visited upon religious groups by other religious groups or in which the violence is random? For the most part, unless one has actually taken the time to answer these questions and to learn of the beliefs and practices of a particular religious community or fellowship, it is unlikely that there will be any understanding of that community. Fear, misunderstanding, and prejudice will become hallmarks of the methods of official policing and penalising. Thus, unless governments, law enforcement agencies,

and the public generally are prepared to address these issues, our world is likely to be subjected to levels of religious violence similar to those that have marred the pages of history to date.

How pervasive is religious violence in the 1990s? Hindu militants in November 1990 attacked a sixteenth-century Islamic mosque in the northern Indian city of Ayodhya (one of India's seven sacred Hindu cities) which they claim was built on the site of the birthplace of Lord Rama. More than fifteen militants were shot and killed as they entered the area of the mosque. The mob finally sacked the mosque on December 6, 1992. Tensions persist in Israel, Lebanon, and Jordan. In Northern Ireland killings continue sporadically yet brutally. The conflict between the Islamic nations of Iran and Iraq, which continued for a decade as a full-scale war, only in 1990 reached a negotiated settlement. Asia and Africa are not immune from sporadic outbreaks of religious violence.

The crisis between Iraq and a U.S.-led military coalition which began in January 1991 and which was rekindled in January 1993 provides another example of twentieth-century violence which can trace its roots to religious fanaticism. Of course, this war found other roots in the world of economics, as the world's major trading blocs manoeuvred with and against each other in order to protect threatened energy resource supplies. But there continues to exist a religious tension as well, as various champions of the opposing causes claim self-righteously that the appropriate deity is on their "side," and that their cause is aligned with ultimate spiritual "truth." The arrogance which usually accompanies such claims carries an equally dogmatic intransigence. Such a mixture provides a fertile field for violence. It does not seem to be abating despite most draconian policing policies and often devastating loss of life. There has to be a process set in motion in which alternatives are employed. Any calls for "more of the same" in relation to official responses to violence will ensure "more of the same" levels of violence as well.

The irony in this situation is that virtually every religious tradition promotes nonviolence at its official level. For example, the famous Mosaic commandment in Exodus not to kill is endorsed by three of the "great" religions: Islam, Judaism, and Christianity. It would appear, however, that the rule against killing may be easily abrogated in circumstances in which *spiritual* justice is at stake. Although a temporal struggle may be bound by these restrictions, elevated to the cosmic realm, they may easily be bypassed. Symbols and mythology of most religious traditions are filled with violence and bloodshed. Any scholar of biblical tradition will remind us that I Samuel, chapter 15, in the Old Testament reveals to the reader that God has been presented to Christians and Jews by the writer as sanctioning the wholesale slaughter of people in a "holy war." Indeed, the so-called "just war" theory has been around since the days of Ambrose and later Augustine of Hippo in the fourth and fifth centuries.[3] Similar allegories are used in most faiths in an attempt to explain the "war" between good and evil. But the disturbing feature of the lives of some religious zealots is that often the allegories pass beyond the allegorical.

One might think that they should prevent violent acts by allowing violent feelings to be channelled into the harmless dramas of ritual, yet we know that the opposite is sometimes the case. The violence of religion can be savagely real.[4]

Some consistent themes can be found when one seeks to uncover the roots of religious violence. I examine briefly the Sikh/Hindu conflict, the Islamic Jihad's battle against zionism, and the fundamentalist Christian fanatics' battles with "heretics." The concept of duty to "cosmic" instructions appears common to all three. In that context they become exceedingly difficult to comprehend let alone contain or prevent.

Sikh violence in India came to recent world attention with the publicity surrounding Sikh leader Sant Jarnail Singh Bhindranwale in his religious campaign to save the Golden Temple in Amritsar from forces marshalled by the Indian government in 1984. Bhindranwale repeatedly reminded his followers that the Sikh tradition has always been filled with conflict and that the latter-day battles are simply the most recent chapters in a long ongoing war with the "enemies" of the faith. "The foes of today are connected with those from the legendary past," claimed Bhindranwale. Compromise is inappropriate and impossible, he said.[5] Thus there cannot be a negotiated peaceful settlement. Juergensmeyer continues:

In a sense, then, Bhindranwale feels that individual Sikh demands can never really be met, because the ultimate struggle of which they are a part is much greater than the contestation between political parties and factional points of view. It is a vast cosmic struggle, and only such an awesome encounter is capable of giving profound meaning to the motivations of those who fight for Sikh causes. Such people are not just fighting for water rights and political boundaries, they are fighting for truth itself.[6]

The symbols and mythology of Sikhism have parallels in the Islamic Jihad or "Holy War," although their leaders do subscribe to the possibility of political solutions.[7] Iran's spiritual leader, Ayatollah Ali Khamenei, has said that the return of the Palestinian homeland to the Palestinian people is a "divine duty" and any compromise is treason both to the nation and to the deity. Presumably a political solution—dialogue on the question of a separate Palestinian state—would go some way to reducing the level of tension and terrorism in the Middle East.

Isolated killings by fanatics, such as those of Jeffrey Lundgren the messianic cult leader who "sacrificed" a whole family in Ohio in 1989 on the "instructions of God," involve a different kind of violence. Yet Lundgren believed, apparently, that he, like Bhindranwale or Ayatollah Ali Khamenei, had discerned the mind of the eternal and was merely acting on divine instructions. In many respects, the arrogance displayed by all such religious fanatics who see violence as a legitimate means to greater cosmic ends breeds an extremely dangerous concoction which must be monitored and policed carefully.

The task for those charged with the responsibility of containing and reducing the violence is to ensure that their response is the most appropriate in all of the circumstances and does not inflame matters. The various responses to the violence of Bhindranwale, the Islamic Jihad, and Jeffrey Lundgren will necessarily be different, considering factors such as the nature of the society and its religious communities, the nature of the threat to the community generally, the political options available, and the deterrent effect upon others, to name a few. It is not sufficient to deal with violence of a religious nature simply by using a measure of force with no thought to the special need of the particular situation.

Juergensmeyer, drawing upon the work of Rapoport,[8, 9] has analysed religious violence and has isolated a number of features of religious faith and belief which appear to be common to groups engaging in such violence. These need to be considered in addressing the policing needs of such groups:

1. *The war between good and evil is seen in historical time and in real geographical location and continues to the present.* This conviction excites, for example, current-day movements such as the radical Jewish militant group Gush Emunim to continue their struggle con-

vinced that the Six Day War was a sign that messianic redemption has already begun. The major religious tradition that appears to lack this characteristic—Buddhism—is characteristically (although not exclusively) devoid of religiously sanctioned violence.

2. *Believers can identify with the struggle personally.*

If one believes that the cosmic struggle is primarily a matter of large contending social forces, one is not likely to become personally identified with the struggle; and if one is convinced that the struggle is solely interior there is no reason to look for it outside. But when the two ideas coexist, they are a volatile concoction.[10]

A contrast of the Islamic Sufis and the Shi'ites illustrates this point. The former see the Jihad within the soul, while the latter do not. Bhindranwale's Sikhs were asked to wage an external cosmic struggle. Jeffrey Lundgren saw his enemy in his immediate community.

3. *The struggle is at a point of apocalyptic crisis.* If religious leaders regard their cause as being poised on a delicate balance between oppression and opportunity and believe that human action can make a difference, then violence is more likely. Of course, that is not always the case, as the life of Mohandas Gandhi illustrates. But those who advocate a violent struggle very often use the rhetoric of uncertainty—that the final outcome is in doubt and a superhuman sacrifice is required in order to win the "battle." Bhindranwale expressed the desire that he die fighting, and his wish was fulfilled on June 6, 1984, within months of being uttered. If the foe is demonic, so the logic goes, even the most violent of aggressors will be saintly in death, and if the ends are so vital, even the most foul of deeds used in the means to reach those ends are justified. The recent posturing in the Salman Rushdie affair—a death sentence was placed on a British author accused of blaspheming the Islamic prophet by Iranian mullahs—saw

that even the most passive of people (British Islamic clerics) would condone Rushdie's execution if the blasphemy were evil enough.

The great promise of cosmic struggle is that order will prevail over chaos; the great irony is that many must die in order for certain visions of that victory to prevail and their awful dramas be brought to an end.[11]

What responses to religious violence are possible by governments and criminal justice agencies when violence is actuated by such a range of beliefs and in circumstances in which the militants are said to be undertaking a task often of cosmic proportions?

The first point to be made is that there must be attempts at understanding the various perspectives of the religious antagonists. The agencies must endeavour to come to grips with the various tenets of all religious orders which are violence-prone. This attitude will go some way to preventing the difficulties presented when one assumes that all religious struggles are alike. It will also help determine which religious struggles are "legitimate" and which are merely shams for opportune ulterior political motives.

Second, there has to be a reluctance to impose order by means of force of arms except as a last resort. A policy of force merely adds fuel to the fire of the martyred, in the same way that some short-term solutions to crime problems—such as harsher punishments—are often counterproductive in the long term. It may merely mean that the state is substituting one form of violence for another. If that substituted violence is justified by the state as being *morally* correct, then the state is playing into the hands of the martyrs who have alleged that their violent struggle is also morally sanctioned, albeit by a different moral ruler.

Third, there is a need for a greater tolerance of religious diversity—one that is encouraged by enquiry and study rather than fuelled by prejudice and suspicion. This re-sponse is, of course, less immediate, although it may ultimately be more effective than rule by the power of the sword. A society that is prepared to accept a variety of religious faiths, and in which religious faiths and orders lay fewer claims to moral superiority and place less emphasis on their absolute rights to moral authority is a society in which less violence will occur, without the need for repressive policing. John Stuart Mill once said that honesty necessitates the recognition that if one had been born elsewhere, one would probably have adopted the religious tradition of that particular culture.[12] Any serious reflection on that fact should forestall religious intolerance. An attitude, rather, of religious tolerance would go some way toward defusing the religious violence perpetrated in the wake of dogmatism, fear, and prejudice.

A corollary of the preceding response is the need for seeking solutions from within the faith itself and using terms which are familiar to the faithful. An example may be found in South Africa, a predominantly Christian nation, where violence has become a way of life in the struggle against apartheid. There, the leaders of many groups are endeavouring to site the struggle within religious frameworks which are compatible with the peaceful resolution of conflict. In contrast, an example of a response which is more likely to inflame tensions rather than reduce them is the oft-quoted (former U.S. President) Ronald Reagan phrase in which he referred to his superpower antagonists as "God-less" communists.

Mesle's discussion of faith, belief, and dogma[13] reminds readers of Bronowski's *The Ascent of Man*. In one scene from the film series, Bronowski waded out into a muddy stream near the Auschwitz prison camp. Kneeling down, he scooped up a handful of mud from the pond into which, very likely, the ashes of some 4 million people were flushed. Reflecting on what people do to one another when they claim dogmatically that they are absolutely right and certain, Bronowski noted that the Nazi atrocity was not done by gas.

It was done by arrogance. It was done by dogma. It was done by ignorance. When people believe that they have absolute knowledge, with no test in reality, this is how they behave.

Finally, he reminded viewers of Oliver Cromwell's words in 1650 to the General Assembly of the Scottish Church, "I beseech you, in the bowels of Christ, think it possible you may be mistaken."[14]

Conclusion

The world is currently dogged with political and ethnic violence. The religious influence on such violence is rarely studied, possibly because of the scepticism of observers who believe that its adherents are using it as a cloak for subversive political ends. Such an attitude ignores the fact that religious struggles are as diverse as they are numerous and require astute and perceptive policing rather than just the mere application of force.

It is Juergensmeyer's view that since religious language and symbolism often speak of the tension between order and disorder (often beyond this world) then religious fanatics are frequently found using violence as a means of explaining and justifying their positions. In those circumstances, treating these violent episodes as political, and policing and punishing them accordingly, may be inappropriate and merely an exacerbation of a violent situation.

The difficulties one must encounter when addressing this issue are numerous. The dynamics of religious conflict are often very difficult to isolate. The task one faces will require a better knowledge of the religious beliefs and faiths involved. If there is going to be any effective and long-term response, agencies and governments must not be so arrogant as to assume that they have the right to speak with moral authority, or to believe that a "whiff of grapeshot" will do anything other than heighten tensions and worsen an already volatile situation. Stone reminds us that it is foolish to expect that we can ever hope to deliver, once and for all, a just distribution of spiritual and temporal resources that will satisfy all people of all religious faiths.[15] But while it is not possible to bring justice down from the heavens, it may be possible to see solutions which may allow those in religious conflicts with themselves or with their state at least to survive together. At the heart of that solution must be a dialogue between religious faiths, the communities of which they form a part, and the governmental agencies which have been given a mandate to control the disorder. The challenge, in the first instance, goes out to those of our faith still vacillating over the merits of an interfaith dialogue. A rethinking of the mission of the Christian Church is essential if the peoples of this world are ever going to foster peace rather than promote violence.

Notes

1. Anthony Zwi and Antonio Ugalde, "Towards an Epidemiology of Political Violence in the Third World," *Social Science and Medicine* 28, no. 7 (1989): 633–642.
2. Mark Juergensmeyer, "The Logic of Religious Violence, The Case of the Punjab," *Contributions to Indian Sociology* New Series, 22, no. 1 (January–June 1988): 65–88.
3. Joseph Fahey, *Peace War and the Christian Conscience* (New York: The Christophers, 1982), 3.
4. Juergensmeyer, 76.
5. Ibid., 71.
6. Ibid.
7. Rudolph Peters, *Islam and Colonialism: The Doctrine of Jihad in Modern History* (The Hague, Netherlands: Mouton Publishers, 1979).
8. David Rapoport, "Fear and Trembling: Terrorism in Three Religious Traditions," *American Political Science Review* 78, no. 3: 658–677.
9. "Why does messianism produce terror?" unpublished paper delivered at the 81st Annual Meeting of the American Political Science Association, New Orleans (27 August 1985).
10. Juergensmeyer, 83.
11. Ibid., 87.
12. John Stuart Mill, *On Liberty* (New York: Liberal Arts Press, 1956), 22.
13. C. Robert Mesle, *Fire in My Bones: A Study in Faith and Belief* (Independence, Missouri: Herald Publishing House, 1984), 203.
14. Jacob Bronowski, *The Ascent of Man* (Boston: Little, Brown and Company, 1973), 374.
15. Julius Stone, *Aggression and World Order: A Critique of United Nations Theories of Aggression* (Westport, Connecticut: Greenwood Press, 1958), 120.

II
Theological Perspectives

II
THEOLOGICAL PERSPECTIVES

Editor's Note

Does it matter how we perceive Jesus Christ and interpret his ministry and message? Does it matter how that message is lived out in human relationships and in response to the Divine? The following authors feel these questions are worth discussing and invite the readers to consider their unique viewpoints.

Anthony Chvala-Smith suggests that when the issue of doctrinal norms in Restoration theology is examined, the tradition's search for its own core beliefs reflects the Protestant model of normativity. He supports this thesis by examining the search for the "essence of Christianity" in light of the early twentieth-century debate between Adolf von Harnack and Alfred Loisy. Harnack's identification of Jesus' message as the normative center of Christianity is comparable to the RLDS tradition of placing the message of Christ central in the church's life and thought.

RLDS Christology is also the subject of the paper by Gregory Prymak. He seeks to identify important strands of recent RLDS Christology within the framework of New Testament thought and practice, indicate how our approach to Jesus tracks and deviates from first-century Christianity, and illustrate how RLDS Christology is influencing the social fabric of the church. Prymak suggests that the church seeks to be true to the life and teaching of Jesus by carrying on his mission of redeeming humankind.

Enid DeBarthe explores how the concept of equal worth has been lived out through the course of history in regard to women's status. She traces trends in society and the church. Scriptures, if understood in their original language and context, can give new insights to long-held beliefs. What we perceive God's nature to be will be reflected in how we view each other and how God's love is lived out through us. New insights will come if the fetters of unexamined traditions are broken.

Our language reflects what we believe. If we believe theologically that all human beings are made in God's image, our language will be carefully scrutinized to see if it hurts or excludes. This includes the need to free God's image from male-exclusive language. God transcends both masculine and feminine characteristics. New metaphors can be created that more clearly communicate the Spirit of Love. Ruth Ann Wood reminds the reader that words are tools which can be chosen to clearly reflect the gospel message of God's unfailing love for all persons.

How the message of the gospel is lived out by the body of Christ is the concern of Rita Lester who envisions a liberating church and a ministry that is inclusive. She also sees that inclusive language, including metaphors about God, is an important corrective but not the whole picture. Significant, also, is how we view priesthood, sacraments, Zion, and scripture. She calls for a theological commitment to develop a "discipleship of equals."

The Harnack/Loisy Debate and Normativity in RLDS Theology

Anthony Chvala-Smith

This paper examines the issue of doctrinal norms in Restoration theology. I hold that the RLDS tradition's inclination to seek its own core beliefs is an expression of a Protestant model of normativity. This thesis is developed against the background of an early twentieth-century debate between Adolf von Harnack and Alfred Loisy on the appropriateness of seeking an "essence of Christianity." Harnack's definition of reformation as a "critical reduction to principles" and his identification of Jesus' message as the normative center of Christianity is parallelled in RLDS thought by a christological norm which the tradition critically applies to itself.

I. Normativity in Theological Perspective

The issue of theological norms appears as early as the Epistle to the Galatians. Paul closes the letter with a blessing: "Peace and mercy be upon all who walk by this rule" (Galatians 6:16 RSV). The word "rule" (Greek: *kanon*) signifies that standard by which the Galatian churches measure their faithfulness to the gospel. They are to walk by the rule of "new creation" (6:15 RSV). In the resurrection of the Crucified One, a new order of things has dawned, and the community's life should measure up to the "canon" of this event.

Paul's words epitomize a task theology continually takes up, for theology must concern itself with truthfulness. As a servant of the church, the theologian seeks to understand and clarify the community's faith. But

implicit in that faith, as the text from Galatians shows, are certain "canons" by which the appropriateness of claims and counterclaims must be measured. Making these norms explicit belongs to the theological task. To ask about "normativity" is to ask about those elements of a community's tradition which have regulative value. Associated with the issue of normativity are questions such as: How appropriate to the Christian story is the proclamation of the contemporary church? By what criteria will the church gauge its faithfulness to its identity and mission? By what warrants will the church measure various doctrinal claims?

Having doctrinal norms does not solve the problem of deciding how to use them. In RLDS tradition the "Three Standard Books" have the status of normative texts, but there is less agreement on how they should be used. Are they to be read through the "Epitome of Faith," Joseph Smith's personal experiences, historical-critical exegesis, popular psychology, or something else? Appeals to scripture or creed (as formal authorities) remain ambiguous without a prior agreement on hermeneutical principles. The community, therefore, needs what Schubert Ogden has called "a canon before the canon."[1] But of what will this canon consist? Will the community read its sacred texts in the light of its developing tradition or probe for a central, persisting symbol to function as the key to the canon?

This paper explores two representative answers to that last question: one Protestant and another Roman Catholic. These answers come from an early twentieth-century

European debate between the liberal Protestant church historian Adolf von Harnack and the Catholic New Testament scholar Alfred Loisy. The dispute focused on the value of seeking the "Essence of Christianity," an important notion in nineteenth-century religious thought. Their exchange illustrates how even among revisionist theologians the issue of normativity in the Christian faith will not go away.

Why turn to an academic quarrel which could hardly seem more removed from the Restoration tradition? First, in this debate two distinct models of normativity appear. "Models" are necessarily abstractions, but Harnack and Loisy clearly articulate typical positions. Their positions, I am convinced, provide a fresh angle from which to think about our experience.[2] Moreover, looking beyond the Restoration framework illustrates the point that theological isolationism is an unsatisfactory posture to assume, as well as an illusion. Responsible reflection on the Christian faith takes place only in conversation with the wider tradition. The discipline known as historical theology is a potent antidote for many theological illnesses, among which amnesia is the most debilitating.

II. Adolf Harnack and the "Essence of Christianity"

Adolf von Harnack (1851–1930) was possibly the greatest church historian of the nineteenth century.[3] A generation of pastors and theologians, including Dietrich Bonhoeffer and Karl Barth, received training in church history from him. From the publication of volume one of his *History of Dogma* (1885) until his book on Marcion in 1921,[4] a storm of controversy, unleashed by his conservative Lutheran opponents, surrounded Harnack's work.

Harnack's unconventional interpretation of Christian doctrinal development occa-

sioned much of the contention. For Catholicism, Eastern Christianity, and Protestant Orthodoxy, the classical dogmas attested by the great creeds (Nicaea, Constantinople, Ephesus, Chalcedon) timelessly express Christian faith. They contain the deposit of revealed truth and re-present the biblical revelation. Harnack raised serious questions about this traditional view. Early in his *History of Dogma*, he observes that dogma has a way of concealing its historicity. Because the dogmas arose in the historical struggles of the fourth and fifth centuries, they naturally reflect the theology of that period. Theology, however, always mirrors its environment.[5] Once doctrines are elevated to the position of revealed truths, their status obscures a real relation to the milieu from which they arose. Harnack holds that this connection between dogma and Greek culture must be explained.[6]

Harnack believed that the rise of dogma was a novelty: these formulas were not present at the inception of Christianity but clothed that religion in new garments.[7] So he penned the memorable words, "Dogma in its conception and development is a work of the Greek spirit on the soil of the Gospel."[8] He did not mean to disparage dogmatic development, for he saw it as a great achievement of the ancient church.[9] Nevertheless, his image of the gospel as the "soil" out of which dogma sprang is not happenstance. This "gospel" is the normative center of all subsequent doctrinal development; to apprehend it is to grasp the "essence of Christianity."

The Essence of Christianity (Das Wesen des Christentums, rendered *What Is Christianity?* in the standard English translation) was Harnack's most popular book. Originally a series of lectures at the University of Berlin in 1899–1900,[10] this book is often characterized as the classic statement of European liberal Protestant theology.

Harnack's aim is to identify in Jesus' message and person the permanent element of Christianity and to trace it through its different historical embodiments. Harnack was heir to the Idealist tradition in historiography, and he, therefore, believed that by grasping the whole historical phenomenon of Christianity, one could discern its *Geist*, its inner driving force.[11] Only then could the historian answer the crucial question: What is Christianity?[12]

Harnack thought this essence of Christianity could be readily identified in the message of Jesus. Something "alive" and "great" had permanently entered history in the gospel.[13] Jesus brought and embodied this reality, which can be summed up as follows:

> Firstly, the kingdom of God and its coming.
> Secondly, God the Father and the infinite value of the human soul.
> Thirdly, the higher righteousness and the commandment of love.[14]

Harnack believed simply that this was the timeless essence of Christianity: "[Jesus'] words speak to us across the centuries with the freshness of the present."[15]

The essence of Christianity has endured throughout history in various contingent forms. Harnack uses several metaphors to distinguish the center of the Christian faith from the periphery. He speaks of the gospel and its "contemporary integument,"[16] the life of the tree protected by its bark,[17] a "red thread in the centre of the web,"[18] and the "kernel and husk."[19] This last metaphor became problematic in the ensuing discussion. Harnack did not mean to imply that this "kernel" was inert, for the gospel was always primarily "life" for him. Rather, he used this image to show that the institutional forms necessary for preserving the gospel were not immutable.

An important corollary of Harnack's position is that knowledge of the gospel must promote a critical assessment of the forms which preserve it. This is the chief import of the phrase "Essence of Christianity." To evaluate the passing, historical manifestations of the Christian faith by its essence is to assume the posture of a *reformer*. Harnack asserts in Lecture 15 that the historical phenomenon of reformation always amounts to a "*critical reduction* to principles."[20] The genius of Protestantism is that it always drives toward the essence of Christianity. And though the essence never expresses itself apart from social structures, knowledge of it can contribute to the ongoing emancipation from old forms: Let the Reformation continue.[21]

III. Alfred Loisy and the Church's Gospel

Among the many rejoinders to *What Is Christianity?* came one book which has the reputation of having demolished Harnack's argument. Alfred Loisy (1857–1940), a Catholic priest and New Testament scholar at the Sorbonne, published *L'Evangile et l'Eglise* [English Translation: *The Gospel and the Church*, hereafter *GC*] two years after Harnack's lectures. Eventually five of Loisy's works, including *GC*, were placed on the Index of Forbidden Books.[22] Loisy strove in much of his work to articulate an authentic vision of Catholicism for the modern world. But the church had not yet caught up to the so-called "Modernists,"[23] and Loisy was excommunicated in 1908.

The argument in *GC* can be readily summarized. In response to Harnack's quest for a central idea in the Christian faith, Loisy doubts if any complex historical reality can be so neatly reduced.[24] The attempt to abstract an essence of Christianity from Jesus' message fails on two counts. First, Harnack's reading of the gospel tradition is supremely unhistorical in that it isolates Jesus from any vital connection with Judaism.[25] Second, the texts Harnack chooses as the quintessence of Jesus' message are too small a sample and possibly arose in the early Christian community.[26] And it was the centrality of the community that Harnack failed to grasp. On this Loisy deserves to be quoted in full:

Whatever we think, theologically, of the tradition, whether we trust it or regard it with suspicion, we know Christ only by the tradition, across the tradition, and in the tradition of the primitive Christians. This is as much as to say that Christ is inseparable from His work, and that the attempt to define the essence of Christianity according to the pure gospel of Jesus, apart from tradition, cannot succeed, for the mere idea of the gospel without tradition is in flagrant contradiction with the facts....[27]

Tradition is not only a mediator of the gospel but the continuation of Jesus' work. Jesus and his gospel cannot be abstracted from either the New Testament or the early church. Loisy agrees with Harnack that "Life" entered history in Jesus Christ; he disputes that this life is only incidentally connected to the developing community. Loisy's organic view of religious experience insists on the identity of the tradition with the gospel and on the importance of *development* as the way the gospel survives historically. "Why not find the essence of Christianity," he asks, "in the fulness and totality of its life, which shows movement and variety just because it is life...?"[28]

From Loisy's perspective, Harnack erred in choosing the metaphor of the kernel and the husk. In its place Loisy substitutes that of a seed growing into a tree.[29] The gospel Jesus planted germinated and grew into the Catholic Church. Isolating some principle of life from this living form is impossible, for life is apprehended in whole, concrete realities.[30] Loisy asserts that Catholicism "had to become what it has become: for it has become what it had to be to save the gospel by saving itself."[31] Harnack would have flinched at this exalted view of the church, not because Catholicism failed to impress him, but because Loisy ignored another fact

of the "law of development": the possibility of the organism's demise. But Loisy's is basically a Catholic vision of normativity. The church's norms are not simply extracted from the original events of revelation, but from the ever-evolving tradition.[32]

IV. Analysis: Harnack and the "Protestant Principle"

Harnack discerns from the whole phenomenon of Christianity its living center. The process of separating kernel from husk never ends, because as long as the phenomenon persists in history, it will clothe itself anew. But the kernel will always be the "gospel": Jesus' timeless message about divine benevolence, God's kingdom as the entry of eternal life into time, and the individual's religious life centering on the love of neighbor. Beyond this, Christianity is irreducible. Knowledge of the essence of Christianity permits a reformist stance toward whatever obscures the gospel.

For Loisy Christianity can never be reduced to an idea, for the individual only experiences the Christian faith historically in community. Because Jesus showed that he intended to form a church by gathering disciples, the evolving community *is* the essence of Christianity. Illumined by the principle of development, Christianity allows no critical reduction to principles.

Or does it? The degree to which Loisy wavers on this point cannot be pursued here. But let me suggest three weaknesses in Loisy's criticism of Harnack.[33] First, his developmental model does not clarify what standards will be used to identify distortions. To push Loisy's metaphor, how could we identify diseased branches in the tree? Second, even Loisy submits the Christian faith to the "critical principle" of development. But is the ever-developing church really above the gospel? In what does Christian *identity* consist? Finally, Loisy is not above using the same kind of essence language for which he rebukes Harnack. For example, he refers to the church's life as "proceeding from an obviously powerful principle."[34] Should not this principle, then, be claimed and given a regulative function? Though his critique of Harnack is incisive, Loisy, like his opponent, yearns for a new embodiment of the gospel in the modern period. In short, Loisy also protests against the tradition in the name of its vitality. That makes Loisy far closer to Harnack than he would have liked to admit.

His "protest" notwithstanding, Loisy remained a Catholic historian, even as Harnack remained a Lutheran. If Loisy's model of normativity reaffirms a traditional Catholic emphasis on ecclesiology and continuity, Harnack's model owes nearly all to Luther. Both Harnack and Loisy, however, had drunk deeply from the wells of modernity and, from the viewpoint of traditionalists in their respective communities, had thus compromised the integrity of Christianity. As a liberal representative of the Lutheran tradition Harnack embraced historical-critical methods, wanted to reinterpret the Reformation for modern German civilization, and found the classical dogmas to be out of step with Luther's purer religious impulses.[35]

For some these divergences banish Harnack from the Protestant circle. That cannot be decided here. But with his essence of Christianity, Harnack believed he was reaffirming Luther's own "critical reduction to principles." Luther lifted Christology and the doctrine of justification to the level of axioms and was thus able to challenge the penitential theology of the late medieval church. This normative center even led Luther to a bold reading of the New Testament, provocatively illustrated by his treatment of the Epistle of James. Luther broke with the long canonical tradition by placing Hebrews, James, and Jude (along with Revelation) at the end of his translation of the New Testa-

ment, and he did not list them in the index.[36] When Luther decided against the apostolicity of James, he gave the following reason:

[The author of James] teaches nothing about [Christ], and only speaks of common faith in God. For it is the duty of a true apostle to preach of the Passion and Resurrection and work of Christ, and thus lay the foundation of faith....All the genuine sacred books agree in this, that all of them preach Christ and deal with Him. That is the true test, by which to judge all books, when we see whether they deal with Christ or not, since all the Scriptures show us Christ...and St. Paul will know nothing but Christ. What does not teach Christ is not apostolic, even though St. Peter or Paul taught it; again, what preaches Christ would be apostolic, even though Judas, Annas, Pilate and Herod did it.[37]

Luther was prepared to distinguish center and periphery even in scripture. In this way he employed a "canon before the canon" as an hermeneutical lens.

In the tradition of his spiritual ancestor, Harnack upholds the gospel (in a truncated form Luther would not have recognized!) as the criterion of all Christian experience. His work bears witness to what Paul Tillich has astutely called "the Protestant Principle."[38]

V. Normativity in RLDS Thought

How does the conflict between Harnack and Loisy illuminate the issue of normativity in Restoration experience? I think a position very much like Harnack's is a *tacit* assumption in the RLDS tradition that needs to be made *explicit*.[39] In other words, the RLDS Church employs a Protestant paradigm of normativity: the extraction of "essential" values from the tradition and the raising of these to normative status.

Substantiating this thesis would require a monograph, but a few questions about some RLDS tendencies will show why the thesis is plausible. What hidden convictions lead the RLDS tradition to be critical of its founder? From where does its chariness of the Nauvoo period come? On what grounds does the church reject those theological and institutional developments of the tradition which are characteristically "Mormon"? What is signified by the general discomfort with Section 107 of the Doctrine and Covenants and ultimately its removal to the historical appendix (A)? (One is reminded of Luther moving Hebrews, James, Jude, and Revelation to the margin of the canon for theological reasons!) What can be made of WCR 222, which separates "the plain provisions of the gospel" from "speculative theories upon abstruse questions."[40] And what is the significance of locating "the *essential* meaning of the Restoration" [emphasis mine] in the task of being a "healing and redeeming agent" (Doctrine and Covenants 156:5e)?

I would argue that these tendencies conceal theological norms and that we see here an example of the "Protestant principle" at work. The RLDS Church, itself a "protest movement," has a Reformation-like propensity to measure doctrinal, historical, and practical claims by a set of core beliefs or values. From its beginning, the Reorganization found it necessary to distinguish itself from Mormonism; a critical reduction to essentials must be presupposed in the act of differentiating oneself from others in the same tradition. But, like Harnack, the church rejected the claim that all historical developments are appropriate.

The church has consistently, though not always reflectively, employed a theological "center" or some "essence of the Restoration" as a standard. Let me cite a few examples. For much of the church's life the canon before the canon was the doctrine of the "one, true church." This belief was the lens through which scripture and experience were interpreted and systematically organized. In addition, the "Epitome of Faith" has also functioned much like the *regula fidei* of the third- and fourth-century church: a "rule of faith" which summarizes the content of scripture and which, in turn, is used to interpret scripture.[41] Another example appears in the once-frequent missionary tactic of proclaiming the "Six Principles of the Gospel" (Hebrews 6:1), a phrase echoing Harnack's notion of "the Gospel in the Gospel."[42] And briefly in the 1970s one commonly heard some RLDS thinkers distinguish ultimate principles from middle principles. There is thus a long precedent in our tradition for distinguishing the essential from the peripheral.

What are the roots of this phenomenon? I would suggest that our "critical reduction to basic principles" shows a deep rootedness in Protestant Christianity.[43] Historically, this paradigm of normativity springs from the various Protestant theologies with which the Restoration has always had some contact. The church did, after all, emerge out of the experience of revivalism and it long drew members from mainline denominations. Except for a few superficial "catholic" tinges in church polity,[44] the RLDS community shares much with the Anabaptist traditions. Furthermore, the centrality of preaching in RLDS worship recalls the Reformed emphasis on the Word, and it is hard to imagine an RLDS hymnal without significant contributions from Isaac Watts and Charles Wesley. It can no longer be supposed that the Restoration, in splendid isolation, was dropped like a stone into the middle of the symbol systems of the historic Protestant churches. From these the "Protestant principle" has been mediated to us.

The clearest expression of this principle, though, is found in the way the tradition has learned to apply to itself a *christological* norm as its own doctrinal standard. "Whatever puts forth Christ" was Luther's revolutionary axiom. To steep oneself in the historical Jesus was Harnack's. Being a "Christ-centered church" has become ours. In the person and work of Christ we have found a central, persisting symbol to function as the canon of the Restoration: "This is my beloved Son; hear ye him." In this respect, it is interesting to note that Section 156 connects the "essence" of the Restoration with Christology.

Could this phenomenon have been possible if the "bark," so to speak, had never been protecting life, or the "husk" its living kernel? Here Loisy deserves to speak. For if the RLDS tradition has come to measure itself christologically, and if its Christology reaffirms the classical doctrines (which can be easily demonstrated), this could not very well occur unless the Restoration from the beginning drew life from the wider Christian tradition. In fact a "catholic" Christology appears as early as the preface to the Book of Mormon. Whatever else one conceives it to be, the Book of Mormon is unashamedly christocentric, which is true despite some confusing trinitarian formulations.[45] When the purpose of the work is proclaimed to be

...the convincing of the Jew and Gentile that Jesus is the Christ, the Eternal God, manifesting himself unto all nations.—Book of Mormon, iii

we can hear with a little imagination the distant voice of Luther avowing that whatever puts forth Christ is genuinely apostolic. The preface contains the critical principle of the RLDS tradition, and it is precisely this norm that links the Reorganization with the universal body of Christ in a way our ancestors were not able to see. A Protestant paradigm of normativity has begotten critical analysis of our own tradition, but the use of the paradigm leads to catholic (universalizing) ends. Harnack's victory is but a moment in the greater triumph of Loisy.

VI. Conclusion

From the analysis of the Harnack/Loisy debate, three important principles emerge. First, the Protestant paradigm of normativity already at work in the RLDS tradition discourages an absolutizing of the church. Tillich's "Protestant Principle" and Harnack's "critical reduction" find the tendency of institutions to identify their life with the divine life to be a distortion: a distortion that the ideology of "the one true church" has often advanced. However, this in no way invalidates the centrality of the church as the chief witness of God's redemptive activity in the world. Secondly, our tradition is inseparably connected with the wider Christian tradition. We cannot avoid the language, hymnody, and story of the Christian experience as we reflect on what we are and ought to become. While we must account for our unique saga, it did not arise in isolation, and we neglect the larger story at our peril. The third principle is that whatever forms the church uses in its proclamation, their adequacy must be measured by their ability to state the central Christian claim, that "God was in Christ" (II Corinthians 5:19 NEB). Some questions must be raised about the appropriateness of theological or philosophical systems that want to limit the place of Christ in the church's life and thought. The church, we may say in conclusion, stands or falls with its Christology.

Identifying a Protestant paradigm of normativity in our tradition will not necessarily pacify Calvinists, Lutherans, and Baptists. Nor will it solve all the church's current problems. If we read our story in the light of was Christum treibet,[46] it must still be asked, Which Christ, amid the plurality of portraits: classical? evangelical? revisionary? liberationist? On this we have been less clear. Moreover, if the RLDS Church still exists as a distinct institution, what is the relationship of the christological center to the church's unique story? In addition, to what extent does the doctrine of the kingdom of God—"the cause of Zion"—deserve a role as a normative principle? These questions suggest future theological tasks. Perhaps identifying our basic paradigm of normativity can help us in the struggle to discern the way ahead.

Notes

1. Schubert M. Ogden, "The Problem of Normative Witness: A Response," *Perkins School of Theology Journal* 41 (1988): 22–26. By a "canon *before* the canon," Ogden means a historically prior norm, which he thinks he can find in the undisputed words of the historical Jesus. I find his position theologically untenable. I have borrowed his phrase, however, because it avoids the notion of a "canon *in* the canon," some biblical idea arbitrarily used as the key to the whole of scripture. I use Ogden's phrase to mean the normative element(s) which is (are) already functioning in the RLDS tradition.

2. A classic text which shows the value of models in theological reflection is H. Richard Niebuhr's *Christ and Culture* (New York: Harper/Colophon, 1951, 1975). A more recent example is Avery Dulles' important study *Models of Revelation* (Garden City, New York: Doubleday, 1983).

3. A number of useful works are available in English for the background on Adolf von Harnack. A first-rate introduction to his thought by Wilhelm Pauck is found under the title "Adolf von Harnack" in *A Handbook of Christian Theologians* ed. Dean G. Peerman and Martin E. Marty (Nashville: Abingdon Press, 1965). Standard histories of modern religious thought that deal with Harnack are Claude Welch, *Protestant Thought in the Nineteenth Century*, Volume 2: 1870–1914 (New Haven, Connecticut: Yale University Press, 1972) and James C. Livingston, *Modern Christian Thought From the Enlightenment to Vatican II* (New York: Macmillan, 1971). An excellent anthology of Harnack's writings with an insightful introduction was recently published by Martin Rumscheidt in the Harper/Collins series, "The Making of Modern Theology: Selected Writings," under the title *Adolf von Harnack: Liberal Theology at Its Height* (San Francisco: Collins, 1989). For a good introduction to Harnack's historical milieu, see G. Wayne Glick, "Nineteenth Century Theological and Cultural Influences on Adolf Harnack," *Church History* 28 (1959): 157–182. A fine treatment of Harnack's thought in the context of nineteenth-century Neo-Kantian philosophy and Ritschlian theology is found in John Macquarrie's *Twentieth-Century Religious Thought*, 4th ed. (London: SCM, 1989).

4. *Marcion: Das Evangelium vom fremden Gott: eine Monographie zur Geschichte der Grundlegung der katholischen Kirche.* Darmstadt: Wissenschaftliche Buchgesellschaft, 1985 [reprint of 1924 ed.].

5. Adolf Harnack, *History of Dogma*, 1:9, translated by Neil Buchanan from the third German edition (New York: Dover Publications, 1961).

6. Ibid., 11: "If dogma is originally the formulation of Christian faith as Greek culture understood it...then dogma has never indeed lost this character."

7. Ibid., 1, 17. Because form criticism was only in its germinal stages, Harnack was unaware of the creedal and "dogmatic" nature of many New Testament traditions. The form critics, whose views Loisy anticipated, were later able to show the artificiality of Harnack's distinction between the simple message of Jesus and Christian dogma.

8. Ibid., 17.

9. Ibid., 22: "I have given quite as little ground for the accusation that I look upon the whole development of the history of dogma as a pathological process within the history of the Gospel. I do not even look upon the history of the origin of the Papacy as such a process, not to speak of the history of dogma."

10. Welch, *Protestant Thought*, 2:146.

11. This is the conclusion of Harnack's contemporary, the historian and philosopher of religion Ernst Troeltsch, in his essay, "What Does 'Essence of Christianity' Mean?" The 1913 edition of the essay is found in Ernst Troeltsch's *Writings on Theology and Religion*, translated and edited by Robert Morgan and Michael Pye (Great Britain: Duckworth, 1977), 124–181. For the section in which Troeltsch traces the phrase to the historiography of German Idealism, see pp. 128–137.

12. Adolf Harnack, *What Is Christianity?*, translated by Thomas Bailey Saunders, Fortress Texts in Modern Theology (Philadelphia: Fortress, 1986 [reprint, New York: Harper & Brothers, 1957]), 6, 9. Hereafter referred to as *WC*.

13. Ibid., 14.

14. Ibid., 51.

15. Ibid. I should also point out that Harnack presupposes a rather static anthropology. Citing Goethe, he insists that "Mankind is always advancing, and man always remains the same" (*WC*, 8). If the individual is always the same, there is no scandal of particularity in the gospel. Mind will always comprehend the products of Mind.

16. Ibid., 14.

17. Cf. Stephen Sykes, *The Identity of Christianity:*

Theologians and the Essence of Christianity from Schleiermacher to Barth (Philadelphia: Fortress, 1984), 2136–2137. I am unable to find this metaphor in *WC*, as Sykes claims. However, Sykes does cite the following from Harnack's *The Mission and Expansion of Christianity in the First Three Centuries*, translated by James Moffatt (New York: Harper, 1961 [from the 1908 German ed.]): "Like every living plant, religion only grows inside a bark. Distilled religion is not religion at all." I presume that this critique of "distilled" religion—religious faith abstracted from its social and historical embodiment—can be traced back to F. Schleiermacher's criticism of natural religion in his work *On Religion: Speeches to Its Cultured Despisers* (1799) (New York: Harper & Brothers, 1958).

18. *WC*, 298.

19. Ibid., 12.

20. Ibid., 270: "In the history of religions every really important reformation is always, first and foremost, *a critical reduction* to principles; for in the course of its historical development, religion, by adapting itself to circumstances, attracts to itself much alien matter, and produces, in conjunction with this, a number of hybrid and apocryphal elements, which it is necessarily compelled to place under the protection of what is sacred."

21. Cf. *History of Dogma*, 1:21: "The Gospel since the Reformation, in spite of retrograde movements which have not been wanting, is working itself out of the forms which it was once compelled to assume, and a true comprehension of its history will also contribute to hasten this process." The idea that the Reformation ought to continue is widely represented in nineteenth-century thought. On Harnack's relationship to this notion, Jaroslav Pelikan deserves to be quoted. He notes that it was Harnack's lifelong aim "to continue the Reformation by applying to dogma the same criticism which Luther had applied to the ecclesiastical institution...." J. Pelikan, "Adolf von Harnack on Luther," in *Interpreters of Luther: Essays in Honor of Wilhelm Pauck*, ed J. Pelikan (Philadelphia: Fortress, 1968), 258.

22. For Loisy in his context and the background of Roman Catholic Modernism, a number of texts are available. My summary relies on Bernard B. Scott's Introduction to the "Lives of Jesus Series" edition of *The Gospel and the Church*, translated by Christopher Home (Philadelphia: Fortress, 1976), xv-lxix. Especially valuable are Welch and Livingston (note 2, above). Perhaps the most perceptive study of the Harnack-Loisy debate is Stephen Sykes' analysis in *The Identity of Christianity*, 123–147. Also useful is Gabriel Daly's book *Transcendence and Immanence: A Study in Catholic Modernism and Integralism* (Oxford: Clarendon, 1980), 51–68. As a point of fact, to speak of a "debate" between Harnack and Loisy is inaccurate in a literal sense, because Harnack was in Berlin and Loisy was in Paris. Loisy offered his criticism of Harnack two years after Harnack's *WC* was published, and though Harnack reviewed *GC*, he never responded to Loisy's critique (cf. Sykes, 123–125). "Debate" is convenient shorthand.

23. "Modernist" is a slippery word, but in scholarly circles it usually means the varied group of Catholic theologians, historians, philosophers, and lay people (from the late nineteenth through the early twentieth centuries) who sought rapprochement with modern European culture. The more notable among them were Friedrich von Hügel, Loisy, and George Tyrrell. The movement was condemned in 1908, but many of the positions taken by Modernists, such as the historical-critical approach to scripture, were welcomed into Catholic theology by and during the time of Vatican II. In some sense the Modernists were ahead of their time.

24. *GC*, 4.

25. Ibid., 10: "It is, therefore, in the highest degree arbitrary to decide that Christianity in its essence must be all that the gospel has not borrowed of Judaism, as if all that the gospel has retained of the Jewish tradition must be necessarily of secondary value."

26. Ibid., 11–12.

27. Ibid., 13.

28. Ibid., 16.

29. Ibid., 16–18.

30. Ibid., 16. Loisy's position may be seen as a reaction to the rationalist tendency to ignore the contingencies of history for the sake of the "eternal truths of reason."

31. Ibid., 150.

32. Ibid., 166: "Jesus foretold the kingdom, and it was the Church that came; she came, enlarging the form of the gospel, which it was impossible to preserve as it was, as soon as the Passion closed the ministry of Jesus. There is no institution on the earth or in history whose status and value may not be questioned if the principle is established that nothing may exist except in its original form."

33. The longer I have studied this debate, the more sympathetic I have become to Loisy's position. Harnack typifies the reductionism of theological liberalism: its disposition to placate the pretensions

of modernity by abandoning whatever in the Christian faith does not fit the latest scientific discovery, political ideology, or philosophical fad. In retrospect Harnack the historian appears ironically to have traded the scandalous, historic particularity of the gospel for the particularity of modern (pre-World War I) bourgeois German culture. Thus he did not solve the very problem he set out to solve, but only shows how intractable it is. Nevertheless, in spite of these serious problems, Harnack's insistence on the need for a critical principle and his search for the roots of Christian identify reaffirm the central theme of the Reformation: that "Christianity" in any form remains accountable to the Word of God.

34. *GC*, 16.

35. Cf. Harnack, *WC*, 282–301.

36. Cf. Werner Georg Kümmel, *The New Testament: The History of the Investigation of Its Problems*, translated by S. McLean Gilmour and Howard Clark Kee (Nashville: Abingdon Press, 1972), 26.

37. Ibid., 25. Lest we be too critical of Luther's treatment of James, the Restoration movement has tended toward the opposite extreme: that of making the *non-pauline* books the center of the New Testament canon. That decision is frought with its own theological problems. Both extremes deprive us of the rich plurality of the New Testament canon.

38. Paul Tillich develops this principle throughout his *Systematic Theology* (Chicago: University of Chicago Press, 1981). The term signifies the prophetic, self-critical dynamic which attacks every identification of finite things (including churches) with their infinite Ground (*ST* 1:37, 227). The Protestant Principle has for its own Ground the Spiritual Presence (Tillich's term for God the Spirit). Critical protest against the tradition is an expression of the prophetic Spirit. On the other hand, Tillich, like Harnack, agrees that the Protestant Principle is always in need of social embodiment, or "Catholic substance" (*ST* 3:245).

39. The terms "tacit" and "explicit" have been borrowed from Avery Dulles' book, *Models of Revelation* (Garden City, New York: Doubleday, 1983), viii. Dulles, in turn, borrowed them from the philosopher Michael Polanyi.

40. *Rules and Resolutions*, WCR 222 (Independence, Missouri, 1980), 43.

41. On the rise of the "rules of faith" in the ancient church, see Frances M. Young, *The Making of the Creeds* (London/Philadelphia: SCM Press/Trinity Press International, 1991), 1–15.

42. On this phrase, see Harnack's essay "The Two-Fold Gospel in the New Testament," reproduced in Martin Rumscheidt's *Adolf von Harnack: Liberal Theology at Its Height*, 146–154.

43. It is not incidental that in Doctrine and Covenants 17:6b-c Joseph Smith pairs "justification" and "sanctification"—the twin pillars of Lutheran, Reformed, and Methodist theologies. What needs to be explored in greater depth is the actual use of Protestant *language* in RLDS thought. All I am able to do here is use Harnack's definition of "reformation" and his paradigm of normativity to suggest that the RLDS connection with the Protestant traditions is more than skin deep.

44. Here I take issue with William D. Russell, "The Latter Day Saint Priesthood: A Reflection of 'Catholic' Tendencies in Nineteenth Century American Religion," *Restoration Studies I*, ed. Maurice Draper (Independence, Missouri: Herald House, 1980), 232–241.

45. An example being Ether 1:77, where Jesus Christ is referred to as "*the Father and the Son.*" This distorts the necessary distinction between the persons of the Trinity and if pressed, makes Jesus into the God of Israel. This confusion of the trinitarian persons approaches the ancient Sabellian heresy. I am not saying that the Book of Mormon is without good trinitarian statements; it is appropriate to call Jesus "God" in the classical trinitarian sense as the preface does. However, it is unacceptable to call the Son the Father, not only by biblical and dogmatic standards, but also by the best intentions of the Book of Mormon itself.

46. A phrase from Luther meaning something like "whatever thrusts forth Christ." This little phrase was Luther's motto for that which is normative (or in his words, "apostolic") in scripture. See the citation at note 37.

Recent RLDS Christology*
Gregory Prymak

I. Introduction

This paper attempts to delineate some of the critical dimensions of RLDS Christology which have emerged during the last two or three decades.[1] To this end, it first briefly sketches four prominent New Testament christological motifs[2] and their social consequences for the early Christian movement, especially the types of communities they generated.[3] Then it highlights a few salient features of prevailing RLDS conceptions of Jesus and compares them with these New Testament antecedents to determine what basic christological orientation they seem to follow. Finally it traces various sociological tendencies of these theoretical premises, particularly their impact on the identity and structure of the contemporary RLDS Church.

This study is intended to do three things:

1. identify some of the important strands of current RLDS Christology and situate them within the larger framework of New Testament thought and *praxis*;

2. indicate how our approach to Jesus tracks and diverges from christological patterns of first-century Christianity; and

3. illustrate how our Christology is influencing the social fabric of the church, especially its philosophy of community.

II. The New Testament Backdrop
A. *Jesus the Apocalyptic Redeemer*

Jewish apocalyptic groups during the time of Jesus were many and their specific systems of belief varied, but in the main they

---

1. To stay within reasonable limits, it will deal not with how that Christology may have shifted in recent years but rather with what its main features appear to be.

2. The New Testament treatment of Jesus is, of course, exquisitely nuanced; the focus on four of its primary *topoi* is not intended to suggest the contrary or to oversimplify the discussion that follows. It seeks instead to articulate a conceptual framework (based on criteria derived from analyzing how Jesus was understood in the New Testament) within which contemporary RLDS Christology may be evaluated.

3. As Helmut Koester has noted:

> Moreover, the question of historical continuity between Jesus and the church has a sociological dimension. Jesus did not found a church or start a social or political movement—much less a revolution. He did not envisage the kingdom of God in any institutionalized form. Yet typical responses to Jesus, and the expressions of faith, the Christologies, which they produced, have very distinct ecclesiological as well as sociological and cultural implications.

Helmut Koester, "The Structure and Criteria of Early Christian Beliefs," in James M. Robinson and Helmut Koester, *Trajectories Through Early Christianity* (Philadelphia: Fortress Press, 1971), 209–210. The correctness of Koester's thesis can be seen in how Paul employs *one particular christological perspective*—that Christ died for us (I Corinthians 15:3–4)—to correct inappropriate *behavior* in the church at Corinth.

In I Corinthians 8:7–13, Paul warns Christian enthusiasts that if they eat meat which has been sacrificed to idols, they may trip up weaker members of the community, brothers and sisters "for whom Christ died" (verse 11). His advice: Do not eat such food if you may thereby offend others (verses 12–13). Paul does the same thing in I Corinthians 11:17–34. He invokes a eucharistic tradition which pivots on the atoning death of Jesus (verses 23–25, especially 24: "This is my body which is for you"); adds the comment, "For as often as you eat this bread and drink the cup, you proclaim the Lord's death until he comes" (verse 26); and cautions the "strong" Corinthians that sharing the Lord's Supper without discerning "the body" makes them guilty of the body and blood of the Lord (verses 27 and 29). His message: Stop mistreating poorer members of the church when you celebrate the eucharist (verses 17–22 and 27–34) In both instances, Christology has definite "sociological implications" because Paul presses it into service to determine Christian *praxis*. This paper, therefore, considers both belief and its social expression in reconstructing the New Testament background and in assessing RLDS Christology.

* All New Testament translations in this paper are by the author.

agreed that the present order was contaminated by evil and under the sway of hostile powers—Satan and his cohorts—who were persecuting God's faithful.[4] God, however, would soon intervene in human history to rectify this situation. Most but not all of these sects[5] expected God to do so by sending a Messiah, a mighty redeemer who would usher in the end of this age, subdue Satan and his allies, return control of the world to God, and reestablish God's reign on earth in which the suffering elect would participate as new, redeemed creatures.[6]

Some early Christians shared a similar perspective and identified Jesus as the coming Messiah.[7] This view runs through several New Testament passages;[8] these two are illustrative:

For if we believe that Jesus died and rose again, so also God through Jesus will bring with him those who fell asleep. For we are telling you this by the Lord's word that we the living who remain until the return of the Lord shall in no way precede those who fell asleep. For the Lord himself will come down from heaven with a shout of command, with the voice of an archangel and with the trumpet-blast of God. And the dead in Christ will rise first; then we the living who are left shall be caught up together with them in the clouds to meet the Lord in the air; and so we shall always be with the Lord.[9]

But in those days, after that tribulation, the sun will be darkened, and the moon will not give its light, and the stars will be falling from heaven, and the powers which are in the heavens will be shaken. And then they will see the Son of Man coming in clouds with much power and glory. And then he will send the angels and gather the elect from the four winds, from the end of earth to the end of heaven.[10]

The apocalyptic Jesus thus comes from heaven at the height of the earthly and cosmic distress of the end-times. He has great power and glory, by which he delivers control over the world to God, resurrects faithful Christians who have already died, and rescues those who are still alive from the present tribulation. His return, moreover, is imminent. This depiction "transcends the significance of the person of Jesus in relation to the summons to decision which he brings,"[11] for it centers on his exaltation and coming back as the heavenly, glorified Lord rather than on his historical life and ministry.

The early church at Thessalonica may have been an apocalyptic sect. In a careful study, Robert Jewett has noted in I Thessalonians various indications that a millenarian movement emerged within the Christian congregation there: a disintegration of sexual taboos, in theory if not in practice (4:1–8); a renunciation of regular employment or other business endeavors (4:10–12; 5:14); and a rebellion against the authorized lead-

---

4. Rudolf Bultmann, *Primitive Christianity In Its Contemporary Setting,* translated by Reginald H. Fuller (Philadelphia: Fortress Press, 1983), 82–85.

5. For instance, in the Psalms of Solomon, God (not a redeemer) is the one who will raise up a righteous king to rule over Israel. See Psalms of Solomon 17:1–3, 7–10, 21–25, 45–46, translated by R. B. Wright, in James H. Charlesworth, ed. *The Old Testament Pseudepigrapha,* 2 vols. (Garden City, New York: Doubleday & Company, 1985), 2: 665–669.

6. E.g., 2 Esdras 8:51–54 and 12:31–34, a Jewish apocalypse from the late first or early second century C.E. Numerous other examples can be cited; e.g., Qumran War Rule 11–12, in Géza Vermès, trans., *The Dead Sea Scrolls in English,* 2d ed. (New York: Penguin Books, 1985), 137–140.

7. Whether Jesus identified *himself* as such has been much discussed but is beyond the scope of the present inquiry. For useful analyses of this subject, see Ernst Käsemann, "On the Subject of Primitive Christian Apocalyptic," in *idem, New Testament Questions of Today,* translated by W. J. Montague (Philadelphia: Fortress Press, 1969), 111–124; Norman Perrin, *A Modern Pilgrimage in New Testament Christology* (Philadelphia: Fortress Press, 1974), 34–36, 57–83, 122–132 (*passim*).

8. Others include I Thessalonians 1:10; I Corinthians 15:51–52, 57.

9. I Thessalonians 4:14–18.

10. Mark 13:24–27.

11. Käsemann, "On the Subject of Primitive Christian Apocalyptic," 115.

ership of the church (5:12–13).[12] For these and other reasons, he concludes that this community had an "apocalyptic orientation" that some of its members converted into a "radical form of millenarism" characterized by a realized eschatology and a repudiation of "the structures of everyday life."[13] On the other hand, however, they appear not to have physically removed themselves from society, even though they rejected its institutions, norms, and activities.

Apocalyptic Christology thus tended to produce sectarian groups in early Christianity.[14] They were inclined toward quietism and neither totally withdrew from, nor aggressively engaged, the societies with which they were in contact.

B. Jesus the Agent or Incarnation of Divine Wisdom

Like apocalypticism, first-century Jewish sapiential theology was multiform. Most systems, however, conceived of Wisdom as a heavenly, preexistent and divine personage: she is the repository of information about the world[15] the one who reveals God to humans,[16] and the instrument by which God created the universe.[17]

Wisdom of Solomon (written in Egypt around the end of the first century B.C.E.) added important soteriological and eschatological dimensions to this picture. Wisdom lives with God and God loves her; hence she "is an initiate in the knowledge of God, and an associate in his works" (8:4). The one who lives with her not only receives knowledge from her (6:14; 7:17–22) but also takes on her very nature, is united with God, and receives immortality (6:17–20; 7:27–28; 8:13, 17). The righteous thus "live for ever" (5:15–16), in that their souls have *already* become immortal; they only appear

12. Robert Jewett, *The Thessalonian Correspondence: Pauline Rhetoric and Millenarian Piety* (Philadelphia: Fortress Press, 1986), 172–176.

13. Ibid., 118–132, 172–177 (*passim*). Koester believes that the primitive church at Jerusalem was also an apocalyptic sect, principally because it seems to have separated itself from the larger society in which it was situated, was "fairly stationary and had only limited missionary ambitions." Koester, "The Structure and Criteria of Early Christian Beliefs," 215–216 and note 19. As he himself recognizes, however, the evidence for this hypothesis is not direct or conclusive. The circumstances of the Jerusalem community are discussed in, e.g., Joseph A. Fitzmyer, "Jewish Christianity in Acts in Light of the Qumran Scrolls," in *Studies in Luke-Acts*, ed. Leander E. Keck and J. Louis Martyn (Nashville: Abingdon Press, 1966), 237–254; Ernst Haenchen, "The Book of Acts as Source Material for the History of Early Christianity," in ibid., 262–263; Sherman E. Johnson, "The Dead Sea Manual of Discipline and the Jerusalem Church of Acts," in *The Scrolls and the New Testament*, ed. Krister Stendahl (Westport, Connecticut: Greenwood Press, 1975), 129–142; and Hans Conzelmann, *An Outline of the Theology of the New Testament*, 2d ed., translated by John Bowden (New York: Harper & Row, 1968), 255–257.

14. Apocalyptic ideas about Jesus in all likelihood molded rather than mirrored patterns of Christian social development. As Käsemann has demonstrated, Paul used apocalyptic theology to refute the realized eschatology and crude sacramentalism of the Corinthian enthusiasts. He opposed the idea that through the operations of the Spirit, Christians have already received and begun to experience their ultimate salvation by arguing that Christ's lordship is only temporary because its objective is to deliver dominion over the world to God (I Corinthians 15:24–28). Jesus is "God's representative over against a world which is not yet fully subject to God"; the issue which underlies this passage is therefore: Who has control over the *cosmos?*—a thoroughly apocalyptic consideration. Käsemann, "On the Subject of Primitive Christian Apocalyptic," 132–133. Paul, moreover, extends this idea to anthropology by asking: To which lordship (God's or God's opponents') will you submit? and by holding that a person must submit to Christ's lordship *in fact* by acting properly as a member of his body, the church. Ibid., 135–136. So Paul's apocalyptic Christology regulates human conduct, not vice versa. Cf. John G. Gager, *Kingdom and Community: The Social World of Early Christianity* (Englewood Cliffs, New Jersey: Prentice-Hall, 1975), 28; Wayne A. Meeks, *The First Urban Christians: The Social World of the Apostle Paul* (New Haven, Connecticut: Yale University Press, 1983), 178–180.

15. E.g., Wisdom of Solomon 7:15–22.

16. E.g., Wisdom of Solomon 7:25–28. See also Sirach 24:3–34 and Baruch 3:9–4:12, in which Wisdom is personified as the Torah who dwells with Israel and fills people with understanding.

17. E.g., Proverbs 3:19–20.

to die because their immortality is "present now and continu[es] unbroken through physical death."[18]

Wisdom thus is at once the archetype and mediator of creation, revelation, and salvation, for she brings her followers into her own intimate relationship with God in their present realm of existence. She is, therefore, a mythic symbol of "the true divine identity of suffering righteous men," an identity which transcends real history, "differs radically from the earthly and human fate of the righteous," and separates them "ontologically from the rest of mankind."[19] So wisdom speculation turns on two key elements: a soteriology which takes the form of the devotee's "mystical repetition" of the union between God and divine Wisdom[20] and a realized eschatology based on the "immortality of the soul."[21]

Some early Christians had a similar understanding of Jesus, which can be seen in two sayings from Q (Luke 7:35-Matthew 11:19b, and Luke 11:49–51-Matthew 23:34–36). In the Lukan version, which is the more original,[22] Jesus acts as Wisdom's representative (as opposed to Wisdom herself) in declaring judgment against the present generation.[23] Matthew, however, redacts this material so that *Jesus* becomes the one who dispatches eschatological messengers and performs powerful works.[24] By transferring Wisdom's functions to Jesus, Matthew fuses the two into one and the same figure,[25] and Jesus now becomes the very incarnation of divine Wisdom.

This Matthean christological intention is also reflected in Matthew 11:25–30:

At that time, Jesus answered and said, "I praise you, O Father, O Lord of heaven and earth, because you kept these things secret from the wise and the understanding and revealed them to babes; yes indeed, Father, because you expressed your good will this way! All things were delivered to me by my Father. No one knows the Son except the Father, nor does anyone know the Father except the Son and the person to whom the Son may wish to reveal him. Come to me, all who labor and are burdened, and I will give you rest. Take my yoke upon you and learn from me, because I am gentle and humble in heart, and you will find rest in your souls. For my yoke is pleasant and my burden is light."

This passage consists of two sayings (verses 25–27 and 28–30) which in Jewish sapiential literature were originally spoken by Wisdom.[26] Matthew, though, attributes them to Jesus and thereby presents him as

18. George W. E. Nickelsburg, Jr., *Resurrection, Immortality, and Eternal Life in Intertestamental Judaism* (Cambridge, Massachusetts: Harvard University Press, 1972), 88–90.

19. Koester, "The Structure and Criteria of Early Christian Beliefs," 220.

20. Ulrich Wilckens, "Sophia," *Theological Dictionary of the New Testament*, ed. Gerhard Kittel, 10 vols., translated by Geoffrey W. Bromiley (Grand Rapids, Michigan: Wm. B. Eerdmans, 1965), 7:499–500.

21. Nickelsburg, *Resurrection, Immortality, and Eternal Life in Intertestamental Judaism*, 88–90, 162–164.

22. M. Jack Suggs, *Wisdom, Christology, and Law in Matthew's Gospel* (Cambridge, Massachusetts: Harvard University Press, 1970), 14–15, 33.

23. Ibid., 24–28, 35–38, 44–55.

24. Matthew modifies the sayings in Luke 7:35 ("Yet wisdom is justified by all her children") and 11:49 ("Therefore also the Wisdom of God said") to read: "Yet wisdom is justified by her deeds" (Matthew 11:19); and "Therefore, behold *I* send you prophets and wise men and scribes" (Matthew 23:34). Ibid., 55.

25. Ibid., 59–61.

26. See Sirach 51:26–27: "Put your neck under the yoke, and let your souls receive instruction; it is to be found close by. See with your eyes that I have labored little and found for myself much rest." Suggs regards both Matthean sayings (verses 25–27 and 28–30) as having originated in Jewish wisdom circles, particularly in view of the resemblance between verses 28–30 and Sirach 51:26–27. Ibid., 77–81, 95–97. Bultmann agrees that the latter is a wisdom saying but holds that the former is a "Hellenistic revelation saying." Rudolf Bultmann, *The History of the Synoptic Tradition*, translated by John Marsh (New York: Harper & Row, 1963), 159–160. Whatever their source(s) may have been, however, *Matthew* clearly sees a nexus between them, which is why he arranges them *seriatim*.

divine Wisdom personified rather than as just her mouthpiece.[27]

The New Testament christological hymns run in the same vein.[28] In Philippians 2:6–11, Paul takes up what was once probably a hymn to Wisdom and recasts it as a drama of Jesus' incarnation:[29]

[W]ho, although he was in the form of God, did not consider that to be equal with God was robbery, but by taking the form of a slave, he emptied himself, becoming in the likeness of humans. And after he was found in a form like a human, he humbled himself by becoming obedient to the point of death, even the death of a cross. Wherefore God also raised him to the highest height and freely gave him the name which is above every name, so that at the name of Jesus every knee may bend, those which are in heaven and on earth and under the earth, and every tongue may confess that Jesus Christ is Lord, to the glory of God the Father.

According to this passage, Christ is preexistent and equal to God (verse 6), comes down from heaven to earth (verse 7), dies in obedience to God (verse 8), is exalted and enthroned in heaven (verse 9), and receives lordship over the entire *cosmos* (verses 10–11).[30] The soteriological presuppositions of this *schema* are implicit but unmistakable: human redemption is a derivative of the close correspondence between Christ's servanthood, enfleshment, and obedience to the point of death.[31]

So like divine Wisdom, Jesus is a preexistent, heavenly redeemer who descends to earth, is rejected by those to whom he is sent,[32] and redeems humankind.[33] This Christology not only reflects the features,[34] but also carries the same latent tendencies, of Jewish wisdom speculation—to dissolve his historical reality into a timeless, mythic figure; to make salvation a mystical reprise of his exaltation and cosmic enthronement; and to develop a realized eschatology in which the wise person already begins to experience immortality.[35]

27. Suggs, *Wisdom, Christology, and Law in Matthew's Gospel*, 95–97.

28. Space constraints preclude considering the related hymns in John 1:1–11, Colossians 1:15–20, I Timothy 3:16, I Peter 3:18–22, and Hebrews 1:3. For excellent analyses of these passages, see Ernst Käsemann, "A Primitive Christian Baptismal Liturgy," in *idem, Essays on New Testament Themes*, 2d ed., translated by W. J. Montague (London: SCM Press, 1960), 149–168; Käsemann, "The Structure and Purpose of the Prologue to John's Gospel," in *New Testament Questions of Today*, 138–167; Jack T. Sanders, *The New Testament Christological Hymns: Their Historical Religious Background* (Cambridge: University Press, 1971), 29–57, 75–95; James M. Robinson, "A Formal Analysis of Colossians 1:15–20," *Journal of Biblical Literature* 76 (1957): 270–287.

29. The background and derivation of this passage are disputed. Bultmann and Käsemann locate it in the stream of Hellenistic religion, particularly the Gnostic Redeemer myth. E.g., Rudolf Bultmann, *Theology of the New Testament*, 2 vols., translated by Kendrick Grobel (New York: Charles Scribner's Sons, 1951), 1:175–176, 298. Dieter Georgi and others, however, set it within Hellenistic Judaism. The point is too complicated to be explored here. For useful reviews of the literature, see Ralph P. Martin, *Carmen Christi: Philippians ii. 5–11 in Recent Interpretation and in the Setting of Early Christian Worship* (Grand Rapids, Michigan: William B. Eerdmans, 1983), 63–95; R. G. Hamerton-Kelly, *Pre-Existence, Wisdom, and the Son of Man: A Study of the Idea of Pre-Existence in the New Testament*, Society for New Testament Studies Monograph Series 21 (Cambridge: University Press, 1973), 156–168.

30. Sanders, *The New Testament Christological Hymns: Their Historical Religious Background*, 24–25; Gunther Bornkamm, "On Understanding the Christ-hymn (Philippians 2.6–11)," in *idem, Early Christian Experience*, translated by Paul L. Hammer (New York: Harper & Row, 1969), 113–116.

31. Bornkamm, "On Understanding the Christ-hymn (Philippians 2.6–11)," 115–116.

32. This feature of the Christ-hymn also appears in Jewish wisdom traditions. E.g., in I Enoch, Wisdom leaves heaven and comes down to earth but is unable to find a dwelling place among humankind. She therefore returns to heaven, where she "settle[s] permanently among the angels." I Enoch 42, translated by E. Isaac, in *The Old Testament Pseudepigrapha*, 1:33.

33. The idea of redemption undergirds the close correspondence between Christ's servanthood, enfleshment as a human, and obedience to the point of death. Ibid.

34. Sanders, *The New Testament Christological Hymns: Their Historical Religious Background*, 73–74, 96–97.

35. Koester, "The Structure and Criteria of Early Christian Beliefs," 222; Bornkamm, "On Understanding the Christ-Hymn," 116, 119–121.

The social results of wisdom Christology are reflected in Paul's first epistle to the church at Corinth. The Corinthians are enamored of "wisdom" (2:1–5; 3:18–19), so much so that one of their favorite slogans is, "We know that we all have knowledge!" (8:1–6).[36] What is more, they think that they have *already* begun to experience God's dominion over the world (4:8),[37] i.e., *they believe that they have attained wisdom and, through it, are now released from death and enjoying the benefits of eternal life.*[38] Worse still, they have divided into competing factions and are expressing loyalty to rival leaders, one of whom is "Christ" (1:10–13; 3:3–4, 21–23).[39]

Paul responds to this situation as follows:

For the word of the cross is foolishness to those who are perishing, but to us who are being saved, it is the power of God. For it has been written, "I will destroy the wisdom of the wise and I will reject the intelligence of the intelligent." Where is the wise one? Where is the scribe? Where is the debater of this age? Did not God make foolish the wisdom of the world? For since in the wisdom of God the world did not understand God through wisdom, God determined to save, through the foolishness of preaching, those who believe. And when Jews ask for signs and Greeks seek wisdom, *we* preach Christ who has been crucified—to Jews an offense and to Gentiles foolishness, but to the very ones who are called, both Jews and Greeks, we preach Christ—who is the power of God and the wisdom of God. For the foolishness of God is wiser than people and the weakness of God is stronger than people.... But on the basis of God, *you* are in Christ, who was made our wisdom by God—both righteousness and sanctification and redemption....[40]

Paul's opponents at Corinth are saying that they possess a wisdom which has salvific consequences. His refutation of their claim is carefully constructed on the premises that Christ is not just one factional leader among several within the community but instead is "the wisdom of God"; that he has been crucified; and that what *really* saves is the Christ of the cross, not the "wisdom" of which they have been boasting.

That Paul casts the debate in such starkly Christological terms indicates that the Corinthians had most likely come to their position through Christology, i.e., that they had derived their belief that they had knowledge and had already begun to reign from a gnosticizing wisdom Christology which emphasized the cosmic (as opposed to the historical) dimensions of Jesus' life and ministry.[41] The outcome was a soteriology based on the individual appropriation of saving knowledge and experience of the Spirit; a realized eschatology; and an ecclesiology which fractured the community into contending theological schools "in which the teacher (Peter, Paul, Apollos, Christ) is considered as the leader into divine wisdom."[42]

C. Jesus the Miracle-Worker[43]

Many people in the ancient world believed that divine power could reside in and

---

36. Hans Conzelmann, *1 Corinthians: A Commentary on the First Epistle to the Corinthians*, translated by James W. Leitch, Hermeneia Series (Philadelphia: Fortress Press, 1975), 140–141.

37. The verb here is βασιλευειν, which means "to receive and exercise the power of a monarch."

38. Cf. Käsemann, "On the Subject of Primitive Christian Apocalyptic," 125–127; Conzelmann, *1 Corinthians*, 260–277 (*passim*).

39. For an excellent discussion of the Corinthian "parties," see Conzelmann, *1 Corinthians*, 31–34.

40. I Corinthians 1:18–24, 30.

41. Cf. Käsemann, "On the Subject of Primitive Christian Apocalyptic," 126–127.

42, Koester, "The Structure and Criteria of Early Christian Beliefs," 223. See also Käsemann, "On the Subject of Primitive Christian Apocalyptic," 125–131.

43. The so-called Hellensitic "divine man" is a disputed topic among New Testament scholars. Commentators, for example, disagree about whether the divine man was a relatively standard or diverse figure in the Greco-Roman period; whether ancient biogrphies of holy men comprised a recognizable literary genre (e.g., the aretalogy); and whether Jewish and/or pagan conceptions of the divine man influenced Christian ideas about Jesus and if so, how and to what extent. These questions are much too complex to be considered at any length here. For contrasting solutions, compare

be manifested by exceptional persons in the form of superhuman phenomena, such as prodigy, outstanding virtue, impressive moral instruction, supramundane insight, exorcism, healing, and miracles of all sorts.[44] Revered men were, therefore, quite popular, and accounts of their amazing exploits circulated widely in both pagan and Jewish circles. The famed mathematician Pythagoras of Samos (sixth century B.C.E.), for instance, was reported to have had extraordinary prescience; to have "uttered proclamations which earthquakes would not transgress [and] spells which rapidly drove off plagues and checked violent winds and hailstorms and calmed the waters of rivers and seas"; and to have passed on his miraculous techniques to his disciples, who produced similar wonders themselves.[45] The itinerant philosopher Apollonius of Tyana (late first century C.E.) was said to have expelled a demon from a young man and to have brought a dead girl back to life.[46] According to the Jewish author Josephus, who lived in Jerusalem and (later) Rome during the latter half of the first century C.E., Solomon possessed wisdom *par excellence*, which included the knowledge of how to exorcise demons and how to cure human illnesses through various incantations. What is more, he wrote these formulae down and left them behind so that:

...[T]his kind of cure is of very great power among us to this day, for I have seen a certain Eleazar, a countryman of mine, in the presence of Vespasian, his sons, tribunes and a number of other soldiers, free men possessed by demons, and this was the manner of the cure: he put to the nose of the possessed man a ring which had under its seal one of the roots prescribed by Solomon, and then, as the man smelled it, drew out the demon through his nostrils, and, when the man at once fell down, adjured the demon never to come back into him, speaking Solomon's name and reciting the incantations which he had composed. Then, wishing to convince the bystanders and prove to them that he had this power, Eleazar placed a cup or foot-basin full of water a little way off and commanded the demon, as it went out of the man, to overturn it and make known to the spectators that he had left the man. And when this was done, the understanding and wisdom of Solomon were clearly revealed, on account of which we have been induced to speak of these things, in order that all men may know the greatness of his nature and how God favoured him,

generally, e.g., Carl R. Holladay, Theios Aner in *Hellenistic Judaism: A Critique of the Use of this Category in New Testament Christology*, Society of Biblical Literature Dissertation Series 40 (Missoula, Montana: Scholars Press, 1977); David Lenz Tiede, *The Charismatic Figure as Miracle Worker*, Society of Biblical Literature Dissertation Series 1 (Missoula, Montana: University of Montana, Society of Biblical Literature, 1972); and Howard Kee, "Aretalogy and Gospel," *Journal of Biblical Literature* 92 (1973): 402–422; with Dieter Georgi, *The Opponents of Paul in Second Corinthians* (Philadelphia: Fortress Press, 1986); Paul J. Achtemeier, "The Origin and Function of the Pre-Marcan Miracle Catenae," *Journal of Biblical Literature* 91 (1972), 198–221; Helmut Koester, "One Jesus and Four Primitive Gospel," in *Trajectories Through Early Christianity*, 187–193; Morton Smith, "Prolegomena to a Discussion of Aretalogies, Divine Men, the Gospels and Jesus," *Journal of Biblical Literature* 90 (1971): 174–199; Hans Dieter Betz, "Jesus as Divine Man," in *Jesus and the Historian: Written in Honor of Ernest Cadman Colwell*, ed. F. Thomas Trotter (Philadelphia: The Westminster Press, 1968), 114–133; and Moses Hadas and Morton Smith, *Heroes and Gods: Spiritual Biographies in Antiquity* (New York: Harper & Row, 1965), 3–97. Placing the following section under the rubric *Jesus the Miracle-Worker* is intended to bypass this thicket of unresolved issues while at the same time considering thaumaturgy as one early Christian criterion for evaluating Jesus.

44. See generally Smith, "Prolegomena to a Discussion of Aretalogies, Divine Men, the Gospels and Jesus," 181–188; Paul J. Achtemeier, "Gospel Miracle Tradition and the Divine Man," *Interpretation* 26 (1972): 175–188. Dieter Georgi has pointed out that in the Hellenistic period, people would also have recognized divinity as being active in those who excelled in other, more this-worldly, pursuits, e.g., literature, rhetoric, music, dance, art, athletics, law, and politics. Georgi, *The Opponents of Paul in Second Corinthians*, 402–405.

45. Porphyry, *The Life of Pythagoras*, Morton Smith, trans., in Hadas and Smith, *Heroes and Gods: Spiritual Biographies in Antiquity*, 115–116.

46. Philostratus, *The Life of Apollonius of Tyana*, 4.20, 4.45, translated by F. C. Conybeare, Loeb Classical Library, 2 vols. (Cambridge, Massachusetts: Harvard University Press, 1912), 1:389–393, 1:457–459.

and that no one under the sun may be ignorant of the king's surpassing virtue of every kind.[47]

Although these accounts differ in their specific form, content, narrative, and religious context, they have several elements in common. They revolve around the hero's singular accomplishments, which they take pleasure rehearsing in considerable detail. Their intention thus is to establish *on the basis of his feats* that divine power was present in and operative through this extraordinary personality. The central character, then, is a man of virtue and divine power, a man who is to be believed in because of what he produces: marvelous things.[48] Perhaps just as important, he can *and does* transmit his preternatural capabilities to others.[49] So equipped, they are able to repeat his powerful deeds in their own experience.

Similar ideas about Jesus arose at an early stage of Christian development. They are fairly transparent in the Markan miracle stories, of which the stilling of the sea (Mark 4:35–41) is typical.[50]

And he said to them on that day, after evening had come, "Let us go over to the other side." And after they left the crowd they took him, as he was, in the boat; and other boats were with him. And a great storm of wind occurred and the waves beat into the boat, with the result that the boat was already filling. And he himself was in the stern, sleeping on the cushion. And they awoke him and said to him, "O Teacher, is it no concern to you that we are perishing?" And after he awoke, he rebuked the wind and said to the sea, "Quiet! Be silent!" And the wind stopped and there was a great calm. And he said to them, "Why are you afraid? Do you not yet have faith?" And they were frightened with great fear and began to say to one another, "Who then is this, that even the wind and sea obey him?"

Like its Jewish and pagan counterparts, this pericope *as Mark found it in his sources*[51] focuses on Jesus' supernatural *facta*, for it recounts what he did and raises the question of who he is in light of it. Absent from the story, on the other hand, is any proclamation *by* or *about* Jesus, e.g., he does not announce the coming of the kingdom, and no explanation is provided as to the meaning of his death and resurrection.[52] Attention instead is riveted on what he accomplishes (stilling the storm and waves) and how he brings it about (rebuking the wind and commanding the sea). The dramatic construction, moreover, heightens the impact of the miracle itself by building tension in the plot: Jesus is asleep and the disciples are afraid. All appears to be lost or nearly so. The question posed is: Is Jesus

---

47. Josephus, *Antiquities of the Jews* 8.2.5, in *Josephus*, translated by H. St. J. Thackeray and Ralph Marcus, Loeb Classical Library, 9 vols. (Cambridge, Massachusetts: Harvard University Press, 1958), 5:593–597.

48. Cf. Smith, "Prolegomena to a Discussion of Aretalogies, Divine Men, the Gospels and Jesus," 176; Kee, "Aretalogy and Gospel," 409, 412–416.

49. George, *The Opponents of Paul in Second Corinthians*, 255–258.

50. For an interesting but (in some respects) problematic analysis of others in Mark 4–8, see generally Paul J. Achtemeier, "Toward the Isolation of Pre-Markan Miracle Catenae," *Journal of Biblical Literature* 89 (1970): 274–91. A broader treatment of miracle stories in all four Gospels is found in Betz, "Jesus as Divine Man," 117–133.

51. In his *redaction* of this material, Mark devalues theurgy as an appropriate foundation on which to construct a faith in Jesus. As Mark 8:14–21 plus 31–38 and other passages show, he is not to be understood as a miracle-worker but as the suffering and dying Son of God. For valuable analyses of this point, see generally Theodore J. Weeden, *Mark—Traditions in Conflict* (Philadelphia: Fortress Press, 1971), 52–69; Betz, "Jesus as Divine Man," 121–133; Leander E. Keck, "Mark 3:7–12 and Mark's Christology," *Journal of Biblical Literature* 84 (1965): 352–358. Matthew and John take a similar approach, albeit to advance their own different christological agendas. See, e.g, Heinz Joachim Held, "Matthew as Interpreter of the Miracle Stories," in Günther Bornkamm, Gerhard Barth and Heinz Joachim Held, *Tradition and Interpretation in Matthew*, translated by Percy Scott (Philadelphia: The Westminster Press, 1963), 253–255; and Ernst Kasemann, *The Testament of Jesus: A Study of the Gospel of John in the Light of Chapter 17*, translated by Gerhard Krodel (Philadelphia: Fortress Press, 1968), 21–22.

52. Keck, "Mark 3:7–12 and Mark's Christology," 350; Betz, "Jesus as Divine Man," 121.

equal to the challenge? The answer of the tradition is obviously, Yes! not only because he achieves spectacular results but also because they are acclaimed as such by onlookers.

Jesus is portrayed here first and foremost as a miracle-worker. He is more than human, for what he does shows that God's power is present in and effective through him.[53] Faith in Jesus is, therefore, predicated on his thaumaturgy, which reveals him to be an epiphany of the divine.[54]

Paul's second letter to Corinth shows the consequences of this theurgic Christology. Dieter Georgi has demonstrated that the adversaries whom Paul criticizes there are itinerant charismatic Christian missionaries, outsiders who have come into the church claiming to be apostles superior to Paul himself.[55] They are convincing speakers (11:6), and they preach pneumatically out in public to impress both curious pagans and interested Christians (2:17).[56] They carry with them letters of recommendation from other Christian congregations, attesting the mighty things which they have done through the Spirit (3:1; 5:12; cf. 12:11),[57] including inspired interpretation of scripture (3:12–18);[58] performance of miracles (12:11–13);[59] and experience of visions and revelations (5:12–13; 12:1–10).[60]

Paul's counterattack is telling: the "hyper-apostles" are actually proclaiming "another Jesus" than the one he does (11:4). His objection becomes clear in light of what he says in II Corinthians 4:5, 7:

For we do not preach ourselves but Jesus Christ who is Lord. But we ourselves are your slaves because of Jesus.... But we have this treasure in clay vessels, so that the outstanding quality of the power may be of God and not on the basis of us.

Viewing Jesus as a thaumaturge, Paul's opponents have themselves become thaumaturges. Now as such, they are extolling their powerful acts as if they were their own personal achievement. Paul responds that Jesus Christ is *Lord*, i.e., he is not a wonder-worker but the one who died for all and was resurrected (4:10; 5:14–15). True apostleship, therefore, consists not of producing miracles but of becoming a slave to others (4:5), even if it requires enduring hardship for their sake (4:7–11; 11:23–29; 12:5–10).[61]

As in I Corinthians, Paul here bases his critique on Christology. The specifics of his point-counterpoint suggest that his rivals held a view of Jesus which concentrated on his theurgy. This understanding in turn caused them to become preoccupied with miracle-working and self-promotion, rather than with obedient servanthood. Christian

---

53. Betz. "Jesus as Divine Man," 120; Keck, "Mark 3:7–12 and Mark's Christology," 349–350; Weeden, *Mark—Traditions in Conflict*, 55; Koester, "One Jesus and Four Primitive Gospels," in *Trajectories Through Early Christianity*, 187–188. Acts 2:22 makes the same point even more bluntly: "O Israelite men: hear those words! Jesus of Nazareth, a man proven to you by God, by miracles and wonders and signs which God did through him in your midst, just as you yourselves know...."

54. Betz, "Jesus as Divine Man," 120–121; Keck, "Mark 3:7–12 and Mark's Christology," 350; Achtemeier, "The Origin and Function of the Pre-Marcan Miracle Catenae," 205–206.

55. *Contra* C. K. Barrett, "Paul's Opponents in II Corinthians," *New Testament Studies* 17 (1970–1971): 233–254. Barrett argues (page 251) that they were "Jews, Jerusalem Jews, Judaizing Jews" who set up "a rival apostolate to Paul's, backed by all the prestige of the mother church."

56. Georgi, *The Opponents of Paul in Second Corinthians, 234–238.*

57. Ibid., 243–245.

58. Ibid., 262–264.

59. Ibid., 281.

60. Ibid., 280–281.

61. Ibid., 273–276. Notice that Paul also couples his discussion of weakness in 11:30 with a reference to "the Lord Jesus" in the next verse.

faith was thereby severed from the "historical revelation in Jesus" and instead became premised on the aspect of the miraculous.[62] The practical outcome was that the super-apostles and those whom they attracted were more concerned with edifying themselves and advancing their own positions through supernatural operations than with building up the Christian community through humble, selfless service to others.

D. Jesus the Crucified and Risen Christ

A widespread Jewish expectation during Jesus' era was that God would one day bring the world to an end, at which time God would redeem Israel and resurrect those who had been persecuted for practicing righteousness.[63] After Jesus was crucified, some of his followers had vivid experiences in which he appeared to them, alive again. They interpreted his return from the dead to indicate that God had inaugurated the redemption of Israel and that the end-times were therefore at hand.[64]

The resurrection of Jesus quickly became an important theme of the early Christian proclamation. In I Corinthians 15:3–5, Paul quotes part of a very early creed which succinctly expresses it:

For I delivered to you among the most important matters what I also received: that Christ died for our sins according to the scriptures, that he was buried, that he was raised on the third day according to the scriptures, and that he was seen by Cephas and then by the twelve.

These verses have a distinctive pattern.

A   Christ died for our sins according to the scriptures.

A, He was buried.

B   He was raised the third day according to the scriptures.

B, He was seen by Cephas and then by the twelve.

This structure highlights the decisive events of the Christian message, i.e., those with salvific consequences—Christ's death for our sins and his resurrection the third day. Each is attested not only by the scriptures but also by the historical data, for his burial confirms that he died, his observation by witnesses that he was raised back to life.[65]

So this creed underscores that Jesus was a real, complete person who actually died and was subsequently resurrected. In so doing, it also produces a soteriology which is bottomed on the *historical circumstances* of his expiatory death.

The social application of this "risen Christ" Christology appears in Paul's first Corinthian letter. As noted above, his opponents suppose that they have wisdom and are, therefore, already experiencing salvation. Paul counters by stressing not only that the return of Christ and the resurrection of the faithful are still future (11:26; 15:12–28, 51–56)[66] but also that Christ died for us and has thereby made all Christians "one body," "the body of Christ."

For just as the body is one and has many members, and all the members of the body (although they are many) are one body, so also is Christ. For indeed we were all

---

62. Koester, "The Structure and Criteria of Early Christian Beliefs," 219.

63. E.g., 2 Maccabees 7:7–9; Esdras 7:26–38, 88–89. These two accounts differ as to exactly when and how the resurrection will occur, but they share the same general expectation that at the end of the world, those who have obeyed the righteousness of Torah will be vindicated and raised to new life.

64. Koester, "The Structure and Criteria of Early Christian Beliefs," 224.

65. Conzelmann, *An Outline of the Theology of the New Testament*, 66. Conzelmann also rightly observes that this tradition does not yet distinguish between Christ's resurrection and exaltation; at this stage of its development, the two are seen as identical. Ibid., 67. See also Bultmann, *Theology of the New Testament*, 1:82.

66. Günther Bornkamm, "Lord's Supper and Church in Paul," in *Early Christian Experience*, 151–152; Conzelmann, *1 Corinthians*, 260–275 (especially 260–263, 269–271); Käsemann, "On the Subject of Primitive Christian Apocalyptic," 132–137.

baptized by one Spirit into one body—whether Jews or Greeks, whether slaves or free persons—and we all were made to drink one Spirit. For indeed the body is not one member but many. If the foot were to say, "I am not a hand; I am not of the body," it is not for that reason not of the body. And if the ear were to say, "I am not an eye; I am not of the body," it is not for that reason not of the body. If the whole body were an eye, where would the hearing be? If the whole body were hearing, where would the sense of smell be? But now God arranged the members—every one of them—in the body just as God wished. If they all were one member, where would the body be? But now there are many members, but one body. And the eye cannot say to the hand, "I have no need of you," or again the head to the feet, "I have no need of you." But the members of the body which seem to be weaker are much more necessary, and the members of the body which we suppose are more dishonorable, we show such the greater honor; and our unpresentable members have greater presentability, but our presentable members have no need of such. But God arranged the body by giving greater honor to the member which lacks, so that there might not be a division in the body but that the members might be concerned about the same thing on behalf of one another. And if one member suffers, all the members suffer together. If one member is honored, all the members rejoice together. Now *you* are the body of Christ and members individually.[67]

The community, according to this formulation, is more than just a group of people with common interests or individual relationships to God. It is, rather, Christ's creation, for he has united "the many" in "one body." Christians are, therefore, equal because he died for them all and they belong to him, i.e., to his body.[68] As a result, they have certain practical responsibilities toward one another (12:25), e.g., to respect the sensibilities of a weaker brother or sister (8:7–13); to celebrate the Lord's Supper together as a true community (11:17–34); to share each other's joys and sorrows (12:26); to live in harmony (3:18–23); to care for others (12:25); to edify the whole congregation in their exercise of charismata (8:1, 12:7)—in sum, to love each other as fully and as genuinely as Christ loved them.[69]

So the concretely historical creed about Christ who was really crucified and who was raised again had concretely historical extensions. It yielded a soteriology which is centered on the reality of his cross and resurrection; a future eschatology which recognizes the here-and-now as the locus in which humanity exists and relates to God; an ecclesiology which affirms the equal dignity and equal rights of all Christians; and a sociology which challenges the community of believers to live together in reciprocal love until Jesus returns.

III. Recent RLDS Christology

A. The Jesus Paradigm

To speak of "the" RLDS Christology is almost to posit a *non sequitur*, for two reasons. First, the church has beliefs about Jesus but does not hold them out as an official creed or dogma to the exclusion of all others. Second, views undoubtedly vary from individual to individual, giving considerable depth and texture to RLDS opinion on this (as well as any other) subject. What follows, accordingly, is an identification of christological leitmotifs, i.e., *topoi* which tend to be most prevalent in sanctioned RLDS literature and which, therefore, reflect the current Christology of the church *qua* institution.[70]

---

67. I Corinthians 12:12–27.

68. Bultmann, *Theology of the New Testament*, 1:310; Conzelmann, *1 Corinthians*, 212.

69. See generally Ernst Käsemann, "Ministry and Community in the New Testament," in *Essays on New Testament Themes*, 63–94.

70. This reconstruction is based primarily on three categories of material:

    1. that in which the church consciously attempts to crystallize its concepts of Christ and to communicate them to "outsiders" as well as to its own constituency;

    2. that which expresses the thinking of church leadership and hence indicates the direction in which they have led or intend to lead the general membership; and

    3. that in which the church asks its participants to order their relationships and to conduct their activities inter se in a certain way.

The preceding caveats notwithstanding, the main ridges of RLDS Christology are reasonably clear. *Exploring the Faith*, a recapitulation of basic church theology and doctrine, makes this statement:

We believe in Jesus Christ, the Only Begotten Son of God, who is from everlasting to everlasting; through whom all things were made; who is God in the flesh, being incarnate by the Holy Spirit for the salvation of all humankind; who was crucified, died, and rose again; who is mediator between God and humanity, and the judge of both the living and the dead; whose dominion has no end.[71]

This synopsis is premised in large part on the New Testament Christ-hymns,[72] and at first glance seems coterminous with wisdom Christology: Christ was preexistent; became incarnate; suffered, died, and was resurected; and (by implication) has been exalted and enthroned in heaven as cosmic Lord. The accompanying commentary, however, takes a very different trajectory, as its opening lines indicate: "The Christian faith is historical," for it "results from the revelation of the living God in specific events in history."[73] Precisely! *The criterion of history pervades the RLDS understanding of Jesus.*[74]

Thus when the christological hymns are quarried, their references to the incarnation are emphasized[75] and Christ is affirmed to be "a man in the fullest sense, sharing truly and completely in the conditions of [our] humanity."[76] Indeed RLDS discussions of Jesus draw far more attention to the historical, earthly ambit of his experience than to any other.[77] For instance, Jesus "came *into*

Cf. the similar approach in Paul M. Edwards, *Preface to Faith: A Philosophical Inquiry into RLDS Beliefs* (Midvale, Utah: Signature Books, 1984), xv-xvi.

71. *Exploring the Faith*, ed. Alan D. Tyree (Independence, Missouri: Herald House, 1987), 28.

72. See the references to John 1:3, Colossians 1:15–17, and I Timothy 3:16 in ibid., 32–36 (*passim*).

73. Ibid., 29.

74. See, e.g., First Presidency, "The Foundation of Our Faith," (Paper delivered at First Presidency Meetings, Independence, Missouri, 9 January 1979), 3, 6 (available RLDS Library-Archives, Independence, Missouri). Paul W. Booth, "Glory to God...Good Will to Men," *Saints Herald* 128 (1981): 584–585; Duane E. Couey, "Come to Christ," *Saints Herald* 131 (1984): 206–207, 213–214; Paul W. Booth, "The Word Was Made Flesh, and Dwelt Among Us...Full of Grace and Truth," *Saints Herald* 129 (1982): 577–578. This notion undergirds the analysis in Clifford A. Cole, "Last of All," *Saints Herald* 126 (1979): 579–580 (through Jesus, "God...made himself one of us and entered into our world as a part of his own creation" to reveal to humankind "the essential nature of God," "the true nature of the universe," and "the truth about ourselves").

75. *Exploring the Faith*, 35–40. Cf. *Leaders Handbook 1989*, ed. A. Bruce Lindgren (Independence, Missouri: Herald Publishing House, 1988), 1.2, which offers this interpretation of Philippians 2:5–7: "Christ, perhaps the greatest leader of all times, took upon himself the role of servant as he sought to minister and lead the people of that time."

76. *Exploring the Faith*, 37. See also ibid., 57; Cole, "Last of All," 580; Wallace B. Smith, "In Christ Shall All Be Made Alive!" *Saints Herald* 127 (1980): 216; Reed M. Holmes, "Arise! Shine!" *Saints Herald* 129 (1982): 222.

77. A short excursus is probably in order here, to clarify the discussion below. RLDS Christology is anchored solidly in the tradition of classical orthodoxy, in that it recognizes Christ to be at once completely divine and completely human. *Exploring the Faith*, for example, quotes the Creed of Chalcedon with approval, rejects "any theory which tends to minimize either the manhood or the divinity of Jesus," and goes on to hold that Jesus is "fully human" as well as "not less than the same God who confronts us in our own real experience" (*Exploring the Faith*, 39–40). Paul Booth, similarly, argues that although Jesus is human, he is not "just a man, like any other man" but instead is "both fully God and fully human" (Booth, "Glory to God...Good Will to Men," 584). Lloyd Hurshman observes, conversely, that Jesus should be understood as God, but that conceptions of him must not "separate him from his human expression" (Lloyd B. Hurshman, "Clothing the Christ," *Saints Herald* 122 [1975]: 749). Booth elsewhere makes substantially the same point: Jesus is "the image of God" but "can never be fully appreciated by those who look only at his relationship to God," for he is also "the [incarnate] word that 'dwells among us'" (Booth, "The Word Was Made Flesh, and Dwelt Among Us...Full of Grace and Truth," 578). So in the RLDS perspective, divinity and humanity are wholly and indivisibly united in Christ—a thoroughly orthodox formulation. See e.g., Council of Chalcedon, *Definition of Faith*, translated by Henry R. Percival, *A Select Library of Nicene and Post-Nicene Fathers of the Christian Church*, 2d series, ed. Philip Schaff and Henry Wace, 14 vols. (Grand Rapids, Michigan:

history, and not out of it";[78] was "fully human";[79] was "a real human being";[80] "was actually born of a woman";[81] "was born as a baby and grew [into maturity] as we did";[82] experienced the full range of human emotions;[83] was "a man from among men";[84] labored as a carpenter;[85] was "a trusted friend who loved parties";[86] had a "youthful enthusiasm for life";[87] taught "utter dependence on God";[88] spoke "through the actual dust and also through the dust that chokes men's souls, sharing the truths that come to him as the Son of God";[89] made radical demands on his audiences;[90] "lived on earth to love and serve others";[91] "healed the sick, fed the hungry, and brought hope to the downtrodden";[92] "suffered as we suffer";[93] was "betrayed by his own people";[94] "suffered under Pontius Pilate, was crucified, dead and buried";[95] actually died;[96] was raised again;[97] is "a savior who is victorious over death."[98] His life, death, and resurrection, conversely, have reconciled humankind to God and effected their salvation.[99] Jesus, therefore, enables people to relate to God and to understand the essential meaning of existence because his "actions in historical events" demonstrate who God is,

Wm. B. Eerdmans, 1983), 14:262–265. Of Jesus' two natures, however, the *human* stands front and center in RLDS christological analysis. The objective here is not to trace or elucidate how RLDS Christology deals with this divine/human dichotomy but rather to assess which New Testament Jesus-paradigm(s) it tends to follow. To this endeavor we now return.

78. *Exploring the Faith*, 39. See also Cole, "Last of All," 579; Booth, "Glory to God...Good Will to Men," 585.

79. *Exploring the Faith*, 39. See also Booth, "Glory to God...Good Will to Men," 584.

80. *A People Who Follow Jesus Christ* (n.p., n.d. [1988]), 2.

81. *Exploring the Faith*, 39. See also First Presidency, "The Nature of the Church" (Paper delivered at First Presidency Meetings, Independence, Missouri, 9 January 1979), 2; Hurshman, "Clothing the Christ," 749.

82. Cole, "Last of All," 579–580. See also Booth, "Glory to God...Good Will to Men," 584.

83. Booth, "Glory to God...Good Will to Men," 584.

84. Exploring the Faith, 49. See also Hurshman, "Clothing the Christ," 757.

85. First Presidency, "The Nature of the Church," 2.

86. Ibid. See also Booth, "Glory to God...Good Will to Men," 584; Hurshman, "Clothing the Christ," 757 (Jesus "is real to us as friend, companion, Lord").

87. Hurshman, "Clothing the Christ," 757.

88. First Presidency, "The Nature of the Church," 2.

89. Hurshman, "Clothing the Christ," 757.

90. Couey, "'Come to Christ,'" 207; Kenneth N. Robinson, "Tell of Christ's Love," *Saints Herald* 132 (1985): 56; Wallace B. Smith, "Follow Christ into the World," *Saints Herald* 133 (1986): 236. Cf. Wallace B. Smith, "Life Is Before Us," *Saints Herald* 136 (1989) 10.

91. *A Christ Centered Church* (n.p., n.d.), 2. See also Holmes, "Arise! Shine!" 233; Robinson, "Tell of Christ's Love," 55–56. Cf. Booth, "The Word Was Made Flesh, and Dwelt Among Us...Full of Grace and Truth," 578.

92. *A Christ Centered Church* (n.p., n.d.), 2. See also Aleah Koury and Reed Holmes, "Follow Me," *Saints Herald* 119 (August 1972): 18–21; Booth, "Glory to God...Good Will to Men," 585; Holmes, "Arise! Shine!" 222–223.

93. Hurshman, "Clothing the Christ," 749.

94. First Presidency, "The Nature of the Church," 2. See also Smith, "Life Is Before Us," 10. Cf. Robinson, "Tell of Christ's Love," 56.

95. *Exploring the Faith*, 45. See also First Presidency, "The Nature of the Church," 2; Hurshman, "Clothing the Christ," 757; Cole, "Last of All," 579; Booth, "Glory to God...Good Will to Men," 585; Holmes, "Arise! Shine!" 223. Cf. Smith, "Follow Christ into the World," 236; *idem*, "Life Is Before Us," 10.

96. *Exploring the Faith*, 45. See also Wallace B. Smith, "I Will Be With You Always," *Saints Herald* 130 (1983): 440.

97. *Exploring the Faith,* 45–47; Smith, "I Will Be With You Always," 441.

98. First Presidency, "The Nature of the Church," 2. See also Cole, "Last of All," 579–580.

99. *Exploring the Faith*, 41–45; First Presidency, "The Nature of the Church," 1–2; *A People of Hope* (Independence, Missouri: Herald House, n.d.), 3–7; Smith, "In Christ Shall All Be Made Alive!" 216–217; *idem*, "Life Is Before Us," 10; Booth, "The Word Was Made Flesh, and Dwelt Among Us...Full of Grace and Truth," 578. Cf. Booth, "Glory to God...Good Will to Men," 585; William T. Higdon, "Christ—And the Future," *Saints Herald* 129 (1982): 604.

that God loves us, and what God "intends us to be."[100]

RLDS Christology also makes some important omissions. For instance, it strongly attenuates apocalyptic as a standard for evaluating Jesus. It simply affirms *that* he will return, without speculating as to *when*.[101] Indeed the nearness of his return is downplayed, for even trying to calculate the end of the age would be "fruitless."[102] Hence eschatology is neither realized nor markedly futuristic. Perhaps even more significantly, Jesus is not depicted as "the messianic warrior," an avenging redeemer who crushes his enemies and redeems the suffering righteous from the tribulation of the end-times.[103]

RLDS Christology also lays virtually no stress on Jesus as a worker of miracles or a guide into saving wisdom.[104]He came not to furnish "a list of statements to guide us" but to uncover "the meaning of all life" in what he did.[105] "Knowledge" is, therefore, not a mystical glimpse into the interiority of divine secrets but "windows of experience through which we see more clearly the depth of truth revealed in Christ."[106] Jesus thus furnishes the *historical* matrix within which we may not only comprehend the significance of his life and ministry but also engage the real world in our own time and place.[107]

So RLDS Christology tracks the New Testament cross-and-resurrection paradigm, in that it presents Jesus as a very real person who lived a complete human life, suffered, died, and rose again. In the process, it anchors soteriology in objective, *historical* criteria.

B. Identity and Structure

If the foregoing conclusions are correct, the sociology which the institutional RLDS Church is advancing should resemble that which Paul advocates in I Corinthians. Such in fact appears to be the case.

Like the Christology of which it is a corollary, RLDS ecclesiology is grounded in the historical dimensions of Jesus' life, death and resurrection:

The church of the future will be formed by the living spirit of the One who gathered around him a dozen plain men and shared with them what it is like to live one's life in community. There were many things about Jesus they could not understand. So far as we know, he wrote no words of instruction to them. His message was his life and its relation to God and to them.... [H]e claimed

---

100. *The Godhead* (Independence, Missouri: Herald House, 1979), 5–6; *A Christ Centered Church*, 2; Cole, "Last of All," 580. A variation on this theme appears in Booth, "Glory to God...Good Will to Men," 584: the full divinity and full humanity of Jesus reveal the relationship between God and people, for they demonstrate "both the nature of God and intended nature of humankind." In him, then, are seen "the source, the personhood, and the destiny of persons." Ibid. See also First Presidency, "The Foundation of Our Faith," 6–9; *Faith to Grow* (Independence, Missouri: Herald House, 1979), 6–7. Cf. Charles D. Neff, "Council Comments on Basic Beliefs," *Saints Herald* 121 (1974): 414; Higdon, "Christ—And the Future," 604; Couey, "Come to Christ," 207; Wallace B. Smith, "Draw Near With a True Heart," *Saints Herald* 131 (1984): 201; *idem*, "The Fellowship of the Mystery," *Saints Herald* 131 (1984): 99; Kisuke Sekine, "Christ Claims Us as His Own—A Living Hope," *Saints Herald* 132 (1985):13.

101. See generally *Exploring the Faith*, 270–278 *(passim)*; Smith, "Life Is Before Us," 9–10.

102. *Exploring the Faith*, 35. See also Smith, "Life Is Before Us," 12.

103. Smith, "Life Is Before Us," 10.

104. See generally the distinctly noncharismatic, non-gnostic approach to the Holy Spirit and spiritual gifts in *Exploring the Faith*, 53–81 *(passim)*. Cf. also First Presidency, "The Nature of the Church," 6; Smith, "In Christ Shall All Be Made Alive!" 218; Hurshman, "Clothing the Christ," 749.

105. *Exploring the Faith*, 269–270.

106. Ibid., 269. Cf. First Presidency, "The Foundation of Our Faith," 6.

107. *Exploring the Faith*, 270; First Presidency, "The Identity of the Church," (Paper delivered at First Presidency Meetings, Independence, Missouri, 9 January 1979), 3. Booth, "Glory to God...Good Will to Men," 585, argues that the authenticity of "Direct sources of information from God" depends on "whether or not the revelation is embodied in the life's history of a person and the community of people." Revealed knowledge must therefore always be given a socio-historical expression. Cf. *Faith to Grow*, 3: "We are called to fellowship and work with Christ and his disciples to bring forth the will of God on earth, not at some indistinct future time but now."

nothing for himself, not even his own life, which was finally offered on a cross. Jesus' death on the cross became to the early disciples a revelation of the love of God's own self exposed to the consequences of human sin. In the cross God is revealed as an offering in quest of the sinful human family. The triumph and resurrection of this life, that did not treat its own goodness as an independent act of human achievement, formed the basis for the creation of the community which became the church, the Body of Christ. The church was the community that formed in response to the One who rejected all ethical heroism and threw himself solely on God's grace. Into it came all kinds of people—Jews, Greeks, bond, free, male and female—but there was no barrier between them because they were one body of sinners, forgiven. The bond that united them was the common confession: "Not I, but the grace of God." This breaks down the barriers between person and person, and the members come to love each other because God first loved them and drew them out of themselves into the unity of "one body," the ecclesia, the church.[108]

The church, which includes both the early Christian movement and modern Restorationism,[109] thus is an outgrowth and ongoing reflection of—and is determined by—the cross

and resurrection. It is Christ's accomplishment. Those who enter it stand on the same footing before God and *vis-à-vis* each other, because he died for them all and God has united them in "one body," the body of Christ. The church must therefore "reveal [Christ's] nature tangibly to the world"[110] by sharing "true love, radical love" and thereby enabling "all persons to be reconciled to God, to each other, and within themselves."[111]

The contemporary RLDS Church, consequently, is called *to live in community* in the here-and-now.[112] It will do so to the extent that it demarginalizes individuals and integrates them meaningfully in its collective experience.[113] Such a process is multifaceted but includes, *inter alia*, dismantling oppressive, hierarchical attitudes and structures;[114] affirming the "true nature and worth of each human person";[115] recognizing the giftedness and utilizing the gifts of all;[116] and ministering selflessly to "the deepest needs" of others.[117]

108. First Presidency, "The Nature of the Church," 1.

109. See generally, *Exploring the Faith*, 145–154.

110. Ibid., 155–157.

111. First Presidency, "The Mission of the Church," in *Leaders Handbook 1989*, 2.5. See also *Exploring the Faith*, 163, 166–167; Smith, "Draw Near With a True Heart," 202–203, 211; Couey, "Come to Christ," 214 (the church is "a mutual ministry of believers, who are a means of grace to each other and to all persons"); Hurshman, "Clothing the Christ," 757; Joe A. Serig, "In Christ the Wounded Are Healed," *Saints Herald* 132 (1985): 28.

112. First Presidency, "The Identity of the Church," 3–4; *idem*, "The Nature of the Church," 2; *Faith to Grow*, 7; *Church Administrator's Handbook* (Independence, Missouri: Herald Publishing House, 1987), 5; Couey, "Come to Christ," 214. This community, according to one observer, must be inclusive enough to encompass conservatives and liberals "in a living fellowship...united in a living tension that produces a growing point." Sekine, "Christ Claims Us as His Own—A Living Hope," 30.

113. Council of Twelve Apostles, "Statement of Commitment," *Saints Herald* 127 (1980): 219–220.

114. E.g., Doctrine and Covenants 156:7a–8b; *Guidelines for Priesthood: Ordination, Preparation, Continuing Commitment* (Independence, Missouri: Herald Publishing House, 1985), 8; *Exploring the Faith*, 207; *Leaders Handbook 1989*, 1.2–1.3. Cf. Council of Twelve Apostles, "Statement of Commitment," 220 (advocating that different cultural expressions of the church be permitted, because "In Christ there are no racial, social, economic, educational, or other barriers to the one great fellowship of all humankind").

115. First Presidency, "The Identity of the Church," 1. See also *New Persons for a New World* (Independence, Missouri: Herald House, 1979), 3; *A People With a Calling* (Independence, Missouri: Herald House, n.d.), 4; *Church Administrator's Handbook*, 5; J. C. Stuart, "Enduring Concepts of the Restoration," *Saints Herald* 127 (1980): 165.

116. *Exploring the Faith*, 147–148, 156, 214–215; *Guidelines for Priesthood: Ordination, Preparation, Continuing Commitment*, 28; Council of Twelve Apostles, "Statement of Commitment," 220; Stuart, "Enduring Concepts of the Restoration," 165. Cf. Doctrine and Covenants 156:9b.

117. First Presidency, "The Nature of the Church," 6, 9; *Leaders Handbook 1989*, 1.2–1.3. See also *Exploring the Faith, 167–168*; Council of Twelve Apostles, "Statement of Commitment," 220; Stuart, "Enduring Concepts of

In short, the identity and mission of the church are defined as being true to the life and teaching of Jesus by living as he himself lived and taught. In so doing, its members will not only transform the cultural and social contexts in which they act,[118] but also construct communities of mutual love which rescue people from the periphery and bring them into the very center of human existence—communities which ever reach out to share the pain of others, to bear their burdens, to satisfy their most fundamental longings, to uphold their value as part of God's great economy, to reconcile them to God, and to rejoice as all together partake of the love of God and the goodness of genuine Christian fellowship.

The church is to be a community of equals. Each person has a special worth, to God and to each other. Everyone is encouraged to enrich the entire Body by sharing her or his unique talents in the work of Christ. Community life is a matter of: service, not status; dialogue, not confrontation; cooperation with, not domination of, others; shared, not retained, power; interchangeable, not rigidly fixed, roles of participation and ministry; love in fact, not doctrine in theory.

This philosophy of community matches the RLDS Christology. Because its conception of Jesus focuses on the actual circumstances of his earthly life within history, the church marks its identity and structure by what its members must do in the real world to be faithful to his example and to carry on his mission of redeeming humankind. It, therefore, neither repudiates the world nor seeks to escape from it.[119] Instead it recognizes all of creation as God's marvelous handiwork and as the *milieu* in which God encounters people.

IV. Conclusion

Of the four New Testament models examined, recent RLDS Christology most closely parallels Paul's cross-and-resurrection *schema*, for its nucleus is the historical dimensions of Jesus' life and ministry. Its ecclesiology and sociology are cut from the same bolt of cloth and, therefore, orient the structure and communal experience of the church toward *being* the body of Christ now.

By making the historical Jesus a linchpin of its theology, the church has launched itself on a historical pilgrimage: living in genuine communion with God and humanity. For that reason, the contemporary RLDS faith has become more than statements of doctrine, more than organization, more than sacred rites, more even than recollection of events which happened millennia ago in ancient Palestine. It is, rather, the dynamic, unfolding effort of its people to make the gospel fact by living it in the present day. Indeed it is their commitment—and struggle—to build enduring communities of reciprocal love.

---

the Restoration," 165. Cf. *New Persons for a New World*, 6; *A Christ Centered Church*, 2; *A People Who Follow Jesus Christ*, 6–7.

118. Smith, "Follow Christ into the World," 237.

119. See, e.g., First Presidency, "The Nature of the Church," 5.

Bonds of Tradition: Concepts of God and Gender Roles*

Enid Stubbart DeBarthe

Shock waves surged through the Reorganized Church of Jesus Christ of Latter Day Saints on April 4, 1984, when President Wallace B. Smith called for reevaluation of concepts concerning the nature of priesthood and the ordination of women (Doctrine and Covenants 156).

Questions abounded: "How can this be?" "It breaks all tradition!" "God does not change. So how can this be the word of God?" "No woman is worthy to stand in the stead of Christ." What does it mean to "stand in the stead of Christ?"[1]

On April 6 the World Conference approved the document. The issue was no longer a matter for debate; it was now law for the church. But the questions continued, launching this researcher into six years of intensive study. On what basis did the centuries-old tradition of the inferiority and unworthiness of women become established? Has patriarchy always existed?

Early Attitudes

The earliest artifacts of worship in the human experience are mother goddess figures in stone, ivory, and clay. These figurines, generally associated with fertility cults, have been found most abundantly in the Near and Middle East but are numerous throughout Europe and the British Isles. One of the most ancient findings is a stone relief figure dating from 19,000 B.C.E. discovered in a cave at Laussel (Dordogne), France.[2]

Scholars have cited far-reaching evidence of these female figurines. Richard and Catherine Clark-Kroeger claim the primary deities of Asia Minor were female. "By 5000 B.C.E. Anatolian artists modeled heavyset mother goddesses from clay....For millennia the matriarchal goddesses reigned supreme, and their images are found in great abundance at archaeological sites."[3] Merlin Stone[4] and Leonard Swidler[5] claim that worship of the mother goddesses existed even earlier.

Marija Gimbutas, linguist and archaeologist, found, in extensive on-site searches, few male figurines among numerous female images. "Male figurines constitute only 2 to 3 percent of all Old European figurines, and consequently any detailed reconstruction of their cult role is hardly possible."[6] Linguistic and artifactual evidence strongly support a growing belief that the Indo-European invasions supplanted goddess worship with male-god dominance.

The Semitic-Canaanite culture created a family group to worship: El, Asherah, and their son, Baal (owner-possessor of all). These names are found in the Hebrew Old Testament but are not translated into English.[7] Hebrew tension over concepts of God's name and attendant nature is evident throughout the Hebrew Old Testament. Joshua reminded his people they were still worshiping the Elohym (gods) your ancestors served beyond the river (Euphrates), or Elah (feminine) of the Amorites in whose land you dwell: but as for me and my house,

---

* All biblical quotes are from the Authorized (King James) Version.

we will serve Yahweh (based on Joshua 24:15).

The story of Job extended debate over whose god is just and worthy of worship. Job yearned for the time when Eloah watched over him with her lamp and intimately cared for him in the family tent. Elihu (meaning El himself) who must "speak to refresh" himself or burst, contends at length for Eloah and El. Finally, Job gives his well-known affirmations for Yahweh. And Yahweh "turns the captivity of Job" and returns double his former fortune.

The earliest Indo-European-speaking peoples to enter the historical record were the Anatolians, about the nineteenth century B.C.E.,[8] around the time of Abraham. Their strongest influence on the Hebrews probably came under the Assyrians. The struggle between the cultures which worshiped the energizing, life-giving, and peace-loving mother-deity and those which worshiped a mighty sovereign, warrior, father-deity has been bitter and costly in its effect on both men and women, but especially on women, as this paper will show.

There seems to have been a fairly high status for women in Minoan-Mycenaean Greek culture (1600–1200 B.C.E.), according to the Linear B Tablets unearthed at Knossos, Pylos, Mycenae, and Thebes. An example of their freedoms is shown in frescoes at Knossos where women in balconies watch the bull-leaping contests, and some in male attire also engage in the bull-leaping activity.[9] At Pylos the records of transactions showed twice as many women as men engaged in crafts. And equal rations of food were given to women and men, whereas in Babylon men were allotted three times the rations given to women.[10]

In early Egyptian culture (about 2700 B.C.E.), some women were queens who owned property, directed the building of temples, and carried on business with other rulers. Such was the case in some degree for centuries. Many priestesses served the goddess Isis, whose cult spread into Greece, Rome, and Palestine. In the first to third centuries B.C.E. Egyptian women had professions, paid taxes, and had some legal rights. Both parents had part in making marriage contracts, and a husband's infidelities were considered as grave as a wife's. Inscriptions of the period indicate both girls and boys were educated.

Babylon's patriarchy probably influenced Abraham, for Babylonian religious beliefs and practices, as well as social organization, are reflected in the Judaic culture as recorded in the Old Testament. Yet the Egyptian influence may perhaps be seen in the early Hebrew prophetesses, such as Deborah, who served as a judge and called herself "a mother in Israel," and Huldah, who served as a prime minister under Josiah.

A mother's lineage counted among the Hebrews, for "his mother's name was" appears twenty-six times in I and II Kings, and fourteen times in I and II Chronicles, though some of these are duplicated recordings from the record of the Kings into the Chronicles.

The genealogical listing for Jesus in Luke is thought to be his priestly line, while that of Matthew gives what is believed to be his kingly line.[11] Matthew's list includes four mothers: Rachab, mother of Boaz; Ruth, mother of Obed; Eliam, wife of Uriah (II Samuel 11:3), and mother of Solomon; and Mary, the mother of Jesus. Matthew 1:3–6a seems to be the genealogy of Ruth (Ruth 4:18–22). Mary's lineage was important for Jesus' spiritual authority among the Jews, and under Roman law, the father's genealogy was necessary to assure citizenship and property rights.

Duality of parental responsibility and honor was recognized in early Hebrew times and is evident in a close study of Hebrew words, such as the word YLD (yalad), translated: "bear," "beget," "birth," "born." The word AB, "father," in the plural is ABVTh (feminine, plural ending) and is translated "fathers," but actually means "ancestors." The Hebrew BNY, translated "sons of" 2300 times, and "children of" 1320+ times, as well as "daughter of" (I Chronicles 11:8) actually meant "offspring of" or "descendants of." These and other findings seem to indicate a greater sense of equality of heritage and mutuality of respect among the Hebrews than has generally been thought. The grammatical dual form was dropped in Greece about 350 B.C.E.,[12] before the Septuagint was translated.

Respect for the rights of women to hold property or serve as leaders was lost under some 750 years of Hebrew subjugation: Assyria, Persia, Babylonia, Greek-Syria, Egypt, and Rome. As had happened in all countries invaded by marauding tribes or nations, women were restricted to the home as a protective measure. This restriction became quite severe in Greece, Rome, and Palestine.

Greek Influence

The Greek belief system did not have a priesthood as such. Women served as oracles and the pantheon of gods served various concepts of Deity. The chief god, Zeus, with his wife, Hera, and their pantheon of gods and goddesses were each given attributes and responsibilities to explain Greek concepts of the universe and human behavior. This family of gods more nearly expressed its sense of human balance than seems evident from the citations of the patriarchy developed under Alexander. The family concept further shifted and hardened under the Romans to become patriarchal Roman Catholicism.

After the Macedonian and other invasions, Athenian women who tried to watch the Olympic games were executed. When Pherenice of Rhodes, attired as a male athlete, slipped in to watch her son, Pisidores, compete in a wrestling match, she took a very great risk. As she ran to congratulate Pisidores on his victory, her disguise was discovered, but she escaped execution because of public clamor in her behalf. A new law was then passed that required all athletes to compete in the nude.[13]

The seventh-century B.C.E. story of Pandora's box illustrated the prevailing concept of woman as "the root of all evil." Most of the myths portrayed women as uncontrollable beings or "as traps for destroying men." Eve, "the mother of all living," joined the list, and all daughters of Eve bore her guilt. Tertullian (A.D. 160?–230?) wrote:

Are you ignorant that you are an Eve? The sentence of God still lives upon your sex even in this present age, and of necessity the guilt lives on too. You are the devil's gateway...the first destroyer of divine law...she who persuaded him whom the devil was not valiant enough to attack directly.[14]

In the sixth century B.C.E., a satire, entitled "The Female Mind," was used as a moral tale to instruct. It claimed that in the beginning the Olympian gods made the female mind separately. Her mind was variously made from "a long-bristled sow" (home in disorder); "a bitch" (wants to hear and know everything); the "earth" (knows nothing, bad or good); "the sea" (as changeable); "an ash-grey ass" (suffers blows, puts up with everything, works against her will but does it satisfactorily); "a ferret" (no desirable traits); "a monkey; this is the biggest plague of all that Zeus has given to men" (the laughing stock of the community, ugly and vengeful); or "a bee" (a blameless wife).[15]

Aristotle (384–322 B.C.E.) made these traits more scientific: women had softness of disposition, were nurturers by nature, and were inclined to passions rather than rationality. Men were strong, hard, spirited, rational beings who could be more savage, simpler, and less cunning than women.[16] Because women were weak they were expected to eat less. Therefore, girls' diets were restricted, especially in protein. He believed women contributed nothing to conception and provided only the field for nurture of the male seed.[17] His followers interpreted this as woman the field, child the crop, and man the owner of both. His claims that women are by nature physically, mentally, and socially (though not sexually) inferior to men pervaded the philosophical, medical, political, and theological writings of later ages. He placed the father over the child, man over woman, master over slave.

Plato wrote that woman was created inferior to man, and that cowardly or sinful men would be reincarnated as women.[18] Demosthenes, a contemporary of Aristotle, wrote, "Mistresses we keep for pleasure, concubines for daily attendance upon our person, wives to bear us legitimate children and be our faithful housekeepers."[19] In his will he gave his wife and daughter to a friend. By doing so he could protect them from falling into unfriendly hands.

Adultery was a serious crime for women but expected of men. As far back as 600 B.C.E., Solon had permitted an adulteress to be stripped of her garments and ornaments and turned out to be beaten by "any man who meets her," only she could not be killed or maimed. "The lawgiver seeks to disgrace such a woman and make her life not worth living."[20] This attitude which freed the men and gave blame to the women spread wherever Greek influence was felt.

Because respectable women stayed indoors, under Greek patriarchal law a woman seen at a banquet or working in the markets could be charged "as notorious to all" and brought before the court and fined. The necessity to keep women chaste so that legal heirs were assured was an economic rule, to preserve lineage rights and assure property staying in the patriarchy.

Roman Attitudes

When the Romans conquered Greece, Rome adopted Greek laws and customs and spread them throughout the empire. However, Rome's own legendary past was often referred to as authority for new laws or existing customs. Clans were set up with the head of each clan serving as magistrate, priest, and owner of all things and persons within it. Guided by his council of kinsmen, the chieftain laid down the law and held power over life and death, justified by his religious position. Through the centuries this became "the divine right of kings."

Romulus was credited with the first marriage laws that made a woman her husband's property and part of his estate for inheritance purposes. If a woman did any wrong, the injured party was her judge and determined the degree of punishment. Adultery or the drinking of wine, considered the source of adultery, could be punished with death.[21]

Solon, the Greek lawgiver (639?–559? B.C.E.) was credited with first making a law whereby women might be prostituted in brothels. The inmates were often daughters of slaves, kidnapped women, or discarded baby girls who were rescued from death by exposure. (Unwanted babies were destroyed in Greece and Rome by exposure to the elements, a custom that continued into the Middle Ages.[22] The exclusion of the unwanted child was the sole decision of the father.)[23]

Widows under the age of twenty-five could not remarry without their father's consent. If the woman objected, judicial authority could be appealed to, and sometimes her choice was approved.[24] Girls were married at age twelve or earlier and were under the control of the father, then the husband, and if widowed, her father or brother. As a widow she was often considered a burden and could be abandoned.[25]

Early Christian Attitudes

When Jesus proclaimed his liberating gospel at Nazareth, his hearers thought his message was "gracious." But when he cited their treatment of widows, the men were wrathful and rose up to kill him (Luke 4:16–30). He frequently chided the Jews for forgetting the days of the prophets when temple funds cared for widows, and he condemned the scribes who "devour widows' houses" (Luke 20–47; Matthew 23:11; Mark 12:46).

Jesus rescued a woman from stoning for adultery, pointing out mutual guilt (John 8:3–71). Under Hebrew laws the men were also culpable, but Roman customs and laws were in force, and Rome's attitude toward women had become acceptable to the men of Judea.

When Jesus allowed a woman to anoint his head "as he sat at meat" (Matthew 26:7; Mark 43:3), he broke three rules: (1) women could not approach a rabbi or leader unattended by husband, father, or older son; (2) women were not allowed in the room where men were gathered (except for dancing girls at Greek or Roman banquets); and (3) women were not allowed where men were eating.

Women found acceptance with Jesus and responded to his ministry. They accompanied him on the journey from Galilee to Jerusalem for his last Passover feast and were present at his crucifixion (Luke 23:49; Matthew 27:55–56). Women witnessed to the disciples the proclamation of the angels at the sepulcher (Luke 24:1–2, 22–24), and Jesus sent a woman to testify of his resurrection (Matthew 28:8–10), although legally, women could not testify.

Jesus used more inclusive language in his

charge to Peter than is commonly recognized from the English translation. Though Peter had denied Jesus and had wept bitterly in remorse, reconciliation had apparently taken place (Luke 24:34; I Corinthians 15:5). Peter and six other disciples returned to the Sea of Galilee to fish. When Peter recognized Jesus on the shore he jumped into the water and swam ashore to be with Jesus.

Jesus first fed his disciples, then recommissioned them, using Peter as an example for all disciples. Jesus asked Peter, *Agapas me pleion touton?* "Do you love me more than these (boats, fishing or fellow fishermen)?" (Agape love is unconditional Christ-like love.)

Peter responded, *Nai, kurie, su oides oti philo su.* "Yes, Lord, you know that I love you." (*Philo* love is spontaneous affection. Peter, having previously denied Jesus could not claim his love as the *agape* kind.)

Jesus said, *Boske ta arnia mou.* "Feed the male lambs of me." (Not *amnos*, lambs undifferentiated by age or sex, but *arnia*, male lambs, old enough to butt. *To arnion* is used in relation to Christ, the Lamb in Revelation 5:6, 8, 12). Jesus repeated the same inquiry and Peter answered as before. Then Jesus said, *Poimaine ta probata mou.* "Be a shepherd to my sheep." (Shepherd, pastor, tend my flock, regardless of age, color, condition or sex.)

The third time, Jesus said, *Phileis me?* "Do you truly have affection for me?" And Peter was grieved (sorrowful) because Jesus questioned Peter's affection for him, forcing him to face his depth of commitment. Peter responded, *Kurie, panta su oidas, su ginoskeis oti philo se.* "Lord, you know (see) all things; you perceive that I truly love you."

Jesus said, *Boske ta probatia mou.* "Feed (promote the welfare of) my female lambs." None are excluded! We are all called to cherish our differences while promoting the welfare of all.

There is continuing debate as to the ordination of women in the apostolic period. Several writers claim women were ordained then, as well as during the first, second, and third centuries A.D.[26]

After Pentecost, numerous evidences of women in ministry can be cited in the Greek New Testament. Most notable is Romans 16:1–2, which commends "Phoebe, a minister of the church." In this chapter nine women are cited by name as Paul's co-laborers in the Lord, with Junia "of note (*episemos*—outstanding) among the apostles, who were also in Christ before me."[27]

In the church's struggle against goddess worship, Gnosticism, and cultural traditions against women, which were reinforced when Constantine reinstituted old restrictive laws, women gradually lost their ecclesiastical status. *The New Catholic Encyclopedia* admits women were ordained in the early church. The first reported martyrdom of a woman minister was in A.D. 55. Peter and Paul are believed to have been killed in A.D. 67. Eusebius' *Ecclesiastical History* is gory in its details of martyrdoms. In A.D. 104 Governor Pliny reported to Emperor Trajan his having had two women tortured and executed. Rome thought women ministers posed a threat by converting their captors and tormentors through their bravery; and also, they set a poor example for other women of Rome.

In A.D. 253 Origen taught that women ministers were both "existent and necessary." And the Council of Nicea in 325 recognized deaconesses serving in the church. After a split in the church following the Nicene Council in A.D. 381, the Eastern Church ordained deaconesses until about 1600. The Western Church ruled at the Council of Laodicea (381) that no more women elders were to be ordained, but deaconesses and abbesses apparently were. At the Synod of Orange (A.D. 441) the Western Church forbade the ordination of women.

The mother-god worship of the Gauls and Celts of East Europe, Spain, Italy, France, Germany, and British Isles persisted into the fifteenth century, carried on by mothers and grandmothers who deeply felt the need of a deity who could understand the peculiar needs of women. Known as Mother Earth, or under Christianity as the Virgin Mary, "the mother of God," almost all nations revered the birth-giver, the source of all life. By the fifteenth century, adherents of female-deity worship were considered witches, and in A.D. 1486, Pope Innocent VIII in a papal bull denounced witchcraft as an organized conspiracy of the devil's army against the Holy Christian Empire. In that same year a handbook for witch hunters, called *Malleus Maleficorum*, or "Hammer of Witches," appeared and became the indispensable authority for terror and murder. More than 300,000 innocent women were tortured and put to death between 1484 and 1782.[28] Under such conditions, women could not serve in ecclesiastical roles.

Even though the Greek New Testament clearly indicates that women clergy were ordained in the early church, cultural traditions continued to rule. It took 700 years to end the church's practice of ordaining women, but a very few women were still serving in the western Catholic Church in isolated areas until the 1400s, primarily as heads of convents.

As the church lost its vision of the liberating gospel of Jesus, and succumbed to the cultural traditions of the times, it became a proscriptive, rather than a liberating gospel. Paul's writings appeared to give authority to restrictive attitudes and practices concerning women, and eventually superseded the example and teachings of Christ. Woman was seen as unworthy, even incarnate evil, condemned by divine decree to be subject to man in every aspect of life.

The Authorized (King James) translation (1611) came forth during a time of tension over women as queens, as well as during the struggle between Protestants and Catholics. Mary, Queen of Scots, was a devout Catholic who desired to return England to Catholicism. She was forced to flee from Scotland, and her son James was reared by Scottish lords.

Shortly before Queen Elizabeth (cousin to Mary) came to the throne, John Knox, Protestant reformer, published an essay against women as monarchs. It was necessary for Knox to apologize to Queen Elizabeth, but she never forgave him.

Mary's son, James, became king after the death of Elizabeth. His court prosecutor, Sir Francis Bacon, condemned many women to death as witches. Such intense animosity against women as rulers or ministers strongly indicates why so many "he" and "man" substitutions and insertions are found in the King James Version, the first edition being called the "He" Bible (because Ruth was referred to as "he"). Modern King James' versions still have 258 insertions of the word "man" where no comparable word is found in Hebrew, Greek, or Latin versions.

Theologians for centuries failed to recognize that Paul's statements which seemed to put women in submissiveness were written to converts in what had been Greek city-states—people who had never known anything other than Greek and Roman traditions toward women. Though Paul said, "all ye are the children of God by faith in Christ Jesus...(and) there is neither male nor female" (Galatians 3:26,28), his converts still had to accommodate to the laws of the state. Paul was first a Roman citizen; second, a Greek and Hebrew scholar; and third, as

a Christian convert, he stood for mutuality of respect and equality of opportunity.

Augustine (A.D. 354–430) had much influence on Christian teaching. "When she is referred to separately in her quality of helpmate, which regards woman alone, then she is not in the image of God; but as regards the man alone, he is in the image of God as fully and completely as when the woman is joined with him."[29]

Saint John Chrysostum (ca. 345–403) taught, "The woman taught once, and ruined all. On this account...let her not teach. But what is it to other women that she suffered this? It certainly concerns them; for the sex is weak and fickle....The whole female race transgressed....Let her not, however, grieve. God hath given her no small consolation, that of childbearing...."[30] The God who condemned women to bear children in "sorrow" (OTsBVN, "worrisome labor") and to give birth in "sorrow" (OTsB, "pangs of pain, travail") could not release them from this sentence and remained unchangeable.

Legal and Academic Attitudes

Legal and academic attitudes reflected general concepts of a God of judgment and condemnation throughout the Middle Ages (A.D. 400 to 1400s). Though legal restrictions had been eased somewhat under the Romans, they varied according to locality and culture. Under the Visigoths, a husband and wife could jointly administer the land either possessed before marriage, but property gained after marriage was considered community property, and the wife could claim a share. If the husband died, the widow retained control of the family property and the inheritance of her minor children. Girls inherited equally with their brothers, even when their parents died intestate. However, this changed under Roman, then church influence.[31]

The Barbarian tribes that overran the Roman Empire and all of Europe were of

Germanic stock, with differing customs and tribal laws. In general, the northern tribes were more strict in regard to women than were the southern, and the Lombards of the north long championed the chastity of women to protect the purity of lineage in inheriting property. No Lombard woman was ever allowed to be her own guardian; she was a perpetual minor.

Under the Saxon code, redacted in A.D. 785:

If any man die and leave a widow, let his son by another wife be her guardian; failing him, let the brother of the dead man be guardian, and if he had no brother, then the nearest of the husband's kinsmen.

When a man dies leaving no sons but only daughters, the inheritance shall go to them, but the guardianship over them shall pass to their father's brother or nearest kinsman.

If a widow with a daughter remarries and has a son, the guardianship over the daughter goes to the said son; if, however, having a son, she then marries and has a daughter, the guardianship over the daughter goes not to the son by her first marriage but to the father's brother or nearest kinsman.[32]

The land always went to the nearest male relative, down to the fifth generation. After the fifth it could go to the daughter, both from the father's and mother's side. "...not until then does the inheritance pass from the spear to the spindle."[33] But if one brother survived, he became guardian and obtained the land. The English laws of primogeniture reflected these old codes.

Germanic peoples observed the custom of bride purchase. Rape or sexual violence was considered theft of property which belonged to the guardian, husband, or overlord. The thief had to pay a monetary penalty to the injured guardian, and the woman remained a pawn.

Under the Burgundian Code (redacted about A.D. 500), if a woman left her husband, she was to "be smothered in mire." But if the man wished to leave his wife without cause, he was to pay her the amount of her purchase price. If a woman was guilty of adultery, witchcraft, or grave-digging, she could be rejected by her husband and must suffer the penalty cited above. If the relative of a violated girl did not wish to have her punished, she could be delivered to the king for servitude.[34]

English law was based on the Germanic codes, and Sir William Blackstone's *Commentaries*, used by law students until quite recent times, defined woman's proper status as:

By marriage, the husband and wife are one person in law; that is, the very being or legal existence of the woman is suspended during the marriage, or at least is incorporated and consolidated into that of the husband; under whose wing, protection, and *cover* she performs every thing.... A man cannot grant anything to his wife, or enter into covenant with her: for the grant would be to suppose her separate existence.[35]

Though a few women were taught to serve as scribes or illuminators of manuscripts during the Middle Ages, or to administer a convent, almost no women (and not many men) were educated. During the Renaissance a few women of the upper leisure class were taught by their fathers or a tutor to read Greek, Latin, or their own language, usually only their own.

Even in America in the nineteenth century only a very few women were educated. The first elementary school for girls was established by Emma Hart Willard in 1823, and she pushed for public education for girls. Though a few girls attended school with their brothers in the nineteenth century, it was not until the early twentieth century that girls were generally taught academic subjects.

Not until the mid-twentieth century could a woman claim her own earnings. Only recently could she make a contract without her husband's signature. As recently as the 1970s a wife had to prove her financial earnings helped pay for the farm or business or pay inheritance tax when widowed, for it was assumed all she possessed in goods or finances came from her husband. This writer was told in 1972 by Iowa attorneys-at-law that she had to have proof by checks that her earnings helped pay for the jointly held property, or else pay inheritance tax on at least half of the property. This law was later changed to a limit of $180,000 tax free. Today, Iowa law grants unlimited inheritance to either spouse.

George Fox (1624–1691) founded the Society of Friends (ca. 1648) which recognized women as spiritually equal to men and opened the practice of preaching ministry to them.[36] Not until the 1800s in other denominations, when beneficent and reform societies were organized, did women really find opportunities for humanitarian service outside the home, and several women served as "missionaries."[37]

The Congregationalist churches had ordained forty women by 1900, the Cumberland Presbyterian Church began to ordain women in 1889. "A Women's Ministerial Conference was formed in 1882 to provide a network of support for women, but it had little power to enact changes."[38] The Lutherans, Presbyterians, and Episcopalians did not ordain women until well into the twentieth century.

The Restoration Movement

Why did not the early Latter Day Saint Church ordain women? Joseph Smith gave a revelation in July 1830 that his wife, Emma, was to "be ordained under his hand to expound Scriptures, and to exhort the church, according as it shall be given thee by my Spirit" (Doctrine and Covenants 24:2c). It has long been denied that she was ever ordained, or that this meant more than a divine calling as a comfort to her husband and to compile a hymnal.

Men and women sacrificed to build the "House of the Lord" at Kirtland, but women were excluded from most religious activities

there. The concept of a strictly patriarchal priesthood did not permit women to be involved in the planning, organization, and functioning of classes, or in conducting worship services. Contrary to tradition, however, women were permitted to attend the dedication service on March 27, 1836.[39]

When the Nauvoo Relief Society was organized at Nauvoo, on March 17, 1842, Joseph Smith recorded the event briefly in his journal:

The revelation was then fulfilled by Sister Emma's election to the Presidency of the Society, she having previously been ordained to expound the Scriptures. Emma was blessed, and her counselors were ordained by Elder John Taylor.[40]

When testimonies of healings under the hands of these women were made public, Joseph Smith attended their meeting on April 28, 1842, and spoke to them concerning the spiritual gifts:

...if the people had common sympathies they would rejoice that the sick could be healed; that the time had not been before that these things could be in their proper order...wherein they are ordained, it is the privilege of those set apart to administer in that authority, which is conferred on them; and if the sisters should have faith to heal the sick, let all hold their tongues, and let everything roll on."[41]

Though women of the Reorganization may have voted earlier than 1864, the earliest documentation so far discovered is a report of the Northern Illinois District in which John Shippy instructed the Saints that "every brother and sister should vote on every resolution which is voted upon."[42] In 1868 a General Conference resolution was passed, ruling that "all the members of the church, male and female, have a right to vote on all questions that may be brought before the General Conferences."[43]

For many years, when women in the Reorganization met it was required that a priesthood member be present. Periodically in the columns of the *Herald* women expressed their desire to have more active and independent participation in church life, and the "Mother's Home Column" became a forum for these women. Eleanor Kearney advised the women to deliver their meetings to priesthood supervision, and listen to what the priesthood member had to say. But any layman could be ignored and they could go on with their meeting. "The mere fact of being a man gives him no authority."[44]

That same year (1890) High Priest D. S. Mills, who was in charge of the Pacific Slope Mission, anointed and set apart Emma Burton, wife of Joseph Burton who had been assigned a mission to the Polynesian Islands, "to administer to the sick among the females of the church."[45] The apostle in charge of this mission, T. W. Smith, objected to this action and requested publication of his protest. In his letter to Bishop E. L. Kelley, he stated,

Say what Sr. Emma may—being very hard of hearing—and not understanding all, even if a portion, of what was said, yet it was a square out and out ordination. It has created confusion, and uncertainty and division in many parts of the church.[46]

According to Madelon Brunson, there is no evidence to bear out the truth of this last sentence; nor was this information widespread. Mills "defended his course by saying, 'What I have said and done in that matter was by the power of the Holy Spirit and I can't go back on that'."[47]

In 1893 Cassie B. Kelley objected to the policy that had ended the Women's Prayer Union, and which still troubled the attempts by the "Daughters of Zion" societies to organize and hold meetings by and for women. She complained, "...everything must be done under the eye of the elder....I protest against such an idea."[48]

This policy was still in force in 1936, as witnessed by this writer when she suggested the women could have a season of prayer for badly needed rain. Some of the older women insisted that because no elder was present we could not do that. They said, emphatically, "That is not allowed!"

This appears to have been a policy based on tradition rather than inspired reason. In relation to the Daughters of Zion conducting their own meetings without the presence of an elder, Joseph Smith III wrote to his daughter, Audentia Smith Anderson, a member of the Daughters of Zion Advisory Board:

My opinion is that the Daughters of Zion should engineer and conduct their annual meeting at Independence entirely within themselves, presiding officers, secretaries, ushers, speakers, and all. Don't ask a *brother* to "peep" a word.... If you go down, go with your colors flying, women on deck in command, women at the guns and at the helm. Don't let an elder, or the son of an elder have a thing to do with it from A to Izzard. That's my opinion.[49]

As scholars came to realize that there really was no scriptural basis for excluding women from ecclesiastical ministry, a few spoke against cultural tradition which denied women equal status with men. Two years before the Nineteenth Amendment to the U.S. Constitution gave women the right to vote in 1920, T. W. Williams (ordained an apostle in 1920) spoke to the Women's Auxiliary about God's intention in creating humans.

There was no embargo upon either sex.
They were equal! They had equal dominion! They had equal privilege! They possessed equal responsibility! Woman was not confined to domesticity! Man was not master. Each was answerable to God! They were comrades!
This was paradise!
Then man fell and male domination commenced....
It is urged that God cannot trust woman and this is the reason why he does not confer priesthood upon her. There is not one word, not one line where God has indicated that woman is unworthy....
Priesthood is not a regalia, it does not consist of bright colors. It is not self-exaltation. It does not consist of an "I am holier than thou" attitude. Priesthood is nothing more than the privilege to serve. Who dare say that God has not called woman to service in his Church....
This church places no embargo on sex. We recognize them as comrades, co-workers with man in a common service.[50]

Garland Tickemyer, a close associate of "Fred M.," testified to the World Conference on April 6, 1984, that President Smith had written a letter to Pauline Arnson saying the day would come when women would be ordained to priesthood in the Reorganized Church of Jesus Christ of Latter Day Saints.[51]

F. M. Smith's interest in providing expanded roles for women in the church was expressed in the *Herald* (November 5, 1935). It suggested at least some concern with ecclesiastical roles:

In Paul's time there existed some form of Order of Widows, who functioned as those to offer special prayers, comforters of the distressed or despondent, and administerers to the sick. More information should be secured on the work of this order for I can see where such an organization could be of great assistance, if rightly conducted in their work, to the priesthood. Care must be exercised, however, in laying down the lines along which their work should be done if at all. So I suggest you should consider a committee to study this matter. I am so interested in this that I have for some time been hoping and trying to find the time to more thoroughly inform myself on this interesting subject having in view the possibility and advisability of effecting a similar order among our women. Perhaps you might be willing to join me in this research.

Allied with this is the question of the Order of Deaconesses. Was there such an order among the former day saints? What were its functions? Should we have one now?[52]

Some RLDS Church leaders continued to try to alert the church membership concerning attitudes: toward women, minorities, other religions, and cultures. In the 1960s when the people of the United States were struggling for more civil and economic rights, an Equality Resolution was presented to the RLDS delegate assembly stating, "The R.L.D.S. concept of equality is a vital aspect of the gathering and Zionic philosophy of the church."[53] Economic equality was part of the thrust of this resolution.

"We believe that the achievement of equality depends on the free cooperation of godly men motivated by an informed aware-

ness of the demands of justice in the social, political, economic and other fields." This resolution was presented by the First Presidency and approved April 3, 1962.[54]

In June 1969 Velma Ruch and Barbara Higdon organized a conference at Graceland College which addressed the problem of women's role in the church. This precedent-setting event was reported in the *University Bulletin* under the title, "Womanhood and Manhood: A New Image."[55] Violette Lindbeck, the keynote speaker, spoke concerning the long-held premise of natural inequality:

In the last two centuries or more, this concept of necessary hierarchical ordering of human relationships based on the premise of natural inequality has come under attack from all quarters. The insights on emerging social values which created the demand for political democracy, for liberal churches, for economic justice, for self-determination of men and nations, for freedom of slaves and emancipation of women are forming the world revolution of social expectations....

The church must stop being a follower of the culture and become a leader, become that body of ministry of reconciliation where all the little walls of separation which are found in our society (black-white, young-old, married-single, male-female) are overcome. The church is only the church when it reflects the glory of the Kingdom.[56]

Barbara Higdon, *University Bulletin* editor, tried to prick the conscience of all in relation to cultural tensions by publishing articles and speeches pertinent to the cultural and theological tensions of the 1960s. In Geoffrey F. Spencer's article, "The Theology of Men and Women as Revealed in Scripture,"[57] he noted that the Hebrew culture was not so much a male culture as a tension culture, tending to reflect the mythological climate which sexualized the world, into a tension of opposite and hierarchical functions.

From 1973 to 1981, the hymnal committee compiling a new hymnal for the RLDS Church worked diligently to eliminate sexist language from all hymns and prevailed in most instances. Several new hymns were written to specifically bridge recognized gaps in communication through song.

In the February 1981 *Herald*, Apostle Charles Neff called for a study of the issue of ordination of men, as well as women. The title of his plea was "Ministers All."[58]

In April 1970 the RLDS World Conference approved a resolution "to make the proportion of women given assignments to committees and commissions more in keeping with the proportion [62 percent] of women who are members of the church."[59] Elders A. H. (Bud) Edwards III and Robert Wood moved a substitute:

Whereas, There is no scriptural, ecclesiastical, theological, or social justification for discriminating against women in the life of the church or society; and

Whereas, There are early and significant precedents of leadership by women in the church; and

Whereas, The church is called to pioneer in achieving just social relationships in the world and is therefore called to set its own house in order to demonstrate its commitment to Zionic principles; and

Whereas, Women constitute over 50 percent of the membership, yet occupy less than 10 percent of the positions of leadership in the church, even though women have demonstrated their ability to lead both in the church and in society; therefore be it

Resolved, That the World Conference of 1970 looks with favor on the accepting of women for leadership in the church who qualify according to their ability and God's divine call; and be it further

Resolved, That leaders of the church at every level be directed by the First Presidency to move with forthrightness in the spirit of resolution to end discrimination on the basis of sex in the life of the church; and be it further

Resolved, That the World Conference of 1970 ask the First Presidency to provide a clarifying statement on the ordination of women to priesthood which can serve as a guideline to the church in this matter.

The mover of this resolution tried to speak to it and was "shouted down." When objection to consideration was overruled, the matter was tabled. A motion to take from the table lost.[60]

Resolutions related to women as leaders or ordained ministers were again presented in 1972. One on female representation in administrative decision-making carried, and in 1974 a Conference report stated there was "...still only minimal degree of increase of women serving on boards, commissions, and committees or working in executive positions."

A resolution from Santa Fe Stake in 1976 noted, "A limited number of recommendations for women to be ordained to the priesthood have been submitted through administrative channels to the First Presidency" and requested that calls for ordination of women be deferred "until such time as prophetic direction might be presented and approved, by common consent, of a World Conference assembled."[61]

Ecumenical Awareness

As some leaders and members of the RLDS Church were active in trying to rectify perceived social injustices, some events of an ecumenical nature are worthy of note. In 1978 a Christian conference at Bangladore, India, called Paul's teachings (as found in the King James version of the Bible) into question and suggested "inter-dependence and mutuality" as the meaning of marriage. From 1978 to 1981, such conferences were held in San Jose, Costa Rica, and Beirut; also in Sandy Point, New York, and Bad Segeberg, West Germany.[62]

In September 1980, at the African Regional Consultation held at Ibadan, Nigeria, thirty-one official participants from eleven countries and about an equal number of visitors, women and men coming in daily from the Ibadan area, met at the Center for Church and Society in Ibadan. This African Regional Consultation, representing a wide range of churches, met to study, "What role does scripture play in establishing Christian identity that is authentically Christian and authentically African?" It was generally conceded that Christianity reinforced its own traditions as to women's being born to suffer and endure. Because "help meet" or "helper" does not infer inferiority, and because man and woman created in God's image does not imply subordination—rather, equality under God—they believed this was the interpreter's problem, not God's. They noted that Jesus' attitude toward men and women was the same, that he went beyond the culture of his day.[63]

In July 1981, the World Council of Churches conference in Sheffield, England, heard the "Third World Women's cry" for recognition, social transformation, and abolishment of sexism. Two hundred and fifty persons from ninety nations participated in that council.

The fifth International Conference met in August 1981 at New Delhi, India, and demanded the release of women from the cultural web of oppression in all Third World countries. The members of this conference declared, "A new theology of all religions must be done."

The All-Africa Conference of Churches at Nairobi declared the Bible was not relevant to African cultures because many of their dialects do have non-sexist words for the reflexive pronoun indicating an individual human being, which makes Bible translation more fair and meaningful. This conference stressed the importance of the extended family. Finally, a resolution was sent from Africa to Geneva stating the need for a "new revelation of God's relation to women."

Summation

Our theological perceptions are limited by our concepts of the divine presence many of us call God. A degendered God is impersonal. A single-gender God tends to limit the inclusive love of God. How can we perceive God as nonanthropomorphic yet as an ever-caring, personal influence? What we individually perceive God's nature to be, we project on ourselves.

The history of the projections of our perceived nature of Deity becomes the evolution of the God concept. It shows stages of development in company with cultural reflections. The mother goddess roots in prehistory associate with the fertility cults. The familial nature of the gods in Greek culture continues to provide us with a study in relationships. Chronos imposed the order of time upon Chaos. Both continue in the struggle for access to and control of Gaia, our mother, the earth. The Macedonian influence, Roman culture, and the Roman Catholic Church profoundly influenced us toward patriarchalism and a male Deity. Hebrew folkways under the influence of these dominating cultural traditions adapted and survived. In the early writings of the church, we see the profound influence on the language of the scriptures as they were translated throughout two millennia.

The Restoration movement has at once been prophetic and subject to cultural traditions hardening into law. As we continue to seek to be in the forefront of organizations promoting the worth of persons, we find ourselves ecumenically involved. We respond to the shock waves shaking traditional priestly forms which have culminated in the reevaluation of the nature of priesthood and our relationship to the Divine.

Projections

Knowing the past helps us to understand the present and to project into the future. The RLDS Church has already experienced improvement in ministry through ordained women and husband-wife teams. Women pastors have brought uniquely nurturing, compassionate listening skills into visiting ministry. While some men also show such skills, the traditional mode which inhibited men from showing emotion still influences both men and women. This hinders many men from using the supportive touch, or the compassionate, nurturing hug many women can give. However, this is changing, as evidenced in the 1992 RLDS World Conference when some men of the leading quorums embraced each other in supportive, *agapic*-bonding gestures.

The church is yet called to break the glass-ceiling of power, currently evident in all-male leadership quorums. A few women seventies and high priests graced the 1992 Conference body, and many women elders could be seen in the elder's quorum. Also, several women were seated in the Aaronic quorum meetings. Currently, no woman or non-Caucasian is a member of the Quorum of Twelve Apostles, First Presidency, or Presiding Bishopric.

The eternal power struggle evident in almost every aspect of social activity (economic, political, ecclesiastical, aesthetic) must be recognized and challenged to promote well-being for all, and for utilizing our diversity of gifts and needs. Our cross-cultural perceptions must be examined and modified to enhance relationships.We need to define, accept, and deal with our diversities.

Our call as a prophetic people requires an understanding of the nature of God in relation to our lives. Empowerment comes as we respond to the call to be reconciled as to cultures, ethnic groups, and racial and economic classifications. As we seek to recognize and accept our diversities, our differing gifts and callings, can we accelerate the coming of a Zionic reality—a synthesis of diversities?

Though changes in attitudes toward women took centuries to achieve, we can expect continued rapid changes, such as we have witnessed in the sciences. As we break the fetters of unexamined traditions and seek greater freedoms, such as the ordination of women has already brought, new insights will come, individually and collectively. Under our old definitions of God, we shuffled along, wearing the shackles of patriarchalism. An exciting new paradigm opens to us as we shake off the bonds and embrace a religious frontier in which we claim membership in the functional family of God.

Notes

1. II Corinthians 5:20—the only New Testament reference using "stead" in a comparable manner. "We pray you in Christ's stead, be ye reconciled to God." Malachi 3:6—"I am the Lord, I change not; therefore, ye sons of Jacob are not consumed [finished]."
2. John Ardagh and Colin Jones, *Cultural Atlas of France* (Oxford: Time-Life Series, 1992), 20.
3. Richard and Catherine Clark Kroeger, *I Suffer Not a Woman* (Grand Rapids, Michigan: Baker Book House, 1992), 50.
4. Merlin Stone, *When God Was a Woman* (New York: A Harvest/HBJ Book, 1976).
5. Leonard Swidler, *Biblical Affirmations of Woman* (Philadelphia: Westminster Press, 1979), 21–73.
6. Marija Gimbutas, *The Language of the Goddess* (London: Thames & Hudson, 1989), 175. William G. Dever, *Recent Archaeological Discoveries and Biblical Research* (Seattle: University of Washington Press, 1990), 157. Dever noted concerning human figurines, "Thousands of these terra cottas have been found at Israelite sites...; there is scarcely a single clear example of a male figurine, bronze or ceramic, from an Israelite site."
7. AL (EL) is translated *God* 212 times, *god* 15 times, *idol* 1 time, *power* 3, *mighty* 4. AShRH (*Asherah*, feminine singular) is translated *grove* 40 times. BOL (*Baal*, meaning owner-possessor) is translated *Baal* 56 times, *god* 15, *man* 26, *husband* 14, *owner* 14, *mighty* 4, *power* 3. Gail Ramshaw, "The Gender of God" in *Feminist Theology: A Reader*, ed. Ann Loades (Louisville, Kentucky: Westminster/John Knox Press, 1990), 170: "Human Language cannot express the essence of God, nor its power effect communication with God, any more than the human mind can grasp at divinity. Different languages and genres use various techniques to varying degrees in their worship and theology." Our names and pronouns used for God can only be metaphoric.
8. J. P. Mallory, *In Search of the Indo-Europeans:*

Language, Archeology, and Myth (London: Thames & Hudson, 1989), 24.

9. Julia O'Faolain and Lauro Martines, eds., *Not in God's Image* (New York: Harper & Row, 1973), 49ff.

10. Jon-Christian Billegmeyer and Judy A. Turner, "Role of Women in Mycenaean Greece," *Reflections of Women in Antiquity*, ed. Helene P. Foley (New York: Gordon and Breach Science Publishers, 1981), 1–10.

11. *The Interpreter's Dictionary of the Bible*, Volume 2 (New York: Abingdon Press, 1962), 2:366.

12. Gimbutas, 159.

13. Richard Schaap, *An Illustrated History of the Olympics*, 2nd ed., rev. & enl. (New York: Alfred Knopf, 1967), 29.

14. Tertullian, *de cultu feminarum*, 1:11–12, *The Fathers of the Church*, Vol. 40 (Fathers of the Church, Inc., 1959), 117–118. Partial quote in Leonard Swidler, *Biblical Affirmations of Woman* (Philadelphia: Wesminster Press, 1979), 82.

15. Mary R. Lefkowitz and Maureen B. Fant, *Women's Life in Greece and Rome* (Baltimore, Maryland: The Johns Hopkins University Press, 1982), 14–16.

16. John Peradotto and J. P. Sullivan, eds., *Women in the Ancient World: The Arethusa Papers* (Albany, New York: State University of New York Press, 1984), 3.

17. Aristotle, *Generation of Animals*, translated by A. L. Peck (Loeb Classics, Harvard University Press, 1943), Bk. 1, 211ff.

18. Dorothea Wender, "Plato, Misogynist, Paedophile, and Feminist," in Peradotto, 219–220.

19. Demosthenes, "Against Neaera," *The Orations*, quoted in O'Faolain, 9.

20. Aeschines, "Against Timarchus," quoted in O'Faolain, 23.

21. Ibid., 36–37.

22. Ibid., 18–19, 115, 225–227.

23. Frances and Joseph Gies, *Marriage and the Family in the Middle Ages* (New York: Harper & Row, 1987), 19.

24. O'Faolain, 48–49.

25. Ibid., 55, 256, 303.

26. Elizabeth Clark and Hubert Richardson, *Women and Religion* (San Francisco: Harper & Row, 1977), 33–34. Jean Daniélou, S.J., *The Ministry of Women in the Early Church* (London: Faith Press, 1961), *passim*. Alice Hageman, ed., *Sexist Religion and Women in the Church; No More Silence!* (New York: Association Press, 1974), 54–57. Arthur F. Ide, *Woman As Priest, Bishop, and Laity, in the Early Catholic Church to 440 AD* (Mesquite, Texas: Ide House, 1984), 24–56. Paul K. Jewett, *The Ordination of Women* (Grand Rapids, Michigan: Wm. B. Eerdmans, 1980), 58–74. Letty M. Russell, *Human Liberation in a Feminist Perspective* (Philadelphia: Westminster Press, 1974), 141–143. G. Rattray Taylor, *Sex in History* (New York: Vanguard Press, 1970), 65. "...in the Early Church they (women) had been allowed to preach, to cure, to exorcise and even to baptize. All these rights had been generally removed, and by the Middle Ages women ceased to have legal existence." M. E. Thrall, *The Ordination of Women to the Priesthood* (London: SCM Press Ltd., 1958), 111.

27. The world translated "servant" in the KJV is *diakonon*, the accusative form of *diakonos*, translated "deacon" five times, "minister" twenty times, "servant" seven times. "Servant" is *doulos* 120 times. The Greek word *prostatis* ("standing before" or "presiding") appears only once and is translated "succouror" in the KJV (Romans 16:2). It comes from *proistemi*, translated "rule" in I Timothy 5:17—"Let the elders [*presbyteroi*, inclusive] who rule well be counted worthy...."

Several Hebrew words are all translated "rule" or "have dominion" or "power." *WShL* (*mashal*), to have "active mental ability" (*Strong's Exhaustive Concordance*) is also translated "parable" and indicates the power to see contrasts and make comparisons. Eve questioned and Adam named the animals, each exhibiting "superior mental action." In Genesis 3:16—"and he shall rule over you"—the phrase "rule over" is *mashal*. "Over" is not present, rather "among" is used. They were each to exercise their intellectual power.

Unilateral power is expressed in the words *ShRR* (*sharar*), *ShLT* (*shalat*), and *ShLTVN* (*shilton*) ["Sultan"], translated "rule," "ruling power," or "prince." Relational power is found in *Rd*, *rad*, or *RDH* (*radah*), translated in Genesis 1:26: "And let us make man [*ADM*=mankind] in our own image, after our likeness: and let them *have dominion over* [*radah*] the fish of the sea, and *over* the fowl of the air, and *over* every creeping thing that creepeth upon the earth." Each "over" is the prefixed *B*—"with" or "among," indicating relational power, accountability, or stewardship.

28. World Book Encyclopedia, *Witchcraft* (Chicago: Field Enterprises, 1965), 310–311.

29. Augustine, *On the Holy Trinity*, translated by a. W. Hadden and W. G. T. Shedd, Select Library of the Nicene Fathers (Buffalo, New York: 1887), 159.

30. O'Faolain, 129.

31. *Legis Saxonem und Lex Thuringorum*, quoted by O'Faolain (in English), 96–97.

32. Ibid., 97.

33. Ibid., 98.

34. Ibid., 105.

35. Frances and Joseph Gies, *Women in the Middle Ages* (New York: Barnes & Noble, A Division of Harper & Row, 1978), 30.

36. Barbara J. MacHaffie, *Her Story: Women in Christian Tradition* (Philadelphia: Fortress Press, 1986), 89–90.

37. Edith Deen, *Great Women of the Christian Faith* (New York: Harper Brothers, 1959), 256.

38. MacHaffie, 112.

39. Madelon Brunson, *Bonds of Sisterhood: A History of the RLDS Women's Organization, 1842–1983* (Independence, Missouri: Herald House, 1985), 11–12.

40. Ibid., 16.

41. Ibid., 19.

42. *Saints' Herald* 6 (July 1, 1864): 3.

43. *Saints' Herald* 13 (April 15, 1868): 126.

44. *Saints' Herald* 37 (July 26, 1890): 487.

45. Brunson, 39.

46. Ibid., 40.

47. Ibid., 41.

48. Cassie B. Kelley, "Daughters of Zions," *Autumn Leaves* (August 1893): 383–384.

49. Joseph Smith letter to Audentia (Smith) Anderson (December 17, 1897), Joseph Smith III Miscellaneous Letters and Papers, RLDS Library–Archives, P13 f555.

50. T. W. Williams, speech delivered April 9, 1918, in *Zion's Ensign* (reported May 2, 1918): 6–7.

51. Garland Tickemyer, oral testimony to RLDS World Conference (April 6, 1984) and statement to Enid S. Debarth (April 9, 1984).

52. Saints' Herald 82 (November 12, 1935): 1452, 1459.

53. RLDS World Conference *Bulletin* (April 11, 1962): 49.

54. Ibid.

55. *University Bulletin* 21, no. 6 (Winter 1969), Barbara Higdon, ed. RLDS Library-Archives.

56. Violette Lindbeck, "In Christ Is Neither Male Nor Female," *University Bulletin* 21, no. 6 (Winter 1969): 5, 85.

57. *University Bulletin* 21, no. 6 (Winter 1969): 47–56.

58. *Saints Herald* 128 (February 1, 1981): 56–57.

59. RLDS World Conference *Bulletin* (1970): 309, 310, 329, 330. Also telephone interview (May 10, 1992) with "Bud" Edwards affirming the "shouting down" and referring to a taped archival record in care of RLDS Church historian, Richard Howard.

60. Ibid., 329–330.

61. RLDS World Conference *Bulletin* (1976): 197.

62. John C. B. and Ellen Webster, *The Church and Women in the Third World* (Philadelphia: Westminster Press, 1985), 12, 105–119.

63. Andre-Dumas, "Biblical Anthropology and the Participation of Women in the Ministry of the Church," *World Council of Church's Statement Concerning the Ordination of Women* (Geneva: The World Council of Churches, 1961), 12–40.

The Power in Language
Ruth Ann Wood

Most of the grounds of the world's troubles are matters of grammar.

—Montaigne (1533–1592)

Language is a powerful influence in human existence. The degree of ability to think and to communicate those thoughts separates humans from animals. Through the use of language, people convey their vision of reality. For example, if the earth is to be "subdued," people want to control and suppress the manifestations of nature. Conversely, if humans are challenged to "preserve" the earth, they strive to identify the rhythm of nature and modulate their lives to its inherent pace. Through communication with others, persons name and give meaning to the world and find their special place in that world.

The French philosopher Montaigne could have been speaking of the troubles that currently plague the Christian Church as it struggles to communicate its message in terms that include all persons. Inclusive language is language that promotes and maintains attitudes that recognize all persons as of equal worth.

Inclusive language is simply a concrete expression of what we say we believe theologically: that all human beings are made in God's image, that salavation [sic] is free to all through the work of Christ on the cross, that in Christ all Christians are one body, one family.[1]

In a social environment in which sensitivity to language has been heightened as never before, Christian churches today are challenged to eliminate sexism in the language used to convey the gospel message. The secular world has made many attempts to eliminate gender-specific nouns from its vocabulary (e.g., mailman, chairman, and po-liceman). The church could likewise promote inclusive language by closely examining the grammar of scripture and metaphor that conveys its theology. As individual Christians, we can be more responsible in examining the language we use to describe our beliefs and then consciously choosing inclusive terms to express that theology.

Many of the "matters of grammar" confronting the church today are rooted in a sexist culture and a manipulated language. Christianity was born into a patriarchal society. Patriarchy is defined as a hierarchical structure which places men at the pinnacle of a pyramid and women below them in power and influence in all areas of life: family, society, and religious institutions. In the patriarchical Hebrew culture, women were treated as possessions whose ownership was transferred from fathers to husbands. There was strong religious confirmation of societal restrictions for women:

One rabbi writing about A.D. 90 said, "If a man gives his daughter a knowledge of the Law it is as though he taught her lechery," and "Better to burn the Torah than to teach it to women."[2]

The general belief was that when a baby boy was born, a bit of heaven came into the world; when a baby girl was born, nothing came. A rabbinical dictum stated,

The world cannot exist without males and females, but happy is he whose children are sons and woe to him whose children are daughters.[3]

There are many examples in ancient Hebrew culture in which a female's very existence was considered repugnant and evil. Men were prohibited from speaking to any woman in public. Each month a woman's God-created bodily functions rendered her unclean according to the dictates of the Jewish religion. Women were forbidden to draw close to the Holy of Holies for worship. The most blatant rejection of females was the Jewish males' ritualistic daily prayer:

Praised be God that he has not created me a gentile; praised be God that he has not created me a woman; praised be God that he has not created me an ignorant man.[4]

Sexist language and attitudes are the norm in the standard books of the church as well as in the Christian tradition—not because God does not value females, but because Christianity grew out of the soil of patriarchy.

The traditional teachings of the church also perpetuated the distortions in attitudes toward women. Much of Christian scripture came directly from the patriarchal society of Israel. Scripture predominately was written and/or edited and translated by men and its very fabric was woven from the strands of patriarchy. It is a miracle that so many of the stories of Jesus' ministry to and through women appear at all. Jesus' ministry to prostitutes, Samaritans, and "unclean women" is clearly recorded. The image of some of these faithful women has been distorted through tradition. For example, many sermons have been preached about Mary Magdalene as a prostitute. But there is *absolutely no evidence* that Mary Magdalene was the woman taken in adultery or the "woman of the streets" who anointed Jesus' head with precious oils.[5] Christian tradition has associated these unnamed women with Mary Magdalene. The only information given in the scriptures about Mary Magdalene is that she was healed by Jesus' casting out devils (Luke 8). Many men underwent similar healing, but none was labeled a prostitute.

The scriptures include many instances in which women represent God, but these, too, have been largely ignored as metaphors for God's action in the world. The woman's search for her lost coin is obviously an example of God's great concern for the lost. It is prominently placed between two other stories (the Prodigal Son and the Good Shepherd) in which God is personified as the father and the shepherd, respectively, but one seldom acknowledges that God is personified by the woman.

As Christianity moved beyond the geographic bounds of Israel and the chronological bounds of the first century, the gospel was often carried by responsible and capable women—Junia, Lydia, Phoebe. In fact, Phoebe is named in Romans 16:1 as a deacon (*diakovos*) which for men was translated as minister. As Christianity became a powerful, political influence, male dominance was reasserted. Moving from the female-led house churches to the powerful church of Constantine, Christianity became a tool of oppression against women. The ingrained patriarchal attitudes of society were reemphasized; and as the church became more formalized, rules excluding authoritative participation of women were formulated.

Another factor which added great weight to the legitimacy of sexist language was the manipulation of English usage in the seventeenth and eighteenth centuries to establish the use of "he, him, man, and mankind" as representative of *all* persons. The preference for male-oriented usage is viewed by many as a deliberate campaign. A grammarian, J. Poole (1646), pushed for the use of "he, him, and man" as generic because as he asserted, "The Masculine is more worthy than the Feminine...."[6] Until this time the plural pronoun "they" had been used regularly with singular referents. Shakespeare used the third person plural with a singular referent: "Everyone to rest themselves." The idea of placing men in a supreme role over women was solidified by the famous British jurist William Blackstone who set a legal supremacy of males:

By marriage...the husband and wife are one person in the law—that is, the very being or legal existence of the woman is suspended during marriage....[7]

Thus, the grammatical subjugation of women was extended into legal subjugation. These ideas were further reinforced by a grammarian of the late eighteenth century. L. Murray (1795) explained the reasoning behind assigning male and female pronouns to grammatically sexless nouns:

Figuratively, in the English tongue, we commonly give the masculine gender to nouns which are conspicuous for the attributes of imparting or communicating, and which are by nature strong and efficacious. Those, again, are made feminine which are conspicuous for the attributes of containing or bringing forth, or which are peculiarly beautiful or amiable. Upon these principles the sun is always masculine, and the moon, because the receptacle of the sun's light, is feminine. The earth is generally feminine. A ship, a country, a city, &c. are likewise made feminine, being receivers or containers. Time is always masculine, on account of its mighty efficacy. Virtue is feminine from its beauty, and its being the object of love. Fortune and the church are generally put in the feminine gender....[8]

The concept of male dominance prevailed in the colonies, too. As John Adams attended the meetings of the Continental Congress, he received an entreaty from his wife, Abigail, who expressed her desire to

hear that you have declared an independency, and, by the way, in the new code of laws, which I suppose it will be necessary for you to make, I desire you would remember the ladies and be more generous and favorable to them than were your ancestors. Do not put such unlimited power into the hands of husbands.[9]

John made it clear that "the Ladies" were not to assume themselves included in "all men." He wrote, "Depend upon it, We know better than to repeal our Masculine Systems."[10] Abigail would not let the matter rest:

I cannot say that I think you very generous to the Ladies, for whilst you are proclaiming peace and good will to Men, Emancipating all Nations, you insist upon retaining an absolute power over Wives.[11]

The manipulation of language was cemented into grammatical usage by the English law of 1850 that declared "he" as generic and legally included "she." Parliament was following a rule established in 1746 by John Kirby, who decreed that the male gender is "more comprehensive" than the female.[12] The English Parliament (an all-male body) in 1850 justified the law "because men should 'naturally' take precedence."[13] This completed the grammatical shift which mandated that pronouns agree in number rather than in gender. Thus females became lost in "he, him, and his" and invisible in "man, mankind, and men." This invisibility was firmly entrenched on this side of the Atlantic, too. In 1894 a woman was denied entry to the Virginia bar when the U.S. Supreme Court ruled that it was *reasonable* for a lower court to decide that a "woman" was not a "person."[14]

With the underpinnings of sexist attitudes, it is no wonder that when the translators of King James began work on the Bible, all Greek, Latin, and Hebrew words were processed through the strainer of male language. When the Hebrew words *'adam* (person), *'enosh* (mortal), and the Greek *anthropos* (human being) appeared, the seventeenth-century translators narrowed these inclusive terms to the English *man*. This grammatical shift rendered females invisible. To compound this grammatical damage, the nineteenth-century church accepted these mistranslations literally as God's words.

The Church spoke with much authority and for the most part commanded women to remain in the limited sphere supposed to be fixed for them by divine decree.[15]

The modern Christian Church's lack of leadership in correcting the distorted views of the Godhead and human relationships to each other and to God perpetuates injustices toward females.

Today women seek acknowledgment as individuals—not as a subspecies of "man." Females are invisible in a language that uses male pronouns and nouns to represent every human. Persons are forced to perform constant mental gymnastics: "Does *Man and Civilization* include the history of women?" "Does the men's volleyball team include my niece?" "Did the angel chorus exclude all women when they sang 'on earth, peace; good will to men'?"

The decisive argument against using masculine terms generically, however, is not that they are often inadequate and sometimes ridiculous, but that they perpetuate the cultural assumption that the male is the norm, the female a deviation.[16]

Sensitive individuals can extract the church firmly and decisively from the distorted grip of sexist language. God's call is to convey the divine presence to every person regardless of race, color, sex, or station. The first step in that process is to scrutinize carefully current linguistic usage to recognize when language is used in inequitable ways. Many people use language unconsciously, without meaning to depreciate or offend. It is vital to the equality of all persons to stop attaching sexist labels to individuals and work harder to recognize each human being as a unique creation of a nonsexist God. Christians who believe that God is no respecter of persons have a responsibility to examine their vocabulary and eliminate inappropriate phrases and terms. Few women who are old enough to vote and pay taxes appreciate being called a "girl." Is the office staff referred to as "boys"? Neither is it appropriate to model language that depreciates another's value: "silly old man," "crazy old maid," "snot-nosed kid." The best

test for appropriateness of a term or phrase is to put oneself in the hearer's place. Are the descriptive words flattering or hurtful? What mental picture is created? Is a standard being perpetuated that no longer reflects society?

Corporate bodies are developing sensitivity to this issue. In 1978 the RLDS Church developed an inclusive language policy to guide the church out of the mire of sexist language. All resource producers were instructed to change all gender-specific references to gender neutral (e.g., spokesman to representative, brother to Saints or brothers and sisters, chairman to chair, etc.). Writers and editors were cautioned to see that all persons were treated fairly and equitably.

As the worth of persons becomes a central concern of both church and society, and as we continually try to understand and use concepts which emphasize wholeness, dealing with language is essential. Every manuscript submitted for publication should contain clear, well-stated, inclusive language.[17]

In another important step, the committee that developed *Hymns of the Saints* (1981) attempted to modify language to include all persons in the gospel message. They were very sensitive to language in traditional hymns that excluded women. They diligently sought and, in many cases, wrote new hymns that fulfilled the church's desire to be inclusive. Many RLDS ministers also have consciously eliminated male-exclusive terms from their sermons.

Changing the language related to humans is only the beginning. Freeing God's image from male-exclusive language is the next desirable step. When male language for God is the standard, this teaches that God is male; the assumption is that men and boys are God-like and women and girls are not. Constantly switching between male-specific and male-generic language is very confusing. Young children create explicit pictures in their minds whether the subject is concrete or theological:

[A] little girl named Sylvia once wrote, "Dear God, Are boys better than girls? I know you are one but try to be fair" (*Children's Letters to God*).[18] A five-year-old playing with friends argued that boys are better than girls. When asked why, he responded, "Because God is a boy, isn't he?"[19]

There are many examples of feminine characteristics of God in the scriptures, but these are obscured by the traditional use of male-specific nouns referring to God (Father, Lord, and King) and the exclusive use of male pronouns (He, His, and Him). References to God as Father are not as pervasive as some assume. "Father" appears less than ten times in the Old Testament and frequently in the New Testament only in Matthew and John.[20] A multitude of feminine references to the Divine have been largely ignored by preachers and teachers of the gospel.[21] In addition, confusing the historical Jesus (who was physically male) with the risen Christ who transcends the physical, further excludes women from identification with the Divine. In the biblical record a man in Palestine preached and taught and was resurrected by God's power as a symbol of redemption. To insist that the maleness of Jesus is inexorably tied to the divinity of Christ is absurd. Furthermore, to translate the Holy Spirit from the feminine noun of Hebrew and Aramaic (*ruach*) and the Greek neuter noun (*pnuema*) with the male pronoun "he" is a direct mistranslation. "...there is no earthly reason for referring to the Spirit as masculine—except for the assumption that God is masculine!"[22]

For Christian leaders to affirm only the fatherhood of God can become just an attempt to buttress their own positions of authority, to identify their own masculinity with God's supposed masculinity, thus making themselves false gods. They not only falsify the image of God but violate the model of authority given us by Christ, who told the disciples they were to lead as he did, as one who serves.[23]

Human language not only forms culture but is a product of culture and, therefore, changes as culture changes. Because the church's traditional language renders women invisible, the modern church through enlightened scholarship and understanding should be in the forefront to guide cultures and societies out of the Dark Ages of sexist language and into the Enlightenment of equality.

For religious leaders to suggest that one should continue to read it [man] and hear it as generic in religious contexts is similar to arguing that services should continue to be conducted in Greek or Latin or German even when not a soul in the congregation understands the language.[24]

Words are not secret incantations that create magical occurrences. Words are tools. Tools are useful, but as the job changes some tools are left behind on the workbench to gather dust. They once may have served a purpose, but as needs change, so must the tools. Once we had only a wood rasp to smooth rough edges, today that job is most often accomplished with an electric sander. The wood rasp is a relic of days gone by and of limited use today.

The language we use about God is not technical jargon that precisely describes the Unknowable. Rather we speak of God in metaphor using the aspects of our human world that we associate with God. Language influences our mental pictures. If God is an old man in a white robe whiling away eternity sitting on a throne, how does one relate God to a peace activist who feels called by the gospel message to stop the production of nuclear weapons? If God is presented exclusively as a father figure, what image is created for children who have been abused by their fathers and see "father" as threatening and hurtful? There is no "loving father" in that child's experience. When we limit the terms used to discuss God, we restrict God's self to those human terms. We limit God to a norm of human society and do not release the Divine from that very small box.

Christians must not be tied down to the specific language of the scriptures. The scriptures are valuable, but they must not be the end of our search for God. The images of the scriptures grew out of a culture that is far removed from the twenty-first century in which we will soon find ourselves.

If men and women are not both made in God's image, then God is male and this is idolatry. To help avoid idolatry and make good theological sense of the fact that God transcends both masculine and feminine characteristics, it is important to experiment with ways that the Bible can be read in an inclusive manner.[25]

The images of a wrathful, to-be-feared, vengeful God in the Old Testament are in great contrast to a loving, kind, tender-hearted God presented by Jesus in the New Testament. Is one a good God and one a bad God? No, rather the differences in the descriptions and the attributes given to God lie in the writers of the material rather than in the essence of God. Some argue that only men can symbolically represent God because Jesus was historically male. If one follows that line of reasoning, all ministers must be born to Jewish women, have olive skin, wear their brown hair long, and dress in robes. No one wants to limit the ministry of the Messiah to those who physically resemble Jesus.

[T]he purpose of inclusive language is to find for ourselves a fuller vision, a deeper understanding of the One we love and to offer to others a relationship with the God who will heal their wounds, satisfy their longings, and make us all whole persons.[26]

How then do we select our images of God? I suggest that we free the gospel message from the male-dominated language of scripture and Christian tradition and create new metaphors to communicate more clearly the Spirit of Love. The church must acknowledge the patriarchy and sexist bias that is inherent in its language and move beyond those limitations. Hymns, scriptures, and traditions that cannot be made inclusive of all persons should be left on the workbench of history and replaced by more inclusive works that take God beyond male language and male symbols. With this renewed consciousness, Christians can then step forward and lead the fight to eradicate sexism which distorts the gospel message of God's unfailing love for all persons. Language is important. It illuminates or clouds thinking, limits or expands expectations, and expresses acceptance or rejection of others.

The last verse of the hymn "Our God Is Like an Eagle" (sung to the tune of "Stand Up, Stand Up for Jesus") sums up the need for new language:

Our God is not a woman; our God is not a man.
Our God is both and neither; our God is I who am.
From all the roles that bind us, our God has set
   us free.
What freedom does God give us? The freedom just
   to be.[27]

Notes

1. Nancy A. Hardesty, *Inclusive Language in the Church* (Atlanta, George: John Knox Press, 1987), 6.
2. As quoted by Joanna Dewey, "Images of Women," in Letty M. Russell, ed., *The Liberating Word: A Guide to Nonsexist Interpretation of the Bible* (Philadelphia: The Westminster Press, 1976), 74.
3. Virginia Ramey Mollenkott, *Women, Men & the Bible* (Nashville, Tennessee: Abingdon Press, 1977), 12.
4. Leonard Swidler, "Jesus Was a Feminist," *Catholic World* (January 1971): 178.
5. Rosemary Radford Ruether, "If Magdalene wasn't a prostitute, what have the men done to her?" *National Catholic Reporter* (May 9, 1986): 13.
6. Casey Miller and Kate Swift, *The Handbook of Nonsexist Writing* (New York: Barnes and Noble, 1980), 63.
7. Susan Brooks Thistlethwaite, "Inclusive Language: Theological and Philosophical Fragments" in *Religious Education* 80, no. 4 (Fall 1985): 561.
8. Miller and Swift, *The Handbook of Nonsexist Writing*, 63.
9. *The Encyclopedia AMERICANA*, Volume 29 (New York: America Corporation, 1950): 445.
10. Thistlethwaite, 562.
11. Ibid.
12. Hardesty, 60.
13. Letty M. Russell, "Inclusive Language and Power," in *Religious Education* 80, no. 4 (Fall 1985): 584.
14. Casey Miller and Kate Swift, *Words and Women: New Language in New Times* (Garden City, New York: Anchor Books, 1977), 75.
15. The Encyclopedia AMERICANA, 451.
16. Miller and Swift, *Words and Women*, 118.
17. Policy of Inclusive Language in Church Publications and Other Written Materials, Approved by the First Presidency (November 1978), 1.
18. Hardesty, 13.
19. Barbara A. Withers, "Inclusive Language and Religious Education," *Religious Education* 80, no. 4 (Fall 1985): 509.
20. Hardesty, 27.
21. There are many such references to be found in the scriptures. The following are a few that may be new to many people. God is compared to
   a woman in labor—Isaiah 42:14
   a nursing mother—Isaiah 49:15
   a midwife—Isaiah 66:9; Psalm 22:9–10
   a mother bear—Hosea 13:8
   a female homemaker—Proverbs 31:21
   a bakerwoman—Matthew 13:33; Luke 13:20–21
   a mother eagle—Deuteronomy 32:11–12; Exodus 19:4; Job 39:27–30
   a mother hen—Matthew 23:37; Luke 13:34
   Dame Wisdom—Proverbs 1:20–33
22. Virginia Ramey Mollenkott, *The Divine Feminine: The Biblical Imagery of God as Female* (New York: Crossroad, 1984), 35.
23. Hardesty, 31.
24. Ibid., 62.
25. Letty M. Russell, "Inclusive Language and Power," 600.
26. Hardesty, 102.
27. Mollenkott, *The Divine Feminine*, 88. Words by Laurence G. Bernier (1974) as they appeared in the UFMCC Trial Hymnal.

Envisioning a Liberating Church and an Inclusive Ministry within an RLDS Context
Rita Lester

Speaking about God

Language for God is never socially neutral: language reflects gender and social power structures. Language can hurt, unlike the childhood retort that says that sticks and stones can break bones but words can never hurt you.[1] Language is a very important tip of the iceberg of misogyny and androcentrism, elitism and classism, militarism and feudalism, hence phrases like "God the Father," "sovereign Lord," and "servants of God." "If God is male, then the male is God"—usually the white upper class male at that.[2]

It is important to note that all language is metaphorical and constructed. All language is metaphorical, including language about God; theology is metaphorical. To only understand and worship God as male is to not recognize the metaphorical nature of such words and is idolatrous. The metaphors we use shape our reality, as Lucy Tatman writes in her *Storied Theological Dictionary*.

[We] see reality as we define it...we understand the world [and] our relationship to the world through the words we use to define the world...*to change our words is to change our world*.[3]

It is my assertion that what is often understood as traditional language about God, Christ, church, and humanity cannot fully integrate a feminist vision, cannot express a fully embodied theology, and cannot accomplish the ethic of love at the center of Christianity or acknowledge other religiously central components of Christianity, such as the resurrection of the body.

A theology that does not effectively express women's experience cannot fully include women, just as a theology which does not effectively deal with our embodied experience cannot accomplish what Meredith McQuire, calls a re-materialization of the body; that is, to make the body matter, or what I would call a resurrection of the body (you cannot resurrect something your theology ignores; i.e., the body).[4] We need language that is attuned to the challenges of feminism and liberation theology and that includes but is not limited to eliminating patriarchal, sexist, militaristic, and feudal language about God, Christ, and the body of the church.

In the text, *Exploring the Faith*, published in 1970 and updated in 1987 by Alan Tyree, it pains me to read the dismissal of inclusive language without any systematic discussion informed by current mainstream Protestant practices and the vision of feminist theologians.[5] Besides the strictly patriarchal language and images for God, the text illustrates little concern for militaristic language and images for God: "God as...sovereign," for example, is rooted in a feudal image of God.[6] I would suggest that there are many creative approaches to correcting patriarchal language, including both alternative images for God, which include female images and associations (which can be found in the Bible and created by communities), as well as language which is not gender specific, like Creator, Redeemer, and Sustainer for the Trinity. My disagreement with the text does not necessarily exclude me from this community in that the stated aim of the editor of *Exploring the Faith* intends this text as a resource, not a creedal position.[7]

This is not to say that the historical church can be transformed merely through inclusive language, because, though language should explicitly evoke female and nature imagery as a corrective principle, further and more profound transformations will occur only through a redefining or renewing of understandings, practices, and worship. Though this is a call to an awareness about language, I do not wish to perpetuate what, in feminist circles, is often called the "myth of nonsexist language," that is, that simply changing "chairman" to "chairperson" gets at any deep androcentric assumptions within our cognitive and social constructs. But practicing a policy of inclusive language is a start. (Consider that seminaries like Garrett-Evangelical Theological Seminary in Evanston, Illinois; Episcopal Divinity School; Iliff School of Theology in Cambridge, Massachusetts, and Denver, Colorado; and Claremont in California regard inclusive language policies within classroom and worship as covenant agreements, in some cases to be signed in agreement with the administration.)

Inclusive language would aid in the reconciliation of feminist women and men, a part of the community which most local churches are losing and have largely lost because of their inability to change. The present pattern of sexist language creates a situation in which the more feminist one becomes, the more offended one becomes in worship, as it is practiced, and more out of place one feels in a church community.

Ministry and Community: Confirmation as Ordination?

Sexism, which includes heterosexism, according to feminist theologians like Rosemary Ruether, is a sin—sin being defined as a structure that perpetuates dominance, rendering one group as the definers/knowers and all other groups as the defined/known. Historical churches can only begin to be transformed through a comprehensive revisioning of the language for God and humanity, liturgical practices, and concepts of ministry. In the RLDS Church, to be specific, the underlying androcentrism and the present misogyny, the "call" system of ordination, and the priesthood hierarchy need to be revisioned. It is no longer a question of whether or not women should be in the ministry, but what is the nature of ministry?

The official statements on the nature of ordination vary, from the nonhierachical statement that "confirmation is an ordination" to the specifically hierarchical discussions of what each priesthood office can and cannot do. Fortunately or unfortunately, the church's text entitled *Exploring the Faith: A Series of Studies in the Faith of the Church, Prepared by a Committee on Basic Beliefs*, is vague enough and inconsistent enough on issues of authority to let the reader decide. What is authoritative? I strongly agree with Carter Heyward as she writes in *Touching Our Strength* that,

the value and meaning of authority…is to shape justice, the *logos* of God. As such, authority is the power to elicit among us, between us, and within us that which already is, to give birth to who we are when we are related rightly. The authority of God is not to create out of nothing (the mythos of patriarchal deity), but rather the power to cocreate out of the fabric of our daily lives who we are when we are related mutually—with justice and compassion.[8]

The priesthood in many ways is not treated as an elite group within the RLDS community. Priesthood members are very rarely, and only at the very top of the hierarchy, paid employees of the church. There are no visible signs, like vestments, to differentiate the priesthood from the laity. There is little difference in the theological language used by priesthood and laity as priesthood is not required to be trained extensively in theology. Finally, no one is forbidden to give testimony. Local churches are relatively free, in comparison with most Catholic and Protestant churches, in that they "do not face constant intervention and coercion from hierarchical authority."[9] It is my hope and the intention of my interaction with the community to use these aspects and interpretations of the RLDS Church's anti-clerical history to present a vision of inclusivity and mutual empowerment within the context of ministry.

In the most recent *Priesthood Manual*, it is acknowledged that "roles which once were well accepted by people are now being challenged" because the "unordained have skills and insights needed by the church."[10] This challenge is, in the above-mentioned text, framed as a concern only of the unordained; i.e., that unordained persons are more concerned now than in former years about the ways in which they may function appropriately in the church and how they should relate to those in the priesthood. But it is my suggestion that this issue is precisely the concern of the ordained prescribing what the unordained can and cannot do from a centralized, hierarchical position; i.e., "…the priesthood have exclusive roles which cannot be performed in the church by anyone else."[11] This centralized authoritative position does not take into account the radical congregationalism which actually characterizes the church at the local level.

This deferring to the authority of the ordained is what has been referred to as our Catholic tendencies. Though this name does imply an assumption about the ordained as more knowledgeable and more connected to God, it is worth pointing out that this is where the similarities stop between Catholic and RLDS practices. RLDS ordained persons do not have to attend seminary for three years in order to learn how to consecrate and distribute the Communion ele-

ments, nor do I believe any should have to, but this educational mandate does provide for the possibility of a theologically informed priesthood. It has been my experience that education is central to revisioning church, because, as Jean Danielson has written, "without knowledge of historical and theological alternatives, we will have a great barrier to change…never expanding our circles of knowing and known."[12]

Laying On of Hands

"Laying on of hands" is an ordinance practiced within the church not just in healing ceremonies but also in confirmation rites and upon the request of any person wishing to participate in this rite. The basic premise appears to be that the touching of the three individuals (two of the priesthood and the person requesting the ceremony) is healing. The power and simplicity of such a ritual also appears in the work of women writers like Shange who, for example, presents her women characters as spontaneously recreating the ritual of laying on of hands in *For Colored Girls Who Have Considered Suicide When The Rainbow Is Enuf*.

Granted, there is a hierarchical assumption at work in the present practice of this ordinance in that the ceremony is performed with two priesthood members. But the point of interest and promise to me is in the possibility of acknowledging the body as a site of knowledge and healing, and not just as dead matter to be transcended for the sake of the spirit. This recognition of the body as a site of knowledge, and the practice of gathering with others (priesthood or not) for the purpose of renewal, healing, affirmation, or guidance, allows for an embodied theology, and has the possibility of affirming feminist concerns and ecological concerns. Whereas, an anti-body theology tends to be anti-women and anti-earth, an embodied theology has the potential to revision classic mind/body, male/female hierarchical dualisms. Such practices, as the laying on of hands ceremony, focus on the here and now, placing confidence and authority in association and bodies, not in aloofness.

Ecclesiastical bodies, rules, or practices hold genuine authority in the lives of people only insofar as we experience them as forged in and concerned with our actual struggles for mutual empowerment and justice. The healing and encouraging power of an ordinance like laying on of hands can be seen, not as a ceremony in which priesthood "call down" and mediate the power of God through their emptied selves to the person being "administered" to, but as a ceremony in which we celebrate the recognition that persons, as embodied selves, whether priesthood or laity, generate the relationships which can be mutually empowering, and reflect the shape of the Sacred in our lives together.

Zion

As the editors of *Restoration Studies I* write, throughout the RLDS "church's 150-year history the cause of Zion has been cherished and pursued."[13] The conceptualizations of Zion have

taken on many dimensions, ranging from that of a haven to which the Saints may flee to escape the judgments descending on a wicked world to that which ascribes to Zion a redemptive, self-sacrificial ministry for the sake of a world which would be lost but for the love of God; from that of an isolated single community to that of a network of communities permeating social body with Christian attitudes and service.[14]

The RLDS Church, like the LDS Church, has—deep and meaningful within its past—the concept of Zion. To a large degree, LDS Zion is manifest in the theopolitical state of Utah and its temple theology. Though the RLDS Church's Zionic theology is at less tension with the surrounding culture than the LDS Church's, Zion is not simply symbolic in either community (though some argue it should be only purely symbolic).

As Geoffrey Spencer discusses in "Symbol and Process: An Exploration into the Concept of Zion," Zion is often interpreted in concrete terms as a place, like Independence, Missouri, or the United States, occurring or achievable at a particular time, or as a spiritual condition, like pureness of heart.[15] Though Spencer is arguing that a concrete interpretation of Zion "tends to limit our vision and lead to confusion, anxiety, and disappointment,"[16] I do agree with him that Zion's role as symbol and process is seen

...as a powerful and significant dimension in the life of the church as it endeavors to bring the ministry of redemption to individuals but more especially to the corporate structures of the societies in which we live.[17]

In other words, Zion can mean the possibility of redeeming, not only individuals, but persons in community. In this way, Zion is not an other worldly hope or system of rewards but is a present striving on earth and within a community of commitment. Consider that the line of the Lord's Prayer[18] reads, "Thy will be *done on earth*, as it is done in heaven" (Matthew 6:11) not "let your will be concerned with heaven, because earth does not really matter either in creation or redemption."

At its best, the Zionic community concept is a call for a "prophetic church [which] participates in the world to embody the divine intent for all personal and social relations."[19] Zion is not static but is a process which involves both theory and practice. It is not necessarily an immanent eschatological apocalypticism but can be a social and theological commitment which involves the totality of life. It manifests itself as work within the Bread for the World campaign, an active support of peace studies as a religious and educational program, and the justice-making efforts of women's groups like the AWARE group.

The concept of Zion interpreted in this way can be used as a commitment to justice, a striving for the eradication of present systems of oppression, the decreasing focus on the "afterlife" as the time of redemption, and an increasing focus on the present community as redemptive and salvific.

Open Canon

In the RLDS Church I see great potential in the notion of open canon, in spite of the fact that, in recent years, the subject of the canon has been largely bureaucratic and administrative. A text is not "sacred" in the traditional sense of being able to stand alone as the direct word of God and, as such, of being immune to critical accountability to the tasks of justice-making today. Though it has been argued within our theological forums that the almost immediate canonization of material (which is presented by the Presidency and voted on by the delegates at World Conference) shows disrespect for the long and time-tested canon of the Bible, I see it differently.

Whereas the Catholic approach seems to be to submit biblical authority to an elaborate understanding of tradition and the Protestant tendency has been to grant scripture the sole place of authority in determining church beliefs, I think the RLDS practice of an open canon allows us to claim a new motif of authority and to reinterpret both scripture and subsequent tradition. We have a forum within which to deal with philosophical and theological issues (open canon). We also have a person responsible for the initiation and presentation of canonical additions (president-prophet), and we have the practice of representational voting on the presented material (World Conference).

In this way, we have the opportunity to evaluate presented material on the basis of the following question: Does it help us real-ize more fundamentally our connectedness to one another and, hence, the shape of our own identities as persons-in-relation within this historical community? We have much in common with Carter Heyward's description of her own tradition. She writes that "we are to draw upon biblical authority in relation to the rest of our faith-heritage (tradition) as well as our own best judgment (reason) in living responsibly in our own generation."[20] The textualized canon is not worshiped or idolized. The radical congregationalism, rooted in the Restoration movement's beginnings in America in 1830, allows for various interpretations and practices within the different congregations without substantial hierarchical interference or a strict policy of adherence even to the canon.

Women-Church

It has been my experience that "the more one becomes a feminist the more difficult it becomes to go to church."[21] One reaction to this is for women to build their/our own organizations. This does not necessarily involve a total rejection of the institutional organization. Like most major U.S. Protestant denominations, the RLDS Church ordains women but has not fully expressed questions about the very nature of ministry.

Women-church, not simply an ideology or protest, is a community of nurture which has and will continue to:

...guide one through [the] death [of] to the old symbolic order of patriarchy to rebirth into a new community of being and living...[and is important because] one also needs deep symbols and symbolic actions to guide and interpret the actual experience of the journey from sexism to liberated humanity.[22]

Though this can refer to neo-pagan, wicca, or post-Christian gatherings of women and men, my focus here is on an intentional community of women with experiences of Christianity and specifically RLDSism who seek to either reclaim tradition through the experience of women or to reject traditional religion as patriarchal. Both approaches reject the anti-modern evangelical crusade to trivialize and negate women's liberation and both reach beyond traditional patriarchal religion. Both approaches, the reclaiming of a tradition or the rejection of a tradition as hopelessly patriarchal, challenge the tradition. The force behind this challenge is "women, specifically feminist women, who ask critical questions about the role of religion in the sanctification of patriarchal societies."[23]

AWARE is a self-gathered community of women that takes responsibility for theological and personal reflection, celebration, consciousness-raising and liturgy.

But why would women want and need a base community like AWARE, especially now that women are understood as incorporated into the ordination structure? The problem is that the priesthood itself is an ambivalent pattern because, though officially women's ordination is accepted, there are significant remnants at the local level who disagree. A feminist base community moves beyond just getting women into the priesthood to *altering priesthood/authority structures themselves.*

Can't women support each other simply through their best friends? Best friends, of course, are very helpful, empowering, and transformative, but women can increase our resources and audience through the megaphone of the church whether we are struggling to transform the existing church or starting anew. And one of the models that can be used is the biblical exodus community.

A different model of God is assumed in women-church, instead of "needing" the authority of an ordained clerical power to evoke and mediate between the laity and the Sacred, the women-church paradigm assumes that the Sacred is already here among us in our lives together. Worship/celebration is about helping us to experience that which is underlying life, our connection to each other and the shape of the Sacred in our lives. It implies a theological commitment to develop a "discipleship of equals" and is an example of religious agency in which women name their own religious experience.[24]

Closing Comments

The issues discussed in this paper are just a beginning and are from the vision of a person who often feels betwixt and between: too RLDS for religion in the academy and too academic for RLDS communities, too feminist for the religious and too religious for the feminists. Thus far, this has been creative tension, and I am thankful to my friends and companions who have chosen to deal with RLDS theology in very different ways.

Notes

1. Julia Penelope, *Speaking Freely: Unlearning the Lie of the Fathers' Tongues* (New York: Pergamon Press, 1990), xiii.
2. Mary Daly, *Beyond God the Father: Toward a Philosophy of Women's Liberation* (Boston: Beacon Press, 1973), 19.
3. Lucy Alice Tatman, "A Storied Theological Dictionary," (unpublished master's thesis at Garrett-Evangelical Theological Seminary, Evanston, Illinois, 1990), 5.
4. Meredith McQuire, "Religion and the Body," *Journal for the Scientific Study of Religion* (September 1990): 284.
5. *Exploring the Faith: A Series of Studies in the Faith of the Church Prepared by a Committee on Basic Beliefs, Reorganized Church of Jesus Christ of Latter Day Saints*, ed. Alan D. Tyree (Independence, Missouri: Herald Publishing House, 1987), 16.
6. Ibid., 17.
7. Ibid., 8.
8. Ibid., 74–75.
9. Rosemary Radford Ruether, *Sexism and God-Talk: Toward a Feminist Theology* (Boston: Beacon Press, 1983), 202.
10. *The Priesthood Manual,* Reorganized Church of Jesus Christ of Latter Day Saints (Independence, Missouri: Herald Publishing House, 1990), 11.
11. Ibid.
12. B. Jean Danielson, "Revisioning Ministry," (unpublished paper at Garrett-Evangelical Theological Seminary, Evanston, Illinois, 1990), 4.
13. *Restoration Studies I: A Collection of Essays about the History, Beliefs, and Practices of the Reorganized Church of Jesus Christ of Latter Day Saints*, ed. Maurice Draper (Independence, Missouri: Herald Publishing House, 1980), 268.
14. Ibid.
15. Geoffrey F. Spencer, "Symbol and Process: An Exploration into the Concept of Zion," *Restoration Studies I*, 278.
16. Ibid.
17. Ibid., 285.
18. The Holy Scriptures (Independence, Missouri: Herald Publishing House, 1959), Matthew 6:11.
19. Exploring the Faith, 194.
20. Carter Heyward, *Touching Our Strength: The Erotic as Power and the Love of God* (San Francisco: Harper, 1989), 80.
21. Rosemary Radford Ruether, *Sexism and God-Talk Toward a Feminist Theology*, 193.
22. Rosemary Radford Ruether, *Women-Church: Theology and Practice and Feminist Liturgical Communities* (San Francisco: Harper and Row, 1985), 3.
23. Ibid., 2.
24. Mary E. Hunt, *Fierce Tenderness: A Feminist Theology of Friendship* (New York: Crossroad, 1991), 160.

III
IDENTITY AND MISSION

III

IDENTITY AND MISSION

Editor's Note

Issues of identity and mission have had prominent places in discussions during the past decade and many questions still seek answers. The following essays will hopefully draw readers into dialogue on four distinctly different topics.

Paul Jones, as a friend of the church who has been drawn to the uniqueness of the RLDS tradition, calls the church to rediscover its heritage in a new way. He says the church faces a classic dilemma, that of the socio/psychological evolution of a movement of "sect" toward the status of "church" through cultural adaptation. His call is to resist the temptation to become a denomination and to remain faithful to its prophetic mission, not as superiority but as special calling in behalf of the whole of Christ's divided church.

Henry Inouye presents aesthetic justice as responsible, originative, motivating, and foundational. He calls the church to develop and practice an inclusive and responsible theory of justice based on beauty as the metaphysical foundation of reality. The questions of racial justice, economic justice, and ecological justice are interpreted in light of aesthetic justice. The "call forward" and "initial aim" he sees as divine activities that require responses of love and forgiveness rather than retribution.

Roger Launius traces the history of black Americans within the RLDS Church and finds that there has been a two-pronged policy, one emphasizing the ideal and the other the practical. There has been a gap between the ideal and its implementation. One can read between the lines as Launius tells the stories of George Graves, Amy Robbins, and others whose lives were affected. He reminds the church that it has an opportunity to make a worthwhile and lasting contribution to society's unfinished history of race relations.

Don Breckon looks at the traditional views that have informed the church's policy on the issue of homosexuality, specifically in regard to ordination to the priesthood. He looks at scriptural and historic statements in light of contemporary views and asks if the church policy on homosexual behavior needs to be reexamined and if members need to adjust their attitudes.

Demythologizing and Symbolizing the RLDS Tradition*

W. Paul Jones

Although I am not a member of the RLDS Church, for more than twenty years I have worked with many levels of its leadership. There is a pleasant irony in the shift of roles that has occurred during this pilgrimage together. Beginning as an outsider, I functioned somewhat as an "objective" respondent for expanding the vantage of the church in its effort to find a basis for balance during its time of transition. Increasingly, however, I find myself drawn with fascination into the uniqueness of this tradition, until during the past decade I have functioned more from within that tradition, calling the church to rediscover its heritage in a new way. The original suspicion by some—that an outsider would be tempted to undercut the uniqueness of the church—has reversed, so that now some express an uneasiness lest my appreciation will provide fuel for increased conservative criticism of church leadership. Whatever my past or future relationship, it appears that I have come to value the RLDS tradition more than some who regard that church as home.[1]

The dilemma facing this church for the last two decades is classic. The necessary framework is well provided by Ernest Troeltsch, with the illustrative dynamic sketched by H. Richard Niebuhr.[2] It is the socio/psychological evolution of a movement of "sect" origin toward the status of "church" through cultural adaptation. This inevitable dynamic begins with a small group of enthusiastic converts, grasped by a unique

vision warranting disciplined faithfulness, called to be intentionally in but not of the world, different in being called to a special mission. But what happens with the second and third generations, especially with offspring in whom the zeal has cooled, and uniqueness is less a calling and more the penalty for being strange? Further, the frugality and hard work of those who originally responded with enthusiasm to the "demanding work of the Lord" has led in the next generation or two to the unintended rewards of comfortable middle-class existence. With such respectability comes a new sense of belonging to the wider society, justified in turn by an adaptation which entails a mellowing of uniqueness. Without particularly intending it, the movement becomes institutionalized, taking on a resemblance to what Niebuhr calls the "church of the middle."[3]

Two reactions are inevitable in time. On the one hand is the reaction of "conservatives," those who sense this process eroding the very uniqueness which attracted them to the Restoration movement in the first place—provoking a fierce fight for preservation. On the other hand is the response of "liberals," those feeling the need to render intentional this demythologizing of tradition, increasingly embarrassed by what purports to be the miraculous features of its origin.

As this alienation grows, conservatives feel backed defensively into a corner where the only option seems to be an increasingly inflexible insistence upon a literalistic reading of the tradition. In turn, the more vocal this insistence upon "fundamentals," the more determined the liberal process of de-

* Scripture references from New Revised Standard Version

mythologizing—insisting that spectacles, gold plates, the Book of Mormon, and even Zion must undergo a process of minimization. Centrally at stake is the place and character of Joseph Smith, Jr., forcing the inordinate poles of idolatry versus charlatanry.

Such dynamics resemble the liberal demythologizing operative in Protestantism for at least fifty years.[4] In fact, even the nineteenth century exhibits efforts to declare untenable the virgin birth, bodily resurrection, infallible scripture, angels, miracles—any part of Christian tradition that depends on breaking natural law.[5] The basic questions that result, whether in Protestantism in general or the RLDS movement in particular, are twofold. (1) What is left that can be claimed as uniquely Christian? (2) Is profession of uniqueness really a value or is it an arrogance that alienates the church from other denominations in particular and other religions in general?

The present dilemma of the RLDS Church is a more narrow expression of this dynamic. Stated as a question, will the movement discover in a new way an acceptable uniqueness or will it continue to mellow into the ethos of general Protestantism as still another denomination? The precedents for doing the latter are legion. Few present-day United Methodists, for example, are any longer Wesleyans, and even fewer Presbyterians are Calvinists. In both cases there is an excluded "fundamentalist" minority calling vigorously for "restoration" of the tradition. My own uneasiness about the Saints continuing in this direction is that we have no need of another mainline Protestant denomination.

Yet recent official documents seem to reflect, along with present-day Protestantism, an emphasis on growth and expansion, as contrasted with the faithfulness and commitment which characterized its origin. A gentle liberalism has provided the World Church leadership with the necessary catharsis to transcend a narrow parochialism. That is no longer at issue. The issue is the degree to which this leadership has been so scarred by the fundamentalistic skirmishes that they cannot resee their tradition with creative eyes—reloving its uniqueness into a new vision. Symbolization is an inadequate name for the process needed. The word points to the difference between dissecting the book of Revelation by a soothsaying mathematician and reading it as a poet, with parts 2 and 3 of Handel's *Messiah* as ambiance.

A place to begin is with the question of "restoration." Most scholarly writings here have been of a reconstructionist orientation—intent on discovering what Joseph Smith, Jr., "really" meant or "actually" did. An analogy from literature suggests an alternative. The "new critics" insist that the task of literary criticism is not to research the life and circumstances of Melville's life in order to determine what Melville "really" meant by and in *Moby Dick*. If Melville "knew," he should have written an essay, not a novel. *Moby Dick* was written to enter the public domain, where the task of the reader is an immersion in the text itself, thereby helping Melville, as it were, to discern its meaning. Over a century ago, Schleiermacher pointed to a similar theological method—insisting that theological texts grow in meaning, enriching whatever intent the original writer might have had. Its intent is an invitation. Thus both texts and traditions take on lives of their own. Freed of the originator's unavailable intent, the genius of a particular tradition is its evocativeness, its open availability for creative discernment of its enfleshed meaning at this point in its history. In this sense, then, attention belongs less on objectifying Joseph Smith, Jr., as on an imaginative appropriation of the Joseph Smith, Jr., saga.

Thus "restoration" can mean a once-delivered content that constitutes the essence of the one true church, called as judge upon the infidelity and unacceptability of other traditions. But it can mean, instead, the call to serve as leaven to the multitraditions of the Church of Jesus Christ, functioning as a faithful plumbline of renewal. Put another way, the restoration task may not mean for the RLDS movement to become still another splintered expression of Christianity claiming, as did every denomination at its inception, to be the one church. This dilemma is precisely that which kept plaguing Israel—whether to understand God's call to be a chosen people as entailing privileged superiority or involving the task of being a suffering servant in behalf of all.

The RLDS Church may need to undergo the same catharsis, renewed to see its mission not as superiority but as special calling in behalf of the whole of Christ's divided church. This task would be one of enabling restoration, the unlikely success of which would remove the movement's need to be. What an incredible model—a church born to die, losing its reason for being by following the One who "came not to be served but to serve" (Matthew 20:28).

But what would it be like to reconsider the fascinating tradition of the RLDS movement, discerning with metaphorical eyes its prophetic mission? This is to ask for the ingredients of a post-demythologizing vision that can reclaim the movement with an excitement sufficient for rebirth. There is reason to believe that if the leadership can get its theological heart together, resolution of many of the present problems will follow.

1. Zion as Multifaceted

I still remember my shock when in opening a book on Nauvoo I found on the inside cover a street map of Zion. While my tradition sometimes speaks of heaven with streets of gold, never had it enfleshed the Christian vision—complete with sewers and streetlights. Here was witness to Christianity's forfeiture of an indispensable dimension of the gospel, pointed to in the key passage from the Lord's Prayer: "Your kingdom come. Your will be done, *on earth* [emphasis mine] as it is in heaven" (Matthew 6:10). That prayer has to do with daily bread and debts. William Temple once called Christianity the most this-worldly religion in history.[6] Against the adaptive and supportive capitulation of most denominations to the present-day socioeconomic status quo, Zion is the insistence that the kingdom of God is countercultural without being other-worldly. No message needs more to be heard in our time.

Zion as kingdom. The fear by some leaders that talk of Zion will encourage those who understand it as meaning one central "gathering place" (namely Independence) dare not permit the church to eliminate Zion as *any* gathering place. Here the "theologians of hope" can give guidance in their insistence upon a linear eschatology. The Christ event is foretaste of the promised end time of history—in history. This vision provides a prophetic fulcrum by which the church can bring judgment on societies for their destructiveness to human life. History has purpose because it is linear—moving toward a goal, calling forth a people committed to this cosmic restoration, undergirded by the divine promise, and disciplined for this mission by both personal and social sanctification. Jesus came precisely to proclaim Zion, in the light of which all are called to repentance (Mark 1:15). In this sense we can understand Joseph Smith, Jr.'s insistence on his people being a separate nation, for radical monotheism requires that there be no rival allegiance. They were a people

111

destined to march to another drummer, in behalf of all. It is little wonder that their opposition to idolatry was interpreted as treason.

Zion as model communities. Yet these very theologians of hope can sometimes be more irritating than useful. What is more tiresome than a person who sits in the back of a meeting, and no matter what idea is proposed, finds fault with it as not good enough—yet having nothing concrete to propose? The church needs recalling to the task of gardening God's creation, but not with some vague ideal that can only function as a disheartening "impossible possibility." The church must create "Zionic communities" as signal experiments in concrete Christian transformation, as the early church felt called to do (e.g., Acts 2:44–47). Such experimentation is on the pioneer edge, on behalf of the world. Against today's rampant individualism, the Saints have understood the biblical concept of a covenant people: pilgrims who are social to the core.[7] Monasticism through the centuries has felt something of this call, but with a tendency toward other-worldliness rather than Zionic witness.

Zionic principles and process. Zion is the goal in which prophetic hope is rooted. It is the leaven emerging as experimental signal communities. But we must speak also of "Zionic principles." Jesus not only pronounced the coming kingdom but gave it fleshly substance through focus—as good news to the poor, release to the captives, liberty to the oppressed. Indeed, the Zionic ideal is the equalization year of Jubilee for all (Luke 5:18–19). Further, he sketched out the principles of this vision in terms of the Beatitudes (Matthew 5:1–11). He did this so clearly that they involved as "woes" their implications for leaders of the status quo (Luke 6:7ff).

These Zionic principles are to function as "salt of the earth," as the "light of the world," as "leaven" to every sector (Matthew 5:13–14, et passim). Such a perspective has two features. On the one hand, Zion has to do with "who" and thus "where." It rests on the awareness that to "inherit the kingdom" means to ask now the question: "Lord, when was it that we saw you hungry and gave you food, or thirsty and gave you something to drink? And when was it that we saw you a stranger and welcomed you, or naked and gave you clothing?" (Matthew 25:37–46). The church is not called to duplicate social institutions but to be where there are none that care.

On the other hand, Zion has to do with the "how." In this age of specialization, individualism, and mechanization, Zion is the insistence upon a holistic approach to every sector—health care, welfare, counseling, architecture, education, legislation, administration, family, sexuality, *ad infinitum*. Zion is a holistic, incarnational method for transforming every segment of social and personal life. For example, it means "doing medicine" by teams, as at the Sanitarium (now known as Independence Regional Health Center), approaching humanness as a preventative and healing whole, spiritually, physically, economically, socially, medically. Every dimension of the human being is a cry to be Zionic. Wherever the movement found itself—Kirtland, Nauvoo, Far West—came the Zionic call: to drain the swamp, to house the people. The present worldwide indigenization of the movement is a centrifugal expression of Zion, a Zion holistically centripetal wherever it touches down. In this time of rampant self-gratification, there is much need for this witness to disciplined faithfulness.

Joseph's interest in alternative politics, his building of a place where kings and queens from around the world could come and learn by seeing the universal implications of Zion as a sanctuary of sanity—in many such ways, the movement witnessed to an open and experimental vision, to be lived as model in behalf of all. So understand, we have a fine expression of the posture H. R. Niebuhr called "Christ transforming culture."[8]

The aesthetic Zion. I have often wondered how to understand the love of music by the offspring of Joseph Smith, Jr.—unmatched in choral and organ expressions as manifestations of glory and praise. Conscious or otherwise, I am coming to sense these as witness to the meaning of Zion as celebrating life under promise.

The personal Zion. I would like to believe that there can be such a reality as a Zionic personality, based on an androgynous wholeness. This image is one the church has only begun to suspect.

2. Functional Theology and Lay Ministry

At this point in the history of many denominations, there is a reaction against elaborate and costly structures of salaried pastors and staff. Instead, there is talk in this "post-Christian" era of a need for the church to return to the biblical image of tent-ministry—self-supporting clergy with minimal institutional overhead. No church has had more experience with such an approach to ministry than the RLDS movement.

Not only does this approach minimize financial expenditure for operating expenses, but it helps to erase the chasm between laity and clergy, rendering congregations more communitarian. Further, it opens the way to conceive (as did Luther) all vocations as ministry, each person called to serve in a special full-time calling, whether doctor or housewife. Here, in witnessing to varied kinds of ordination and calling a number of ministers in each congregation, is an expansion of the idea of priesthood—toward

the largely untried Reformation ideal of the "priesthood of all believers."

This phenomenon relates to the movement's resistance to become an institution—for the tradition centers more on action than doctrine. Faith has been a total orientation of one's being, not a departmentalized dimension of normal living. This approach rests on a deep sense of grace, although this has not always been recognized. The "Saints" are those called, chosen, set aside—not because they are better but because God has taken the initiative in calling them to a special task requiring authentic faithfulness. The call is not to receive but to cross the Red Sea with hot pursuit, to endure the desert and often fail, to enter Zion only to be exiled. Obedience is not in order to receive, but a thankful response to being needed by God.

3. A Marginal People

Related is the fact that the Restoration has been composed of a people exiled—persecuted, hunted down, feared, exploited, mistreated, violently abused—whose leader was finally martyred. If ever there is a people whose movement stands within the biblical tradition of the remnant, it is the RLDS Church. Thus no church should understand better, from within, the meaning of liberation theology[9]—God's preferential love of the marginalized and oppressed—expanding prophetically Joseph's insistence on "concern for the poor in your midst."

4. Sacramentalization

There is no more sacramental movement than the RLDS Church. Even Roman Catholicism's seven sacraments have been done one better. At each hinge point of human existence is a sacrament of divine-human intersection as blessing. Strangely, however, RLDS worship today has almost nothing to distinguish it from the word-saturated worship of most Protestantism, which has only two sacraments. Avoiding the temptation to use sacrament as magic, the movement is ripe today to see the implications of its tradition for affirming the sacramental nature of all of life. This means acting out Christianity's unique incarnationism.

Tillich wisely observed that evidence of the fall rests in the fact that there is a distinction between baptism and one's daily shower, Holy Communion and the family's evening supper, the altar and one's desk for work. Sacraments so focus the senses of the believer that they may be opened to perceiving every material thing as a vessel of transparency, and every act a gesture of ultimate meaning. This goal—of a culture in which everything is symbolic for the Ground of Being—he called "theonomy."[10] This is another name for Zion.

5. Storehouse and Stewardship

In this day of frightening individualism, the Saints make common cause with what has lately been called the need for "communitarian democracy." The movement's past encourages economic sharing rather than the competitive exploitation of narrow self-interest.[11] There is witness to the stewardship of resources, a mutual responsibility for each other, and encouragement of a lifestyle consistent with a world in need. This is not a eulogizing of poverty but a commitment to be good stewards in behalf of all.

This special approach to income—whether with stewardship forms, discouragement of biological inheritance, or oblation—is lived out in the radical practice of church leaders who are paid not according to title, ability, prestige, or promotion, but on the basis of need. Such socialist tendencies are on the edge of testing the Christian meaning of "to each according to one's ability, from each according to one's needs." Contrasted with the approach to money in secular society, the RLDS Church is an illustration of Jesus' parable in which the first may be the last, the last first, with the laborer hired at 4 p.m. receiving comparable wages to the one who worked from early morning (Matthew 20:1–26).

6. Ongoing Revelation

It has always seemed strange to me that a religion that sees the work of God moving toward a crescendo in Pentecost—with the descent of the Holy Spirit into our midst—closed the canon of revelation, and did it so quickly. No matter what situation you will be in, said Jesus, "the Holy Spirit will teach you at that very hour what you ought to say." Even more, "the Advocate, the Holy Spirit, whom the Father will send in my name, will teach you everything" (John 14:26). The RLDS movement is special in bearing witness to this reality. Revelation does not stop, God does not "leave you orphaned"—but continues to lead, both with the large brush strokes of vision and the small brush intended for portrait painting. This process need not be autocratic but can be the discernment of a prophet who so lives with the people that the declarations are spoken in their collective behalf, offered as gift to those empowered to discern the wisdom of the discernments. Richard Foster correctly insisted that the church is not an institution of majority rule. It is a theocracy, for it is to be Spirit-led. Its primary sin is "opposing the Holy Spirit" (Acts 7:51). Indicatively, then, at the crucial Jerusalem Conference no vote was taken. The decision is recorded this way: "it has seemed good to the Holy Spirit and to us..." (Acts 15:28).

In a real sense, the RLDS movement was a rediscovery of the Holy Spirit. While at times this led to physical-like visions and graphic ecstasies, at its best it was rooted in an ecclesiology. In contrast to most present churches as static institutions living according to spiritual truths, the movement was rooted in a firm trust in providence—rendering life a process and history a becoming.

7. Native American Magnetism

There is a special relation between the RLDS movement and native Americans. While this has sometimes led to confusion of mission and ambiguity of attitude, there is something in this intriguing passion and compassion that is worth exploring. Christendom is in need of learning from native Americans a holism of lifestyle, a sacramental spirituality, an ecology for the earth, a sensitivity to the rhythm of living and dying, a respect for the wisdom of the elderly, and the profound oneness of spirit and body. That is, it needs help in exploring Zion.

A Conclusion

In no way do I intend this article to be a eulogizing of the RLDS Church, as if blind to the tensions and hypocrisies that plague it, and all of us functioning within the human condition. I confess the advantage of creative distance, in which, by being able to enter and leave, come and go, I may have more freedom for unhampered dreaming with a purified tradition. I do not have to live daily with the reality. Yet this vantage is the only gift I have for the church that I have come to love. May it be a luring toward a vision that may be difficult to see, when the pressures all around tempt a movement to seek the safety of becoming a denomination.

Notes

1. There was a secret taping and transcribing of a talk I gave in 1980 at the invitation of staff members on an official RLDS document. My remarks have been widely circulated among conservative members of the RLDS Church, totally without my permission. Interesting, however, has been their positive response. There is apparent openness by both poles of the present controversy to some of the ideas developed in this paper.
2. Ernest Troeltsch, *The Social Teaching of the Christian Churches* (New York: Harper Brothers, 1966); H. Richard Niebuhr, *The Social Sources of Denominationalism* (Hamden, Connecticut: Shoe String Press, 1954).
3. H. Richard Niebuhr; *Christ and Culture* (New York: Harper and Brothers, 1951), chapter 1.
4. See Rudolf Bultmann, *New Testament and Mythology* (Philadelphia: Fortress, 1984).
5. For example, see Adolph von Harnack, *What Is Christianity?* (Philadelphia: Fortresss Press, 1986) and the work of Albrecht Ritschl.
6. William Temple, *Nature, Man and God* (London: MacMlllan and Co., 1934).
7. See H. Richard Niebuhr, *The Kingdom of God in America* (Chicago: Willett, Clark, and Co., 1937).
8. Niebuhr, *Christ and Culture*, final two chapters.
9. See Gustavo Gutiérrez, *A Theology of Liberation* (Maryknoll, New York: Orbis Books, 1973).
10. Paul Tillich, *The Protestant Era* (Chicago: University of Chicago Press, 1948), 206ff.
11. Book of Doctrine and Covenants, Section 42 (Independence, Missouri: Herald House, 1958).

Zionic Justice: Increasingly Aesthetic?
Henry K. Inouye, Jr.

Introduction

On April 24, 1832, Joseph Smith, Jr., and his party arrived in Independence, Missouri, from Hiram, Ohio. The journey had taken twenty-four days. On the twenty-sixth, he convened a general council of the church in which inspired instruction was given concerning the poor and the enlargement of Zion.

Within these instructions, beauty and justice were brought together in a distinctive way.

...Zion must increase in beauty, and in holiness...Zion must arise and put on her beautiful garments;...you are to be equal...to have equal claims on the properties...every man according to his wants and his needs, inasmuch as his wants are just.[1]

Beauty, beautiful, equality, equal claims, and just wants signify in their juxtaposition the aesthetic justice that this essay addresses. Beauty and justice were, of course, only an ideal at this point in the history of the church and in ensuing years a beautiful Zion and a distributive justice proved difficult to normalize.

As early as 1834, Joseph Smith, Jr., seemed to be against retribution in the form of just war, yet he sanctified holy war as "the vengeance of the Lord." God would fight along with the Saints if need be.[2]

By 1838, church leaders were becoming increasingly belligerent in response to the rising conflict between the Saints and gentiles. Joseph vowed to be "a second Mohammed" in leading the Saints into war against the enemy.[3] Thus retributive and distributive justice emerged early in the church.

The worldwide history of beauty and justice began before written accounts. Space does not permit a summary here. Suffice it to say that ideas of beauty and justice had existed for thousands of years before Protestant and RLDS concepts emerged. Concepts of justice and beauty shaped largely by modern scientific, economic, social, and religious ideas have only recently been influenced by postmodern science and spirituality.

This essay describes a postmodern justice. It is responsible and inclusive and emerges from an aesthetic matrix.

Justice must be more than retribution, i.e., in the eyes of the beholder. When justice is retributive, a victim mentality emerges that can be very destructive, as we all know. Though a victim should have remedies for an injustice, this should be in legislation, legal enforcement, and the courts rather than in personal retaliation by the victim. It seems that some of us feel justified in pursuing retribution first, rather than finding remedies in the legal system (which admittedly can be frustrating).

The ordering and distribution of benefits and burdens among the members of the RLDS Church has tended to be tentative rather than consistently normative. Distributive justice according to need has been problematic since the church's inception. An impartial and even-handed consideration of competing claims has been hampered by fluctuating economic conditions and the constant hegira of the church from one part of the country to the other.

Much of what has been said here preliminarily about retributive and distributive justice can be said about beauty. Beauty has

116

been an erstwhile and sometime companion of the RLDS Church and often considered a nonessential part of basic beliefs. Beauty has been for the most part derivative and secondary in importance in the church and it has been mainly in the eye of the beholder. This is understandable when modernity conceived beauty as a transient quality to be purchased rather than metaphysically foundational. My claim is that beauty, like justice, should be located first in the subject (the original source of beauty) and only secondarily in the eye of the beholder. Why this is so will be more fully clarified in the explanation below.

Besides positing beauty and justice as primary and responsible activities, this essay explores the possibility for an originative aesthetic justice and its power for motivating responsible just activity. Further, aesthetic justice is presented here as being imaginatively and creatively foundational for individual and group freedoms.

An aesthetic justice is responsible, originative, motivating and foundational; its greatest value is as a source of relational power that integrates the various typologies of justice. Thus no valid model for justice is deliberately ignored. My belief is that any one absolutized theory of justice is limited and a derived justice, and actual only in a secondary sense, i.e., in the eye of the beholder.

My thesis is that postmodern RLDS justice could be distinctive in the coming century only if the church develops and practices an inclusive and responsible theory of justice based on beauty as the metaphysical foundation of reality. Beauty, truth, and goodness would work together in an aesthetic justice.

In theory and practice, an aesthetic justice includes a concern for human needs such as health care, housing, food, and clothing.

This justice seeks freedom for the oppressed and mercy for the accused and imprisoned.

An aesthetic justice is concerned for the entire creation and works toward ecological justice and respect for all forms of life.

What is an aesthetic justice? It is based on feelings for inclusiveness and rightness. Because it is an inclusive justice cooperative with other types of justice, Zion would likewise be inclusive and cooperative. Yet Zion would not relinquish its distinctiveness or lapse into widespread relativity.

Why an aesthetic justice? In part because there needs to be an exploration of more effective models of justice in theory and practice. The beginning for this endeavor is the imaginative, creative, and aesthetic transformation of the concept of justice. This is important because the practice of justice in the past has been exclusive and inadequate. Justice has been informed in quite different ways from an aesthetic justice; old solutions are not stemming the slide to the destruction of humankind and all other creatures.

An aesthetic justice is important because it is a broader justice allowing "feelings" as well as reasoning in theory and action. Furthermore, justice is given a more universal character because of the commonality of the aesthetic drive. The aesthetic drive is universal, and harmony of contrasting views is encouraged in a justice based on beauty.

In addition, a broader base for justice is needed because justice must no longer be for humans alone but must include all creatures and forms of life. Humans must recognize an obligation and responsibility to every creature as ends in themselves and not merely a means to human ends. We must uphold the intrinsic value of every creature, while not overlooking the instrumental values of creatures for each other. To do this requires a holistic aesthetic perspective involving the ability to appreciate differences and contrasts. "Just living is an art, and more than a science—therefore, aesthetic."

An aesthetic justice is responsible for originative creative solutions. It is imaginative—not simply retributive. A retributive justice is derivative and largely irresponsible. Creative justice corrects injustices in holistic, healthy ways, e.g., by discussion and persuasion rather than divisiveness or fighting. It is also creative in solving economic, ecological, and nuclear problems in ways that keep the total picture in mind. It is originative in righting racism by affirmative action and fair legislation.

How is aesthetic justice possible? This essay proposes three ways: by prehension, by the aesthetic drive, and by beauty.

Prehension

Aesthetic justice is possible first because of inward feelings and perceptions of rightness and oughtness, called by Alfred North Whitehead "prehensions."[4]

Two hundred years before Whitehead, Jonathan Edwards connected beauty with morality and equated aesthetic feeling with an ability to sense the rightness of things. He wrote, "When a holy and amiable action is suggested to the thoughts of a holy soul; that soul, if in the lively exercise of its spiritual taste, at once sees a beauty in it, and so inclines to it, and closes with it."[5] His concern for feeling (affection) indicates a deep affinity for beauty.

In 1829 Joseph Smith, Jr., entreated Hyrum Smith to trust in the Spirit which leads "...to do good; yea, to do justly, to walk humbly," and to "...judge righteously."[6] This was an appeal to Hyrum's innate feelings for "rightness" or "oughtness." That Hyrum must have felt deeply this obligation and responsibility is not in doubt as he was to trust in the Spirit right up to the moment that he and Joseph were murdered by the mob at Carthage.

Joseph Smith III was aware of a sixth sense of "apperception." In an 1888 sermon at Independence he claimed this sense of rapport allowed for experiencing of angels and the spiritual world.[7]

Recently, David Griffin wrote:

Most empiricism, equating perception with *sense* perception, has concluded that there can be no direct experience of God. However Whitehead portrays sense perception as derivative of a more basic kind of relatedness, called "prehension," in which one directly grasps previous events, which themselves have prehended previous ones. This non-sensory preconscious prehension is at the root of our response to reality and is a kind of response which we share with all other events—from animals, cells, and atoms below to God above.[8]

In Whiteheadian theory, "right" and "ought" are obligatory responses. John Cobb wrote,

If I feel that I ought to do something, that means that my sense of obligation attaches to my idea of myself as performing that act....The prehension of this kind of proposition is an "imaginative feeling."[9]

The imaginative feeling of a proposition for "oughtness" and "rightness" is basic to aesthetic justice. These prehensive activities might be better understood by RLDS members as a kind of "discernment." Aesthetic prehension responds to and synthesizes moral principles, situational factors, consequences, and general insights from all religious traditions and cultures in an effort to illuminate and discern just behavior.

Experiencing the past and God's just aims for us in each novel occasion of life are possible because of this basic kind of responsiveness called "prehension." This is a metaphysical response and is foundational to all experience.

The importance of prehension to justice is the implication that one can "feel" rightness and "oughtness." This aesthetic feeling, together with the consideration of all relevant factors, addresses the justice this essay describes.

Edwards' "new inward perception,"

Joseph Smith, Jr.'s awareness of rightness and justice, and Joseph Smith III's sixth sense of "apperception" are all "feelings" similar to what Whitehead and Cobb refer to as "prehension" and what I have proposed as the first way an aesthetic justice is possible.

Creativity

The second way aesthetic justice is possible is because of what Whitehead calls creativity. The aesthetic drive is one type of creative activity. It is the striving for completion and satisfaction. This is similar to Aristotle's "entelechy." The creative or aesthetic drive refers to the conditioning of possibilities so that abstract ideals become actual. It also refers to prehending past actualities so that reality becomes theoretically abstract. In aesthetic activity, both actualities and abstractions are relevant factors. Both theory and practice are important in aesthetic justice. The theory and practice of justice are always a struggle, and we usually fall short of the ideal.

The aesthetic drive, besides being volitional, is also the feeling for "rightness." In our daily activities we all know this feeling. It is that certain struggle to get things "just right." Artists know the feeling well. So do cooks. It is when we strive to "do justice" to a thing or activity.

Our feelings for rightness are always referenced in a mixed mode of symbolism. Most human experience is causally preconscious. This means that most of the time we are dimly aware (if at all) of the formative factors of our past. This is called "causal efficacy" by Whitehead. What we are immediately aware of consciously is referred to as "presentationally immediate." Causal efficacy deals with what is real, while what is referred to immediately are abstractions of reality. Causality is originative and real, whereas presentational immediacy is derivative and abstract. An aesthetic justice is aware of both symbolic modes. It strives not to be abstract where actuality is crucial, yet sees the necessity for abstract theory, e.g., the study of justice. This means that what we *feel* to be right or just emerges from a dim reality (or past) and should always be held tentatively. Whereas what *appears* to be right and just may be simply an abstraction of justice or a mere theory. The guiding principle is a prehension or discernment that does not mistake abstract justice for actual justice and a justice that actually serves all creatures.

Everything in our past (our training, the tools and materials we use, our recipes) are all "propelling causes." What we add to our inherited past are "finite causes" which are our own unique responses and creative contributions to whatever we are doing or becoming. Aesthetic feelings are also responsive to divine cause. John Cobb calls this "God's call forward."[10] Whitehead termed it "God's initial aim."[11] While God's call or aim for us is persuasive influences or "lures," we are subjectively free to pursue our own creativity or finalize our own cause.

The importance of this aesthetic drive for completion is in the universality of our common "striving." All creatures, including humans, strive for completion or satisfaction. This universal drive unites all of life in a common activity, and human awareness of this activity ought to help us realize our connectedness to the rest of nature. This should give us a more inclusive sense of justice. Interdependence and acting for the other's good is at the same time acting for one's own good. The diminishing of one is the diminishing of all.

The theories and practice of justice in the past have failed because people have not seen the interrelationship of power and justice. Power has been generally thought of as coercive; consequently, justice has been largely retributive and destructive. If justice is to be constructive and positive, power will have to be understood as reciprocal and relational. The problem has been twofold. First, justice is usually in the eye of the beholder, and second, people usually employ coercive force in achieving what they wrongly perceive to be justice. Therefore, there is an urgent need to redefine power as well as justice. Rather than coercion, power should be redefined as the ability to be *affected*, to be *creative*, and to be *influential*. This is a relational power, receptive and persuasive rather than coercive. The power of an artist, and others, emerges in relationality. Relational power is the power to be "affected" by nature and other humans, and the power to "affect" (i.e., to create, to influence others). This is a reciprocal power rather than a unilateral one-way power exhibition. The power of Zion should likewise be found in reciprocal, rather than unilateral, relations. A basic definition of aesthetic justice might then be expressed as:

Aesthetic justice is the striving for beauty in all human and creaturely relationships in imaginative and creative ways such that responses to the past and contributions to the future enrich the lives of one and all.

Relational power, as described above, is crucial because aesthetic justice is also receptive, active, and persuasive. Aesthetic justice attempts to be:

1. receptive and aware of all relevant factors and types of justice prior to making judgments; responsible, informed, and inclusive, avoiding retribution, unequal distribution, and disproportionate emphasis;

2. creatively active in collecting and analyzing all relevant factors as the informed basis for just actions; inner-directed, authentic, and free; and

3. persuasive, contributory, compassionate, mixing love and concern with just practices—avoiding unilateral power and force.

Prehension, creativity, aesthetic drives,

rightness, completion, satisfaction, causes, God's call or aim for us, and relational power make aesthetic justice possible by definition and in practice.

Beauty

The third way aesthetic justice is possible is because of the value of beauty. Beauty has been defined as the mutual adaptation of the several factors of experience.[12] For example, in an RLDS wedding it has been tradition for both parties to "mutually agree" to various factors important to companionship and legal rights. Mutual adaptation is encouraged throughout the marriage and when there is absence of inhibitions between husband and wife so that intensities of feelings do not inhibit each other, there is the minor form of beauty—the absence of painful clash and vulgarity. The major form of beauty is defined as the harmony emerging from the introduction of new contrasts, new intensities natural to each partner, which in turn increases the empathetic feelings of each. Thus each experience contributes to the whole, and the whole contributes to each experience. Therefore, the perfection of beauty is the perfection of harmony.[13]

Furthermore, aesthetic justice is possible because beauty is the metaphysical foundation of reality. Hartshorne believes that "...the basic idea of beauty as integrated diversity and intensity of experience is metaphysical, valid for any possible state of reality."[14]

Paul Edwards, in *Preface to Faith*, says "the metaphysical foundations of the RLDS church are often confusing, unrelated, and sometimes exclusive."[15]

While this essay addresses justice in particular, it also proposes a general metaphysical foundation (the aesthetic) that is coherent instead of confusing, related rather than unrelated, and inclusive rather than exclusive. Hopefully an aesthetic foundation is applicable and adequate.

A way to understand beauty as foundational to a metaphysical system is to imagine the world as a puzzle. In a puzzle, the individual pieces influence the player. Further, *all* the pieces together influence the player. But the player is not totally directed by the pieces. The player feels a piece is missing. The player supplies the missing piece of the puzzle.[16] Now that the puzzle is satisfactorily completed, and if the player is quite conservative, the finished puzzle might be framed. Of course the problem with this is that a completed puzzle is not puzzling anymore. The world is boring because of its static being. On the other hand, there are those who might choose to break down the completed puzzle immediately without fully appreciating or enjoying the total completed picture.

This third way an ideal justice is possible then finds beauty to be the mutual adaptation of the several factors of experiences; that is, beauty relates all the pieces of the world similar to the pieces of a puzzle. This is the power of beauty to hold a variety of experiences in contrast.

The importance of beauty for justice is not only in the minor and major forms of beauty and the harmony they engender but in the art of assimilating contradictory positions and points of view. An artist is well aware of the montage as an effective art form. In a montage it might well be that there are many elements that contrast with each other. However, these are not separate contrasts. In an authentic work of art the multiple contrasts emerge as one single contrast. This is the emergent evolution of a work of art and "the doctrine of real unities being more than a mere collective disjunction of component elements."[17]

To answer the question, what makes an aesthetic justice possible then, this essay has considered three reasons: by prehension, by aesthetic drive, and by the value of beauty. These three have been considered in separate sections above.

The rest of this essay will consider aesthetic justice as related to racism, economics, ecology, hunger, the sick, and the homeless. Finally, some questions regarding a just Zion will be asked.

Racism and Justice

I have suggested that an aesthetic justice is located in both the eye of the beholder and in the person beheld. This is similar to beauty being in the eye of the beholder, as well as in the beheld. An inclusive aesthetic justice will, therefore, be both subjective and objective. The danger arises when either justice or beauty is exclusively perceived to be entirely subjective or entirely objective.

This paper has proposed that justice must be more fundamental than mere retribution. When justice and racism are located only in the eye of the beholder, this is a secondary justice, and a victim mentality emerges that can be very destructive. Do not get me wrong. I feel the victim has every right to expect justice. My contention is, however, that justice and the remedy for racism lie in legislation and legal enforcement (up to a point) rather than in the retaliation by the victim. *Responsibility* for racial justice should be originative and not simply in the eye of the beholder or derived. The worldwide problem is that everyone feels justified in pursuing retribution in the first place, and relegating a responsibly just attitude to second place. Until this is reversed, there will be no racial justice.

We must take responsibility for ourselves including whatever color we happen to be. What I have suggested is that we should all take another look at racism and rise above a victim mentality. Responsible behavior in a racist world will be impossible otherwise.

We are all racist in some way and victims of racism also. What is important is that we rise above both mentalities to a responsibly just position. We must realize that justice, like beauty, originates with us as individuals. I am just only in acting justly. A person is beautiful first of all in acting beautifully.

An aesthetic awareness, besides being helpful in engendering personal just behavior, should also be helpful in promoting tolerance and dialogue among proponents of various types of justice. My intuition is that any one absolutized type of justice might be a relative justice and obtained only in the eyes of the beholder. This would then be a derived justice rather than responsibly originative.

I agree with Kant that motives for justice are crucial (deontology), with the view that doing what is appropriate for the occasion is important (cathekontic), with the utilitarian view that the ends of justice are important (telelogy), *and* with an inclusive and originative view of justice (aesthetic).[18]

An inclusive and originative aesthetic justice would help persons to be more fully informed and responsible for just obligations and duties and bring God back into the process. A final just principle could then be formulated to allow all four of the above types to exist and to promote rigorous debate among their proponents. An aesthetically just imperative could then be expressed as follows:

An aesthetically just person ought to act in that way in which a person would will, on full consideration of all relevant factors, that all people should act, given just these relevant factors.

A responsible theory of justice enhanced by aesthetic feelings for rightness would greatly increase the persuasive power needed for timely just decisions and just acts. An aesthetic justice, because of its metaphysical foundation in beauty, has the power to *move* people to appreciate diversity and the power to enhance the quality and richness (*shalom*) of life.

Economic Justice

A just society, motivated and moved by aesthetic aims, would pursue economic justice as well as racial justice. An economic system that treats each person as "persons" and not as mere "things" and also encourages a more sustainable world for those persons would be normative. A good example of an aesthetically just economic theory is Herman Daley's economic approach. He calls it a "steady-state economy" and claims we currently have a "malady of growthmania." He defines the steady state as:

...an economy in which the total population and the total stock of physical wealth are maintained constant at some desired levels by a "minimal" rate of maintenance throughput (i.e., by birth and death rates that are equal at the lowest feasible level, and by physical production and consumption rates that are equal at the lowest feasible level). The first part of the definition (constant stocks) goes back to John Stuart Mill, and the second part ("minimal" flow of throughput) goes back to 1949 vintage Kenneth Boulding. Minimizing throughput implies maximizing the average life expectancy of a member of the stock.[19]

Daley goes on to explain how the steady state may be attained in areas such as population, physical wealth, and distribution. He feels the present economy is unrealistic because, in its disregard for natural laws, it is attempting the impossible. The steady-state paradigm, unlike growthmania, is realistic because it takes the physical laws of nature as its first premise. Daley cites the Old and New Testaments as supportive of a steady state.

Economic understanding *and* immediate action is required if we are to save our world from economic destruction. We already have left an enormous national debt to our grandchildren, and our natural resources are being depleted at an alarming rate because of growth demands. The challenge for us today as a nation is to somehow turn around our economic machine so as to "pay off" our national debt. An aesthetic justice could be an important factor in our economic recovery because of its motivational power for action.

Ecological Justice, World Hunger, the Sick and Homeless

"All of creation is interrelated. Every creature, every element, every force of nature participates in the whole creation. If any person is denied *shalom*, all are thereby diminished."[20] Because of this, we must all take on the responsibility for originating justice. This should be an inclusive aesthetic justice. There must be ecological as well as human justice. We must realize that everything is interconnected, fragile, and sensitive as a delicate web. A responsible society is inclusive and participatory. Individuals must be allowed their places in the world. Emerging life forms must be allowed to evolve with a minimum of human intervention. There must be a participatory attitude in our partnership with God and with each other in creative activity. We must be responsible aesthetically (holistically) for a sustainable and regenerative stewardship over all resources: forestry, mining, agriculture, fishing, etc.

Jorgan Randers and E.F. Schumacher argued in 1971 and 1972 that the world could not maintain its present growth in production and consumption.[21] Later, Cobb and Birch collaborated on *The Liberation of Life* in which they brought together, for the first time in one book, the insights of modern biology with the wisdom of holistic philosophy and liberal theology in a way that challenges outmoded approaches to science, agriculture, sociology, politics, economics, and liberation movements.[22] These prophetic voices must be heard and taken seriously. It is urgent today because humans are destroying one entire species of life each day and are bent on destroying humankind.

The deteriorating relationship between expanding populations and natural systems is a worldwide problem contributing to world hunger. Human beings have caused changes in atmospheric chemistry, air pollution, acid rain, ozone depletion, and the buildup of greenhouse gases. In the last decade, the earth's temperature has begun an upward climb—this is affecting agriculture. The sea level is rising with catastrophic results for sea level areas. Those who do not see the relationship between our dwindling rain forests and the destruction of the world's diverse plant and animal life would seem to be unfeeling, greedy, or simply ignorant of the interconnected and cooperative web of life. Ignorance is threatening the world's food chain and destroying the beauty of our world.

Here at home, cooperative steps must be taken to relieve the burdens of the hungry, sick, and homeless. Legislators must be urged to take immediate action in several areas: strengthening the food stamp program as well as school and other meal programs. Health care and income-support programs are urgent. Congress also must be asked to pass legislation to create a permanent and independent body to monitor the nutritional status of the population.

Those who bemoan aid to the needy would hardly miss an aircraft carrier or two, the cost of which would go a long way to remedy hunger and homelessness in America.

A responsible justice would place those in the forefront who are working imaginatively and creatively for legislative and social action to end hunger. Health care should be for those who need it, not just for those who can pay.

There must be a conscious choosing of a responsible aesthetic justice and for *shalom* (harmony). Zionic planning now for justice could *originate* responsibility for aesthetically satisfactory solutions to humanity's problems in the coming century.

Some Questions on Zion and Justice

1. Could an aesthetic justice unite the various factions of the church? Could we emphasize beauty and harmony as well as truth and goodness?

2. In lieu of "growthmania" in the RLDS Church, could a "steady-state" or steady membership policy be considered? Is quality and intensity of membership as important as quantity and massiveness?

3. Instead of developing church properties for the highest and best economic use, could church lands surrounding the Independence area be conserved for parks, trees, and the beautification of Zion?

4. Should the church become more active in social service? Could various mixes of private and public facilities be stepped up to serve the needy?

5. Could "enclaves" of Zion be instigated such as: schools that teach, hospitals that serve the sick rather than those who can pay; rest homes for the aged based on need, not financial ability; inclusive health plans that really work for all members; etc.?

6. Could Zion be inclusive (sharing rather than acquisitive), be tolerant of diversity, see differences as assets, welcome contrasts between liberals and conservatives, encourage discussions, encourage feeling as well as thinking, encourage imagination and breadth of vision, encourage change amid permanence—can Zion put on her beautiful garments?

Conclusion

More and more thoughtful people are realizing that the search for justice is destroying the world (as well as many marriages). It seems that justice is mostly retributive and mainly in the eyes of the beholders. Responsible objective standards of justice seem lacking. Consequently only retribution and force remain to mediate differing claims.

All of us in today's world must promote justice in a responsible way. We must all, beginning with me as an "I," somehow originate a sensitive, intelligent feeling for justice in the world and in the family. We must develop frugal lifestyles and ethically responsible economic policies. The justice I have written about is an originative justice.

What an originative position is regarding responsibility, aesthetics, and justice has been, in part, the topic of this essay. However, a theoretical stance and perspective are not sufficient to save our world from ecological and economic destruction. Understanding *and* immediate action are required.

Because we have left an enormous national debt to our grandchildren, and our natural resources are being depleted at an alarming rate, the challenge for us Americans today, as a nation, is to turn around somehow our economic machine so as to "pay off" our national debt. We must also conserve our resources and heed Herman Daley's "steady-state" ideas. His theme that growth for growth's sake is destructive and unsustainable, plus his alternatives to "growthmania," should be taken seriously.

Jesus' exclamation from the cross at his crucifixion, "Father, forgive them; for they know not what they do" (Luke 23:35 IV) is in my estimation, the clearest expression of a responsible and just human being. (Of course, the Crucifixion is much more than an illustration of responsibility and justice). In his plea to God to forgive his accusers, Jesus gives us a beautiful pattern of personal responsibility for living in today's broken world.

The "call forward" and the "initial aim" that I wrote of above are divine activities requiring responses of love and forgiveness rather than retribution. The divine "lure" is not simply a hypothetical "ifness" in the sense that "if" a person loves and forgives, happiness will follow. A response to divine persuasion carries with it an obligation that the individual be just by forgiving and loving. "Do unto others as you would have them do unto you" is a just imperative of continuing beauty.

Notes

1. Book of Doctrine and Covenants, Section 81:4c, e (Independence, Missouri: Herald House, 1978).
2. Graham St. John Stott, "Just War, Holy War, and Joseph Smith, Jr." in *Restoration Studies IV* (Independence, Missouri: Herald House, 1988), 137.
3. Ibid., 134.
4. For a good nontechnical explanation of Whitehead's "prehension" and "feeling," see John Cobb's *A Christian Natural Theology* (Philadelphia: The Westminister Press, 1965). For a more technical definition, see Alfred North Whitehead's *Process and Reality* (New York: The Free Press, 1978).
5. Jonathan Edwards, *Religious Affections* (1746), ed. John E. Smith (New Haven, Connecticut: Yale University Press, 1969), 281.
6. Book of Doctrine and Covenants, Section 10:6.
7. Joseph Smith III, Sermon on God's Justice delivered at Independence, Missouri, April 15, 1888 (Lamoni, Iowa: Lambert & Hansen); in vault, RLDS Library-Archives.
8. David Ray Griffin, "John B. Cobb," in *A Handbook of Christian Theologians*, eds. Martin E. Marty and Dean G. Peerman (Nashville, Tennessee: Abingdon Press, 1989), 698.
9. John B. Cobb, Jr., *A Christian Natural Theology* (Philadelphia: The Westminster Press, 1969), 114–115.
10. John B. Cobb, Jr., *God and the World* (Philadelphia: The Westminster Press, 1969), chapter 2.
11. Alfred North Whitehead, *Process and Reality* (New York: The Free Press, 1978), 108, 224, 283.
12. Alfred North Whitehead, *Adventures of Ideas* (New York: The Free Press, 1933), 252.
13. Ibid.
14. Charles Hartshorne, *Creative Synthesis and Philosophic Method* (New York: University Press of America, 1970), 307.
15. Paul M. Edwards, *Preface to Faith* (Midvale, Utah: Signature Books, 1984), 3.
16. Whitehead, *Adventures of Ideas*, 253–255.
17. Whitehead, *Process and Reality*, 229.
18. For a good discussion on aesthetics and various types of ethical systems, see John B. Spencer's two essays, "Meland as a Resource for Political Ethics" and "Whitehead as a Basis for a Social Ethic." Both essays are in *Process Philosophy and Social Thought*, ed. John B. Cobb, Jr., and W. Widick Schroeder (Chicago: Center for the Scientific Study of Religion, 1981).
19. Herman E. Daley, "The Steady-State Economy," *Toward a Steady-State Economy*, ed. Herman E. Daley (San Francisco: W. H. Freeman and Co., 1973), 152ff.
20. The United Methodist Council of Bishops, *In Defense of Creation* (Nashville, Tennessee: Graded Press, 1986, 1986), 24.
21. Leon Howell, *Acting in Faith* (Geneva: World Council of Churches, 1983), 6.
22. Charles Birth, John B. Cobb, Jr., *The Liberation of Life* (Cambridge: University Press, 1984).

Second Among Equals: The Reorganized Church, Black Americans, and the American Mainstream[1]

Roger Launius

In his brilliant novel *The Invisible Man*, Ralph Ellison described the dilemma of black Americans. "I am an invisible man," the hero of Ellison's novel cried in anguish, as he crystallized centuries of race relations in a single phrase. "I am invisible," he went on, "simply because other people refuse to see me." Ellison believed "the long habit of deception and evasion" had soured black-white relations in America.[2] His criticisms describe race relations in the Reorganized Church of Jesus Christ of Latter Day Saints. The Reorganized Church never imposed official restrictions on black members as did the Latter-day Saints under Brigham Young. Yet Reorganization leaders and members have generally accepted the American middle-class racial concepts and this tacit decision has hampered its operations among black Americans.[3] The church's black membership, therefore, has been a minority within the institution without a constituency or sympathetic champions among its upper echelons.

Currently, there are probably less than 1,000 active African-American Reorganized Latter Day Saints on the church's rolls. While this is probably the largest number of black members at one time in the church's history, it is not an impressive statistic. The church's black membership is still smaller than the ratio of blacks to whites in American society.[4]

The Reorganized Church has always pursued something of a two-pronged policy concerning black members, one emphasizing the ideal and the other the practical. The first prong has remained unchanged since the church's organizational meeting: the gospel is offered to all humankind. This position, documented in Restoration scriptures, asserts that the gospel of Jesus Christ is for all humanity, promoting universal Christian salvation without regard to race, color, or condition. The atonement of Christ is available to all. According to the Book of Mormon, "...he invites them all to come to him...black and white, bond and free, male and female...all are alike to God."[5] The Doctrine and Covenants contains similar statements: "[T]he voice of the Lord is unto all men, and there is none to escape, and there is no eye that shall not see, neither ear that shall not hear, neither heart that shall not be penetrated."[6]

The Reorganized Church early on adopted an official policy that accepts this basic scriptural position, as a review of General Conference Resolutions on race reveals. The half-dozen statements following an 1865 revelation providing for black ordination in the Reorganized Church stressed similar views. For example, a 1956 resolution said: "The gospel is for all mankind. It knows no distinction of race or color." There may have been additional paragraphs appended to these various resolutions on race relations, but the fundamental official position, with the emphasis on *official*, is expressed in those two sentences.[7]

This official position tells less than half the story. The second prong of the church's racial policy suggests a wide divergence between the ideal and its implementation. Like Orwell's *Animal Farm* where all the pigs are equal but some are more equal than others, the Reorganized Church has allowed larger social conceptions to impinge on its implementation of the official policy of complete racial equality. And these issues have shifted significantly over the last century and a half. Equitable treatment of blacks in the 1860s was significantly different from what would be accepted in the latter part of the twentieth century, and the changes in the Reorganization mirror those in mainstream American society. The forays and rebuttals, bobs and weaves, ins and outs of these practical shifts form a delta between the ideal racial policy stated in scripture and Conference resolutions and the empirical evidence of race relations in the Reorganization.

There is a cognizance in this discussion that the Reorganized Church has been since its inception in the 1850s and continues to be a white, American, Midwestern-based religious movement. It has also been a relatively conservative organization, despite whatever radical conceptions it might have inherited from early Mormonism. Its story is largely one of the American mainstream. Its leaders have been firmly incorporated into the American value system. Because they either were or aspired to be middle-class, they accepted, by and large, the racial attitudes of that social stratum.[8]

Joseph Smith III is one example of the embracing of middle-class racial ideas by a church leader. He was very much a product of his Midwestern society. Like others in antebellum Illinois, he became an early and vocal advocate of the abolition of slavery. As early as 1848, when he was not yet sixteen, Smith went out of his way to serve as the Nauvoo guide of Owen Lovejoy, an antislavery congressman from Illinois, so he could tell Lovejoy how he admired his stand against slavery. In the mid-1850s he carried on a spirited correspondence of slavery's evils with his adopted sister, Julia, who had married a Texan and struck a pro-slavery position. In 1858 he became a lifelong devotee of Abraham Lincoln and the antislavery politics of the Republican Party.[9] At the same time, Smith was not interchangeable with a 1960s urban liberal campaigning for desegregation. He always held blacks in an inferior position to whites. He sometimes referred to them in derogatory terms. He commented during the Reconstruction era that whites must not "sacrifice the dignity, honor and prestige that may be rightfully attached to the ruling race," implying a basic black inferiority.[10] While Joseph Smith III and other church leaders of his era subscribed intellectually to the ideal of racial equality within the church and larger society, they and most of those they led were no more liberal than the larger society.

When the Reorganized Church first began to send missionaries into the South immediately following the Civil War, it affirmed an egalitarian racial policy. In 1865 Joseph Smith III announced a revelation providing ordination of black males to the priesthood, a courageous decision that stood up to the ideal but an easy one at the time for there were no black members.[11] Virtually the same was true in April 1866 when the Council of Twelve Apostles considered "whether Coloured Members should be organized by themselves into Branches or in connection with the White Brethren." After considerable discussion they "Resolved that as the Author of Life and Salvation does not discriminate among His rational creatures on account of Colour neither does the Church of Jesus Christ of Latter Day Saints."[12] This was an admirable position, and perhaps it reflects the heady racial utopianism during the first years of Reconstruction.

The ideal was soon subsumed, however, in the reality of racial tensions in the United States. Perhaps spirited on by the opportunities in the immediate postwar period, the church began missionary outreach among blacks and sent appointee ministers to the South to preach among them. They had some success; the most significant of the first blacks baptized were Benjamin and Caroline Booker. They and their family became members of the Lone Star Branch in Alabama, until then a white Reorganized Church congregation, on 13 July 1868. They had two sons, Perry W. and E.R. Booker, who became black leaders in the church during the latter nineteenth century, and many members of the family have remained active in the Reorganization to the present.[13] But the very success of such activities sowed the seeds of racial strife.

Despite good intentions, the church hierarchy was largely ignorant of race realities in the South and it misinterpreted the depth of racist ideology. To direct that congregations be integrated was easy, to accomplish it in a world where racism was rampant both within and without the church was another problem. Moreover, from the early days of Reconstruction virtually all Protestant churches in the South were segregated and for the church to buck this tradition was quite ingenuous.[14]

Although the Reorganization's official racial policy remained unchanged, as its missionaries gained experience in the South and made black converts, conditions in the nation shifted during the latter nineteenth century and the implementation of the policy shifted radically.[15] From the outset, racism from both the white and black quarters in the South made a truly egalitarian policy toward black members impossible. Virtually every letter from missionaries in the field complained of the difficulties inherent in working with blacks and whites.

Thomas W. Smith, a full-time church missionary in Alabama in the 1870s, ran into this problem. In a letter of 5 February 1871 he wrote:

There is a feeling of reluctance on the part of the white people to mingle with them [blacks] in social worship, and to show them…brotherly and sisterly affection due all saints from each other….It will require a great deal of prudence and wisdom to act just right, so as to neither offend the whites while this prejudice exists, (and it is no use to ignore the fact of its existence), nor hurt the feelings of the believing blacks….To educate the white saints to remove this "I am holier than thou" idea…requires much wisdom, (and whether I shall attain to the measure required I know not).

He concluded it was difficult "to be able to understand how far one should yield, and how far [to] oppose this prejudice against the race."[16] Because of his experience in the South, Thomas Smith, unlike most other Reorganization leaders, perceived the race issue as most delicate both for the church membership and for the larger society.[17]

L.F. West, a church member from Alabama, expressed eloquently the difficulties of circumventing racial mores in 1872. He wrote, "…to break down the middle wall of partition from between the two races is beyond the power of mortal man, this can only be done by time." He sadly concluded, "To cultivate too much familiarity with the blacks, offends the whites, to neglect the blacks, will offend the Lord."[18] The dilemma of race relations forced the Reorganization to take a path less visionary than originally intended.

These concerns forced a rethinking of the *implementation* of the church's policy of complete racial equality and, in ways that were important, practical considerations chipped away over time at the implementation of the ideal of racial equality among the Reorganized Latter Day Saints. This led to the adoption of an informal policy of racial segregation in Reorganized Church congregations in the South by at least 1881. Because of racial tensions in their mostly white congregation in that year, Benjamin and Caroline Booker removed their family from the Lone Star Branch and began meeting in a largely black congregation at St. Joseph, Alabama. The church hierarchy backed this move. It illustrated in graphic terms the acceptance of the racial status quo.

From this expedient racial segregation sprang a whole series of compromises concerning race relations. For example, the Reorganized Church used blacks to minister almost exclusively among blacks. It also accepted a de facto second-class position for the race by not standing up as forcefully for black rights within the church as it might have otherwise.[19]

The same type of problem prompted Joseph Smith III to compromise on his policy of black ordination dating from 1865. He described in his memoirs how some members of the church hierarchy claimed that its wording—"it is expedient in me that you ordain priests unto me, of every race who receive the teachings of my law"—restricted blacks to the office of priest, only. That was neither Smith's intent nor the way it eventually turned out, but Joseph Smith III was unwilling to stir up what he believed would be a divisive and brutal controversy within the church over this issue. "I did not contend for my own understanding very strongly, as at the time there was no apparent necessity for making any such serious discrimination"; he recalled in his memoirs, "...since the office of Priest would permit the preaching of the Word, I felt that time would either soften asperities or the Lord would make the matter still plainer by further direction."[20] Because of this compromise, no blacks were ordained to the office of elder until a generation later when George F. Crawley was ordained in 1893.

Between Reconstruction and World War II the church's *official* policy of racial equal-ity remained completely unchanged. It was reaffirmed periodically in church publications and official correspondence, if not in Conference action. If members raised the issue of racism in the church, they were promptly told that none existed. The Reorganization welcomed all who wished to join its ranks. Blacks could conceivably hold any priesthood or administrative office in the church and could participate on an equal footing with white members.

If one scratched the surface of this official policy, however, he or she would find an unquestioning acceptance of the nation's racial caste system. The injustice of this *a priori* acceptance of standard racial conceptions was generally unknown to the Reorganization's rank and file and remarkably hidden even among the church leadership. About the only people who were aware of it were the few black Saints who suffered all types of abuses because of their race. Some complained, like appointee missionary George H. Graves and stalwart convert Amy E. Robbins, but it was nearly always met with a deaf ear in the administrative system. Most black members endured in silence or withdrew from the movement.

This era was the most trying of any experienced by black Saints of the Reorganization. Because of the lessened status of blacks in larger society, they suffered in the church as well. In this environment Graves made important contributions until he, too, was driven off by the race issue. Born in 1847 to former slaves who had escaped to Canada on the Underground Railway, in 1877 Graves joined the Reorganization, was soon ordained to the Aaronic priesthood, and in 1880 was appointed as a full-time minister to blacks in Alabama and Florida. For many years Graves served as a missionary until his de facto retirement in 1908.[21] Although he worked principally among the members of his own race, building up small enclaves of black Saints wherever he preached, Graves never believed that his responsibilities were limited to his own race and often founded interracial missions.

This sometimes got Graves into trouble. On one occasion he ran afoul of the officials in charge of his mission in Chicago for orienting his efforts toward converting whites. Graves responded that it was not his intention to deemphasize his own race, but the curiosity of whites about a black preacher brought him into contact with many who embraced the Reorganization. He did not care what attracted seekers, Graves rebuffed those who criticized him; he would minister to all who came. "I will tell you," he wrote in July 1900,

that I preach to 10 white people to 1 colored person. For the white people think it is very foxey to hear a colored Mormon preach, as they call us here on the street. They gather around us in great crowds and ask questions about Joseph Smith, whether he stole sheep or was he a prophet of God. And so goes the fight. We are willing to stand up and fight for Joseph the Prophet and this blessed latter day work while I live.[22]

Graves turned off the controversy by suggesting that perhaps God used his skin color to bring in seekers, and if God sent them he would teach them the gospel.

Graves' treatment ensured that he eventually became disaffected. After he left appointment in 1908, he gradually drifted out of association with the church. On 4 October 1916 the Central Chicago Branch minutes reported that the London, Ontario, District had removed him from the membership roles of the church.[23] There was no indication that he was guilty of any wrongdoing; the action appears to relate to inactivity brought on by his unwillingness to accept the second-class position he felt in his home branch. Nothing is known of his life after that time. Graves represented in microcosm the experience of many black members within the Reorganized Church, accomplishing much but never being fully accepted and finally having to assume a second-class position or abdicate the church.

Amy Robbins, a black who had joined the Reorganization in 1905, was typical of the next generation of devoted black members during the early twentieth century. As a young woman, she joined the Reorganization in Michigan. She summarized her basic commitment to the church in her recollection of her baptism, as "the highest mountain peak of my life." While only four people were at that service, that did not diminish its significance: "A motley group to be sure, for there was a Mr. Black, who was white and my aunt, Mrs. White, was black, and Amy...I was brown and the Elder was white. These different colors were one in Jesus Christ."[24]

While Amy Robbins remained a strong advocate of the church until her death, it was not always an easy task. She reported several instances of abuse and neglect by her fellow members in her largely white Battle Creek congregation, and church authorities took no action to resolve the controversies. In a hundred small ways she and her family were made to feel unwelcome. Many of her children were quite talented musically, and the congregation wanted their voices in its choir. Yet some members refused to allow them to be seen in the choir loft during the service. They worked out a curtain arrangement at the back of the loft with the black singers seated behind it. It was an exceptionally belittling episode. Most members would not have accepted such a plan and would have been gone in short order never to return. Amy, too, considered staying away from the church. That she did not speaks volumes about her. Although she had no doubts about her own commitment, she wondered about her children. "I realized that the salvation of my children was at stake when they mingled with the world and were denied the privalege [sic] of hearing and association with the gospel."[25]

The problems of prejudice extended to the highest levels of the church, and this especially troubled Amy Robbins. She remarked on an incident at the Indian Lake reunion which Reorganization President Frederick M. Smith, the grandson of the founding prophet, attended. "I was very anxious to meet the prophet of God," she wrote, "as it had always been my wont to place saints upon a pedestal, and the president was on the highest of them all, and I felt greatly honored to have this opportunity of meeting him." She commented that when she finally met him the Spirit of God confirmed his prophetic ministry and "As he stood to speak that morning, he was, in my eyes, a little lower than an angel; a chosen representative of Christ; a man of God who was to lead us, the people of God, to Zion." Then Smith began to speak. He first began talking about having a "nigger" working for him and how he came to have "one." Robbins' recollection was moving:

I did not remember anything more that was said in that talk. I don't think in all my life I ever had such a hurt, such a bitter disappointment, my angel, or saint, or prophet had fallen from the pedestal on which I had placed him. Many eyes were turned on me and my aunt, the only colored people on the grounds. My eyes were filled with tears, my face burned with shame and humiliation and I at once felt like an outsider, an outcast with no part in the Zionic scheme because I was what the Prophet would call a "nigger." As soon as the benediction was pronounced I fled to my tent where I gave way to my bitter tears; my week-end was spoiled and I wanted to go home.[26]

She left the reunion as soon as she could get a ride, disappointed and chagrined that the prophet could be just a "man" subject to all the prejudices of any other.

Amy Robbins' powerlessness in the face of these discriminatory actions was very real. She felt that as a black woman she was closed off from the normal channels of administration. But even with all internal mechanisms for justice shut in her face, she was unwilling to leave the church. Why? The most satisfactory answer is that Robbins was firmly committed to the ideals of the Reorganization even in the face of internal prejudices. Her writings were laced with statements of belief and commitment. Perhaps the most telling evidence of this was her poetry, primitive but emotional and powerful. One poem, "The Restoration," captured the angles of Amy Robbins' life and belief.

The church was brought out of the wilderness,
    The gospel gifts have all been restored.
Showing forth God's love and great tenderness,
    To all those who put all their trust in the Lord.

If man will have faith and truly repent,
    Be baptized and his sins washed away,
The gifts from above will surely be sent
    As promised in this latter day.

True to form the prophet in this latter day
    Gave his life as a martyr for Truth.
He searched in the scriptures to find the true way
    And God called him while yet in his youth.

And so God has in these latter days,
    Made available to man the new birth,
Faith, repentance, baptism, just as in old ways
    When Jesus was here on the earth.

Let us spread glad tidings of the restoration
    And work while it is yet called today
Until we have reached out into every nation
    And spread the gospel of truth all the way.[27]

She was never willing to do what at least one of her sons suggested, "Leave those ungodly, sinning, scornful church members alone," although some of her children were driven away.[28] She remained an active member, and she searched for ways to better the situation.

This search became more active as time passed. Perhaps she became less timid, perhaps maturity brought greater appreciation of what was at stake, perhaps the changes in the larger American society made it easier to speak out on these issues, perhaps she eventually decided that the issue was significant enough for her to injure others' feelings. Certainly, she went a long way toward overcoming the church's conservative strictures on her race and gender in her efforts. For example, she proposed an alternative branch in Battle Creek that would meet in her house. While she explained this should not have been necessary, it was better than suffering abuse from the local Saints, especially the propensity it had to alienate her children. She wrote:

Since God has accepted us as members of the body of Christ and has acknowledged us as His children, I am unable to understand why the rest of His children would assume the attitude that they were better than their father.[29]

She obtained this permission, but the mission was never successful at attracting enough attendees to satisfy the local church leadership and was eventually discontinued. It was later revived under the direction of her son, Arnold Robbins, who was a priest, but it was again discontinued after several months of futile effort.[30]

As racial consciousness in American society rose in concert with the changes of World War II, some black Saints—like Amy Robbins, who died only in 1956—and a large number of white members began to address the inconsistency between the official racial policy and its less than egalitarian implementation. Without the shifts in larger society, however, Reorganization members probably would never have come to grips with this inconsistency. It was not, therefore, a move toward leadership in social issues but a natural following of the American mainstream. Although not the first to comment on the discrepancies, Wilford G. Winholtz, a young city planner in Chicago, was the first to offer something tangible aimed at alleviating churchwide racial injustice. During the

latter 1940s he became interested in the black members in his area of responsibility. He documented a legacy of, at best, neglect and, at worst, mistreatment of black Saints in the Chicago Congregation. He tracked down several black members, almost none of whom were still active in the church and collected information about their treatment. Winholtz concluded that the church was unwilling to recognize its poor treatment of blacks. As he wrote to Graceland College sociologist Raymond D. Zinser in January 1950, "[I]t is not uncommon to find...Melchisedec Priesthood who would 'just rather not talk about the problem.' It's too big a job to tackle, and we just make it worse by attempting to."[31]

Winholtz sponsored resolutions aimed at admitting church culpability in racial discrimination and urging more equitable treatment for blacks at the General Conferences of 1948 and 1950. His lengthy description of abuse in the church and positive statement of the Reorganization's commitment to racial equality was transformed into the same general official position: "all people are fundamentally equal before God." Removed were all possible inferences that the Reorganized Church had ever experienced any racial turmoil or that it needed to do anything more to ensure equality of all Saints. President Israel A. Smith, summing up the position of the church leadership, wrote:

There is nothing in the law of the church which creates or tends to create racial inequality or racial discrimination. To legislate with respect to a specific race raises, by implication the presumption that that race has heretofore been unjustly dealt with in our church law and discipline, which we cannot and do not admit.[32]

He wrote to Winholtz privately that he could never acknowledge the church's involvement in anything less than the lofty principles of complete racial equality as stated and restated in church scripture and resolutions.[33]

Church leaders adopted a similar position in 1963, some fifteen years later, when William D. Russell, then an assistant editor of the *Saints' Herald*, published "Martin Luther King: Satan or Saint?" By that time the United States was fully wrapped up in the civil rights crusade, with King as an extremely controversial spokesman for equal rights. The author pointedly advocated support of King's activities and challenged the Reorganization's membership to involve themselves in the crusade, "for [not] to do so is to make the gospel irrelevant to today's needs." King, he argued, was a voice of nonviolent change in a nation of unrest. King's goals were just and his methods were laudable. With those combinations how could the Saints not support his activities?[34]

The church hierarchy's answer was an emphatic no. Prompted partly by a negative reaction from certain church members, the First Presidency chastised the *Herald* editorship and singled Russell out for criticism. They then wrote an official statement for the 1 August 1963 *Saints' Herald*, "Our Position on Race and Color." It was essentially a reiteration of the official policy of the church with no admission that there were ever any racial differences. "The internal racial problems in our church have been very minor," they wrote. "Integration has been such a natural process that there would be no need to discuss it in these columns were it not for the national attention that has resulted from the tense integration question."[35]

This view was shared neither by the blacks in the church nor by very many white liberals. The facts of race relations at the local level did not bear out the lofty principles of the official position. Many Saints thought the policy statement a travesty and urged greater commitment on the part of the institutional church to support racial equality. Even the First Presidency was not fully united on the statement. Maurice L. Draper, one of the quorum's members, admitted later that it was a cautious statement but was the most he could get the other members of the First Presidency to accept.[36]

To that date the Reorganized Church as an institution had never explicitly suggested that it might tolerate anything but the most egalitarian of racial interaction, a stand not unusual among modern organizations. It did undergo a shift in the mid-1960s from a basic lack of concern about racial questions to moderate and legal attempts to bring about change during the civil rights crusade. For instance, by the latter 1960s the church was officially supporting nonviolent civil rights activism, a position advocated without success by Winholtz in the 1950s and Russell in 1963, while questioning the more militant expressions of the "Second Reconstruction."[37] The Reorganization's publications, its conferences, and its local jurisdictions took action designed to foster a certain egalitarian racial treatment. There was also a renewed interest in evangelism among black Americans.[38] This has been too often at a superficial level, however.

Throughout the 1970s a number of racial *firsts* were ballyhooed by the institutional church, which on deeper consideration have had limited impact. The ordination of the first black to the office of high priest in 1970, the setting apart of the first black to an office on a stake high council also in 1970, the prominent use of black church members in the World Conferences throughout the decade, the first ordination service in America in which all the participants were black in 1975, and the placing under appointment of the first American black in more than sixty years in 1978 were notable examples of such action.[39] Although I do not want to diminish the importance of these episodes, they all bear the marks of tokenism. There have been, however, a few expressions of substantive gains in the church's approaches toward race relations since those occasions. These include concerted efforts to conduct missionary work and social assistance programs in largely black sections of Chicago, St. Louis, Kansas City, and Detroit, and the establishment of dynamic and growing Reorganized Church congregations there. It has also been manifested in missionary work among blacks in the deep South and the incorporation of black members into largely white RLDS congregations.[40]

Despite these efforts, the Reorganized Church's historical commitment to genuine racial equality has generally been no greater than the level acceptable in polite American society. This is true for several reasons. First, the church has never been able to transcend the larger society in which it resides. In all but a few cases the membership has not been dedicated to moving beyond the norms of society; it has not been important enough to shoulder the weight of American disapproval. Even if the movement as a whole wanted to do so—which is not usually the case—any far-reaching commitment to racial equality would invite suspicion from outside the movement. The Reorganization's small size, its dissenting nature, and its membership's desire to fit in with neighbors made it imperative that the church reflect larger social perspectives. The Reorganized Church embraced the racial ideas of larger society during its formative period, most of which accepted the inherent inferiority of blacks. As those ideas changed during the twentieth century, the position of the Reorganized Church's membership evolved to keep pace.

Additionally, the basic moderation of Reorganized Church presidents contributed to the movement's racial position. In an effort to ensure the greatest goodwill for the greatest number of members, all extremes in the race issue have been avoided with great care throughout the history of the Reorganization.

This moderate position was motivated in part by an overwhelming concern for the welfare of the church as a corporate institution. Those occupying the prophetic office have considered the church's stability and growth of paramount importance. For them, this was synonymous with relative unity and both external and internal harmony. All have been essentially practical men—with Joseph Smith III and Israel A. Smith especially cast in that mold—who recognized that without some semblance of church unity the larger objectives of the church as a vehicle for converting humanity and establishing Zion could not be accomplished. They have each demonstrated a certain pragmatism laced with principle in the ordering of priorities and the pursuit of objectives.[41] They were willing to forego issues that had less support or were potentially divisive if they did not appear the most critical to the movement's overall welfare.

All the church presidents have sought to deal with the race issue from the perspectives of their personal opinions, the members, and the larger society without damaging appreciably the fragile unity of the Reorganized Church. Each had to ask whether if a particular decision on race created controversy, how critical was its adoption to the movement's larger mission? Joseph Smith III decided that ordering the ordination of blacks to the Melchisedec priesthood was not sufficiently important to warrant upsetting church unity. W. Wallace Smith and the First Presidency in the early 1960s said support of Martin Luther King's activities in the civil rights movement was not sufficiently important to justify internal dissention or external suspicion. Because there was no churchwide consensus on the issue, and the possibility of a loss of external prestige existed, they took a cautious position. Later, as the more moderate aspects of the civil rights crusade became more acceptable, the church encouraged them.[42]

F. Henry Edwards, a long-time church official during the twentieth century and member of the First Presidency between 1946 and 1966, offered this assessment of the position of the church hierarchy on the race issue. He insightfully commented in a 1979 interview, "Socrates was a gadfly, but gadflies don't build nests."[43] The implication was clear: the First Presidency, as the leading quorum of the church, must anticipate all possible ramifications of its statements and actions and rest them upon a solid foundation of support. To act incautiously would be to invite controversy among and toward the membership. Depending on how deep that controversy went and the stature of whatever malcontents it created, it could shake the very roots of the church.[44] Consequently, even if some members demanded that the church take a stand on an important and just issue, the First Presidency would refuse to do so until a consensus of support could be built at the grassroots level.

The church, therefore, has a divided legacy in race relations: the ideal and the application of policy that compromises on that ideal. This is perhaps a paradox and certainly one which makes us stand Janus-like assessing the nature of both sides and seeking to appreciate each equally. There are reasons, however, to believe the Reorganization may be interested in working on the race issue more adequately than in the past. Perhaps the most important development in this arena has been the creation of a core of leadership as a special interest group working largely behind the scenes to effect change. Built around the small Ethnic Ministries Office at church headquarters in the early 1970s, this interest group succeeded for the first time in the Reorganization's history in building a dialogue with the larger church. Through this focal point black Saints could trade information, build consensus, and present a united front to the larger church community. Its *Black Ministries Newsletter* has served to cement together the small black membership of the church and to present a united position to church authorities. Several unifying and bonding retreats, services, and other activities have aided in this process. This has been an incredibly important development within the church. Clearly nothing of this type has been tried before. The result has been the elevation of the racial issue, if only a little, above its earlier place without engendering the negative connotations of earlier efforts through the latching on of "Black Power" rhetoric and images.[45]

Although the black ministries coalition in the Reorganized Church has recently enjoyed increasing visibility and status, there are many issues yet to be decided about the future role of blacks in the church.[46] What will happen in the future? The church's history suggests that the Reorganization would accept the mainstream status quo, whatever that might be at the time. Clearly, the challenges of race relations, both in America and, with increasing criticality, in non-white parts of the globe forces the Reorganization to consider anew its role as a force for good in the world. The informal black ministries coalition developed in the 1970s is an important and positive aspect of this reconsideration. Race relations in the church and world is an unfinished and crucial history and one toward which the Reorganized Church has an opportunity to make a worthwhile and lasting contribution. If it seizes that opportunity then black Saints will no longer be second among equals.

Notes

1. An earlier version of this paper was presented at the John Whitmer Historical Association Spring Lecture Series (13 March 1988), Graceland College, Lamoni, Iowa. A more in-depth and extended treatment can be found in my book, *Invisible Saints: A History of Black Americans in the Reorganized Church* (Independence, Missouri: Herald House, 1988).

2. Ralph Ellison, *The Invisible Man* (New York: Random House, 1963), as quoted in William Manchester, *The Glory and the Dream: A Narrative History of America, 1932–1972* (Boston: Little Brown, 1974), 899.

3. For excellent introductions to the study of blacks in the Reorganization see William D. Russell, "A Priestly Role for a Prophetic Church: The RLDS Church and Black Americans," *Dialogue: A Journal of Mormon Thought* 12 (Summer 1979): 37–49, and Arlyn R. Love, "The First Presidency's Response to the Civil Rights Movement," *John Whitmer Historical Association Journal* 4 (1984): 41–50.

4. The 1,000 member statistic is the estimate of Richard W. Hawks, the only black American serving as a full-time appointee of the church as of 1988. Hawks is in a particularly strong position, because of his responsibilities with the church, to offer this estimate. Interview with Richard W. Hawks (15 September 1987), East St. Louis, Illinois.

5. Book of Mormon (Independence, Missouri: Herald House, 1966 ed.), II Nephi 11:113–115.

6. Book of Doctrine and Covenants (Independence, Missouri: Herald House, 1970 ed.), Section 1:1b.

7. There were resolutions relating to race adopted in 1875, 1948, 1950, 1956, and two in 1968. These have been conveniently published in *Rules and Resolutions* (Independence, Missouri: Herald House, 1990 ed.). The quoted resolution is number 995.

8. Although no demographic studies of church population have been done for the nineteenth century, it appears that most members were white, of middle-class origin, and reflective of society in general. Certainly they were mostly located in the Midwest and sought to blend into larger society even while seeking to create distinctive communities. See Roger D. Launius' discussion of church growth and development, "The Golden Years," chapter 13, *Joseph Smith III: Pragmatic Prophet* (Urbana, Illinois: University of Illinois Press, 1988); Roger D. Launius, "Quest for Zion: Joseph Smith III and Community-Building in the Reorganization, 1860–1900," in Maurice L. Draper and Debra Combs, eds., *Restoration Studies III* (Independence, Missouri: Herald House, 1986), 314–332; Norma Derry Hiles, "Lamoni: Crucible for Pluralism in the Reorganization Church," in *Restoration Studies III*, 139–144. The perceptions of white nineteenth-century America toward blacks has been analyzed in William Stanton, *The Leopard's Spots: Scientific Attitudes Toward Race in America, 1815–1859* (Chicago: University of Chicago Press, 1960), and George M. Fredrickson, *The Black Image in the White Mind* (New York: Harper and Row, 1971).

9. Joseph Smith III, "The Memoirs of President Joseph Smith (1832–1914)," *Saints' Herald* 82 (12 February 1935): 207–208; 82 (23 April 1935): 529–530; 82 (30 April 1935): 559–562; 82 (7 May 1935): 589–590; Joseph Smith III, "Undue Strife," *Saints' Herald* 40 (13 May 1893): 289–290; Edward Magdol, *Owen Lovejoy: Abolitionist in Congress* (New Brunswick, New Jersey: Rutgers University Press, 1967), 45; *Carthage (Illinois) Republican* (14 November 1856, 30 September 1858, 14 October 1858, 28 October 1858).

10. Joseph Smith III, "All One in Christ," *True Latter Day Saints' Herald* 22 (15 February 1875): 112. See also, Joseph Smith III to Israel A. Smith (8 July 1905), Miscellaneous Letters and Papers, Reorganized Church of Jesus Christ of Latter Day Saints Library-Archives, Independence, Missouri.

11. The revelation providing for black ordination is in Doctrine and Covenants, Section 116. The background of the decision can be found in Diane Shelton, "The 1865 Revelation," unpublished paper presented at the 1978 annual meeting of the John Whitmer Historical Association, Plano, Illinois, copy in Restoration History Manuscript Collection, Frederick M. Smith Library, Graceland College, Lamoni, Iowa; Roger D. Launius, *Invisible Saints*, 111–133.

12. Council of Twelve Minutes, quoted in Russell, "A Priestly Role for a Prophetic Church," 40.

13. This has been discussed in Roger D. Launius, *Invisible Saints*, 135–138.

14. The segregation of churches in the South has been documented exhaustively in Eugene D. Genovese, *Roll, Jordan, Roll: The World the Slaves Made* (New York: Vintage Books, 1974), 236–237; John Samuel Ezell, *The South Since Eighteen Sixty-Five* (Norman, Oklahoma: University of Oklahoma Press, 1975 ed.), 344–345; John Hope Franklin, *From Slavery to Freedom: A History of Negro Americans* (New York: Alfred A. Knopf, 1967 ed.), 309–310; Winthrop S. Hudson, *Religion in America* (new York: Charles Scribner's Sons, 1981 ed.), 226–227. Contrary to this view, William D. Russell suggests that religious segregation among Christian churches in the South did not take place until the post-Reconstruction era. Citing as evidence an important study— Kenneth K. Bailey, "The Post-Civil War Racial Separations in Southern Protestantism: Another Look," *Church History* 46 (December 1977): 453–473—Russell concludes that after Reconstruction "the churches, which had been somewhat integrated in the 1870s, moved toward complete segregation" (Russell, "A Priestly Role for a Prophetic Church," 42). Unfortunately, Russell overstated the evidence marshaled by Bailey. Bailey's concern was not so much with segregation in individual churches, which was a common practice by both races in the South during the Reconstruction era, but more with the establishment of separate and distinct religious associations. Bailey suggests that the rush to establish racially restrictive conferences, synods, or other ecclesiastical jurisdictions was not nearly so cut and dried as previously thought, but he wrote that "a clear sentiment favoring racially-discrete congregations quickly developed among whites in most localities" (Bailey, "The Post-Civil War Racial Separations in Southern Protestantism," 456). It was a suggestion, for Bailey, of segregation at the district level rather than one of segregation at the congregational level. This is contrary to Russell's use of the evidence for the Reorganization's experience.

15. To list all the published defenses of the church's racial policy would be impracticable; however, the remarkable consistency in each of these representative articles over the years is exceptional. See, as examples, W. W. Blair, "The Negro and the Priesthood," *True Latter Day Saints' Herald* 12 (1 August 1867): 35–36; Joseph Smith III, "Pleasant Chat," *True Latter Day Saints' Herald* 13 (1 May 1868): 137–139; Joseph Smith III, "All One in Christ," *True Latter Day Saints' Herald* 22 (15 February 1875): 112; Joseph Smith III, "No Color Line in Heaven," *Saints' Herald* 25 (1 December 1878): 367; Joseph Smith III, "Undue Strife," *Saints' Herald* 40 (13 May 1893): 289–290; Elbert A. Smith, "The Negro Problem in America," *Saints' Herald* 60 (15 October 1913): 997–999; Elbert A. Smith, "Some Racial Minority Problems in the United States: III, The Negro," *Saints' Herald* 90 (25 December 1943): 1631–1633, 1635; Israel A. Smith, "A Sane View of the Race Question," *Saints' Herald* 100 (30 March 1953): 291; Israel A. Smith, "Race Relations," *Saints' Herald* 104 (8 July 1957): 8; First Presidency, "Our Position on Race and Color," *Saints' Herald* 110 (1 August 1963): 506; Paul A. Wellington, "The Restoration Attitude Towards Race," *Saints' Herald* 110 (15 November 1963): 770.

16. "News from the South," *True Latter Day Saints' Herald* 18 (15 April 1871): 235, 236.

17. "Away Down South," Ibid., 18 (1 September 1871): 524–527.

18. Letter of L. F. West, from Escambia, Colorado (21 April 1872), *True Latter Day Saints' Herald* 19 (1 August 1872): 469–471.

19. This argument is laid out in detail in Launius, *Invisible Saints*, 219–254.

20. Quote from Doctrine and Covenants 116. Joseph Smith III, "The Memoirs of President Joseph Smith (1832–1914)," *Saints' Herald* 84 (24 July 1937): 944.

21. For a general discussion of Graves' career, see Roger D. Launius, "George H. Graves: The First Black Missionary," *Saints' Heritage: A Journal of the Restoration Trail Foundation* (1988): 11–31.

22. George H. Graves to E. L. Kelley (18 July 1900), typescript in Anne Graves File, Reorganized Church Library-Archives.

23. Central Chicago Branch Minutes and Reports (1914–1951), 36, Reorganized Church Library-Archives.

24. Amy E. Robbins, "Just Amy, Autobiography" (n.d.), 23, typescript reproduction in possession of author.

25. Amy E. Robbins, et al., to Elder A. C. Barmore, president of Battle Creek Branch (1930?), 5, in notes from materials from library of Amy E. Robbins (n.d.), typescript by Richard W. Hawks (14 June 1979), copy in possession of author.

26. Robbins, "My Experience as a Negro in the Battle Creek Branch" (n.d.), 4, copy in possession of author.

27. Excerpt from Amy E. Robbins, "The Restoration," in "Amy's Pomes" (n.d.), part 3, 13–15, photomechanical publication of typescript, copy in possession of author.
28. V. Russell Robbins to Amy E. Robbins (21 February 1950), copy in possession of author.
29. Amy Robbins, et al., to Elder A. C. Barmore, president of Battle Creek Branch (1930?), as quoted in Launius, *Invisible Saints*, 205.
30. Amy E. Robbins to Wilford G. Winholtz (17 February 1949), copy in possession of author.
31. Wilford G. Winholtz to Raymond D. Zinser (20 January 1950), copy in possession of author. This is also supported in Wilford G. Winholtz to the First Presidency and members of the Joint Council, "Report on Relations Resolution and Background Correspondence" (15 March 1950), copy in possession of author.
32. *Saints' Herald Conference Daily* (1948): 105; telephone interview with Wilford G. Winholtz, Independence, Missouri (23 September 1987).
33. Israel A. Smith to Wilford G. Winholtz (4 February 1948), copy in possession of author.
34. William D. Russell, "Martin Luther King: Satan or Saint?" *Saints' Herald* 110 (1 July 1963): 434.
35. First Presidency, "Our Position on Race and Color," *Saints' Herald* 110 (1 August 1963): 506.
36. William D. Russell to author (15 December 1987), copy in possession of author.
37. See the position taken on this issue in Reed M. Holmes, "The Mild and the Militant," *Saints' Herald* 113 (15 June 1966): 401; Verne Sparkes, "Sinful Man and the Civil Rights Dilemma," *Saints' Herald* 113 (15 October 1966): 690-691, 701–702; Lloyd R. Young, "A Perspective on Racism," *Saints' Herald* 116 (15 July 1968): 479, 492; Bob Smith, "The Churches and White Supremacy in America," *Saints' Herald* 116 (15 July 1968): 480–485, 496.
38. This theme is presented in Launius, *Invisible Saints*, 209–254.
39. "First Negro Is Ordained in Los Angeles," *Saints' Herald* 108 (24 July 1961): 717; Charlotte Graham, "A Reflection on World Conference: A Time of 'Firsts'," *Black Ministries Newsletter* (n.d.), copy in possession of author; "Stake Creates Inner-City Mission," *Saints' Herald* 118 (March 1971): 54; photograph in News section, *Saints' Herald* 117 (November 1970): 55; "A Prayer for Conference," *Saints Herald* 121 (May 1974): 333; photograph in News section, *Saints Herald* 122 (February 1975): 127; "Authella and Richard Hawks," *Saints' Herald* 127 (February 1980): 61–62.
40. These have been documented in Launius, *Invisible Saints*, 256–259.
41. For a discussion of Joseph Smith III's practicality see Launius, *Joseph Smith III*, especially 361–374.
42. Launius, *Invisible Saints*, 219–254.
43. Quoted in Love, "The First Presidency's Response to the Civil Rights Movement," 42.
44. Examples of instances in which church leaders sought to move the membership in directions for which little consensus existed included the Supreme Directional Control controversy of the 1920s and the New Curriculum controversy of the 1960s. On these see Paul M. Edwards, "Theocratic-Democracy: Philosopher-King in the Reorganization," in F. Mark McKiernan, Alma R. Blair, and Paul M. Edwards, eds., *The Restoration Movement: Essays in Mormon History* (Lawrence, Kansas: Coronado Press, 1973), 341–357, and William J. Knapp, "Professionalizing Religious Education in the Church: The 'New Curriculum Controversy,'" *John Whitmer Historical Association Journal* 2 (1982): 47–59.
45. Interview with Richard W. Hawks, East St. Louis, Illinois (15 September 1987); Apostle Alan Tyree, "Introducing the Black America Ministries Newsletter," *Black America Ministries Newsletter* 1 (1980): 1; Launius, *Invisible Saints*, 260–262.
46. Launius, *Invisible Saints*, 262–265.

The Issue of Homosexuality and the Priesthood Reexamined
Donald J. Breckon

Introduction

Sex and sexuality are often in the news. The centrality of sexuality in the lives of people, regardless of how it is expressed and the wide range of advocated expressions, results in ongoing controversy. Controversy exists because churches and governments often attempt to prescribe "correct behavior," which necessarily labels other behavior immoral or illegal.

The appropriateness of various sexual expressions is a major theme that runs through the scriptures and church history. Various aspects of this theme receive emphasis at different times. In the early 1990s, two of the most controversial sexual topics for churches and governments are abortion and homosexual behavior.

The purpose of this article is to reexamine the basis for the prevailing position on homosexuality. Scriptural and historic statements will be examined, as will contemporary views. Necessary questions will be raised for readers to consider: Does the official position of the Reorganized Church of Jesus Christ of Latter Day Saints on homosexual behavior need to be reexamined so as to be more relevant to the 1990s? Does the membership need to adjust its attitudes to more closely comply with the existing position of the church?

Terms and Issues Defined

Homosexuality will be used in this article to refer to individuals whose sexual orientation is toward members of the same sex. No attempt will be made to differentiate between males with an affinity toward males or females with an affinity toward females. Likewise, except where expressly indicated, no attempt will be made to differentiate between homosexual orientation and homosexual activity. Rather, homosexuality will be used collectively to refer to all these variations.

Current Issues

A recurring issue in the news recently is whether homosexuals should be ordained to the priesthood. Several Protestant denominations are struggling with policy matters on this subject. The United Church of Christ is among the most liberal in stating that a ministerial candidate's sexual orientation by itself is not grounds for denying ordination. This denomination has ordained homosexual ministers for many years.

However, George W. Cornell, religion writer for the Associated Press, reported in June 1991 that the Episcopal Church, Presbyterian Church, American Baptist Church, Southern Baptist Convention, United Methodist Church, and Evangelical Lutheran Church in America were all poised for heated battles. In the Episcopal and Presbyterian churches, study commissions recommended that their churches be open to ordaining homosexuals and also to developing rituals for blessing same-sex unions. All the above referenced denominations (except for the United Church of Christ) have ruled against admitting homosexuals to the priesthood.

Violation of state or federal laws is not at issue with these religious bodies: churches usually advocate obeying laws. However, what is done in private between consenting adults is at issue. Also an issue in several denominations is expressed sexual preference, even among nonpracticing individuals.

The RLDS Position on Homosexuality

The church's current position was adopted a decade ago (document adopted by Standing High Council, March 18, 1982). The position acknowledges that "the issue of homosexuality is demanding increased attention in Western society today."[1] (Certainly this is also true of the 1990s.) The statement continues to hold to the norm of heterosexuality and marriage. Interestingly, it acknowledges that an "anti-homosexual bias" still exists and that "homosexuals ... still are denied social justice."[2] It also affirms that homosexual and heterosexual Christians "are all brothers and sisters and share in common the love and grace of God."[3] Among the guidelines is that homosexuals who refrain "from homosexual acts should be fully accepted into the ongoing life of the congregation."[4]

Yet another guideline is, "The church should not admit a practicing homosexual to the priesthood....If a member of the priesthood admits to, or is found to be engaged in homosexual behavior, the administrative officer having jurisdiction should institute procedures for silencing."[5] The position, however, holds open the possibility of ordination for nonpracticing homosexuals.

Thus, the RLDS Church's position seems fairly liberal, at least as judged by the standards of 1982. Paraphrased, it states that practicing homosexuals should not be ordained and, if already ordained, should be silenced. Nonpracticing homosexuals, however, can be ordained and can continue to minister.

As with many church positions, this practice has not always been followed. This author has personal knowledge of practicing homosexuals being allowed to continue in ministerial roles. Conversely, others have not been ordained, and some have been encouraged to withdraw from the ministry.

The Basis for Antihomosexual Stances

There are three commonly used bases for antihomosexual stances. Each can be debated and argued persuasively on both sides. The three bases are: (1) It is expressly prohibited in the scriptures. (2) It is against nature and is contrary to natural law. (3) It is not a good church policy to select and elevate homosexuals to role-model status.

Scriptural Prohibition

Those who use the scriptures as the basis for being against homosexuality are adamant that the scriptures are clear. The usually quoted Leviticus 20:13 states, "If a man also lie with mankind, as he lieth with a woman, both of them have committed an abomination; they shall surely be put to death." Romans 1:24–27 makes passive reference to homosexuality as "vile," "unseemly," and "uncleanness," in the context of a treatise on glorifying God and to "dishonor their own bodies."

Those who challenge the scriptural prohibition of homosexuality might label Leviticus and Romans as the thinking of that day, for that society, and of those authors, questioning the relevancy for today's changed world. However, more importantly, they would charge that antihomosexuals have conveniently selected verses that support their point of view while also conveniently ignoring other instructions with which they disagree. A closer look at Leviticus will illustrate this concern.

First of all, Leviticus pertains directly to the duties of the Levitical priests, a more or less nonexistent priesthood today.[6] However, descendants of the tribe of Levi included Aaron, for whom the Aaronic priesthood was named, so the book of instructions could logically be construed as applying to the Aaronic priesthood, but not the Melchisedec priesthood. At one point in time, Levites were regarded as servants of priests, who cared for and transported the Ark.[7] Certainly that priesthood subgroup has passed out of existence. Significantly, the vast majority of the instruction directed to this currently nonexistent priesthood group is also irrelevant and is ignored by nearly all practicing Christians.

Chapters 1–7 of Leviticus deal with the rituals associated with sacrifices, all of which is ignored today. Chapters 8–10 provide instruction on installation of Levitical priests, all of which is ignored today. Chapters 11–15 provide instruction on cleanness and uncleanness, nearly all of which is ignored today. Chapter 16 discusses the Day of Atonement and is ignored today. Chapters 17–27 discuss the Holiness Code for Priests, most of which is ignored. Of the 823 verses in Leviticus, this author concludes that fewer than a dozen verses are even remotely used to evaluate behavioral standards for today's priesthood. A simple mathematical calculation indicates that timeless verses are 1 percent of the total. It is somewhat amazing that people can intentionally disobey 99 percent of the verses because they are irrelevant, and yet give blind obedience to the 1 percent with which they agree. Yet precisely that phenomenon occurs.

As further example, rules in Leviticus that prohibit divorce are largely ignored, as are the purification rites. For example, women are said to be ceremonially unclean for seven days after giving birth to a son and for fourteen days after giving birth to a daughter and are not allowed into the sanctuary until their waiting period is concluded with a burnt offering (Leviticus 12:2–6). Women are prohibited from church while menstruating (Leviticus 15:19–33). Men are prohibited from wearing clothes made of two different materials (Leviticus 19:19) or to shave their beards (Leviticus 19:27) *except* for leprosy (Leviticus 14:9) or to marry non-virgins (Leviticus 21:13). We ignore all these scriptures, and we do not refuse to ordain blind people or those with broken bones (Leviticus 21:18–21). Nor do we require an eye for an eye or a tooth for a tooth (Leviticus 24:20).

It is also interesting to note that there are problems when Leviticus 20:13 is examined closely. The scripture does not refer to non-practicing homosexuals but only to those who engage in homosexual activity, as well as being directed specifically to a currently nonexistent priesthood group. Moreover, it does not reference females engaged in homosexual activity. Moreover, most supporters of this scriptural injunction demand that only half of the scriptural injunction be followed, declining to put both offending parties to death. This author concludes after a careful analysis that the scripture is an opinion of that generation and does not necessarily apply today. Logic is defied by those who use this scripture as proof, while ignoring or considering irrelevant the other half of the verse and 99 percent of the other verses in Leviticus. Without commenting on the merits or demerits of homosexuality, this author concludes that Leviticus is irrelevant to today's social problems, including but not limited to homosexuality.

In a more general sense, readers must also remember that scriptures used in similar ways have been taken out of context to justify the Inquisition, the Holocaust, and slavery. Even more pertinent to this topic, scripture has been used to ban both women and black people from priesthood in some churches. Perhaps homosexuals are being similarly discriminated against at present, by those who conveniently ignore contextual issues and instead focus on literal interpretation and application.

Against Natural Law

The argument that homosexuality is against natural law assumes that sex is only for procreation. It also assumes "nature" is established and exists as a divine blueprint for the cosmos and that nature, therefore, dictates certain roles and patterns of behavior for people. Contrary to the scriptural prohibition, the logic for this position is more defensible. Homosexual activity does not produce offspring.

Another way of approaching this issue, however, is to believe that sexuality and sexual expression are pervasive influences that condition much of life, regardless of if, or how, expressed. Where logic and consistency break down, however, is that most people do not act as if sex is only for procreation. A side issue is that many species engage in some form of same-sex sexual activity at some time or other.

If one concedes that reproduction is only one of several appropriate sexual functions, then same-sex activity is harder to condemn, as long as that expression is in private between consenting adults. Stated differently, if it is an expression of love (rather than lust) as part of an ongoing, committed relationship, homosexuality is harder to consider as sinful because expressions of love are generally constructive, not destructive. This argument borders on the ethical stance of "the greatest good for the most people" and includes some aspects of situation ethics.

Perhaps the most troublesome emerging issue is that the cause of homosexuality may be biological. Researchers claim to have found a biological basis for homosexuality. The Salk Institute's Simon LeVay claims to have found an anatomical difference between the brains of homosexual and heterosexual men.[8]

Scientists are still debating whether brain structure differences are the cause of homosexual activity rather than the result. The relevant question of a physical cause is still unanswered, but it poses another question. If homosexual behavior has a physical cause, should it be the basis for excluding church members from the priesthood, any more than other physical factors like skin color or gender? An even more difficult question to answer is: Even if the behavior is learned, should it be the basis for exclusion from the priesthood any more than obesity, automobile speeding tickets, alcoholism, or other learned behaviors? A related question is: Does any form of sexual activity inhibit ability to provide ministry or, in fact, does any form of sexual expression between consenting adults enhance the ability to minister?

Poor Role Models

The issue of poor role models is relevant, primarily if ability to serve as a role model is the overriding criterion for priesthood, as contrasted to the ability to minister. A related question is whether that criterion is applied to other role model issues.

The Priesthood Guidelines that emerged after the revelation that called for the ordination of women but before implementation suggests that pastors should consider congregational needs and the ability of the candidate to minister.[9] That advice is still relevant today.

If a homosexual individual has so alienated himself or herself from the congregation that ministry will not be accepted, then ordination should not occur, regardless of the nature of the alienation. More specifically, if sexual orientation inhibits ability to offer good ministry, then ordination should not occur.

A related but unexplored question is whether homosexual priesthood members are better able to provide ministry to a growing homosexual subgroup. In a church of lay priesthood, one premise is that priesthood do not have to be all things to all people and that all members need to receive specialized ministry from those with whom a bond has been established. However, when the need for specific ministry matches the ability to provide ministry, sexual orientation should not logically preclude ordination. Perhaps the key issue is not whether potential priesthood has an appropriate sexual orientation but rather that they have "gifts and potential in their lives to match the needs for ministry among the people to whom they were sent."[10]

Consider the following: "The most basic and substantial evidence of a person's call is in the nature of the person. What are his or her priorities, desires, and interest in life?"[11] Should sexual orientation override other considerations usually thought to be more important? Moreover, should variations of heterosexual experience be similarly held up as an essential standard of practice?

The related issue is whether other role-model issues are also considered. Would obesity preclude ordination? How about a divorce? Would a never-married individual of marriageable age be considered? Would we preclude ordination from someone who went through bankruptcy? Would we preclude ordination to anyone who engaged in premarital sex? Would we preclude ordination of a nonpracticing alcoholic?

None of these characteristics are espoused as the norm that we want to hold up as a role model. On the other side, however, we do select current abstinence from alcohol and tobacco as precluding factors. The author suggests that these policies ought to be reexamined.

The ability to serve as a role model is an important consideration for all priesthood. However, the question of whether standards of practice related to sexuality should be the "litmus test" that makes ordination possible or impossible is still debatable, as is the question of whether the role-model issue is applied uniformly to other role-model criteria. It appears as if we are being selective, and thus discriminatory.

General Comments about Priesthood

Is it possible that the attempt to legislate "correct" sexual expression is a human initiative that has its basis in misunderstanding divine will? Is it possible that too much emphasis is put on sexuality and that society should downgrade that emphasis, simply letting nature take its course?

Is it possible that just as homosexuals are expected to unlearn their behavior or sublimate it, that they have an equal right to expect society to unlearn their discriminative attitudes toward their behavior? Should people who are prejudiced (against people of color, for example) be confronted with their prejudice so that they have an opportunity to change? Certainly the attitude that homosexuality is a sin is in itself a learned response and could be unlearned over time. Finally, is it possible that just as we have learned there are no gender-based reasons to prohibit women from the priesthood, that it is now time to conclude that sexual expression between consenting adults in private should no longer be the basis for barring them from the priesthood, even if they are of the same sex?

"Simply stated, priesthood is designed to facilitate the witnessing, revealing, redeeming ministry of the gospel."[12] Do we do God or each other a favor when we insist that those who facilitate the witnessing, revealing, and redeeming ministry of the gospel have a specific sexual orientation, or must conform to a socially acceptable standard of practice?

Further instruction to pastors processing priesthood calls is that: "Division over issues should never affect the love of persons or the recognition of their worth."[13] Perhaps we should no longer allow a division over this issue to affect priesthood calls.

Concluding Comments

Two questions were raised in the early paragraphs of this article: Does the official position of the Reorganized Church of Jesus Christ of Latter Day Saints on homosexual behavior need to be reexamined so as to be more relevant to the 1990s? Does the membership need to adjust its attitudes, in order to more closely comply with the existing position of the church? This author concludes that the answer to both questions is "Yes." It is the hope of this author that this article provides affirmative data to answer both questions.

Notes

1. Donald J. Breckon, *Matters of Life and Death* (Independence, Missouri: Herald House, 1987), 34.
2. Ibid.
3. Ibid.
4. Ibid., 35.
5. Ibid.
6. *The Interpreters Bible* Volume 2, ed. Nolan B. Harmon (Nashville, Tennessee: Abingdon-Cokesbury Press, 1953), 3.
7. *Harper's Bible Dictionary*, Paul J. Achtemeier, general editor (San Francisco: Harper SF, 1985), 558.
8. *The Chronicle of Higher Education* (September 4, 1991): A9.
9. *Guidelines for Priesthood: Ordination, Preparation, Continuing Commitment* (Independence, Missouri: Herald House, 1985), chapter 4.
10. Ibid., 25.
11. Ibid., 32.
12. Ibid., 25.
13. Ibid., 28.

IV
SCRIPTURE STUDIES

IV

SCRIPTURE STUDIES

Editor's Note

The enduring controversy of the Apostle Paul's views about women is studied by Keith Norman. One problem is the difficulty in determining just what Paul actually said. Secondly, and equally difficult to deal with, are the inconsistencies in what Paul probably did write. On one hand, Paul has been hailed as the champion of women's liberation while on the other hand he is credited with some of the most sexist passages in the Bible. Essential to understanding Paul's views is to have a clear understanding of the culture and the context of his writings.

Angela Crowell suggests that to understand the Book of Mormon's message more clearly and to appreciate the beauty of its ancient literary style, it must be viewed in relation to its poetic structure. She shares her original research on the Book of Mormon which covers a twelve-year period of study. This paper outlines her research on biblical Hebrew poetry, homiletics, and narrative midrash. While study in the Book of Mormon's Hebrew literary structure is in its infancy, the author feels it provides impor-

tant clues to understanding and appreciation of the book's message.

A unique and personal perspective on the Book of Mormon is provided in the article by Piotr Klafkowski. Having heard about the book as a youth, the interest and desire to know more about it has been with him for more than two decades. Through barriers of language, oppressive government, lack of study materials, and anti-Mormon feelings, he searches both the RLDS and LDS churches to discover those editions that most clearly present the message that he feels has a profound relevance today.

Another personal perspective is shared by Wayne Ham, this time about the Book of Abraham and why it has not attained the status of scripture within the RLDS Church. A brief history of the book shows it to be a product of the Kirtland experience with a rather brief acceptance, followed by a solid rejection by the Reorganization. To know its history, the questions it raises, and the way it has been responded to by the Reorganization is to know more of who we are as a people.

Let Your Women Keep Silent: Was Paul a Misogynist?*

Keith E. Norman

As feminist issues have emerged as a frequent topic of debate among biblical scholars and concerned Christians in recent years, the attitude of St. Paul with respect to women has become increasingly controversial. Because his epistles are the earliest documents produced by the Christian movement, as well as the fact that they form the largest single body of work by one author in the New Testament, Paul's influence on the formation of the new religion and its subsequent development has been enormous.

Determining just what Paul actually said or wrote, however, can be problematic. When I refer to "Paul" in this article, I confine myself to the epistles generally agreed by scholars to be authentic; i.e., directly written or dictated by the apostle. Several New Testament writings commonly attributed to Paul are now thought to have been written later, perhaps by devoted disciples who meant such attribution as a tribute. The seven undoubted Pauline epistles are: I Thessalonians, I and II Corinthians, Galatians, Philippians, Philemon and Romans. Scholars still debate the authenticity of the remaining epistles, which must be classed only secondarily as Pauline. A comfortable majority credits II Thessalonians as genuine, while the view on Colossians is about evenly divided. Most now reject the authenticity of Ephesians, and almost all agree that Paul did not write the pastoral

epistles: I and II Timothy and Titus. The view that Paul is not the author of Hebrews is virtually unanimous. Furthermore, Acts, in which Paul is prominently featured, was written some decades after his death and can thus give, at best, only indirect information about the apostle's thought and words. All of this is not to say that these writings are of questionable value, or that we should revise the canon to exclude any of them from scripture, only that we have assumed too much in attributing them to Paul. For purposes of this article, I will exclude the secondary epistles and Acts from consideration, confining myself to the recognized authentic or genuine epistles listed above.

Unfortunately, the apostle never sat down and wrote, "Now concerning females, here's what I think of them." When he mentions women, it is usually in the context of another subject: proper decorum, marriage, or simply within a personal greeting. Because Paul did not set down his views methodically, we need to take the clues he gives us and analyze them in context before constructing an overview.

The warning of II Peter 3:16 that Paul is something of a slippery character, and easily misunderstood, applies to his writings on women. Just when you think you have the apostle pegged, he turns around and says something clearly contradictory. If Emerson was right that "a foolish consistency is the hobgoblin of little minds," then Paul's place among the larger intellects of Western thought must be reckoned as secure.

On the one hand, Paul has been hailed as a champion of women's liberation, who

*A longer version of this article by the author was published as "The Writings of Paul about Women" in *Women of Wisdom & Knowledge* (Salt Lake City, Utah: Deseret Books, 1990), 202–221. Used by permission.

advocated the complete abolishment of distinction between the sexes. In one of his earlier epistles, Galatians (chapter 3) he wrote, in verse 28, of those who had been baptized, "...there is neither male nor female; for ye are all one in Christ Jesus." At the other extreme, I Timothy 2:11–13, he is credited with one of the most blatantly sexist put-downs in the Bible: "Let the women learn in silence with all subjection. For I suffer not a woman to teach, nor to usurp authority over the man, but to be in silence. For Adam was first formed, then Eve." But, as we noted, I Timothy can no longer be ascribed to Paul, however sincere the disciple was who "dedicated" the epistle in his honor.

Nevertheless, Paul is not so easily exonerated from the charge of sexism. In fact, the passage from I Timothy 2 was probably based on, or inspired by, a passage from one of the genuine epistles, I Corinthians 14:34–35: "Let your women keep silence in the churches; for it is not permitted unto them to rule, but to be under obedience, as also saith the law. And if they will learn any thing, let them ask their husbands at home; for it is a shame for women to rule in the church." Generations of male churchgoers over the age of fifteen have diligently underlined this passage in red in their Bibles! It has been argued[1] that these two verses in I Corinthians are not from Paul, but that they were inserted by a later editor, perhaps the same disciple who wrote I Timothy. Unfortunately, because there is absolutely no manuscript evidence to support this theory of a later interpolation, most scholars accept the verses as genuine. Earlier in the same epistle (11:3–10), Paul had pointed out that "the head of the woman is the man," (i.e., her husband), and then exhorted women to cover their heads when praying or prophesying in church, because woman was made from man and created for his glory, not the other way around. Apart from the obvious contradiction of Paul approving of prayer and prophecy by women in church as long as they are dressed for it, and then telling them to keep quiet until they get home, one can hardly credit Paul with advocating full equality of the sexes in church life.

Nevertheless, set against the background of an unashamedly sexist patriarchal society arising from both Jewish and Greco-Roman traditions, Paul stands out as much more than a moderate. His advice on marital relations in I Corinthians 7 tends to focus on equal rights and duties to a surprising degree. This chapter begins a section in which Paul is responding to questions or assertions put to him by the Corinthian church. The first question (verse 1b) is often read erroneously as Paul's opening statement, rather than as the question he is dealing with. Here we should note that the Greek word most commonly translated as "woman" in Paul's writings, *gune*, can mean either "wife" or "woman," and the context here seems to indicate the former connotation. Paraphrasing their proposal, what the Corinthians were asking was, "It's better for a man to abstain from sex with his wife, isn't it?"

Why such a question? Paul's views on the imminence of the end of the world (I Thessalonians 4:15; I Corinthians 7:29 and 15:51–52) and the transformation of life in Christ were taken up enthusiastically by some of the Corinthian saints, who wanted to live the life of the Spirit here and now. From Paul's comments, we can infer that these earnest disciples understood they had already attained the angelic state which would supersede marriage (cf. Luke 20:35), making sex obsolete. That women were the most prominent and probably also the most numerous among this group of enthusiasts seems apparent from the discussion of problems in chapters 7, 11, and 14.[2] If, as Paul said, there is neither male nor female in

Christ (Galatians 3:28), why, these women were apparently asking, should we be required to submit to our husbands' carnal demands? Anyone who is or has ever been married will easily imagine the level of tension that existed in the church at Corinth, particularly in view of the other extreme evident in chapters 5 and 6, where Paul refutes some—perhaps the frustrated husbands of these same women—who were arguing that because all things are lawful to the Christian, there was nothing wrong with visiting prostitutes!

Hold it! Paul said, Let's not get carried away. Each husband (vss. 2f, supplying the alternative reading of *andros*) should stick with his own wife and vice versa; otherwise the temptation to immorality will be too strong. Note how balanced the duties that follow between the husband and the wife are. The KJV's peculiar phrase "due benevolence" here in verse 3 is based on an obsolete Greek text. Earlier and better manuscripts correct this to read literally "debt," what is owned—in this context, to give or render the spouse's conjugal rights; in plain language, sex. Both partners owe this debt; neither has exclusive control over his or her own body. Verse 5 specifies the only exception to normative sexual union within marriage allowed by Paul, when both agree to devote themselves to prayer for a short time. This was apparently a concession to those who could not get over the idea that sexual intercourse involved cultic impurity (Leviticus 15:18) and would, therefore, hinder prayer. Paul, who resisted applying the strictures of the cultic law to gentile converts, refused (vs. 6) to make such abstention mandatory and further warned couples not to prolong their celibate prayer vigils to the point that they became self-defeating.[3]

Paul's even-handed advice on mutual obligations and rights within marriage was certainly at odds with his male-oriented Jewish heritage, and this tone continues when he speaks of divorce in verses 10–11: in accordance with what Jesus ("the Lord") had taught, the husband had no more right to initiate divorce than did the wife.

But what of mixed marriages—a Christian yoked to a nonbeliever? Here in the absence of explicit guidance handed down from Jesus, Paul must give his own opinion ("to the rest speak I, not the Lord"—vss. 12–16): the believer, whether it happens to be the husband or the wife, should not dissolve the marriage just because the spouse is not a believer. "For the unbelieving husband (vs. 14) is sanctified by the wife, and the unbelieving wife is sanctified by the husband." The efficacy of the faith and faithfulness of a wife in sanctifying her unbelieving spouse was just as great as that of a believing male with regard to his wife who had not seen the light. Similarly, in verse 15, the husband in such a marriage should no more force his spouse to remain, if she wished to end the marriage, than should a wife expect to control her husband so inclined; neither is bound. Such equal consideration was hardly the norm in Paul's culture[4], and the fact that this counsel comes from his own authority, rather than from scripture or from the authorities in Jerusalem, is all the more telling.

Paul seems to value the service of female missionaries equally with that of his own sex when he commends the unmarried who are devoted to the Lord's work (vss. 32–35). Unmarried disciples are undistracted from holy endeavors by the worry of pleasing a spouse. While Hellenistic philosophers of Paul's era often decried the burdens of marriage, they usually pinpointed women as the disturbers of intellectual tranquility. Paul's concern, by contrast, is to free believers, male or female, to wholeheartedly fulfill their missions.[5]

If we could end I Corinthians right here,

and add only Galatians to the book of St. Paul, we could perhaps portray him as the apostle, if not of feminism, at least of equal status of the sexes. But from here on things get a bit more sticky. Continuing on to verse 36, Paul lapses into talking about marriageable women as though they were the property of their fathers (or fiancés—it is not entirely clear whom he is addressing). He can marry her off or not, as he chooses, Paul says (vs. 38). Of course the subject here is what to do with the little time remaining before the imminent end of the world, not how to achieve social justice. Verse 39 addresses the widow no longer bound to her late husband—she at least does have control over whether or not she will remarry. Neither here nor in Romans 7:2–3, where Paul repeats the principle in the context of explaining the limits of the Law of Moses, does he mention a reciprocal relation or obligation on the part of the male. The subordination of the wife is taken for granted, as we would expect given the Jewish background. Similarly, in I Thessalonians 4:4, Paul speaks to the brethren of "possessing a vessel"—by which he means a wife. This was "a common idiom in both Hebrew and Greek usage, reflecting the view of both cultures that the wife passed into her husband's possession at marriage."[6] Again, we should not make too much of this in light of the context, which is sexual morality, not patriarchy or women's lib. But it is precisely the unconscious attitudes revealed at the periphery of an argument that betray cultural biases. Paul had to *work* at overcoming his upbringing.

Returning to I Corinthians 7, although Paul's advice on marital relationships on the whole pushes for a more balanced treatment, we note in 1b that the starting point is from a male perspective: whether or not it is good for man to touch his wife. Furthermore, his insistence that only the unbeliev-ing partner could exercise the divorce option presented greater difficulties for women than men, since the legal prerogative to control the religious practices of members of the household remained the man's. Thus, in a pattern still familiar today, a female believer from a part-member family could be seriously hampered in her religious and social freedom.[7]

Further along in I Corinthians we seem to confront even clearer indications that Paul had not cast off the sexism of his culture to the extent that his ideals would apparently warrant. It is difficult to read chapter 11 without seeing a fairly blatant underlying commitment to a patriarchal subjection of women. Verse 3 begins an argument for women to keep their heads covered when they pray or prophesy in church. Now this cuts both ways, because it clearly shows that women participated in the worship of the Corinthian church, and Paul does not, at least not yet, voice any objection to their doing so. Rather, his concern is only that they dress appropriately, with a head covering of some sort, to distinguish them clearly from the men. With this rather curious argument, the context is critical.

The traditional view of chapter 11 is that women were being insubordinate to their husbands due to their understanding of freedom in Christ. Thus Paul was putting them in their proper place with the head covering as a symbol of subordination. But Gordon Fee, in his exhaustive commentary on I Corinthians, argues that, as with chapter 7, Paul is confronting a group of women who feel they are ready to live the higher law, and who want to abolish all distinctions between the sexes *now!*[8] If there is neither male nor female in Christ, we imagine them saying, why should we be required to dress differently? Paul's answer indicates that they were going too far too soon, and the indications are that he was motivated by missionary

150

concerns. Unkempt hair in women was a sign of religious frenzy among Greco-Romans and could mark an adulteress in Jewish culture.[9] To behave in the present reality as though gender no longer mattered could be seen as disgraceful or scandalous by potential converts, and Paul's concern above all was to avoid offending anyone unnecessarily, as we see in I Corinthians 9:19–22; 10:32–33. He sums up his rather convoluted argument for modest female head attire by asserting in verses 14–15 of chapter 11 that even nature (read "custom") itself teaches us that men should have short hair and women long. Flaunting your freedom in Christ to the point of scandal is to pervert it. "If any man seem to be [i.e., is disposed to be] contentious" on this point, Paul adds in verse 16, "we have [or recognize] no such custom [or practice], neither [do] [any of] the [other] churches of God."

If this analysis is correct—that Paul was not in fundamental disagreement with these free spirits, but just wanted them to be more conscious of the effect they were having on others—why does the apostle go to such lengths to shore up his instruction with such sexist-sounding arguments?

At first reading, it does seem that a Jewish belief in the inferiority of women, adduced from the Genesis 2 creation account which Paul cites, underlies the whole discussion.[10] But this is to read modern cultural and linguistic assumptions into the text. Take the word "head" in verse 3: obviously, a double meaning is intended here, but it is not the same pun we might assume in English. The Greek kephale does not connote the idea of authority or rulership so much as that of source; in this context, the source of life, as verses 8 and 12 indicate. "Thus," according to Fee, "Paul's concern is not hierarchical (who has authority over whom), but relational....Indeed, he says nothing about man's authority; his concern

with the woman is being the man's glory, the one without whom he is not complete (vss. 7c–9). To blur that relationship is to bring shame on her 'head;'" i.e., her husband.[11]

In Paul's understanding, a man, as the image and glory of God, ought to leave his head uncovered (vs. 7). Just why disregarding this stricture would dishonor God is unclear to us; it appears to be a cultural bias. We are reminded that men today remove their hats as a token of reverence during prayer or the Pledge of Allegiance, but that is hardly the same thing. The crucial question, however, is why Paul thought it was important to maintain the visible distinction between the sexes in worship. Paul does not mean to imply, when he alludes (vs. 7) to the creation of humanity in the image of God (in Genesis 1:26–28), that woman is not included in that divine image, but he does appear to blend the first creation account with that in Genesis 2, where the man is created first and the woman is taken out of his side afterward. Nevertheless, Paul's focus is on man's relationship to his creator; man brings out the glory of God. Likewise, woman, created from and for man as the only living being suitable to be his companion, is his glory. Because man is the source (head) of woman and she is his glory, to disregard this visible mark of distinction, the head covering, when praying and prophesying, is to bring shame on him by negating the appropriate male/female relationship still a reality in the present age.[12] Thus, when Paul reminds us, in verses 11 and 12, that men and women are interdependent, he is not switching gears but expanding on the meaning of the relationship he has been talking about all along. These verses show that 8 and 9 are not arguments but subjection: the fact that woman was created "for man's sake" does not entail male dominion, but signifies that man without woman is incomplete, missing something vital. "She is not thereby subordinate to him, but necessary for him."[13]

In verse 11, the King James version's translation of *choris* as "without" can be misleading. More frequently, *choris* is used in the sense of "different from," "unlike," "of another kind," Thus, Elisabeth Schüssler Fiorenza translates verse 11: "In the Lord, woman is not different from man nor man from woman."[14] This variation on Paul's "there is neither male nor female in Christ" certainly fits the context better, leading more logically into verse 12: since both are from God, neither man nor woman has ultimate priority. The point that men and women are "of the same kind" also fits nicely with the allusion to Genesis 2. Of all created beings, woman is the only suitable companion to man (Genesis 2:18–24); as we would put it, they are the same species.

Verse 10 is perhaps the most puzzling and deserves somewhat closer scrutiny. The KJV has Paul telling women that they should have "power on their heads;" literally, "authority" is a better rendering of εξουσια (*exousia*). Generally, this has been taken to refer to the head covering of which Paul has been speaking, and some later manuscripts amend the word to καλυμμα (*kalumma*), a veil. More likely, "authority" should be taken in a more literal fashion, as freedom or the right to choose. In other words, women, particularly the ones who are causing problems in Corinth, should indeed take authority upon themselves, but responsibly, by covering their heads with decorum, so as to honor their relationship to their husbands and to God.

How, then, does the phrase "because of the angels" fit in? Possibly there is some reference to tempting or offending angelic beings who watch over them,[15] but it seems more likely that Paul alludes to their eagerness to live "as the angels" here and now.[16] Note how smoothly this leads into verse 11:

Okay, Paul concedes, you should exercise your freedom as the angels, but that does not make you independent of your husbands. All things are from God, and that includes your relationship as men and women. In the final analysis, certainty about the meaning of verse 10 eludes us, but the idea of exercising angelic or spiritual freedom responsibly seems to fit Paul's overall argument best.

We turn now to chapter 14, the notorious "silence in church" passage. As we noted, a number of scholars have argued, on the basis of its inconsistency with most, or at least the best, of the rest of Paul, that these two verses, 34 and 35, are not genuine—they were added by a later editor. But since every early manuscript includes these verses, such carping looks suspiciously like those who object are picking what they like, what they would want Paul to say, and throwing out the rest. The command to silence on the part of women is undeniably inconsistent with chapter 11, where Paul makes absolutely no suggestion that women who pray or prophesy in church should stop, but inconsistency in itself does not rule out a single author. Even apostles can have off days.

But why would Paul tell the Corinthians something so obviously at odds with his earlier counsel and, we may venture, rather out of character for him? He even appeals (at the end of verse 34) to the Law of Moses, which elsewhere he dismisses as irrelevant to the believer "in Christ." Here again, the context goes a long way toward explaining this seeming anomaly. Chapters 12 through 14 are concerned with a situation in which certain of the Corinthian saints are flaunting their spiritual gifts and thereby claiming superiority to those less demonstrably spiritual. Chapter 14 addresses those who are speaking in tongues, a form of ecstatic utterance in an unknown language, which impressed its hearers as a most dramatic manifestation of the Spirit. But Paul decries such activity as meaningless babbling meant only to impress, not to edify. In the absence of an interpreter, he admonishes, those possessed with such a spirit should restrain themselves. God is not the author of confusion, he contends in verse 33, but of peace. We can easily picture Paul as being quite upset over these vain-glorious saints. If we can conjecture that the persons involved consisted of or included the same group of overly eager women in Corinth who considered themselves beyond the legalisms and strictures of conventional society, then the following outburst on Paul's part is quite understandable. To paraphrase, "If that's the way these women are going to act, let them just keep quiet altogether in church. They can stay subordinate to their husbands, just as the law says they should. If they must talk, let them do it at home; their husbands can tell them what is going on. The way these women carry on in church is shameful!" Let us admit that the sentiment is extreme: Paul overreacted, falling back on the marital ethos of his Jewish-rabbinic upbringing and the Greco-Roman sentiment against public demonstrations and speeches by matrons.[17] Our conjecture is strengthened by I Corinthians 12:13, which essentially repeats the baptismal formula of Galatians 3:28: in [the body of] Christ we are neither Jew nor Gentile, bond nor free. But the "male nor female" pair is conspicuously omitted in this context; the zealous Corinthian women needed no reinforcement on that score.

While we cannot be entirely sure just which woman Paul had in mind in the chapter 14 passage, it is clear he is addressing an unusual situation in Corinth. Just as competitive prophets and those possessed with tongues were told to control themselves, certain married women—perhaps those same ones who wished to negate their marriages and dress like men—were told to keep quiet in the public assembly. As verse 40 shows, Paul's main concern was that "all things be done decently and in order." Again, Paul's missionary zeal probably underlies this passage. He may well have been upset with the prospect of alienating prospective converts or giving ammunition to critics, who were prone to confuse Christians with one or another of the licentious mystery cults of the time. Such fanatical groups were viewed as foreign and subversive of public order and morality, in part because they blurred sex roles.

Having now covered what Paul said about women, what can we learn further of how he interacted with them? Here again, we do not have a lot from the authentic epistles, but what we have is quite tantalizing. In Philippians 4 Paul mentions two women, Euodia and Syntyche, whom he describes in verses 2–3 as having labored side by side with him and his companion Clement. Apparently these women had a falling out with each other, and the apostle entreats an unnamed intercessor to try to reconcile them. Because Paul's labors were focused so much on missionary work, we can fairly surmise that these two were companion laborers in the field. Paul speaks of them with no hint that their service was any less valuable than that of Clement and himself; they are among those whose names are inscribed in the book of life. Certainly, as his experience with Barnabas shows,[18] Paul could understand a serious disagreement between missionary companions.

Similar to Euodia and Syntyche, in Romans 16:3–4 Paul refers to Priscilla, along with her husband, as "my helpers in Christ Jesus." But this chapter contains even more striking references to women's roles in the church, and they are mentioned by Paul with obvious approval. In verses 1–2 he describes

Phoebe as a *diakonos*, literally, a "deaconess," and he urges the Christians in Rome to assist in whatever effort she engages, implying that she had been given an official capacity, and a rather wide-ranging one at that. But the real bombshell comes in verse 7. In a list of notable and beloved people in Rome deserving special salutation, Paul includes Junia as someone "of note among the apostles," who had also been imprisoned with him.[19] Before we get too excited about this situation, we need to remind ourselves that Paul's writings are the very earliest we have from the new Christian movement, and they reflect an organization in which hierarchy, titles, and priesthood offices were not yet formalized. "Apostle," in its root meaning from the Greek verb *apostello*, denotes someone who is sent out in a representative capacity, as an ambassador. *Diakonos* is literally one who ministers to the needs of others; thus the KJV rendering of "servant." It is not hard to see how these descriptive words took on the status of specialized titles, but with Paul, we are still in the formative period, when status in the ministry was more on the basis of manifestations of the Spirit than of hierarchical appointment. However, the context of Paul's usage of these terms makes it clear that women could be important functionaries in the early church. As one prominent scholar has pointed out, referring to Romans 16:1, since Phoebe apparently had a permanent and recognized ministry, "one may at least see an early stage of what later became the ecclesiastical office."[20]

Having now surveyed the passages referring to women which can be confidently ascribed to Paul, what are we to conclude about his attitude to women? The apparent discrepancy in his remarks has resulted in the standard view that Paul's nonsexist ideals, capsulized in Galatians 3:28 ("there is neither male nor female in Christ"), were focused on the future kingdom of God, when sex would be abolished and his own preference for celibacy normalized, but that for the present, in the real world, the sexual or gender roles of the culture prevailed and should be obeyed. In this view Galatians 3:28 is an aberration, not representative of Paul's day-to-day dealings with women or his *real* attitude toward them. Our analysis indicates that such a reading of Paul is seriously flawed; on the contrary, closely considered in context, the epistles indicate that Paul went to considerable lengths to inculcate the ideal stated in Galatians into church life, and that it is the statement at the other extreme, I Corinthians 14:34–35 ("women keep silence in the churches"), that is the aberration.

But the one passage we still need to subject to careful scrutiny is, in fact, Galatians 3:28. Just what *did* Paul mean by his assertion that male and female become one in Christ? The standard view, that Paul anticipated the sexless condition to come in heaven, is based on a similar interpretation of Jesus' statement that there will be no marriage in the resurrection.[21] Whether Paul was familiar with this saying is questionable in itself, but there is certainly more going on here.

Galatians is a tract justifying the universal applicability of the gospel, the power of God unto salvation (Romans 1:16), against the so-called "Judaizers," those who insisted that no one could be saved who did not first become a Jew and submit to the demands of the Law of Moses. Paul's argument is that the distinctions made under the law are no longer applicable; through faith and baptism, Christ has freed us from the bonds of the law and made us his. The old divisions do not matter anymore; they have ceased to count. Unlike circumcision, the former sign of the covenant, which was for Jewish males only, the new sign, baptism and the clothing

154

donned afterward as a token of putting on Christ, is for all.[22] Race is irrelevant to salvation, as is social standing, as is gender: all are equally the children of God by virtue of their faith in Christ Jesus. Correctly understood, Paul is not hinting here that we will all be neutered in the Resurrection. What he *is* saying is that you do not have to be a male to be saved, or a Jew, or a free person.

We have seen that working out the practical applications of this theological equality presented challenges to Paul, particularly among the Corinthian saints, some of whom took it seriously indeed, and wanted to abolish gender distinctions entirely. In response, Paul delineated the roles and relation-ships between men and women appropriate to his time and culture, specifying behavior that would not give needless offense to others. In that context, Paul's attitude to women is remarkably liberal. Only by isolating selected pronouncements from their cultural setting and missionary motivation can he be cast as a misogynist. For Paul, Christ Jesus makes birth, social standing, and gender ultimately irrelevant. He proclaimed the liberating effect of the gospel from every kind of bondage, and our analysis shows that he struggled to make his vision a reality with respect to women. In some ways, we have yet to catch up to him.

Notes

1. See Hans Conzelmann, *Der Erste Brief an die Korinther* (Gottingen, Germany: Vandenhoeck & Ruprecht, 1969), 290. See also Gordon D. Fee, *The First Epistle to the Corinthians* (Grand Rapids, Michigan: W. B. Eerdmans, 1987), 699; and Jerome Murphy-O'Connor, *I Corinthians* (Wilmington, Delaware: Michael Glazier, 1979), 133.

2. See Robin Scroggs, "Paul and the Eschatological Woman," *Journal of the American Academy of Religion* 40, no. 3 (September 1972): 283–303; and Fee, 269f.

3. See O. Larry Yarbrough, *Not Like the Gentiles: Marriage Rules in the Letters of Paul* (Atlanta: Scholars Press, 1985), 99–101.

4. Wayne A. Meeks, "The Image of the Androgyne: Some Uses of a Symbol in Earliest Christianity," *History of Religions* 13 (1974): 1991.

5. Yarbrough, 106. We might note that many commentators have taken Paul's advice here as the voice of experience, inferring that Paul had been previously married, although apparently he now enjoyed celibacy as a kind of spiritual gift.

6. Wayne A. Meeks, *The First Urban Christians: The Social World of the Apostle Paul* (New Haven and London: Yale University Press, 1983), 23–25. The usage is similar to that in I Corinthians 7:2.

7. Elisabeth Schüssler Giorenza, "I Corinthians," in James L. Mays, ed., Harper's Bible Commentary (San Francisco: Harper SF, 1988), 1177.

8. Fee, 497ff.

9. Fiorenza, 1183.

10. James L. Price, "The First Letter of Paul to the Corinthians," in Charles M. Laymon, ed., Acts and Paul's Letters (Nashville, Tennessee: Abingdon Press, 1983), 214.

11. Fee, 503–504.

12. Ibid., 518.

13. Ibid., 517.

14. Quoted by Yarbrough, 116. Taken from Elisabeth Schüssler Fiorenza, *In Memory of Her: A Feminist Theological Reconstruction of Christian Origins* (New York: Crossroads, 1983), 229.

15. Genesis 6:2–4 is often cited as a reference point; see also Joseph A. Fitzmyer, "A Feature of Qumran Angelology and the Angels of I Corinthians 11:10," in *Essays on the Semitic Background of the New Testament* (Missoula, Montana: University of Montana Scholars Press, 1974), 187–204.

16. Fee, 522.

17. Fiorenza, 1186.

18. Acts 15:36–40.

19. Some manuscripts read "Junias," the masculine form of the name, but this is most likely an emendation by a later scribe who was bothered by the idea of a female apostle.

20. Ernst Käsemann, Commentary on Romans, translated by Geoffrey W. Bromiley (Grand Rapids, Michigan: W. B. Eerdmans, 1980), 411.

21. Luke 20:35–36. On the historical development of celibacy as the ideal spiritual state Elaine H. Pagels, *Adam, Eve and the Serpent* (New York: Random House, 1988), esp. 13–1; 28–31; 78–97, 140–144.

22. William Baird, "Galatians," in *Harper's Bible Dictionary*, 1208.

The Hebrew Literary Structure of the Book of Mormon

Angela M. Crowell

This article will examine biblical Hebrew poetic structure and midrash (ancient Jewish interpretation and commentary) that have been identified in the Book of Mormon. Also, Isaiah variants will be commented upon.

Biblical Hebrew Poetry

The Society of Biblical Literature (SBL) is composed of 5,000 professors, Jewish and Christian, from universities and seminaries throughout the world. Each year biblical scholars present their latest research in the field of biblical Hebrew poetry at the society's annual meeting. This topic continues to be of current interest in biblical circles, and as new research findings are brought forth, they enlarge our understanding of the Hebrew Bible.

Knowledge of biblical poetry helps us to see the Hebraic literary structure found in the Book of Mormon. The poetic structures in the book are equal to and, in some cases, surpass the examples found in the Bible.

To understand the Book of Mormon's message more clearly and appreciate the beauty of its ancient literary style, it must be viewed in relation to its poetic structure.

In George Buchanan Gray's book, *The Forms of Hebrew Poetry*, the author states that in the past, failure to understand the structure of Hebrew poetry has "frequently led to misinterpretation of Scripture."[1] An understanding of the forms of Hebrew poetry becomes a valuable, if not necessary, means to correct interpretation.

David Noel Freedman points out in his book, *Pottery, Poetry, and Prophecy*, that "perhaps a quarter to a third of the Hebrew Bible, must be reckoned as poetry or poetic in character." In the ancient Near East, "poetry [was] the traditional means of expressing and transmitting religious experience."[2]

Freedman states that while the "word of God is predominantly [written down in] the prose narrative...the original medium was poetry...a product of the divine spirit." He reiterates "that from the beginnings of prophecy in Israel at least until the exile, poetry was the central medium of prophecy...in subsequent centuries the revival of prophecy brought with it a revival of poetry."[3]

Wilfred Watson states in his book, *Classical Hebrew Poetry*, that:

[S]ince the discovery of poetic texts in Ugaritic [dating to about about 1400 B.C.] and Akkadian [written 1000 B.C. to 800 B.C.]...certain techniques of poetry...[can now] be recognised in Hebrew. This knowledge is still expanding: [and] at the same time...these techniques are becoming better understood....[4]

Since 1952 modern versions of the Bible have begun to utilize indented lines to clearly identify poetry. Hebrew poetry, like Akkadian, Egyptian, and Chinese, has no rhyme.

This article will cite a small number of examples of different kinds of Hebrew poetry that have been identified by Hebrew scholars. The study of Hebrew poetry is still an open field, and many Hebrew scholars worldwide continue to research in this area. This activity will, in time, bring more light to our present understanding.

Parallelism

While traditional English poetry is characterized by rhyme and meter, Hebrew poetry differs in that its most distinctive feature is a parallel structure of words or lines that relate to each other. Parallelism occurs when two or more lines correspond to each other in both meaning and structure.

It is remarkable that parallelism can be retained almost unimpaired in a translation. Ancient Hebrew poets used many techniques for variation and had lists of established word pairs (i.e., night/day, heaven/earth) to choose from. These word pairs were handed down from one generation to another and were usually used in the same order.

The following examples compare various kinds of poetry identified in the Bible and the Book of Mormon.

Synonymous Parallelism

This type of parallelism occurs when "the second line of a couplet [two-line unit] repeats the thought of the first line in different words"[5] (emphasis added here and in all following examples). The highlighted words illustrate the synonymous word pairs.

Old Testament
O *magnify* the LORD with me,
and let us *exalt* his name together.
—Psalm 34:3 KJV (King James Version)

Book of Mormon
For his *soul* did rejoice,
and his whole *heart* was filled.
—I Nephi 1:14

Antithetic Parallelism

This kind of parallelism occurs when the second line of a verse contrasts or opposes the first line.

Old Testament
For the LORD watches over the way of
the *righteous*,
but the way of the *wicked* will perish.
—Psalm 1:6 NIV (New International Version)

Book of Mormon
Ye are *swift* to do iniquity,
but *slow* to remember the Lord your God.
—I Nephi 5:144

Alternating Parallelism

This type occurs when the first and third lines and the second and fourth lines, etc. correEspond or balance each other with an ABA'B' pattern. (Scholars use an identification system of capital letters and accent marks to identify parallel words, phrases, or lines that correspond to each other.) This type of parallelism has been identified sixty-four times in Psalms, and 135 in the Prophets.[6] There are also numerous examples in the Book of Mormon.

Old Testament
A The **LORD** is my light and my salvation;
  B whom shall I *fear*?
A' The LORD is the strength of my life;
  B' of whom shall I be *afraid*?
—Psalm 27:1 KJV

Book of Mormon
A And the gospel of **Jesus Christ** shall be
    declared among them;
  B Wherefore, they shall be restored unto the
    knowledge of their *fathers*,
A' And also to the knowledge of **Jesus Christ,**
  B' which was had among their *fathers*.
—II Nephi 12:82

An extension of this pattern is (ABCA'B'C'):

Old Testament
A Open to me the *gates of righteousness*;
  B I shall *enter through* them,
    C I shall give *thanks* to the LORD.
A' This is the *gate of the LORD*;
  B' The righteous will *enter through* it.
    C' I shall give *thanks* to Thee, for Thou hast
      answered me;
    and Thou hast become my salvation.
—Psalm 118:19–21 NASB (New American
Standard Bible)

Book of Mormon
A And he that shall breathe out wrath
      and strifes against the *work of the Lord,*
    B and against the *covenant* people of the Lord,
      C who are the *house of Israel*, and shall say,
A' We will destroy the *work of the Lord,*
    B' and the Lord will not remember his *covenant*
      C' which he hath made unto the *house of
        Israel*...
—Mormon 4:26

Staircase Parallelism

This type of parallelism repeats one or more words and advances the thought in successive lines, step by step to a climactic conclusion.

Old Testament
Ascribe to the LORD,
O mighty ones,
Ascribe to the LORD
glory and strength.
Ascribe to the LORD
the glory due his name;
Worship the LORD
in the splendor of his holiness.
—Psalm 29:1 NIV

Book of Mormon
Believe in God;
Believe that he is,
and that he created all things
both in heaven and earth;
Believe that he has all wisdom,
and all power,
both in heaven and in earth;
Believe that man doth not comprehend all things
which the Lord can comprehend.
And again:
Believe that ye must repent of your sins
and forsake them,
and humble yourselves before God;
and ask in sincerity of heart
that he would forgive you:
And now, if you believe all these things,
see that ye do them.
—Mosiah 2:13–17

ABCB Parallelism

In 1963 Stanley Gevirtz first identified this pattern of nouns or verbs, etc. in a parallel relationship. The second and fourth words in this sequence result in an ABCB pattern[7] (i.e., justice, righteousness, salvation, righteousness). Later in 1971 and 1982 scholars identified further examples, bringing the total to thirty-two examples located in the Old Testament.[8]

Old Testament
Thus says the LORD,
A Preserve **justice**,
B and do **righteousness**,
C for my **salvation** is about to come
B And my **righteousness** to be revealed.
—Isaiah 56:1 NASB

Book of Mormon
A Therefore come and be baptized unto
repentance,
B that ye may be washed from your **sins**,
C that ye may have **faith** on the Lamb of God,
B who taketh away the **sins** of the world.
—Alma 5:25

Inverted Parallelism or Chiastic Structure

A chiastic verse has a sequence of words in the first clause reversed in sequence in the second clause. Simple chiastic sentences have a word pattern of ABB′A′ (i.e., day, night, night, day).

Old Testament
He shall **open** and none shall **shut**;
and he shall **shut**, and none shall **open**.
—Isaiah 22:22 KJV

Book of Mormon
The **soul** shall be restored to the **body**,
and the **body** to the **soul**;
—Alma 19:58

Longer structures have a ABCB′A′ or ABCC′B′A′ etc. with a center point emphasized. These structures cover paragraphs, chapters, and books with the first line corresponding to the last line and the second line to the next to last line, etc.

The following example illustrates a center point, the main point the author wishes to emphasize.

Old Testament
A Then he shall take the **cedar wood**,
and the **hyssop**, and the **scarlet string**,
B with the **live bird**,
C and dip them in **the blood of**
the slain bird, as well as
in the running water,
D and **sprinkle* the house** seven times.
D′ He shall thus **cleanse the house**
C′ with **the blood of the bird**,
and **with the running water**,
B′ along with the **live bird**
A′ and with the **cedar wood** and with the
hyssop and with the **scarlet string**.
—Leviticus 14:51–52 NASB

---

*The Hebrew word for sprinkle here is *nazah*, which means sprinkling to purify or cleanse.

Book of Mormon

A Yea, having a great **knowledge**,
  of the goodness and the mysteries of God,
  B therefore, I make a **record** of my
    proceedings in my days;
    C yea, I make a record in the **language**
      of my father,
      D **which consists of the learning of the**
        Jews
    C' and the **language** of the Egyptians.
  B' And I know that the **record**
    which I make is true;
    and I make it with mine own hand;
A' and I make it according to my **knowledge**.

—I Nephi 1:1–2

Chiasms with Matching Center Terms with First and Last Lines

In 1943 Nils Lund identified a type of chiasm commonly used in which the center contains a single line with parallel or identical terms in the first and last lines.[9]

New Testament

A For even as the **body** is one
  B And yet has _many_ members,
    C And all the members of the **body**,
  B' Though they are _many_,
A' Are one **body**, so also is Christ.

—I Corinthians 12:12 NASB

This type of chiasm is also in the Book of Mormon.

Book of Mormon

A And now it came to pass that when Jesus
  had **expounded** all the scriptures in one,
  B which they had _written_,
    C he _commanded_ them that they should
      teach the things
      D which he had **expounded** unto them
    C' And it came to pass that he _commanded_
      them that they should write the words which
      the Father had given unto Malachi, which he
      should tell unto them.
  B' And it came to pass that after they were _written_
A' he **expounded** them.

—III Nephi 11:1–3

Chiasms within Chiasms

In 1977 J. de Waard wrote on the chiastic structure of Amos 5:1–17 in *Vetus Testamentum*, a quarterly published by the International Organization for the Study of the Old Testament. He points out that within the greater chiastic structure of seventeen verses, there are three smaller chiasms of two, four, and seven lines.[10]

Duane L. Christensen, professor of Old Testament languages and literature at American Baptist Seminary of the West in Berkeley, California, reported in 1985 in the *Journal of the Evangelical Theological Society* that the entire book of Jonah (chapters 1–4) is chiastic and contains smaller chiasms within the larger chiastic unit. Christensen identifies four levels of chiastic arrangement within the book of Jonah.[11] The pattern is chiasms within chiasms within chiasms within chiasms.

The recent research of these two scholars identifies a chiastic pattern in the Old Testament that is also prevalent in the Book of Mormon. The chiastic structure of Alma 17:1–30 illustrated in Figure 1 (see page 160) contains examples of smaller chiasms within a larger chiastic structure. Alma presents in thirty verses the experience of his conversion to Jesus Christ. In his chiastic arrangement he places Jesus Christ at the center or turning point and balances his description of events preceding and following his conversion experience.

```
A words (v. 1)
  B commandments of God (1)
    C prosper in the land (1)
      D as I have done (2)
        E remembering (2)
          F captivity (2)
            G bondage (2)
              H deliver them (2)
                I deliver them (2)
                  J I do know (3)
                    K trust in God (3)
                      L supported (3)
                        M God (4)
                          N born of God (5)
                            O unto me (5)
                              P feet (6)
                                Q stood (7)
                                  R limbs (8)
                                    S angel (9)
                                      T pains (10)
                                        U pains (14)
                                          V racked with torment (15)
                                            W harrowed up (15)
                                              X remembered (15)
                                                Y Jesus Christ, Son of God (15)
                                                Y' Jesus, Son of God (16)
                                              X' remember (17)
                                            W' harrowed up (17)
                                          V' filled with joy (18)
                                        U' pain (18)
                                      T' pains (18)
                                    S' angels (20)
                                  R' limbs (21)
                                Q' stood (21)
                              P' feet (21)
                            O' unto me (23)
                          N' born of God (23)
                        M' God (24)
                      L' supported (25)
                    K' trust in him (25)
                  J' I know (26)
                I' delivered them (27)
              H' delivered them (27)
            G' bondage (27)
          F' captivity (28)
        E' remembrance (28)
      D' as I have done (28)
    C' prosper in the land (29)
  B' commandments of God (30)
A' word (30)
```

Figure 1—Chiastic Structure of Alma's Conversion to Jesus Christ found in Alma 17:1–30

One example of a smaller chiasm within the larger chiastic unit follows:

A for they were **in bondage**, (G)
  B and none could **deliver them**, (H)
    C except it was the **God of Abraham**,
      and the **God of Isaac**,
      and the **God of Jacob**:
  B′ and he surely did **deliver them** (I)
A′ in their **afflictions**.[12]

—Alma 17:2

Alma's description of his conversion to Jesus Christ is a literary masterpiece, not casually written but designed with great care, giving us a perfect form of Hebraic artistry.

Chiastic Structure of Entire Books in the Bible

Recognizing a chiastic structure which covers an entire book can show the reader a book's purpose or theme by what is brought out in the chiasm and emphasized in the center point.[13]

Duane Christensen, in addition to identifying the entire book of Jonah as chiastic, also identifies the book of Deuteronomy as chiastic in his newly published commentary.[14] Yehuda Radday identifies I and II Kings, Ruth, and Esther as totally chiastic.[15]

M. Philip Scott's study of the Gospel of Mark identifies a chiastic pattern for the entire book. He states:

Having tried to understand Mark's gospel through his chiasmus, I now wonder if, in those places where he differs from Matthew and Luke and where the differences allowed the slotting of an event into the chiasmus, he is not less the eyewitness than Matthew and Luke. For a chiastic plan necessarily creates a priori needs to chisel and carve the material.[16]

In other New Testament studies Charles Lohr[17] and J. C. Fenton[18] cite the entire Gospel of Matthew as chiastic. David Deeks[19] and William E. Hull[20] identify the entire Gospel of John as chiastic. Nils Lund has pointed out the chiastic structure of Philemon.[21] Lund[22] and Elizabeth Schüssler Fiorenza demonstrate the chiastic structure of Revelation.[23]

Chiastic Structure of Entire Books in the Book of Mormon

John Welch, professor of law at Brigham Young University, first identified chiastic structure in the Book of Mormon in 1967. In his book, *Chiasmus in Antiquity*, published in 1981, Welch identifies the books of I and II Nephi and Mosiah as being entirely chiastic.[24]

Poetic Devices

Inclusio

When the same word or phrase is repeated at the beginning and end of a verse or composition, it is called inclusio.

Old Testament
In **booths** shall ye dwell seven days;
All that are Israelites born shall dwell in **booths**.

—Leviticus 23:42
Hebrew Masoretic Text

Book of Mormon
And my **soul** hungered;
  and I kneeled down before my Maker,
And I cried unto him in mighty prayer
  and supplication, for mine own **soul**;

—Enos 1:5

Keywords

Some poems contain repeated words which may be synonyms or the same word on a dominant theme.

Old Testament
Near is the great **day** of the LORD,...
Listen, the **day** of the LORD!...
A **day** of wrath is that **day**,
A **day** of trouble and distress,
A **day** of destruction and desolation,
A **day** of darkness and gloom,
A **day** of clouds and thick darkness,
A **day** of trumphet and battle cry,...
On the **day** of the LORD's wrath;...

—Zephaniah 1:14–18 NASB

Book of Mormon
Now this was what Ammon desired,
for he knew that King Lamoni
  was under the power of God;
He knew that the dark veil of unbelief
  being cast away from his mind,
and the **light** which did **light** up his mind,

which was the **light** of the glory of God,
which was a marvelous **light** of his goodness;
Yea, this **light** had infused such joy into his soul,
the cloud of darkness having been dispelled,
and that the **light** of everlasting **light**
was **lit** up in his soul;
—Alma 12:132–134

Merismus

This poetic device divides a subject into two or more parts. For example, the expression "heaven and earth" means "all creation,"[25] and "sea and dry land" mean "the universe."[26] The two parts joined together represent the entire unit.[27]

Old Testament
The **sea** is His, for it was He who made it;
And His hands formed the **dry land**.
—Psalm 95:5 NASB

Book of Mormon
Behold I am Jesus Christ, the son of God.
I created the **heavens** and the **earth**,
and all things that in them are.
—III Nephi 4:44

Secondary Techniques: Lists

A list consists of a group of nouns set out consecutively. Three types of lists have been identified: (1) the simple list uses a short or long list; (2) a list with a final total has a summary line at the end; and (3) a list with an initial total has a summary line at the beginning of the list.[28] The following examples illustrate lists with an initial total.

Old Testament
In that day **the Lord will snatch away their finery**:
the **bangles** and **headbands** and **crescent necklaces**,
the **earrings** and **bracelets** and **veils**,
the **headdresses** and **ankle chains** and **sashes**,
the **perfume bottles** and **charms**, the **signet rings**
and **nose rings**, the **fine robes** and the **capes** and **cloaks**, the **purses** and **mirrors**,
and the **linen garments** and **tiaras** and **shawls**.
—Isaiah 3:18–23 NIV

Book of Mormon
And he laid a tax of one fifth part of all they possessed;

a fifth part of their **gold** and of their **silver**,
and a fifth part of their **ziff**,
and of their **copper**, and of their **brass**
and their **iron**;
and a fifth part of their **fatlings**;
and also, a fifth part of all their **grain**.
—Mosiah 7:6

Verse Pattern: Sorites

A sorite is a group of statements which proceed, step by step, logically to a climactic conclusion, "each statement picking up the last key word (or key phrase) of the preceding one."[29]

Old Testament
Then shall all the trees of the wood rejoice before
the LORD: **for he cometh**,
for he cometh to **judge the earth:**
He shall judge the world with righteousness,
and the people with his truth.
—Psalm 96:12–13 KJV

The following example found in the Book of Mormon is clearer than all the examples given in Watson's *Classical Hebrew Poetry* textbook which cites Habakkuk 1:8, Psalm 78:3–8, 116:16, 133:2–3a, Amos 5:19 and II Kings 4:16.[30]

Book of Mormon
And the first-fruits of repentance
is **baptism**;
And **baptism** cometh by faith unto
the **fulfilling the commandments**;
And the **fulfilling the commandments**
bringeth the **remission of sins**;
And the **remission of sins** bringeth **meekness and lowliness of heart**;
And because of **meekness and lowliness of heart**, cometh the visitation of the **Holy Ghost**,
Which **Comforter** filleth with hope
and perfect **love**,
Which **love** endureth by diligence
unto prayer,
Until the end shall come, when all the saints shall dwell with God.
—Moroni 8:29

These examples are just a sampling of many that have been identified in the Bible and the Book of Mormon.

Midrash: Ancient Jewish Interpretation and Commentary

The word "midrash" (derived from the Hebrew verb *darash*—"to search out," "inquire") has been traditionally defined as rabbinic interpretation of the Old Testament.

In Jacob Neusner's book, *What Is Midrash?*, the author explains that "Midrash refers to the types of scriptural exegesis [scholarly interpretation] carried on by diverse groups of Jews from the time of ancient Israel to nearly the present day."[31]

Biblical scholars have had an increased interest in identifying midrash in the Old and New Testament and Qumran Scrolls in the last forty years.[32]

Three Types of Midrash

Scholars have identified three types of midrash. The first type, exegetical, is a verse-by-verse explanation of Old Testament books. A second type, homiletic, consists of sermons or discourses which explain scriptural texts or subjects in the Old Testament. A third type, narrative, works "the interpretative material...into the biblical text to form a continuous narrative."[33]

Following are examples of homiletic and narrative midrash that have been identified in the Bible and in the Book of Mormon.

Homiletic Midrash

Proem and Yelammedenu Homilies

Two important sermon patterns—the proem and the yelammedenu—have been identified in rabbinic literature. These two patterns have also been identified in the New Testament[34] and in the Book of Mormon. The Greek word *proem* means "prelude." The proem homily or sermon begins with a key Old Testament introductory (proem) text followed by a sermon built on the initial text and additional supporting texts. The sermon ends with a final text that repeats or alludes to the initial text. Keywords which link the sermon together are found in the initial and final texts, as well as in the exposition itself.

The yelammedenu homily or sermon is identical to the proem except that it begins with a question or problem which is answered in the exposition.[35]

Proem Homily in the New Testament

Romans 9:6–29 is one example that E. Earle Ellis, research professor in theology at Southwestern Baptist Theological Seminary, has identified in the New Testament as a proem homily:

> **Initial Text/Theme:** Genesis 21:12 [21:10 IV] (Romans 9:6–8); keywords: seed, children, called
> **Second Text:** Genesis 18:10 [18:9,10 IV] (Romans 9:9)
> keyword: son
> **Exposition**: Romans 9:10–28
> additional citations (13, 15, 17, 25–28) linked to the initial text by keywords: call, sons (12, 24ff., 27)
> **Final Text:** Isaiah 1:9 (Romans 9:29)
> alluding to the initial text with the keyword: seed[36]

Proem Homily in the Book of Mormon

Notice the impressive proem homily pattern of Jesus' sermon found in III Nephi 9:52–106:

> **Initial Text:** Micah 5:8–9; 4:12–13 (III Nephi 9:52–55); keywords: midst, cut off, gather, people, together, father, covenanted
> **Exposition:** III Nephi 9:56–98
> additional citations (Deuteronomy 18:15, 18–19; Genesis 22:18; Isaiah 52:1–3, 6–15) linked to initial and final texts by keywords: Father, people, covenant, midst, cut off, gather, together
> **Final Text:** Micah 5:8–15 (III Nephi 9:99–106)
> links the initial text and exposition with keywords: people, midst, cut off, Father

Jesus' sermon is an excellent example of a proem homily. More extended examples of proem homilies can also be found in the New Testament and the Book of Mormon. These will be identified as extended commentary patterns.

Extended Commentary Pattern in the New Testament

The Apostle Paul used an extended commentary pattern that is found in Romans 1:17–4:25. He used this technique of midrash to communicate his interpretation of scriptures:

Initial Text: Habakkuk 2:4 (Romans 1:17)
keywords: just/righteous, faith
Exposition: Romans 1:18–3:3
keywords: to judge, just/righteous, faith
Supplementary Text: Psalm 51:6 (Romans 3:4)
keywords: righteous, to judge
Exposition: Romans 3:5–9
keywords: righteousness, to judge
Supplementary Texts: Ecclesiastes 7:20; Psalm 5:10;14:1–3; Isaiah 59:7 (Romans 3:10–18)
Exposition: Romans 3:19–31
keywords: righteous, righteousness, just/righteous, fai**th**
Final Text: Romans 4:1–25
keywords: righteous, righteousness, faith[37]

Extended Commentary Pattern in the Book of Mormon

A similiar pattern is found in II Nephi 8:17 through 12:100. Nephi also used this technique of midrash to communicate his interpretation.

Initial Text: Isaiah 2–14 (II Nephi 8:17–10:54)
keywords: mountain(s), secret, nation(s), knowledge
Exposition: II Nephi 11:1–81
keywords: mountains, nation(s)
Supplementary Text: Isaiah 29:3–5 (II Nephi 11:82-88)
keyword: sealed
Exposition: II Nephi 11:89–116
keywords: secret, nation
Supplementary Text: Isaiah 29:6–24 [29:6–32 IV] (II Nephi 11:117–160);
keywords: reveal(ed), nation, sealed
Exposition: II Nephi 12:1–87
keywords: nation(s), sealed, knowledge
Final Text and Application: Isaiah 11:4–9 (II Nephi 12:88–100)
keywords: mountain, secret, revealed, nation, sealed, knowledge

Significance of the Extended Commentary Pattern

The preceding portion of scripture, which contains long quotes from the book of Isaiah, can bog readers down when they are reading in II Nephi. Identification of this extended commentary pattern which covers forty-five pages (pp. 116–160) in II Nephi, clarifies the structure of this portion of scripture. We now understand this ancient Jewish extended commentary form of midrash Nephi used in his teaching.

Yelammedenu Homily in the New Testament

One example Ellis identified as a yelammedenu homily is found in Matthew 15:1–9. This type of homily begins with a question or problem that is answered in the exposition. Verse two begins with the Pharisees and scribes questioning Jesus concerning his disciples' transgression of the tradition of the elders. The organization of the rest of the homily then follows the same pattern as the proem homily:

Question/Dialogue: Matthew 15:1–3
keywords: tradition, commandment
Initial Texts: Exodus 20:12,21:17 (Matthew 15:4)
keywords: honour
Exposition/Application: Matthew 15:5–6
keywords: honour, tradition
Final Text: Isaiah 29:13 (Matthew 15:7–9)
[15:7–8 IV];
keywords: honoureth, commandments[38]

Yelammedenu Homily in the Book of Mormon

A remarkable example of a yelammedenu homily is found in Mosiah 7:76 through 8:69. Here Abinadi answers King Noah and his priests' question in this ancient Jewish sermon pattern:

Question/Dialogue: Mosiah 7:76
keywords: meaneth, words, taught
Initial Text: Isaiah 52:7–10 (Mosiah 7:77–80)
keywords: beautiful, mountain, feet, good tidings, peace, salvation, people, redeemed, earth
Exposition: Mosiah 7:81 through 8:46
counter questions and additional citations (Exodus 20:2–17, Isaiah 53) linked to the initial and final

text by keywords: teach, mean, taught, people, salvation, words, earth, redeem, peace

Final Text/Application: Isaiah 52:7–10 (Mosiah 8:47–69)

keywords: peace, good tidings, salvation, beautiful, mountains, feet, redeemed, people, earth

In this yelammendenu pattern, Abinadi used Isaiah 52:7–10 for both the initial and final texts. Another example of the yelammendenu homily pattern from the Book of Mormon is I Nephi 6:8–56. Here Nephi teaches his brethren from Isaiah. The initial text is Isaiah, chapters 48 and 49. The question is found in I Nephi 7:1–2 where Nephi's brethren ask him the meaning of the Isaiah text. The exposition is I Nephi 7:3–68. Verse 69 has the concluding allusion to the initial text with the keywords "commandment(s)" (also in 6:25) and "save(d)" (6:55).

Narrative Midrash

Narrative midrash works "the interpretative material...into the biblical text to form a continuous narrative."[39] Narrative midrash has been identified in the Old and New Testaments and in the Book of Mormon.

George Wesley Buchanan, professor of New Testament Studies at Wesley Theological Seminary, has identified both homiletic and narrative midrash in the Bible. He states in his Anchor Bible Commentary *To the Hebrews* that the book of Hebrews (chapter 1–12) is homiletic midrash based on Psalm 110.[40]

In Buchanan's paper, "Isaianic Midrash and the Exodus," presented at the Annual Meeting of the Society of Biblical Literature (November 1990), he stated that:

...unless all of this Isaianic literature can be proved to have been composed by later authors, midrashic literature was already an accepted literary genre as early as the seventh or eighth century B.C. This fact has not been widely recognized.[41]

Buchanan further commented:

This is only the tip of the iceberg. Midrashic composition was more widely practiced in the Hebrew Scriptures than anyone has imagined, but some will not be surprised....This method deserves more attention than it has received.[42]

Narrative Midrash in the Book of Isaiah

James Sanders, professor of Intertestamental and Biblical Studies at the School of Theology at Claremont, and George Wesley Buchanan have both identified Isaiah 43 as narrative midrash on Exodus 15. Buchanan has also identified Isaiah 12 as narrative midrash on Exodus 15, Psalm 88:2, and Psalms 105:1–2; another example is Isaiah 11:11, 14–16 on Exodus 15.[43] This example will be illustrated in the next section.

Narrative Midrash in Isaiah 11

Buchanan has identified Isaiah 11:11, 14–16 as narrative midrash on Exodus 15. Note the exact words found in Exodus 15 are woven into the Isaiah text forming a continuous narrative.[44]

Isaiah's Narrative Midrash on Exodus 15

Isaiah 11

11 the Lord shall set his
hand again the second time to
recover the remnant of

his **people**, which shall be left, from Assyria,
and from Egypt, and from Pathros, and from
Cush, and from Elam...

14 they shall fly upon the shoulders of the
Philistines...they shall lay their hand upon
Edom and **Moab**

15 the **LORD** shall utterly destroy the tongue of
the Egyptian **sea**; and
with his mighty **wind** shall he shake his **hand**
over the river...

16 there shall be an highway for the remnant of
his **people**...

(Regular italics are used in the King James version to
indicate words not found in the Hebrew text.)

Exodus 15

6 Thy right **hand**, O LORD...
thy right **hand**, O LORD...

12 thou stretchedst out thy right
hand

13 the **people** which thou hast redeemed...

16 thy **people** pass over, O LORD, till the
people pass over, which thou hast
purchased.

14 sorrow shall take hold on the inhabitants of
Palestina [**Philistia**].

15 **Edom**...**Moab**, trembling shall take hold upon
them...

19 the **LORD** brought again the waters of
the **sea**...

12 thy right **hand**

10 Thou didst blow with thy **wind**...

16 thy **people** pass over...till the **people** pass
over, which thou hast purchased.

13 the **people** which thou hast redeemed...

Moroni's Narrative Midrash on Isaiah 52:1–2: 54:2, 4, 10

In Moroni 10:27–28 the author uses the text of Isaiah 52:1–2; 54:2, 4, 10 in his
exhortation in narrative midrashic form. This example is illustrated below.

Moroni 10:27–28

27 And again I would exhort you,
that ye would come unto Christ,
and lay hold upon every good gift
and touch not the evil gift,
nor the **unclean** thing.

28 And **awake**,
and **arise from the dust**
O Jerusalem; yea
and **put on thy beautiful garments**,
O daughter of Zion,
and strengthen thy stakes,
and **enlarge** thy borders for ever,
that thou mayest no more be
confounded,
that the **covenants** of the eternal
Father
which he hath made unto thee,
O house of Israel,
may be fulfilled.

Isaiah 52:1–2; 54:2, 4, 10

52:1 the uncircumcised
and the **unclean**
Awake, awake

2 **from the dust**; arise,
O Jerusalem

1 **put on thy beautiful garments**

2 O captive **daughter of Zion.**

54:2 **and strengthen thy stakes**,
enlarge the place of thy
tent

4 neither be thou **confounded**;

10 neither shall the **covenant** of
peace be removed

Isaiah Variants in the Book of Mormon

When dealing with the Hebrew literary structure of the Book of Mormon one comment should be made concerning the Isaiah variants in the book. John Tvedtnes, former Hebrew instructor at the University of Utah, pointed out in his article "Isaiah Variants in the Book of Mormon" that of the 478 verses quoted from the book of Isaiah, 207 show variations from the King James reading. Some of those variations agree with more ancient versions of Isaiah.

One example is found in the spelling of the word "Ramath" in the Book of Mormon (II Nephi 9:110, which is a quote from Isaiah 10:29). The King James rendering is "Ramah." The Book of Mormon rendering is the more ancient form of the spelling reflected in the Hebrew.

This example and others "provides evidence that the brass plates are from an older source than the MT" [Hebrew Masoretic text from which the King James Version is derived].[45]

Tvedtnes concludes his study by saying that "one of the more remarkable linguistic evidences for the authenticity of the Book of Mormon as a translation from an ancient text lies in the Isaiah variants found in it."[46]

Conclusions

We have impressive examples of Hebrew poetry and authentic homiletic and narrative midrash in the Book of Mormon. These illustrations of poetic artistry and midrash exhibit well-established ancient Jewish patterns of poetic expression, interpretation, and exposition. These patterns, which are recognized by current Biblical scholarship, continue to clarify the ancient Hebrew literary structure of the Book of Mormon.

Some readers consider the literary style of the Book of Mormon awkward and repetitive. What many have thought was King James English is actually good Hebrew language structure. The Hebraic idioms and grammatical forms are what give the book its unique style.

In research published on "Hebraisms in the Book of Mormon"[47] one can see the literal translations of Hebrew words and syntax found in the book.

I have found the Book of Mormon translation to be closest to the Hebrew Masoretic text [i.e., the accepted Biblical Hebrew text by Christians and Jews] in retaining the purest Hebrew form, even closer in some cases than English translations of the Bible because of translators' changes.[48]

We are just now opening the door in our understanding to be able to appreciate the Book of Mormon as an impressive example of Hebraic literature. One of the most profound evidences we have today for the validity of the Book of Mormon is found in its Hebrew literary structure.

Notes

1. George Buchanan Gray, *The Forms of Hebrew Poetry* (Hoboken, New Jersey: KTAV Publishing House, 1972), 3.
2. David Noel Freedman, *Pottery, Poetry, and Prophecy* (Winona Lake, Indiana: Eisenbrauns, 1980), 1, 16.
3. Ibid., 16, 18–19.
4. Wilfred G. E. Watson, *Classical Hebrew Poetry* (Great Britain: JSOT Press, 1984), 1–2.
5. F. B. Huey, Jr., and Bruce Corley, *A Student's Dictionary for Biblical and Theological Studies* (Grand Rapids, Michigan: Zondervan, 1983), 182.
6. John T. Willis, "Alternating (ABA'B') Parallelism in the Old Testament Psalms and Prophetic Literature," *Directions in Biblical Hebrew Poetry*, ed. Elaine R. Follis (Great Britain: JSOT Press, 1987), 49, 71.
7. Stanley Gevirtz, *Patterns in the Early Poetry of Israel* (Chicago: University of Chicago Press, 1963), 43–44.
8. John S. Kselman, "The ABCB Pattern: Further Examples," *Vetus Testamentum* 32:2 (April 1982): 224, 228.
9. Nils W. Lund, "The Significance of Chiasmus for Interpretation," *The Crozer Quarterly* 20, no. 2 (April 1943): 107–109.
10. J. de Waard, "The Chiastic Structure of Amos V 1–17," *Vetus Testamentum* 27, no. 2 (April 1977): 176.
11. Duane L. Christensen, "Andrzej Panufnik and the Structure of the Book of Jonah: Icons, Music and Literary Art," *Journal of the Evangelical Theological Society* 28, no. 2 (June 1985): 133–140.
12. John W. Welch, "Chiasmus in Alma 36," working paper (Provo, Utah: Foundation for Ancient Research and Mormon Studies), 16.
13. Ronald E. Man, "The Value of Chiasm for New Testament Interpretation," *Bibliotheca Sacra* 141, no. 562 (April-June 1984): 153.
14. Duane L. Christensen, *Word Biblical Commentary, Deuteronomy 1–11* (Irving, Texas: Word Books, 1991), xli.
15. Yehuda T. Radday, "Chiasmus in Hebrew Biblical Narrative," *Chiasmus in Antiquity*, ed. John W. Welch (Hildesheim: Gerstenberg Verlag, 1981), 54, 62, 71.
16. M. Philip Scott, "Chiastic Structure: A Key to the Interpretation of Mark's Gospel," *Biblical Theology Bulletin* 15 (1985): 17–18.
17. Charles H. Lohr, "Oral Techniques in the Gospel of Matthew," *The Catholic Biblical Quarterly* 23, no. 4 (October 1961): 427.
18. J. C. Fenton, *Saint Matthew* (Philadelphia: The Westminster Press, 1963), 15–16.
19. David Deeks, "The Structure of the Fourth Gospel," *New Testament Studies* 15, no. 1 (October 1968): 122.
20. William E. Hull, "John," *The Broadman Bible Commentary*, ed. Clifton J. Allen, vol. 9, Luke-John (Nashville, Tennessee: Broadman Press, 1970), 200–201, 210.
21. Nils Wilhelm Lund, *Chiasmus in the New Testament* (Chapel Hill, North Carolina: University of North Carolina Press, 1942), 219.
22. Ibid., 325–326.
23. Elizabeth Schüssler Fiorenza, "Composition and Structure of the Revelation of John," *The Catholic Biblical Quarterly* 39, no. 3 (July 1977): 364–366.
24. John W. Welch, ed., *Chiasmus in Antiquity* (Hildesheim: Gerstenberg Verlag, 1981), 201, 205.
25. Huey and Corley, 123.
26. Watson, 323.
27. Ibid., 321.
28. Ibid., 351.
29. Henry A. Fischel, "The Uses of Sorites (Climax, Gradatio) in the Tannaitic Period," *Hebrew Union College Annual* 44 (1973): 119.
30. Watson, 213.
31. Jacob Neusner, *What Is Midrash?* (Philadelphia: Fortress Press, 1987), 8.
32. Addison G. Wright, "The Literary Genre Midrash," *The Catholic Biblical Quarterly* 28, no. 2 (April 1966): 105.
33. Ibid., 128.
34. E. Earle Ellis, "How the New Testament Uses the Old," *New Testament Interpretation*, ed. I. Howard Marshall (Exeter, England, and Grand Rapids, Michigan: William B. Eerdmans, 1977), 203–204.
35. Ibid., 205.
36. Ibid., 204.
37. E. Earle Ellis, "Biblical Interpretation in the New Testament Church," *Mikra*, ed. Martin Jan Mulder (Philadelphia: Fortress Press, 1988), 708–709.
38. Ellis, "How the New Testament Uses the Old," 206.
39. Wright, 128.
40. George Wesley Buchanan, *To the Hebrews* (New York: Doubleday, 1972), XXI.

41. George Wesley Buchanan, "Isaianic Midrash and the Exodus," paper presented at the Annual Meeting of the Society of Biblical Literature, New Orleans, Louisiana, 26 November 1990, 2. (Paper in possession of author.)

42. Ibid., 32–33.

43. Ibid., 28; 6, 3 (handout).

44. "King James Version," *The Comparative Study Bible* (Grand Rapids, Michigan: Zondervan, 1984), 174, 176, 1656, 1658.

45. John A. Tvedtnes, "Isaiah Variants in the Book of Mormon," *Isaiah and the Prophets*, ed. Monte S. Nyman (Provo, Utah: Religious Study Center, BYU, 1984), 172.

46. Ibid., 176.

47. Angela M. Crowell, "Hebraisms in the Book of Mormon," *Recent Book of Mormon Developments*, vol. 2 (Independence, Missouri: Zarahemla Research Foundation, 1992), 4–11.

48. Angela M. Crowell, "A Comparative Study of Biblical Hebrew Sentence Structure in the Old Testament and in the Book of Mormon" (master's thesis, Central Baptist Theological Seminary, 1989), 68–69.

Twenty-Two Years with the Book of Mormon: Thoughts and Reflections

Piotr Klafkowski

Greetings to you from distant Drammen! Allow me to introduce myself. My name is Piotr Klafkowski. I am a Polish researcher living in Norway. This contribution is the result of Velma Ruch's suggestion that I write of my long experience and interest in the Book of Mormon. I was happy for the privilege. However, I feel I must begin by saying that I am not a member of any of the Restoration churches. The following pages, therefore, outline my personal views and are not conditioned by any religious loyalties. In the course of my studies I have always followed an independent path, asking help of those churches and individuals whom I believed could provide the information I needed. I would like to thank them all.[1]

I have called this contribution "Twenty-two Years with the Book of Mormon— Thoughts and Reflections." I realize it is not a meaningful title. I chose it deliberately, trying not to promise something I cannot deliver. For more than two decades I have been increasingly interested in the Book of Mormon, but my life's circumstances never favored any concentrated research on it. It is not easy to have such interest while I am in a place where even the basic works on the subject are unknown and unavailable. What's more, my fragmentary knowledge of current Book of Mormon scholarship is limited to the works of Brigham Young University scholars, whose premises, for all I know, may be very different from yours of the Reorganized Church. On the other hand, my limited acquaintance with Restoration churches makes it now easier to concentrate on the Book of Mormon itself and to avoid deviating into comparing the churches or arguing with quotations.

I remember the first time I came to know about the existence of the Book of Mormon. I think I was about fourteen or fifteen at that time. The source was a lengthy feature in a popular Polish illustrated weekly *Przekrój*. It was written by Melchior Wankowicz, a respected Polish journalist who was then touring the United States. His visit to Salt Lake City resulted in the article I read. I remember I was first attracted by the photograph of a huge and strange building which proved to be the Salt Lake City Temple. In his article, Wańkowicz described the origin of the Book of Mormon and mentioned that two groups of witnesses claimed to have seen the golden plates and issued statements to that effect. A brief summary of the Book of Mormon followed, illustrated with a few pictures. One of them showed the cover of the then standard missionary blue edition of the Book of Mormon of the Utah Church (replaced since 1981 by the "New Triple"), while another was Arnold Friberg's painting "Lehi and His People Arrive in the Promised Land."

The article left me with a burning curiosity about that strange book. For some reason or another, I felt I simply had to get it and read it some day. Some years later, when Wankowicz published a book about his U.S. tour, I learned more about the LDS Church, its structure, priesthood ranks, and hierarchy. The book itself, though, proved very difficult to obtain.

Sometime at the turn of 1969–1970, I suddenly encountered a copy of the Book of Mormon in an antiquariat. There it stood, on a shelf of English paperbacks, at a price which was unbelievably low. I could hardly believe my eyes. It was a copy of the same edition I used to dream about while looking at Wakowicz's photographs. I began reading it on the tram taking me home. In the book I found the testimonies of the witnesses, Joseph Smith's own account of how he came to translate the book, and for the first time I saw the titles *Doctrine and Covenants* and *Pearl of Great Price* referred to but not included. When I tackled I Nephi, however, I realized the book's English was beyond me. Reading with a dictionary seemed an obvious solution, but I soon found it was not enough. Having to check several words in the same verse was too distracting. I kept losing the continuity. I decided that now that I had the book, I should not read it by force. I kept it close at hand, returning to it from time to time, each time able to read more fluently. At long last, I read it through. I found it both interesting and impressive, more than enough to return to it every now and then.

In the meantime I became a student. At about the same time when I first read the Book of Mormon without a dictionary, a copy of the new Polish translation of Goethe's *Faust* by Feliks Konopka fell into my hands. Konopka's long and masterly introduction was my first direct contact with the theory and practice of translation. I had already realized that languages were one of my main fascinations. Konopka's words added a totally new dimension to my interests. I began asking myself whether a language could impose its own pattern of thinking and structuring on a translation from it. Could the strange English of the Book of Mormon actually reflect its original language? Because the arguments by Feliks Konopka were based on his translation of *Faust*, I began by making a systematic study of all the available Polish renderings of it.

Shortly afterward, during my first research stay in India in 1972–1973, a rare complete Tibetan Bible fell into my hands. I read it first merely to practice my reading skill on a text I could control in another language, but soon with increasing interest as it became clear that the Buddhist vocabulary used to render Christian technical terms and the distinct Tibetan way of thinking and narrating made the book I read very different from the one I thought I knew in Polish. While trying to explain my observations, I had reached my first conclusions on what is known as "Whorf and Sapir" or "linguistic relativity" hypothesis long before I heard about it. Trying to apply the same ideas to the Book of Mormon, I got my first glimpses of its underlying complexity.

Unfortunately, my personal life at that time took a rather unexpected turn. In January 1980 I found myself in Norway, rather unwillingly and without anything except my clothes. My library, my collection of Tibetan and Mongolian historical texts and dictionaries assembled at great effort over the years, and all my research papers and manuscripts had to be left behind. Just six weeks earlier, having passed my Ph.D. exams, I thought that at last I could start making full use of my materials. But instead, I was in a strange country which understood little and cared even less for such interests as mine. What I had hoped to be my future became my past.

I missed my library, but strangely enough, I felt that the loss of my copy of the Book of Mormon was in a way apart from the overall misfortune. Fortunately, a convenient coincidence put me in contact with Utah missionaries just a few weeks after I came to Norway. One of my new friends was not merely hunting for converts but was also a scholarly type who read a lot and was very perceptive about many things. He realized that while I was not going to join his church,

I was genuinely interested in the Book of Mormon as a subject. He introduced me to names and works of Hugh Nibley, John L. Sorenson, Paul R. Cheesman, and to many other helpful works.[2]

Needless to say, I took the first opportunity to buy a new copy of the Book of Mormon, even though I knew nothing could ever emotionally replace the copy I left behind. Years later, I realized that it was the first book I bought in a new country, the beginning and the cornerstone of a new library. I treasure that copy so much now that I hardly ever use it, basing my daily reading on another copy.

In the course of my reading I soon learned that the Utah church was not the only one and that the second largest branch was known as the Reorganized Church. In the summer of 1980 I came to know that the Reorganized Church, too, had an office in Oslo. My Utah friends were understandably not too eager to talk about the RLDS, but just one statement—"They have their own Book of Mormon, and their own Doctrine and Covenants, both different from ours"— was enough. A few days later I was ringing at the door of the RLDS Oslo office. When I left it, I carried a bag of books which would soon become my daily tools: the 1966 "Readers' Version" of the Book of Mormon, the 1970 RLDS Doctrine and Covenants, A. G. Koury's *The Truth and the Evidence*, R. E. Weldon and F. E. Butterworth's *Criticisms of the Book of Mormon Answered*, and the one that proved truly indispensable, Richard P. Howard's *Restoration Scriptures: A Study of Their Textual Development*.

Intensive correspondence followed. I was unemployed in a strange country and could not afford books, but I could write to whomever I wanted with no postal censor in the way. Those to whom I wrote, almost as a rule, answered my questions and gave me further bibliographic references. Some even enclosed copies of materials they thought I ought to know. Professor Hugh Nibley solved a lot of my problems by presenting me a detailed bibliography of his works. Paul R. Cheesman contributed his collection of *Purported New World Inscriptions*. Richard P. Howard, in his turn, provided me with a copy of Douglas D. Alder and Paul M. Edwards' "Common Beginnings, Divergent Beliefs," of which I understood very little in 1980 but which was of increasing importance as I began to get a broader view of the entire Restoration movement.

At the same time I first came face to face with the violent reactions against the Book of Mormon. My Lutheran friends felt it was their duty to "save me" from the Mormons. I must give it to them, they were even ready to admit that the *Roman Catholic* Church had some good points—but not the Mormons! Brought up in a family where religion was respected but not in any way dominant, I was amazed by the intensity of anti-Mormon feelings. It seemed that the Book of Mormon was a menace on a par with the Bomb. Merely mentioning it was enough to evoke passionately eloquent reactions so unexpected from cool, taciturn, reserved Norwegians. Why did they object to this book so much, I wondered? It did not take long to realize that it was not the book itself, but its popular—and totally unfounded—image that was being attacked. More often than not, the person arguing against the book had never even seen it, let alone read it—he was merely convinced that he knew everything he needed to know about it and acted according to his genuine convictions.

For the first time I began to see what amount of anti-Mormon books and pamphlets were in circulation. Well-meaning friends piled me with this literature. I read it all and asked for more. Not only did it help me to increase my knowledge and understand many different viewpoints, but the very variety of it forced me to systematize all material and arrange it in categories meaningful to those I wanted to argue with. It is not too much to say that I owe a lot to many of the anti-Mormon books I encountered.[3]

Strange, I thought. Everyone felt certain that the Book of Mormon was evil, but so very few based their judgement on the actual reading of it. What's more, the most vitriolic critics of the book all too often accused it of statements and doctrines it simply did not contain! My three years of research in India (1975–1978) taught me to respect the Indian universalism and coexistence of all religions in the overall tolerance. After all, it was Akbar the Great who convened the world's first Parliament of Religions as early as 1575 in Agra. The Sunni and Shia Muslims, the Hindus, the Zoroastrians, the Jains, the Sikhs, the Buddhists, the Jews, and the Christians were all invited and eagerly participated in what is probably the world's most supreme example of what an enlightened attitude toward religion *may be*. This made the white man's squabbles seem even more parochial. I remembered the Soviet's furious campaign against Alexander Solzhenitsyn's *The Gulag Archipelago*, and I knew that under certain conditions people could be *forced* to condemn a book they had never read. But now for the first time it appeared to me that the Marxists were not the only ones clamoring for monopoly on truth.

The commonest accusation leveled against the Book of Mormon was that thousands of changes have been made in its text, altering it in some rather unclear but definitely sinister way. The Mormons would never show anyone the original edition, I often heard, because it was so different. This seemed to pose a clear, tangible problem. I was, as a researcher, used to comparing various editions of the same text. I felt

challenged to test the accusations. No Norwegian library had a copy of the first edition of the Book of Mormon, but fortunately the year was 1980 and the sesquicentennial facsimile of the 1830 First Edition had just been announced by Deseret Books. Even though unemployed, I managed to scrape up enough money to order it.

A few weeks later the parcel arrived. I opened it with mixed feelings. I was not entirely ignorant of the First Edition. Richard P. Howard had described it at length in my daily tool, *Restoration Scriptures*. On the other hand, all the anti-Mormon publications accused the Mormons of altering the First Edition beyond belief, (I often wondered if they would be more willing to accept it *without* those alterations) and focused on the title page and preface signed by Joseph Smith as "Author and Proprietor." Could he have been so careless first to take years to invent the story of the gold plates and then to "spill the beans" on the title page? And with all these hundreds and thousands of changes between the First Edition and the current ones, would I be able to recognize the text I knew only in its "altered" form?

But here it was—the facsimile of the First Edition, Palmyra 1830. Someone suggested that *it* surely had been altered as well, but I could not take the accusation seriously. Though a rare book, it certainly wasn't unknown, and more than enough authentic copies of the First Edition were surely available to safeguard against altering a well-advertised reprint. Besides, I had Richard Howard's description of the text in *Restoration Scriptures* and a number of quotations from various anti-Mormon publications to use as controls.

I opened the cover and found that the title page *did* say in no uncertain terms: "By Joseph Smith, Junior, Author and Proprietor." The Preface, too, was *really* signed "the Author." However, none of the anti-

Mormon publications I knew mentioned the copyright declaration signed by R. R. Lansing, the statement which makes the apparently surprising title page self-explanatory. Another surprise—the testimonies of the Three and Eight Witnesses were placed at the end of the text, not at the beginning. Once I noticed that, it seemed a much more logical place for them—the text first, collaterals later.

I began reading and was thrilled as never before. The text seemed to come alive with elemental power totally absent from the editions I knew. For the first time I not only read it but experienced it. I lived through the entire narration as if it all happened to me. I shared the joys and sorrows, doubts and elations of the heroes. Was it the same book that Mark Twain described as "chloroform in print" and of which Sir Richard Burton said,"…there never was a book so thoroughly dull and heavy; it is monotonous as a sage-prairie"?[4] It seemed nothing like that to me, so the immediate question was obvious: What was it that caused such a different reaction to the First Edition, when I already knew the text well enough?

I now see that the answer is simple but presupposes both the knowledge of the Book of Mormon and an unbiased attitude. The current editions of the book, divided into chapters and verses, with references, visually convey a Bible-like character. As soon as we open the book, we have a vague feeling of something familiar. We have seen this before, have we not? The current editions are like well-tended, orderly parks with clear paths, regularly alternating thickets and open spaces, resting places and all the like conveniences. Compared with them, the First Edition is a primeval jungle, maybe a wilderness, but it emanates such tremendous force that he who feels it will never get enough of it. The text of a modern edition, in its outer corset of chapters, verses, and numbers of all kinds, could conceivably be the result of laborious planning. On the other hand, the First Edition is clearly in a class of its own, a torrential flood of misspellings, awkward punctuation, gigantic sentences paragraphed totally unlike the text we know from the contemporary editions.

I am aware that what I have written is a subjective, individual appreciation, but the First Edition gives precisely *this* clear feeling of a spontaneous outburst that the more structured editions do not and cannot give. I would even go so far as to say that anyone seriously interested in the Book of Mormon—friend and foe alike—should read the First Edition first. Not only will it bring him closer to Joseph Smith, but it will also preempt whatever doubts may be raised later by the study of the modern editions.

As I look back now, twelve years later, I can see that the arrival of the First Edition concluded my period of groundwork. Everything that I have read and found out since I received the book added more and more details and opened new aspects of study, but once I had the facsimile of the First Edition, the preparatory work was completed.

* * *

Here some words are necessary on the various editions of the Book of Mormon. I have already presented my view of the First Edition. In *Restoration Scriptures*, Richard Howard mentions that the complete printer's manuscript in possession of the Reorganized Church was successfully microfilmed in 1968, and I hope that some day I shall be able to obtain a copy of this microfilm or a set of prints. Before I go on, I must repeat that my viewpoint is independent of religious faith and churchly loyalties. With this in mind, I shall now outline my views on the various editions of the Book of Mormon that I know from direct contact.

It is quite clear that the text we use today is very different from the First Edition. It is praiseworthy that both of the main Restoration churches, LDS in Utah and RLDS in Missouri, have reprinted the First Edition and made it available for study. It would be *most* advisable, though, for identical facsimiles to be published of the Second, Kirtland 1837, and Third, Nauvoo 1840, editions. These were prepared by Joseph Smith himself, and together with the First Edition and either the microfilm or a facsimile of the printer's manuscript they comprise the Book of Mormon corpus which should be available in one set.

Too many myths surround the translation process preceding the First Edition. The LDS missionaries often stress the absolute and revelatory character of it, exposing the book to easy accusations as soon as the changes in the text become a point.

Let us say it loud and clear that the First Edition was *the first* edition, neither a perfect nor an ultimate one. It does not undermine the book if Joseph Smith was not satisfied with the First Edition and spent a decade, 1830–1840, revising and improving it. Has there *ever* been anyone with more authority to do it?

A facsimile reprint of the 1837 and 1840 editions of the Book of Mormon would at once remove all the myths of the text being "altered beyond recognition." I take this chance to make a personal appeal to those who will hear or read my words. Please consider reprinting those two editions. You will render the book a great service.

I must give full credit to Richard P. Howard for his straightforward discussion of this problem in *Restoration Scriptures*. As he points out, there are both changes and *changes* in the three editions that appeared during Joseph Smith's lifetime. While many of them are minor, not to say cosmetic, the relative weight of many other ones will depend on each reader's individual convictions. For example, I consider adding the words "Son of" to the First Edition's "Behold the Lamb of God, yea, even /the Son of/ the Eternal Father!" to be something so obvious that it needs no further comment.[5] The same passage would evoke a very different reaction from a Protestant theologian to whom its relative weight is much higher.

No friend of the Book of Mormon should be unaware of these kinds of changes between the first and the current editions, and I think all the Restoration churches could benefit by studying Howard's exemplary work. It does not in any way undermine the authority of the book but does just the opposite.

The underlying reason for accusing the Mormons of altering the text of the Book of Mormon is the question of establishing *authenticity*. In the absence of the original, we feel something else has to act as the obvious starting point. Unless one knows about, or can consult the manuscript, any doubt cast over the First Edition casts a shadow over the book as a whole. The problem of various editions' reliability and authenticity is, therefore, of paramount importance.

Not many people interested in the Book of Mormon realize that the First Edition was preceded not by a *single* manuscript but by *two* complete ones. Of the first one, the "dictated manuscript," only some portions survive in possession of the LDS Church in Utah. They have never, to the best of my knowledge, been made available in their entirety. The second one, the "printer's manuscript," has survived intact and is now in possession of the Reorganized Church. As I have mentioned already, this manuscript is known to have been successfully microfilmed, so it will eventually become available to researchers. In the meantime, Howard's *Restoration Scriptures* contains the basic information for all to examine.

I need not list here the editions bearing

Joseph Smith's authority and the major editions, both from the Utah LDS and the Missouri RLDS, after the death of Joseph Smith. Suffice it to say that some editorial changes occurred which account for differences in how the books of the LDS and of the RLDS are presented.

We might ask, how reliable are the editions prepared after the death of Joseph Smith? Again, the answer will vary according to one's premises or church loyalties. As an outside observer, I am convinced that the Authorized and the 1966 Readers' (now referred to as Revised Authorized) editions by the Reorganized Church are superior on three different counts:

1. They follow the chapter division of the First Edition.

2. They do not overload the text with often unnecessary references.

Instead of explanation, a simple comparison.

Text: I Nephi 1:1–5

LDS edition, copyrighted 1959—three references, to the words "language of the Egyptians," "first year of the reign of Zedekiah," and "many prophets."

LDS 1981 "New Triple"—fifteen references, to the words "born," "goodly," "parents," "taught," "afflictions," "record," "language," "true," "first year," "Zedekiah,"

"Jerusalem," "prophets," "repent," "Jerusalem" (for the second time), and "heart."

RLDS 1966 Readers' Version—no references.

3. They do not introduce any extratextual matter into the text. Until the advent of the "New Triple," the popular Utah editions of the Book of Mormon attempted to influence the readers' view of the world of the book in two ways, one harmless but the other academically irresponsible.

The first approach was to include a number of illustrations, based on Arnold Friberg's paintings, throughout the book. This was probably well-intended but suggested a certain image of the world of the Book of Mormon which by no means seems probable or plausible. Huge, walled cities, gigantic towers, bulging muscles, Viking helmets and confused Greek and Roman armors look more like shots from *Conan the Barbarian* than anything else. To be fair to the LDS, it was their own preeminent scholar Hugh Nibley who as early as in the first edition of his invaluable *An Approach to the Book of Mormon* pointed out that all the book's internal evidence suggests a civilization wholly unlike its popular image.

The second way of imposing preconceptions on the readers was far more serious. Even before I describe it, I want to say that to the best of my knowledge, this is no longer practiced. The approach was to append to the text several photographs which quite openly identified the world of the Book of Mormon with the classical civilizations of Central and South America. An untold number of such copies have been distributed and keep creating false impressions, providing ground for easy attacks by those opposing the book. Lest I am accused of dramatizing, let me give a full example. In my copy of the Utah edition (copyrighted 1959, reprinted in England 1978) the following illustrations precede the first page of the text:

1. "When Jesus Christ organized his church, he called and ordained his disciples." The picture shows Jesus laying on hands on a bearded man dressed in white shirt with rolled-up sleeves and jeans-like pants.

2. "The Prophet Joseph Smith. He translated the ancient writings inscribed on gold plates from which the first edition of the Book of Mormon was published in 1830."

3. "The Hill Cumorah, near Manchester,

New York, where Joseph Smith obtained the gold plates from which the Book of Mormon was translated."

4. "This beautiful monument to the Book of Mormon prophet Moroni was erected on the top of the Hill Cumorah in July, 1953."

5. "Gold tablet found in Persia in 1961, dating to the time of Darius II (fourth century B.C.), covered with cuneiform engravings. This tablet is about the size of the gold plates of the Book of Mormon. As described by Joseph Smith, the Book of Mormon plates were about six inches wide, eight inches long and about the thickness of common tin."

6. "Ancient copper and bronze tools dated from the book of Mormon period." Which period—of the reign of Darius II?

7. "Gold plates from Peru fastened together with gold rings. Ancient Americans were skilled craftsmen in gold and precious metals." The picture shows some jewelry-like object.

8. "Textiles from Peru, dated from the Book of Mormon period." Dated by whom and to what precise period?

9. "Egyptian-like murals found on the temple walls in Mexico." Distinctly un-Egyptian, though, since both the faces *and the bodies* are shown in profile.

10. "General view of the sacred city of Machu Picchu—'Jewel of the Andes,' believed to have been built over 2000 years ago." Are we to understand this is a Book of Mormon location?

11. "Temple of the Cross in Mexico. This temple, believed to have been erected during the Maya classic period, contains the famous cross of Palenque. Many archaeologists now agree that these artistic masterpieces date back to the beginning of the Christian era." The picture shows a large ruined building on top of a hill. The actual cross is not shown.

I do not think I am wrong to see a clear pattern in the above. From Joseph Smith it leads to the inscribed metal plates in the ancient Near East, equates them with the Book of Mormon, hammers in the desired message, and concludes with a picture of some ruins and the explanation that "the famous cross of Palenque" (whatever it might be) is inside it. Unless the reader has an active interest in pre-Columbian America, he will not know what the "famous cross of Palenque" is nor what its connection with the Book of Mormon might be. But when the First Book of Nephi begins on the facing page, the reader has already been told what to expect. If he still has some doubts, a helpful page of "A Few Interesting Book of Mormon References" will clear them. Now he knows he is actually reading a history of the Mayas, Aztecs, and Incas, all of whom descended from the Hebrews. Simple, isn't it? How sad it is that though this kind of forcing of facts has been largely eliminated, it is still practiced in some places.

The LDS authorities still do not seem to believe that the Book of Mormon is good enough to stand on its own. Some time in the early 1980s, a subtitle was added to the title page, "Another Testament of Jesus Christ." Has someone forgotten that right from the First Edition the Book of Mormon had its own title *and* subtitle? The Utah missionaries never tire of explaining how all the assorted "great and abominable churches" apostasized by adding to, and deleting from, the once-pure Bible. It is remarkable that at the same time the book containing "the fullness of the everlasting gospel" seems too weak to stand on its own, even its title page requires a suggestive interpolation.

The Reorganized Church's editions of the Book of Mormon should be commended for the fact that in them the original chapters are not chopped into shorter pieces, thus respecting the integrity of the original text; for the fact that the references are limited to where they are absolutely necessary, without pedantry which distracts the eye and affects concentration; and for the fact that they do not introduce any extratextual material, allowing the reader to draw his or her own conclusions.

What's more, the RLDS foreword to the 1966 edition and preface to the 1908 Authorized edition are factual and to the point, giving the basic information concerning the text itself and how it was prepared. The introduction to the LDS "New Triple" of 1981 does not contain even one word pertaining to how the text was edited and how it differs from the previous editions.

I give full credit to the Utah editions for including the story of the coming forth of the Book of Mormon, now titled "Testimony of the Prophet Joseph Smith." *This* kind of extratextual material has all rights to be included. This, however, does not—to me—balance the addition of an explicatory subtitle.

Strangely enough, Joseph Smith's own preface to the First Edition, important both as historical evidence and as a sample of *his own* writing (the Book of Mormon, after all, claims to be a translation), is missing in all the LDS and RLDS editions known to me. I can only guess that it might be missing in the Kirtland 1837 and Nauvoo 1840 editions, and thus deemed no longer necessary. Not having access to those editions I can only guess.

On the basis of the above, I conclude that unless the reader of the Book of Mormon has access to the First Edition facsimile, he should regard the 1908 and 1966 editions by the Reorganized Church as more authentic and authoritative than the LDS editions from Utah. I do not wish to please or annoy

any of the two churches. I speak as a researcher working with a variety of editions of the same text, who faces the problem of their reliability and follows the methodology most applicable under given circumstances.

As a more personal conclusion, I would like to add that the 1966 RLDS Readers' Version of the Book of Mormon is comparable only to the breakthrough caused by the *Good News for Modern Man Bible* in its own day. Just like the *Good News* Bible, it proves that the same message can be retold in a form equally elegant but free of solemnly archaic "Biblicisms." Even though its foreword states, "No conscious attempt has been made to modernize the language of the text," and although I know from *Restoration Scriptures* that the 1966 RLDS World Conference rejected the 1966 edition as the authorized edition, I feel certain it remains an unparalleled achievement. Paraphrasing what Richard Howard wrote, I think it not only *aimed at*, but actually *produced* a text superior to any previous edition. As a researcher in religious history I know that stepping away from any tradition-sanctioned wording is a difficult decision. However, to quote what the Polish philosopher Alfred Korzybski was fond of saying, "Words are not things."

* * *

The starting point of the discussion of various editions of the Book of Mormon was the question of their authenticity. This logically brings us to the question of whether the book is "true." To answer this, let us begin with a seemingly superfluous question: What *is* the Book of Mormon, really?

This question is much less absurd than it may at first appear because our reaction to the book will largely be conditioned by what we find it to be. I think there are only three possible answers:

1. The Book of Mormon is a forgery perpetrated either by Joseph Smith himself

or by someone else with his knowledge and full agreement.

2. The Book of Mormon is a historical record which is factually true and can be proven by scientific means.

3. The Book of Mormon is a *modern* (as opposed to *ancient*) scripture, and, as such, it is totally outside the impersonal domain of scientific proof.

Let me say a few words about each point:

1. Every few years since 1830, someone has tried to prove that the Book of Mormon is a forgery. Sidney Rigdon, Solomon Spaulding, Ethan Smith, and many others have been postulated as the book's real authors or chief sources. None of these theories has stood the test of time, even though each still claims a number of supporters. I myself have come across people who are so certain the Book of Mormon is based on Spaulding's *Manuscript Found* that they consider it unnecessary to examine a copy of Spaulding's book, easily available at Oslo University Library. If the Book of Mormon is a forgery, nobody has proven it so far, and some of the attempts are so elaborate that it somehow seems easier to believe Joseph Smith's own words.

2. This attitude may appear reasonable at first, but as soon as we enter the domain of scientific proofs, we find it far from certain. An imposing amount of scholarly research relevant to the Book of Mormon is currently available, mostly by the painstaking efforts of Brigham Young University scholars who deserve highest praise for their efforts. We now know that there are countless parallels between the Book of Mormon and ancient Near Eastern scriptures of almost all kinds, that a few unquestionably Egyptian names appear in the book, that it contains the literary figure known as chiasmus, etc. All this, when put together, is extremely impressive—but only as *circumstantial*, not direct evidence. All we can safely conclude on its

basis is that all these parallels, names, and literary figures *are there*. I do not think it is safe to go further than that.

An example: II Nephi 1:80–100 in the RLDS 1966 edition, and II Nephi 2:10–17 in the Utah "New Triple" of 1981, interpret the fall of Adam in a way strongly reminiscent of a certain class of Buddhist texts which argue not in the positive ("It is ...") but in the negative ("What if it wasn't"). Shall we conclude that the Book of Mormon is influenced by Buddhist philosophy?

If the Mark Hofmann story teaches us anything, it shows what may happen if material proofs are given absolute priority. Demanding a material, tangible, and unquestionable proof is a sign of weakness, not strength. It is this insecurity that I see underlying the photographs identifying Nephites with Mayas or Aztecs, which I described above. This attitude is not responsible, neither as science nor as religion. The more we lock ourselves into it, the more dogmatic—not to say myopic—we become.

A responsible Book of Mormon scholarship should not try to provide any "proof" of the Book of Mormon. It should gather and edit all the available material, point the direction it leads in, and leave the reader to form his or her own conclusions. After all, did not Joseph Smith say, "The glory of God is intelligence" (Doctrine and Covenants 90:6a)? Such milestones as Hugh Nibley's writings, John L. Sorenson's recent annotated bibliography on pre-Columbian contacts with the Americas, or Paul Cheesman's collection of *Purported New World Inscriptions* are to me the best examples of responsible Book of Mormon scholarship. This is a far cry from showing a picture of some ruins on a hill and telling us that a presumably important piece of Book of Mormon evidence is inside.

What I will say now may hurt many, but it must be said. *If the people of the Book of*

Mormon were known to the *native* Ancient Americans—be they Incas, Aztecs, or Mayas—it is not impossible that the records of that knowledge were destroyed by Christian missionaries. Who knows, indeed who shall ever know, what untold wealth of knowledge was destroyed by Christian savages when the entire corpus of Mayan literature was burnt? If some missionaries today point to Quetzalcoatl and say he is really the Jesus of III Nephi, one can only shake his head. But, of course, sharing instead a piece of responsible Book of Mormon scholarship like John L. Sorenson's carefully worded masterpiece, *An Ancient American Setting for the Book of Mormon*, would take so much more time.

A relevant plea: friends of the Book of Mormon should be the first ones to come out with the reprints of such texts as Spaulding's *Manuscript Found*, Ethan Smith's *View of the Hebrews*, Howe's *Mormonism Unvailed*, yes, even *Joseph Smith's Egyptian Alphabet and Grammar*, particularly because many of such reprints come from those opposing the Book of Mormon. Those interested enough to be willing to read such materials will certainly be able to draw their own conclusions. Showing all the available evidence is strength, not weakness.

3. If we assume that the Book of Mormon is first and foremost a scripture, the burden of "scientific proof" disappears. However, this approach demands we define the key word. In my research, I assume that a scripture is a text containing messages relating to God, humanity, good, evil, way of life, and the hereafter as conditioned by the given text's own teaching. I do not regard cosmology or eschatology as necessary components of a scripture, even though they figure prominently in the three main traditions of the Old World—Judaism, Christianity and Islam—which are closely related. On the other hand, I assume that a scripture candidate invariably claims a divine origin or inspiration, optionally accentuated by some form of organized worship.

The Book of Mormon fulfills the above requirements. Its historical aspect seems beyond any possibilities of proving or refuting. Its message is such that it easily dominates the historical details. Would the great speech by King Benjamin lose any of its power if someone proved Benjamin never existed? If the Book of Mormon is a scripture, would it be any less so if someone managed to prove it is not what Joseph Smith said it was?

* * *

Opponents of the Book of Mormon all too often stoop to undermine it by attacking the man who gave it to us. An avalanche of charges has been heaped upon Joseph Smith. Until this day, historians argue about the validity of this or that affidavit signed for or against him a century and a half ago. Is this really so important? Do personal accusations affect the message of the book? Let us recall what Brigham Young said on similar charges at the time when the Book of Mormon was just a few weeks old:

I recollect a conversation I had with a priest who was an old friend of ours, before I was personally acquainted with the Prophet Joseph. I clipped every argument he advanced, until at last he came out and began to rail against "Joe Smith," saying, "that he was a mean man, a liar, money-digger, gambler, and a whoremaster"; and he charged him with everything bad, that he could find language to utter. I said, hold on, Brother Gillmore, here is the doctrine, here is the Bible, the Book of Mormon, and the revelations that have come through Joseph Smith the Prophet. I have never seen him, and do not know his private character. The doctrine he teaches is all I know about the matter, bring anything against that if you can. As to anything else I do not care. If he acts like a devil, he has brought forth a doctrine that will save us, if we will abide it. He may get drunk every day of his life, sleep with his neighbor's wife every night, run horses and gamble, I do not care anything about that, for I never embrace any man in my faith. But the doctrine he has produced will save you and me, and the whole world; and if you can find fault with that, find it.[6]

The world does not change all *that* much, it seems.

The Book of Mormon is greater than Joseph Smith and all the Restoration churches together. It deserves to be treated on its own terms, not in connection with any single man, even Joseph Smith. It has stood the test of time. It does not teach history, but life itself. It is, first and last, a *modern*— as opposed to an *ancient*—scripture. If it has any proof, it is in Moroni 10:4–5 and in the reader's own heart.

* * *

But a perfectly reasonable question must be asked. If we speak about a *modern* (rather than *ancient*) scripture, we have to agree that God may and does speak to and through chosen ones today just as in days of old. One of the earliest and longest-surviving arguments against Joseph Smith was that "such things" do not happen anymore. But don't they really?

Let us look at a man as amazing as he still is unknown at large, Emanuel Swedenborg, a Swedish scientist, inventor, anatomist, and theologian who lived 1688–1772. His long life can be divided into three periods. In his youth he worked in mechanics, metallurgy, geology, mineralogy, and engineering, and he left contributions in all these fields centuries ahead of his time. In his midlife he suddenly turned away from the field in which he was an acknowledged authority and applied himself to the study of anatomy. Few have ever set themselves a higher task. Swedenborg set out to locate the soul in the body—and along his new path he became a supreme authority on anatomy and the brain, again contributing discoveries and works which modern science finds prophetic and amazing beyond belief. At the age of fifty-six he again turned away from the field in which his authority by then was universally acknowledged and devoted the rest of his life to set out a system of Christi-

anity which is complete, coherent, and unlike anything ever postulated in the Western world.

Swedenborg claimed nothing less than having been used by God to tell those willing to listen, that both the Catholic and Protestant churches were wrong and had departed from the original truth. The greatest mistake of both churches was to take the entire Bible at literal, face value, wrote Swedenborg, claiming that "the things which I have learnt...are from the Lord alone" (*Spiritual Diary*, 1647). Not only does the Bible have an internal meaning, once generally known but now lost and in need of restoration, but also, claimed Swedenborg with the quiet authority of the one who knows, only *some parts* of the Bible are the Inspired Word. Many other ones may contain several good points but emphatically are of more dogmatic than divine character.

In Swedenborg's system, the New Testament consists of only five inspired books, the four Gospels and the Revelation of John. Let us briefly recapitulate some of Swedenborg's other teachings:

- God is very Man.
- He created the universe from himself, not from nothing.
- There is no trinity.
- There is no predestination.
- No church nor any religion has truth-monopoly.
- Non-Christians reach heaven as well as Christians.
- What makes the decision about reaching heaven is the kind of life we lead and not the church or the religion to which we belonged.
- When we enter the spiritual world, we will be asked not what our faith was, but what was the nature and quality of our life.
- There are three distinct kingdoms in heaven and in hell.

- Nobody goes to hell except by his own choice.
- Heaven is the domain of love of God; hell is the domain of love of self.
- Both heaven and hell are inside each one of us.
- Both the Last Judgment and the Second Coming are spiritual, not material events, and both have already been accomplished.

And to end the list, the most astonishing statement: The true system of Christianity, revealed through Swedenborg on God's own wish, expressly does *not* have to be organized into a church, nor must the whole world be converted to it. No. It ought merely be available to whomever might be interested in it. Otherwise, the greatest wisdom is that everything goes on just as it used to.

Even this all too sketchy outline of Swedenborg's astounding system brings to mind a number of tantalizing parallels from Joseph Smith's own revelations. Can the teachings of the Swedish seer and the American prophet originate from the same source? And if so, can we still doubt that God can and does speak to us through chosen ones now, just like in days of old?

* * *

But let us return to the Book of Mormon, which we now view primarily as scripture. To the large majority of Western people, "scripture" means the Bible, and whatever is claimed to be a scripture but is not found in the Bible is automatically suspect. In the popular view, the Book of Mormon is a second Bible, full of doctrines that are both false and dangerous. It often happens that someone turns down an offer to examine the Book of Mormon saying, "We do not need a second Bible." But if the book is scripture, is it also a Bible or its counterpart?

One can go through the Book of Mormon time and again without finding it to claim parity with the Bible or its own absolute character. In its historical part, it is merely a record of a civilization apparently lost without out a trace. In only one passage, and here the writer is quoting words spoken in prophecy, does the book contain the assertion that further light and truth might yet come forth through inspiration. The words are, "... because I have spoken one word, ye need not suppose that I cannot speak another; for my work is not yet finished; neither shall it be until the end of man, neither from that time henceforth and forever" (II Nephi 12:63, RLDS 1966; and II Nephi 29:9, Utah 1981 "New Triple"). Strong words, no doubt, but do they assert any ultimate authority or supremacy of the Book of Mormon?

The average opponent of the Book of Mormon does not really know anything concrete about Mormon doctrines. He sees only that they are very different but feels vaguely threatened by them and defends himself by rejecting the book he sincerely believes to contain them. And here is the real problem. One can comb the Book of Mormon for any length of time without finding any special and characteristic "Mormon doctrines" in it. Baptism for the dead, eternal progression, plurality of both wives and gods, marriage for eternity, preexistence of humans as spirits, even the dietary advice which the Utah Church elevated to a commandment, none of these doctrines is even mentioned in the book.

Trying to be the devil's advocate, I spent a lot of time hoping to locate any of the most criticized Mormon doctrines in the book of the same name. I succeeded on one count only. The book's explanation of the Fall of Adam[7] is clearly very different from the traditional ones of both Protestant and Catholic teachings. Let us add that Swedenborg, too, did not accept the Protestant interpretation of the Fall. If the Book of Mormon's interpretation gives the book a distinctly optimistic character, does that then automatically mean the book is a fraud? We *do* have Swedenborg as a controlling reference. Maybe it is just that some questions are older and more universal than "American frontier disputes" which so conveniently explain away any given teaching in the Book of Mormon.

As far as I understand the book, it neither contains any of the distinctive features of the Mormon Church in Utah nor does it claim any superiority or universal status for itself. If some missionaries make such claims, they harm both the book and their own cause. The book stands on its own authority. It needs no pedestals or any suggestive subtitles. It has stood the test of 160 years, and it will surely survive much longer, even if some wish to kill it with kindness.

Here I see a remarkable paradox. The Utah Church reaches out to the world in the name of the Book of Mormon, while none of its most distinctive doctrines is found in it. The Reorganized Church, on the other hand, disclaims these doctrines but at the same time does not mention the Book of Mormon in its own "Statement of Faith and Beliefs," at least as far as Steven L. Shields reprinted the statement in *Divergent Paths of the Restoration* (Bountiful, Utah: Restoration Research 1982, 67–71).

* * *

Let me pass on to a different but closely related field. A scripture is often defined or is definable by the art it inspires. Can we imagine Christianity without Michelangelo, Rafael, and Leonardo? (I *do not* mean Teenage Mutant Ninja Turtles!) Has the Book of Mormon inspired *such* art which could in retroflex be used as an argument in its favor?

For a long time I have been willing to make a study of art inspired by the Book of Mormon, but none of the necessary sources or facilities are available to me. However, my answer to the above question is a clear "yes." The Book of Mormon has already proved to be the source of inspiration for works that stand any comparisons in the domain of scripture-inspired creations. Not many of them have reached my hands in remote Norway, but let me list the most impressive ones that did.

1. In the RLDS orbit: the amazing tetralogy published by Herald Publishing House, *Deus, Nativity, Christus: the Life of Jesus, the Christ*, and *Terra Nova* by Wallace B. Shute, who in my subjective opinion can only be compared with Milton in the sweep of his vision, the intensity of his experience, and the unbelievable grandeur of his language.

2. In the LDS orbit: Orson F. Whitney's *Elias, an Epic of the Ages*, a terse, immensely concentrated, thought-provoking poem which more than deserves a new edition; and R. Paul Cracroft's *A Certain Testimony, a Mormon Epic*, a highly readable attempt to present the complete story of Latter-day Saints' standard works and history from the star Kolob to the Woodruff Manifesto.

3. In the universal language of music: Leroy Robertson's *Oratorio from the Book of Mormon*. If someone objects because the composer belongs to the Utah Church, let him try to decide whether Bach's *Matthäus-Passion* is more Protestant than Catholic.

* * *

No matter who gave us the Book of Mormon or how it was given, it is here to stay. It will not disappear because some may not like it. In all likelihood we shall never be able to lay our hands on a comfortable, tangible proof that the Book of Mormon is "true." It has a message which is of profound relevance today, if only because our world is still dominated by truth-monopoly claimants. Those who do not want it can just pass it by. To others, it will remain a challenge, a fascination, a test of both scientific and religious convictions, a mirror in which we can see ourselves and our attitudes both grow and mature. Searching for a "proof," trying to bend facts to fit a theory, using impressive gimmicks to cover up an underlying uncertainty and insecurity are all so much like a youngster who pins all sorts of buttons on his leather jacket hoping it makes him look tough. But figures and statistics do not prove any truth monopoly, nor anything else for that matter.

The Book of Mormon does not need any additional support. It is strong enough to stand on its own. It is like an adult who maybe is not so resplendent but is secure in knowing what he is, tested by life itself, not in need of being constantly reassured of how wonderful he is.

In the final count, we turn to the Book of Mormon yet again—and it dawns on us that it alone carries the ultimate test of itself—those few wise words of Moroni, "And if you shall ask [if these things are true] with a sincere heart, with real intent, having faith in Christ, he will manifest the truth to you by the power of the Holy Ghost" (Moroni 10:5).

This is the Book of Mormon's greatest challenge—and its highest teaching.

Afterword

The above paper was completed in September 1991. In the year that passed, some new and very important materials came to my hands, thanks to the kindness of Velma Ruch, Tom Morain, and Wayne Ham, to whom grateful thanks are due. I have no space here to make full use of these materials, and I hope they will form the basis of another paper in the future. However, I think that I must make two comments, particularly because I pursue Book of Mormon studies in total isolation from both Restoration scholars and libraries.

1. At the time of writing my paper, I had no access to a copy of the 1908 Authorized RLDS Edition of the Book of Mormon, only to a copy of the 1966 Readers' Edition. I received a copy of the Authorized Edition the day before my paper was posted to Velma Ruch. It is a copy of the edition printed in 1986, with a foreword by the First Presidency of the Reorganized Church. In this connection I want to say that my arguments in favor of the Book of Mormon being primarily a scripture are not in any way influenced by the current thinking of the Reorganized Church. I simply did not know about the First Presidency's position stated in the foreword to the 1986 printing. However, I am very glad to see that my own conclusions seem to be so close to the words of the First Presidency. This is a great encouragement for one working in conditions like mine.

2. Thanks to the inefficient information service of the University of Illinois Press, it was only in December 1991 that I finally obtained a copy of B. H. Roberts's *Studies of the Book of Mormon* (Urbana and Chicago: University of Illinois Press, 1985). Roberts's book is of fundamental importance to a Book of Mormon researcher (be he friend or foe), and without two brief comments on it, my paper cannot be complete.

a. One feels an enormous respect for B. H. Roberts's integrity which made *him* of all LDS scholars say it loud and clear that Joseph Smith had all the knowledge and imagination which "would make it possible for him to create a book such as the Book of Mormon is" (Roberts, page 250 and particularly 243–250).

b. Roberts's starting point was an attempt at answering a set of questions concerning subjects which often turn up in Book of Mormon controversies (American Indian languages, horses, Nephi's steel bow, the word "scimeter" and the knowledge of silk culture by the Nephites; cf. Roberts, 36).

When he realized these problems could not be answered by scientific evidence, and that their further consideration would only increase the difficulties connected with them, the LDS Apostle Richard R. Layman answered, "Then I do not know why we should consider them" (Roberts, 57, cf. 57–60). I think this comes close to my words on the danger inherent in accepting the Book of Mormon as a historical record verifiable by scientific means. The "scripture attitude" removes both problems, as it focuses on the spiritual teaching of the text as we now have it and not on the questions of its authorship or its technical details subordinate to the book's main aspect.

Notes

1. My thanks are extended to the scholars of Brigham Young University, Hugh Nibley, John L. Sorenson, and Paul R. Cheesman; the offices of the Church Historical Department and Church Information Center at Salt Lake City, Utah; Richard P. Howard, the church historian of the Reorganized Church, Independence, Missouri; the Foundation of Ancient Research and Mormon Studies (FARMS) at Provo, Utah; Bruce B. Flanders, the presiding elder of the Strangite branch of the LDS Church, Burlington; and especially, Steven L. Shields, whose books and letters have always provided a sure guidance through both the center and the distant peripheries of the Restoration movement.

2. Among the works to which I was introduced were Bruce McConkie's Mormon Doctrine; James Talmage's The Articles of Faith and Jesus the Christ; LeGrand Richard's A Marvelous Work and a Wonder and The Book of Jasher; Francis W. Kirkham's A New Witness for Christ in America; and most of all, to two books which more than anything else charted the course of my own future studies: J. M. Sjodahl's An Introduction to the Study of the Book of Mormon and Hugh Nibley's An Approach to the Book of Mormon. I was a voracious reader—maybe that was a way of compensating for the loss of my library—and I read absolutely everything I could lay my hands on, filling up notebook after notebook with bibliographic references, remarks, reflections, and questions for future study.

3. The books of particular interest were A. A. Hoekema's Four Major Cults, Gordon Fraser's Is Mormonism Christian?, Harry L. Ropp's The Mormon Papers—Are the Mormon Scriptures Reliable?, and particularly to Ira T. Hanson's sweeping list of a hundred questions Ask Your Bishop.

4. M. R. Werner, Brigham Young (New York: Harcourt, Brace and Company, 1925), 48–49.

5. First Edition, page 25; Utah LDS 1981 "New Triple," I Nephi 11:21; RLDS 1966, I Nephi 3:62.

6. Werner, 66.

7. II Nephi 1:90–128 and Alma 19:81–117 in RLDS 1966 edition; II Nephi 2:14–30 and Alma 42:1–31, Utah 1981 "New Triple."

Bibliography

The Book of Mormon (Manuscripts and textual history)

Howard, Richard P. *Restoration Scriptures: A Study of Their Textual Development.* Independence, Missouri: Herald House, 1969.

Jessee, Dean C. "The Original Book of Mormon Manuscript," in *Brigham Young University Studies* 10 (Spring 1970): 259–278.

The Book of Mormon (Printed editions)

First Edition, Palmyra 1830—Facsimile, Salt Lake City 1980, Deseret Books.

Missionary Edition LDS, copyrighted 1959 by President David O. McKay, reprinted in England 1978, illustrated.

The New Triple Combination, Salt Lake City 1981, published by the LDS Church, the present standard text for Utah LDS.

The Book of Mormon, Another Testament of Jesus Christ, Salt Lake City 1985, published by LDS Church, the 1981 text with a new subtitle.

Book of Mormon—Authorized Edition, Independence, Missouri: Herald House, 1908.

Book of Mormon—Readers' Edition, Independence, Missouri: Herald House, 1966.

Historical background

Alder, Douglas D., and Paul M. Edwards. "Common Beginnings, Divergent Beliefs," *Dialogue: A Journal of Mormon Thought* 11, no. 1 (Spring 1978): 18–28.

Arrington, Leonard J., and Davis Bitton. *The Mormon Experience: A History of the Latter Day Saints.* London: George Allen and Unwin, 1979.

Brooks, Melvin R. *LDS Reference Encyclopedia.* Salt Lake City, Utah: Bookcraft, 1960.

Koury, Aleah G. *The Truth and the Evidence, A comparison between the doctrines of the Reorganized Church of Jesus Christ of Latter Day Saints and the Church of Jesus Christ of Latter Day Saints.* Independence, Missouri: Herald House, 1965.

Meyer, Eduard. *Ursprung und Geschichte der Mormonen.* Halle: Verlag Max Niemeyer, 1912.

O'Dea, Thomas F. *The Mormons.* Chicago: University of Chicago Press, 1957.

Shepard, William, Donna Falk, and Thelma Lewis, eds. *James J. Strang. Teaching of a Mormon Prophet.* N.p.: Church of Jesus Christ of Latter Day Saints (Strangite), 1977.

Shields, Steven L. *Divergent Paths of the Restoration,* third edition revised and enlarged. Bountiful, Utah: Restoration Research, 1982.

Biographies

Brodie, Fawn M. *No Man Knows My History: The Life of Joseph Smith, the Mormon Prophet.* London: Eyre and Spottiswoode, 1963; originally published 1945.

Werner, M. R. *Brigham Young.* New York: Hartcourt, Brace & Co., 1925.

Book of Mormon scholarship

Bingman, Margaret. *Encyclopedia of the Book of Mormon.* Independence, Missouri: Herald House, 1978.

Cheesman, Paul R., ed. *Purported New World Inscriptions* N.p.: distributed by the editor, n.d.

Cheesman, Paul R. *The World of the Book of Mormon.* Bountiful, Utah: Horizon Publishers, 1984.

Hanson, Paul M. *Jesus Christ Among the Ancient Americans.* Independence, Missouri: Herald House, 1945.

Hauck, F. Richard. *Deciphering the Geography of the Book of Mormon.* Salt Lake City, Utah: Deseret Books, 1988.

Kirkham, Francis W. *A New Witness for Christ in America: The Book of Mormon,* new enlarged edition, 2 vols. Salt Lake City, Utah: Utah Printing Company, 1960–1963.

McConkie, Bruce R. *Mormon Doctrine.* Salt Lake City, Utah: Bookcraft, 1966.

Nibley, Hugh. *An Approach to the Book of Mormon.* Salt Lake City, Utah: Deseret News, 1957.

Nibley, Hugh. *Since Cumorah: The Book of*

Mormon in the Modern World, Salt Lake City, Utah: Deseret Books, 1967.

Reynolds, George. *A Dictionary of the Book of Mormon, comprising its biographical, geographical and other proper names.* Salt Lake City, Utah: Jos. Hyrum Parry, 1891.

Richards, LeGrand. *A Marvelous Work and a Wonder*, missionary edition. Salt Lake City, Utah: Deseret Books, 1976.

Sjodahl, J. M. *An Introduction to the Study of the Book of Mormon.* Salt Lake City, Utah: Deseret News Press, 1927.

Sorenson, John L. *An Ancient American Setting for the Book of Mormon.* Salt Lake City and Provo, Utah: Deseret Book Co. and FARMS (Foundation for Ancient Research and Mormon Studies), 1985.

Sorenson, John L., and Martin H. Raish, eds. *Pre-Columbian Contact with the Americas across the Oceans*, an annotated bibliography, 2 vols. Provo, Utah: Research Press, 1990.

Talmage, James E. *A Study of the Articles of Faith, being a consideration of the principal doctrines of the Church of Jesus Christ of Latter-Day Saints*, missionary edition. Salt Lake City, Utah: published by the LDS Church, 1977.

Talmage, James E. *Jesus the Christ: A study of the Messiah and his mission according to Holy Scripture both ancient and modern.* Salt Lake City, Utah: Deseret Books, 1954.

Warren, Bruce W., and Thomas Stuart Ferguson. *The Messiah in Ancient America.* Provo, Utah: Book of Mormon Research Foundation, 1987.

Weldon, Roy E., and F. Edward Butterworth. *Criticisms of the Book of Mormon Answered.* Published by authors, 1973.

Basic anti-Mormon books used

Fraser, Gordon H. *Is Mormonism Christian?* Norwegian translation: *Er Mormonenes laere kristen?* Oslo: Filadelfiaforlaget A/S, 1980.

Hoekema, Anthony A. *The Four Major Cults: Christian Science, Jehovah's Witness, Mormonism, Seventh-Day Adventism.* Exeter: Paternoster Press, 1975.

Hoekema, Anthony A. *Mormonism.* Exeter: Paternoster Press, 1973.

Ransom, Ira T. "Ask Your Bishop" (a pamphlet of a hundred questions). Sacramento, California: *United Missionary Fellowship*, no date.

Ropp, Harry L. *The Mormon Papers - are the Mormon scriptures reliable?* Downers Grove, Illinois: InterVarsity Press, 1977.

Best ongoing information on Book of Mormon scholarship

"Insights, An Ancient Window"—quarterly newsletter of the Foundation for Ancient Research and Mormon Studies (FARMS), P. O. Box 7113, University Station, Provo, UT 84602.

"Annual Review of Book of Mormon Books"—vol. 1, 1989; vol. 2, 1990; vol. 3, 1991; to be continued—published by FARMS (see above).

Emanuel Swedenborg and his system

Sigstedt, Cyriel Odhner. *The Swedenborg Epic, the life and works of Emanuel Swedenborg.* London: The Swedenborg Society, 1981.

Swedenborg, Emanuel. *A Brief Exposition of the Doctrine of the New Church.* London: The Swedenborg Society, 1952.

Swedenborg, Emanuel. *The True Christian Religion; containing the universal theology of the New Church*, new translation by John Chadwick, 2 vols., London: The Swedenborg Society, 1988.

Swedenborg, Emanuel. *Heaven and Hell, also the world of spirits or intermediate state from things heard and seen.* London: The Swedenborg Society, 1958.

Swedenborg, Emanuel. *Divine Providence.* London: The Swedenborg Society, 1949.

Swedenborg, Emanuel. *The Last Judgment, and Continuation concerning the Last Judgment.* London: The Swedenborg Society, 1961.

Warren, Samuel M. *A Compendium of the Theological Writings of Emanuel Swedenborg.* New York: Swedenborg Foundation Inc., 1974.

General framework

Choudhury, Makhan Lal Roy. *The Din-i-Ilahi or*

the religion of Akbar, 3rd edition. New Delhi: distributed by Munshiram Manoharlal Publishers, 1985.

Korzybski, Alfred. Science and Sanity; an introduction non-Aristotelian systems and general semantics, 4th edition. Lakeville, Connecticut: distributed by The Institute of General Semantics, 1980.

Art inspired by the Book of Mormon

Cracroft, R. Paul. "A Certain Testimony, a Mormon Epic in Twelve Books," Salt Lake City, Utah: Epic West, 1979.

Cracroft, Richard H., and N. E. Lambert, eds. "A Believing People; Literature of the Latter-day Saints," Provo, Utah: Brigham Young University Press, 1974.

England, Eugene, and Dennis Clark, eds. "Harvest. Contemporary Mormon Poems," Salt Lake City, Utah: Signatures Books, 1989.

Robertson, Leroy. Oratorio from the Book of Mormon, conducted by Maurice Abravanel, MBPC 403 music cassette, available from Deseret Book Express, Salt Lake City, Utah.

Shute, Wallace B. Deus. Independence, Missouri: Herald House, 1989.

Shute, Wallace B. Nativity. Independence, Missouri: Herald House, 1990.

Shute, Wallace B. Christus: The Life of Jesus the Christ. Independence, Missouri: Herald House, 1971.

Shute, Wallace B. Terra Nova. Independence, Missouri: Herald House, 1988.

Whitney, Orson F. Elias, an Epic of the Ages, revised edition. Salt Lake City, Utah: n.p., 1914.

Comment on the Book of Abraham:
A Personal Reflection
Wayne Ham

In February 1991 I had an experience that I wouldn't wish on anyone. President Wallace B. Smith received an invitation to go to Trinity Evangelical Divinity School in Deerfield, Illinois, to spend a day with students and faculty talking about the "Joseph Smith Restoration Movement." President Smith declined the invitation (prophetic soul that he is!) and instead sent a church bureaucrat who happens to be an amateur historian. That was me. I was provided with a schedule and list of topics to discuss, but that was essentially all the information I had on this event.

When I arrived at the seminary, I noticed a big banner across the main entrance to the chapel where the sessions were to be held: "The Annual Tanner [read that 'Gerald and Sandra Tanner'] Lectureship on Cults." Several years previously, I found out later, the Tanners had come to Trinity to expose Mormonism. The lectures went over so well that the faculty decided to invite other cult busters to come to Trinity to bash the Moonies, Scientologists, and anyone calling themselves a mahatma or maharishi. Now, perhaps seeking to breathe new life into an old tired format, someone had suggested, "Let's not bring in a cult buster. Let's bring in some cults that are trying to become respectable."

And so here I was in Deerfield, Illinois, wishing I were anywhere else in the world. I was sharing the spotlight with a former evangelist from the Seventh-day Adventists and a public relations team from the Worldwide Church of God. These two groups plus the RLDS were the cults of the hour.

I sized up the situation rather quickly and, as it turned out, unfairly. I imagined that they viewed me and my cultic colleagues as puny lions in a den of fierce Daniels. After all, this was not your typical Protestant seminary, dedicated to the pursuit of knowledge and the quest for truth, I said to my paranoid self. This was an archconservative, rabidly fundamentalist bastion of extremism. Some of the professors had taught courses on sects and cults. Some had written books against Mormonism. I decided that my only recourse among such knowledgeable anti-Mormons was to be absolutely honest, open, and aboveboard in my responses to any inquiries. No hedging, no bluffing, no evasion, no mental reservations.

To head off trouble at the pass and to avoid being snared in Mormon-baiting, I did my careless little historical sketch that suggests that three early stages of Latter Day Saint development can be experienced today by visiting the three churches that occupy the Temple Lot in Independence. The little white church on the quadrangle is the Church of Christ (Temple Lot). The members of this church like what Joseph Smith, Jr., did in bringing forth the Book of Mormon and in restoring the priesthood and in reestablishing Christ's Church in 1830, but in their eyes he erred seriously—he apostatized—when he introduced the high priesthood into the church in June 1831. So if you want a sense of what it is like to spend your energies preserving the Restoration church of the early New York period, visit the "Hedrickites," to use an old-fashioned term.

The "Josephites" are represented on the Temple Lot by the Auditorium and the Temple with a seashell top. If you want to know the polity, the theology, and the religious practices of the church at Kirtland, I usually say, here is where you would look, among the RLDS.

And if Nauvoo is your cup of tea, look to the "Brighamites" through the Mormon Visitors' Center on the Temple Lot for enlightenment. With this somewhat sloppy trisection of the early church's history, it is easy for RLDS to sidestep a lot of uncomfortable topics. Well, what about plural marriage, baptism for the dead, Temple endowments, the Council of Fifty, and so on? "Oh, well," we say, "that's Nauvoo, you see. Just talk to us about Kirtland."

Then came the Deerfield bombshell. A distinguished professor emeritus with a white shaggy mane got the microphone during a question- and-answer session. "Tell us about the Book of Abraham," he said. "That's a product of the Kirtland era. How does your church relate to the Book of Abraham?"

I was caught off guard. I had my usual historical analyses of the First Vision, the Gold Plates, and the Restoration of priesthood ready to parade. I was even prepared to spend a few hours telling the many ways that we are not like the Mormons (RLDS have been doing that for 140 years, so we are well practiced). But the Book of Abraham? Give me a break!

And yet that question is a valid question. And the data generated by responding to that question has since been useful to me in reexamining some of the identity crises that seem to plague my own religious institution from time to time. So let me share with you, as best I can, my honest, open, and aboveboard response to that inquiry about the Book of Abraham.

Yes, I confessed, it was in the summer of 1835 that Michael Chandler came to Kirtland with four Egyptian mummies and several rolls of papyrus with Egyptian hieratic writings and pictographs. This event coincided with a burst of interest on the part of church leadership in studying biblical languages. Joseph Smith, Jr., in a diary entry of that period (February 17, 1836, *original spelling retained*) recorded:

my soul delights in reading the word of the Lord in the original, and I am determined to persue the study of languages untill I shall become master of them, if I am permitted to live long enough, at any rate so long as I do live I am determined to make this my object, and with the blessing of God I shall succed to my sattisfaction.[1]

With Hebrew and Greek already on the agenda, it was natural for Joseph to add Egyptian, especially with the papyri newly acquired from Chandler. The difference was that Hebrew and Greek were classical languages with dictionaries, lexicons, and grammars readily available. The ancient Egyptian language was shrouded in mystery. It is true that seventeenth-century Jesuit scholar Athanasius Kirsher, professor of mathematics and Oriental languages at the University of Wurzburg, devoted many years to deciphering Egyptian hieroglyphics, but his *Oedipus Aegyptiacus*, written in Latin in forty-four volumes, is totally discredited nowadays. It was full of guesswork, and Kirsher just plain guessed wrong. We know this now because of the Rosetta Stone.

Napoleon's soldiers found the Rosetta Stone in 1799 while digging the foundations for a fortress near the Egyptian town of Rashid (called by Europeans "Rosetta"). Its text was in three columns with Egyptian hieroglyphics (unknown) and Egyptian demotic (unknown) and Greek, which could be interpreted.

Work began in earnest to decipher the unknown scripts. Thomas Young worked on the demotic, and Jean-Francois Champollion worked on the hieroglyphics. Champollion's grammar and dictionary were published to the world from 1836 until 1844. But in the meantime, any enterprising young scholar with a penchant for languages could consider Egyptian fair game and have a go at it. And that is exactly what Joseph Smith did. For the last half of 1835 and the first few months of 1836, Joseph's diary is replete with references to exhibiting the mummies and the papyri, laboring on the development of an Egyptian dictionary and grammar, and translating portions of the records that he had identified as the writings of Father Abraham. All of the Kirtland community of believers must have been ecstatic to know that the Prophet Joseph possessed Abraham's record, older than the oldest extant biblical manuscript by a thousand years, and its message was about to come forth in translation. And perhaps the writing of Joseph of Egypt, Abraham's great-grandson, might not be far behind.

Joseph Smith established a "translating room," a cubicle on the third floor of the Kirtland Temple where he could often be found on his hands and knees examining the papyri spread across the floor. Many in the community believed that Joseph was divinely assisted in the task of translating. Early in his career as prophet, Joseph had translated the Book of Mormon from Reformed Egyptian, had he not? So why should Heaven's Gate be closed at this important juncture of revelatory history? And so the first church historian, John Whitmer, could write that "Joseph the Seer saw these record[s] and by the revelation of Jesus Christ could translate these records, which gave an account of our forefathers."[2]

The contents of the Book of Abraham, made public in 1842 in the pages of the *Times and Seasons* (volume 3, no. 9 [March 1, 1842]) at Nauvoo, seem also to support some of Joseph Smith's changing theological perspectives. Only two items will be noted here. The unitary view of the Godhead so evident in the 1830 Book of Mormon's Sabellian theology where the Father *is* the Son has by the time of Kirtland given way to the duality of Godhead explicated so clearly in the "Lectures on Faith." The Father is a personage of glory and power; the Son is a personage of tabernacle, with the Holy Spirit the combined will of Father and Son. So now the monotheism of the creation passages in Joseph Smith's earlier translation of Genesis give way in the Book of Abraham account to a plurality-of-gods notion of Father and Son, two divine entities, separate and distinct but working together to organize and form the heavens and the earth.

The other belief relates to one of the most perplexing social issues of the day—slavery. After some years of uncertainty about how the church leadership, many of whom were of Yankee stock, felt about slavery, Joseph Smith in a letter to Oliver Cowdery published in the *Messenger and Advocate* advocated slavery as a social institution in the United States of America.[3] The curse is not yet taken off the sons of Canaan, Joseph affirmed, and that curse is a veil of darkness,[4] and the descendants of Ham must live under a special burden of being "cursed [him] as pertaining to the Priesthood."[5]

Yes, the Book of Abraham, while associated in some minds with the doctrinal peregrinations of the church on the banks of the Mississippi, was in fact a product of Kirtland.

So if it is a product of Kirtland, what has been and what is the position of the Book of Abraham in the RLDS Church? The position was shaky at first, followed by disengagement, followed by rejection. In the first document of the Reorganization, co-founder Jason W. Briggs affirmed the lineal principle of priesthood by citing the Book of Abraham.[6] An article affirming the plurality of gods appeared in the December 1860

The True Latter Day Saints' Herald by editor Isaac Sheen referencing the Book of Abraham,[7] as does another article on Brigham Young's alleged idolatry.[8] The Book of Abraham itself was reprinted in the Reorganization periodical in 1862.[9] Obviously the Book of Abraham was accepted by some early RLDS leaders as divine revelation in the same category as Joseph Smith's writing in the Book of Doctrine and Covenants. But the situation was soon to change. Perhaps formalizing the opening of RLDS priesthood ranks to blacks in May 1865 put the first nail in the coffin, while the canonizing of the Book of Abraham by the rival church in Utah slammed the coffin lid shut.

Church leaders and members allowed the book to drop out of sight, except when external forces intervened. In 1912 the Rt. Rev. F.S. Spalding, D.D., of Salt Lake City published "Joseph Smith, Jr., as a Translator" (Salt Lake City, Utah: The Arrow Press, 1912). His target was the Book of Mormon, but the good bishop used the Book of Abraham as a test for Joseph Smith's translating expertise, and when Spalding arrayed against the prophet the opinions of eight world-acclaimed Egyptologists, poor Joseph seemed to fail miserably as a translator of Egyptian.

Spalding's attack on Joseph Smith, Jr., drew the attention of the national media. And the RLDS were forced to respond. Elbert A. Smith, grandson of Joseph, Jr., and editor of *The Saints' Herald*, noted that "we may not be particularly interested in the fate of the Book of Abraham, yet when any defects that are supposed to have been found in it are used as a basis for an argument that the Book of Mormon is of spurious origin, the matter becomes one of common interest."[10] The editor was quick to point out that the Book of Abraham is different from the Book of Mormon. For the

Book of Abraham, Joseph Smith studied out an Egyptian alphabet and grammar, whereas the Book of Mormon is a product of divine revelation, and the RLDS Church has never endorsed the Book of Abraham as anything more than a human performance. But even so the *Saints' Herald* editor went on to say that the Episcopal bishop was not entirely successful in his attempt to discredit the book, since the eight noted Egyptologists themselves disagreed on the translation of the facsimiles from the Book of Abraham text published in *The Pearl of Great Price*. If the scholars could give such different interpretations of the text, why not give Joseph Smith a hearing? Apparently in 1913, despite the noncanonical status of the book, there was still an openness to the possibility of its legitimacy as a translation of an ancient text.

Basically silence then in the RLDS press until the recovery of the papyri from the Metropolitan Museum of Art in 1967.[11] LDS Apostle Alvin Dyer presented to RLDS President W. Wallace Smith photostatic copies of the reclaimed papyri fragments. President Smith announced through the pages of the *Saints' Herald* that the Book of Abraham is simply speculative writings of the author and is not inspired.[12]

A three-part series on the book was presented by church historian Richard Howard, the bottom line of which reads as follows:

The Book of Abraham is neither a scholarly translation (Joseph Smith appears to have had no credentials as an Egyptologist) nor any sort of "inspired translation," as the church has affirmed the Book of Mormon to represent.[13]

And so the verdict has crystallized for most RLDS, at least for those few who have heard of the Book of Abraham. The Book of Abraham came out of a period when Joseph Smith was fascinated with antiquity and fancied himself a world-class translator. The text is the product of a rich imagination and nothing more. The text has no philological connection to the hieratic symbols inscribed on the ancient papyri. The theological speculation inherent in the book bears no resemblance to any theological musings of late twentieth-century RLDS thinkers. Finally, the apologetic work of Hugh Nibley's "parallelomania" methodology seeking to shore up the view of Book of Abraham as ancient literature falls far short of meeting scholarship standards for our times.[14]

So what does all this signify to RLDS now confronting the Book of Abraham? Two thoughts consistently creep to the fore in church history classes that I have taught in which the Book of Abraham has been given its rightful place as a product of the Kirtland experience. First of all, if Joseph could create what our faith community now considers to be a spurious document, what might this say about the Book of Mormon? The time is probably not too far distant when the leadership and the membership will have to take a serious look at the role of the Book of Mormon in the modern church. The other question often encountered is, "Whose church are we after all?" After the expected affirmations are uttered that we are Christ's Church or at least one part of the body of Christ, then the original question reasserts itself. Are we Joseph Smith, Jr.'s church, or are we secure enough now in our own identity to bequeath that distinction to our LDS sisters and brothers? Are we instead the Church of Emma Smith and her son, Joseph the Third? While Briggs, Gurley, Sheen, and others assumed a certain legitimacy for the Book of Abraham, Emma and Young Joseph and other influential members held their peace. And the Book of Abraham, along with many notions that came to fruition at Nauvoo sometimes from an uncertain birth at Kirtland, began its slip into institutional oblivion.

I want to say one final thing about the folks at Trinity Seminary: I misjudged them. Yes, they have some hard-shell notions about biblical inerrancy and other Protestant fundamentalist dogmas that I do not relate to at all, but as soon as the day's explorations began, they turned out to be a gracious, inquisitive, and kindly audience. I believe I convinced most of them that the RLDS Church is not a cult, but I was less convincing about the fact that we are Christian. But then their definition of Christian seemed a bit restrictive to me. I got in a few licks myself about how evangelical Christians should not be so quick to name-call: to call other Christian bodies "cults" simply over differences in theological perspective. As we reasoned together all the day long and on into the evening hours, I found it easy to sense the grace that was alive and working in their community as they engaged in the great struggle to understand from their point of view God's intentions for the human family. I was surprised how the Book of Abraham became such a pivotal point of discussion. In some ways I was shocked to discover that these evangelical Christians were perhaps more open to the *message* of the book than was I. As we talked on, it reconfirmed to me that my present heritage in the Reorganization makes me, in some respects, more Protestant Christian than Restorationist. What a long pilgrimage we have been on, struggling to be faithful to the gospel of Christ on the one hand while attempting to be open to the unsettling demands of modern scholarship at the same time. What strange byways this has led us in.

Despite being written off by the Reorganization, the Book of Abraham undoubtedly has a lot of life left in it yet. Generations of faithful LDS yet to come will no doubt find it instructive and inspirational, and perhaps a renaissance of Book of Abraham scholarship will yet emerge in the near future. Meanwhile, the RLDS have more or less pronounced the Book of Abraham dead to relevancy and have buried it. But unlike so many other funerals for early Restorationist distinctives, now banished by the RLDS to the nether realm of irrelevance with a great sense of loss and trauma, with the demise of the Book of Abraham there have been no tears at parting.

Notes

1. Dean C. Jessee, ed., *The Personal Writings of Joseph Smith* (Salt Lake City, Utah: Deseret Book, 1984), 161.
2. Book of John Whitmer Kept By Commandment, manuscript, p. 76, RLDS Library-Archives vault, Independence, Missouri.
3. *Latter Day Saints' Messenger and Advocate* 2, no. 7 (April 1836): 289–291.
4. Genesis 9:29–30, *The Holy Scriptures, Inspired Version* (Independence, Missouri: Reorganized Church of Jesus Christ of Latter Day Saints, 1974), 29.
5. Book of Abraham 1:26, *Pearl of Great Price* (Salt Lake City, Utah: The Church of Jesus Christ of Latter-day Saints, 1957), 31.
6. *A Word of Consolation to the Scattered Saints* (Janesville, Wisconsin: D. W. Scott & Co.'s Job Office, 1853), 11.
7. *The True Latter Day Saints' Herald* 1, no. 12 (December 1860): 280–283.
8. Ibid., 283–285.
9. *The True Latter Day Saints' Herald* 3, no. 1 (July 1862): 1–10.
10. *The Saints' Herald* 60, no. 23 (June 4, 1913): 541.
11. *Saints' Herald* 115, no. 2 (January 15, 1968): 43.
12. *Saints' Herald* 117, no. 3 (March 1970): 5.
13. *Saints' Herald* 117, no. 12 (December 1970): 26.
14. Edward H. Ashment in his article, "Reducing Dissonance: The Book of Abraham as a Case Study," 221–235, published in Dan Vogel, ed., *The Word of God: Essays on Mormon Scripture* (Salt Lake City, Utah: Signature Books, 1990). References "parallelomania" and refers to Samuel Sandmel in *Journal of Biblical Literature* 81 (1962): 1–13 for an enlightening discussion of "parallelomania."

V
BIOGRAPHICAL
REFLECTIONS

V
BIOGRAPHICAL REFLECTIONS

Editor's Note

Two articles give readers some insight into the lives of two pioneers, their work, and their time in history.

Kenneth M. Walker, Jr., outlines the missionary work of a man who devoted his entire life in missionary activity. Many who are members of the Restoration movement today find their spiritual roots in the work he did. John J. Cornish with evangelistic enthusiasm used the missionary techniques appropriate to his day, and his work was marked by a fruitful harvest. The author tells the story of this man who enjoyed the fellowship of people and the opportunity to share the gospel.

Using the relatively new medium of photography, G. E. Anderson left his home and family to journey to England on a mission for the LDS Church. On the way he spent several months visually recording the history of the Restoration. He was challenged by the lack of money and inadequate housing and places to develop his photographs, but he found many who offered a helping hand and enjoyed the satisfaction of his work. The story of Anderson is told by Richard N. Holzapfel and T. Jeffery Cottle, drawing from the diary and photographs of Anderson.

John J. Cornish: Study of a Missionary 1872–1937

Kenneth M. Walker, Jr.

Introduction

It is hoped that the following study of the missionary techniques of John J. Cornish will be a help to members and missionaries within the Reorganized Church of Jesus Christ of Latter Day Saints (RLDS Church). John Cornish, better known as J. J., baptized more than 1,500 people into the church in Michigan, Indiana, Ontario, and Saskatchewan.[1] His ministry was marked by many miraculous blessings which strengthened the faith and increased the hope of those he brought into the church. His enthusiasm and dedication was unsurpassed in the sixty-five years he served the church as a full-time and self-sustaining minister. He is a role model for those who witness of the Christ, share God's love, or seek to build the kingdom of God on earth.

Cornish will be long remembered for the efforts he made bringing the restored gospel to the people he met. A fellow minister said:

He devoted almost his entire life to the missionary work of the church, mingling with people and telling the gospel story in the way which stamps upon his hearers the conviction that he believes with all his soul that which he is saying to them.[2]

Living in Michigan and baptized in one of the branches that J. J. Cornish organized, I had the opportunity to discover some of the stories and legends of this extraordinary missionary from Ontario. One particular Cornish missionary pattern that I remember hearing was that he would walk into a small town in Michigan, preach a few days, baptize a number of people, ordain a few of those people, and then walk to the next town to start the process all over again. From this experience a branch of the RLDS Church would arise. It was easy to believe such a story because Cornish started so many branches in Michigan.

Although it seems likely that this could have happened and may have occurred on a few occasions, my research was unable to verify this story. Sources cite J. J. Cornish making repeated trips to the places where he organized groups. He baptized more people each time he returned. This happened over a period of years as he brought ministry to that area.[3] I was unable to find one example of Cornish baptizing and ordaining someone as well as organizing a branch in the same week. The shortest interval I found between someone being baptized and ordained by Cornish was ten days.[4] A more common time frame between the first baptism and the organization and ordination of the first members of a new branch was three months to one year.[5]

J. J. Cornish was a productive writer. He wrote more than ninety letters to the *Saints' Herald* that were printed as reports from the field. He wrote an autobiography, *Into the Latter-Day Light*, many articles for church publications, and numerous church missionary pamphlets. He also published a Bible synopsis. There is much that he wrote, but little written about him. This paper is based to a large extent on his writings, letters, and branch records located in the RLDS Library and Archives in Independence, Missouri.

Historical Background

J. J. Cornish traveled twenty-five years as a self-sustaining elder (1875–1884 and 1922–1937) as well as thirty-eight years as a full-time appointee minister (1884–1922). His early years were spent in Ontario and Michigan while his latter years were in Saskatchewan and Alberta. He began his missionary outreach as a newly baptized member of the church in 1872 and continued until the day he died sixty-five years later in 1937.

His spirit of evangelism and missionary work had the wholehearted support of his wife and his children.[6] During his many years of ministry, Cornish and his family sacrificed much. They were separated a considerable amount of the time and were given very little compensation while he worked full-time for the church. In 1884 Cornish accepted full-time General Church appointment, receiving $15 a month for his family allowance.[7] He was a dedicated minister. Cornish once said:

I had a desire to spend all of my time in the preaching of the gospel to my fellow men, to give them an opportunity to know what I knew, that the willing and obedient might have an opportunity to come and occupy. So I was glad and happy in the thought that I was permitted to preach as circumstances would permit, and my dear little wife was willing to sacrifice with me and share the joys and sorrows incident.[8]

John J. Cornish overcame many adversities in his lifetime. His mother died when he was three years old, and his father was unable to provide for the four children by himself. Cornish was bonded to another family and separated from his own. He did not get along with his abusive stepfather, and his caring stepmother died when he was ten.[9] Cornish was not allowed to attend school on a consistent basis, thus causing him to have a reading problem. He ran away from home at the age of twelve to stay with a family a few miles from his stepfather's home. He went to live with relatives when he was seventeen.[10] Cornish had many other hardships during his life, but something very positive became a part of his life in 1872.

His uncle, John Taylor, was an active member of the RLDS Church. He exposed his nephew to the restored gospel. J. J. Cornish's conversion experience came soon after he moved in with his Uncle John. After several worship and prayer meetings, he was so touched by the Holy Spirit that he spent one day praying in a secluded woods that he might be told if the Reorganized Church really was Christ's Church.[11] Cornish was spoken to that night by the Holy Spirit through the very person that he had specified. After that experience there was no doubt in his mind that he was involved in Christ's Church. He soon was baptized and began his life of servanthood. The church remained a positive influence for the rest of his life.[12]

After his baptism, Cornish was excited and determined to share his testimony with others. He moved to London, Ontario, got a job at a mill, and moved into a boarding house. Through his efforts an RLDS branch was established in London. In 1875 Cornish was ordained a priest, married Jannie Stratton, was ordained an elder, and selected the first pastor of the newly organized London branch. By the summer of 1876, he was involved in full-time ministry, while his family was supported by relatives and Saints in London. Cornish traveled from town to town in Ontario and Michigan sharing the restored gospel, baptizing people, and organizing new branches.

His missionary work in southeastern Michigan was very successful in 1878. He walked 1100 miles, preached about 126 sermons, baptized ninety people, and organized four branches.[13] He felt confident there were many able ministers in Ontario but very few to carry on the work in Michigan.[14] In March 1879 his family moved to Richmondville, Michigan, to be closer to his missionary field as well as to witness to his father who lived in the area.

Cornish had to sell his household furniture in Ontario to make ends meet while he was committed in full-time ministry. He decided to open a small sawmill business in Richmondville to provide an income for his family while he continued his missionary outreach. The seasonal work of the sawmill gave him time to travel.

There was a devastating fire in September 1881 while he was on a missionary trip. It caused tremendous damage to Richmondville and destroyed the Cornish home and mill.[15] Fortunately his family was not hurt. Although heavily in debt, Cornish was able to lead the recovery of the fire-damaged area with his refurbished mill. He rallied the whole community of Richmondville into a Zionic endeavor that brought life back to the area.[16] He continued to preach every Sunday. In the three years of rebuilding, Cornish baptized 146 people into the church. From 1875–1884 as a self-sustaining minister he baptized about 450 people.[17]

J. J. Cornish accepted General Church appointment in 1884 and was assigned to Michigan for the next twenty-seven years.[18] These became enjoyable years for Cornish and his family, as he shared his testimony with thousands of people in the Great Lakes state. By 1912 Michigan had many able ministers to carry on the work,[19] and Cornish was assigned to the prairie provinces of western Canada. In April 1910, he had moved his family to Senlac, Saskatchewan.[20] In all, thirty-seven adults and children made the trip. It was there that he would finish the remaining years of his life. Social ethics within the United States were evolving and his methods were not as effective. He was older and times were changing.[21] However, in the frontier land of the Canadian prairies, Cornish was able to carry on his work. In 1922 he retired from church appointment but not from witnessing and missionary outreach. He continued to be a significant influence and enduring voice of faithfulness for the church and the restored gospel in western Canada until his death.

Social Conditions

It is important to recognize the social conditions that existed in Michigan in the late nineteenth century and their part in Cornish's effectiveness. Most people were not very mobile. If a family had a horse and buggy, they were lucky. They stayed home unless there was something special going on in their local area because there was limited entertainment. Michigan in the 1880s was a frontier land with few cities and many small towns.

When he came into a town to preach, Cornish arranged to use a local building. Most townships had their own hall or school. If he had trouble getting permission to use a building, Cornish had a local person obtain approval. They were public facilities, built by the local people, so it was easy to rent or use them for free.

He participated in more than twenty-five debates during his lifetime.[22] It was an effective way of exposing people to the restored gospel. There was a great deal of prejudice against Mormonism by the Christian community and apathy among unchurched people. A debate created enough excitement to be entertainment. Cornish was an excellent speaker and debater. He was able to win many people to the Restoration through his gifts.

Once there were enough people interested in the church, a small group would begin to meet at someone's home, the school, or the township hall. It was typical for them to worship all day Sunday. Sunday school started at 9:30, preaching at 11:00, lunch, preaching at 2:30, dinner, and preaching again at 7:30. A baptismal service was normally scheduled before dinner, after the 7:30 preaching service, or after the Wednesday evening prayer meeting.[23]

When Cornish was baptized in 1872, there were about 8,300 members in the church and 160 members in Canada.[24] When he retired from full-time ministry in 1922, there was little he had not done in respect to missionary outreach. In addition to the baptizing of more than 1,500 souls, he was involved in the organization of at least seventy branches of the RLDS Church. By 1937 the church had 115,000 members, with 6,500 members in Canada.[25] This was the setting that J. J. Cornish was most effective in during his years of ministry. He was a man of his times who fit the culture and related to the people. He lived in poverty most of his life but was willing to share anything he had. Cornish was a straightforward person who told you where he stood. He was a person people liked and trusted. Let us look at the methods he used to persuade so many people to join his church.

Missionary Techniques

J. J. Cornish was an exceptional missionary and church planter. When he went into an area, he intended to plant a church if people responded to the restored gospel. This happened time after time in Michigan and Canada. J. J. started planting churches before he was ordained into the priesthood. He witnessed to many people that he met each day. Two of these individuals responded to the Holy Spirit and were baptized into the church. One was a young woman who boarded in his boarding house and the other worked with him.[26] Cornish invited elders to visit London and arranged

a place for them to speak. He advertised their speaking times in three local newspapers and paid all their expenses out of his own pocket. He even joined the local Temperance Club, so he could qualify to use their hall for $1 a night. He acted as the janitor and cleaned up the hall each night they used it.[27] Through his efforts more than 100 souls were baptized into the church in London from 1872 to 1876. Much can be learned from his witnessing methods.

J. J. Cornish was Christ-centered. He had compassion for those in need and spent time caring for them. People's needs were always important to him. He was people oriented. He cared about them and talked their language.[28] J. J. liked to shake hands, be friendly, kiss babies, and do whatever it took to make people feel at home with him. He wanted people to feel good about themselves. He liked to talk, stay in homes, and share meals.[29]

Cornish was involved in the lives of people with whom he came in contact. He enjoyed fellowship with people. He had people come to his home, but it was not his normal method of contact. He was usually on the road, visiting in someone else's home. He invited people to the home he was staying in, then relied on the hosts to provide a meal and fellowship. Home ministry was important in his relationships with people. When he walked from town to town, he did not have money to stay in hotels or eat in restaurants. He stayed with Saints and their friends and was always satisfied with what they provided.

J. J. Cornish believed in the power of prayer. He lived the gospel every day and expected God's presence in his life. He was open to the workings of the Holy Spirit.[30] He participated in many healings and miracles. His book, *Into the Latter-day Light*, is filled with phenomenal blessings that occurred in his ministry. Many people were blessed by Christ's healing Spirit through him.

J. J. Cornish lived the life that Jesus wanted him to live. He was humble and lived a subservient lifestyle.[31] He did not swear, drink alcohol, smoke, or do anything that brought discredit to his church.[32] He was called to bring the restored gospel to common people. When he was baptized at the age of eighteen, Cornish couldn't read. This, however, did not stop him from bearing his testimony.[33] He talked about religion to whomever listened and especially to those who were not involved in religion. Cornish had a way about him. He could make talking about religion appealing even to those who were not interested. He could convince them to stay and listen as he shared his testimony of Jesus Christ working in his life, the good news of the restored gospel, and Christ's Church here on earth.

J. J. Cornish witnessed to neighbors, family, and fellow workers on a one-to-one basis[34] and to total strangers as he passed them on the street. He had repeated contacts with people who were interested in what he had to say. He also made contact with the network of friends and relatives of baptized members, recognizing that new members had many friends and family. He made it a point to encourage newly baptized Saints to share the good news with others. He sometimes baptized whole families over a period of weeks, months, and years.[35]

J. J. Cornish was scripture-based in his witnessing. He studied the scriptures and put them into action as he lived the gospel. He studied, fasted, and prayed to prepare himself to go and tell. He had a great memory and the ability to recall scriptures that he had read.[36] He stood up for what he believed and was willing to debate anyone in defense of his church. Cornish had a special way of proving what he believed. The scriptures supported his religious beliefs. He used charts, scriptural notes, and whatever it took to persuade someone the church was right.[37]

When J. J. Cornish went into areas he usually knew someone. In his early years, he did not know anyone because he was the first to bring the restored gospel to those areas.[38] However, he was most effective when there was someone established in an area who gave his work stability. Cornish received many invitations from Saints to establish the church where they were living.[39] Knowing his time and abilities were limited, he concentrated on the most receptive areas.

J. J. Cornish always returned to places that were receptive to the Holy Spirit and the gospel message. He identified individuals who were interested in joining the church and responded to their needs. He was prepared to baptize someone when they were ready. A baptismal service could follow his debates, preaching services, or prayer meetings. Over the years he taught, preached, baptized, and ordained members to the priesthood who responded to his ministry. He devoted himself to these new openings until they were well-established and he could go on to another town. He was involved in several of these openings at the same time, making repeated trips back to each group to bring ministry where needed.[40]

J. J. Cornish was willing to travel anywhere at any time, and he did. He traveled many miles to bring the gospel to people in rural areas of Michigan and Canada. He would travel to a nearby town, preach, and then walk home on the same day. He usually traveled by foot because he did not own any form of transportation. One day on the way back from a missionary trip, he and Willard J. Smith walked fifty-three miles.[41]

J. J. Cornish used teamwork as one of his missionary methods. From the beginning of his missionary outreach, he took people to help him.[42] He was not a one-man show.

He recognized the ministry other disciples could provide the Saints and knew it was a team effort.[43] He utilized people's talents. When he first started to preach he couldn't read, so he had someone read the scriptures for him. Music was an important part of his worship, and it was an effective way to use people's talents. If there were gifted vocalists available, they sang. Cornish used his son, William, at an early age because he was a good singer. Traveling with Cornish to participate in missionary experiences was an excellent training ground for many young ministers and provided energetic support.[44]

J. J. Cornish's greatest strength was his enthusiasm and the ability to pass his passion on to others. He was filled with enthusiasm and zeal. He bore an affirmative testimony of Jesus Christ working in his life and shared that testimony whenever he preached, debated, or witnessed.[45] He was excited about sharing the good news with others. His enthusiasm made him a great preacher. He kept everyone's attention: men, women, and children. It was hard to fall asleep when Cornish was preaching, debating, or just talking. When he was preaching, he could almost hypnotize people.[46] His passionate devotion and positive outlook made his Christian discipleship apparent to anyone who knew him.

Conclusion

This paper has discussed John J. Cornish's missionary methods. He was a man of his times—simple, but complex. He be-

came the most prolific missionary in the history of the Reorganization. He related to people at their point of need and administered to their physical, mental, or spiritual needs. His best ministering to spiritual needs came through one-to-one witnessing, preaching, or debating. He enthusiastically witnessed for Jesus Christ and God's love for all people. Cornish, with his co-workers, made Michigan and Ontario two of the church's strongest areas of membership today.

There will never be another J. J. Cornish because North America will never be like it was in the late nineteenth century. However, his evangelistic spirit will endure through the thousands of Saints he encountered and the lives they have since touched. J. J. explained his work in these words:

I have preached the gospel to thousands of people, many of whom have obeyed the same. Many who obeyed have been called to preach the gospel and to administer to those who are in need of the helping hand of the Almighty.... All have their friends, who also have their friends, and so the gospel is being preached by others, and the blessings follow the preaching of that gospel all over the world. I have obeyed it. I have tried it, and *I Know.* Let the readers who have not obeyed it, obey it and live it, and they will know that like blessings are for us now.[47]

The study of J. J. Cornish's missionary techniques can help us learn to share the gospel. As we use those methods that are most effective in our relationships with others, they help us become better missionaries and disciples of the Lord Jesus Christ.

Appendix A: Life in the Cornish Era

The following is an original story based on my reading about the life of J.J. Cornish.
It is told so that you might experience the times and ministry of John J. Cornish.

I remember seeing a poster up at the post office three days ago. It said that there was going to be a debate between a minister named Reverend M.D. Rogers of the Church of Christ and someone named John J. Cornish of the Reorganized Latter Day Saints Church. The debate was going to be held here in our little village, Farwell, at the Gilmour Township School over on Ohio Street. That's usually where people go to have any fun around here. We don't really have much else to do except go swimming in the mill pond or watch the cows come home in the evening.

I had a hard time making a decision to go that first night. I don't know much about religion or God. We don't have many churches around here, and I haven't been to one in ten years. I had never been to a debate before so I decided I'd go ahead and go. I thought it would be something to do. This is the third night in a row that I've been to this debate between J. J. Cornish and the Reverend Rogers. Reverend Rogers is highly educated, and I am very impressed with all the book knowledge that he has and all the big words that he uses. But I don't like the man, he seems to think himself better than the rest of us here in Farwell.

But J. J. Cornish is something special. I'm not sure what it is. He is not very educated and the language he uses is like ours. He sure is polite to that preacher. I don't understand why Reverend Rogers is so much against J. J. and his church. Reverend Rogers is so negative. He is telling us and J.J. that we will all be going to hell if we don't join his church. He is downright rude about it. But Mr. Cornish just gives him an answer for everything he says. I like J.J. He seems to be a real caring man. I like the way he says things. They make sense

to me. He is honest, straightforward, and a hard-working family man. He is so positive when that Reverend Rogers is mean to him.

Last night a group of us followed J. J. out to the old mill pond after the debates, and he baptized three women, two boys about ten years old, and an old man. It was a beautiful thing to see the smiles on the faces of those people when they came out of that water. My cousin Sally was one of those people. That's really why I went. We grew up together, and she asked me if I would like to come along. She and her husband Bob think the world of J.J. Cornish. Bob was baptized the night before at Littlefield Lake. They had to walk several miles, but that was where he wanted to be baptized and J.J. said he was willing to go anywhere at anytime to baptize someone into his church. J.J. had been to their house for dinner last night and they invited me to come too. They talked a lot about Jesus Christ and then went to the debate together. I went to the baptism because I like Sally, she is almost like a best friend to me, and she is family.

We were both born in Richmondville and moved up here with our parents eleven years ago after the '81 fire. Our aunt Liz and her husband, Wil Thomas, came to visit two years ago and ended up staying here. We soon found out that she was a part of some "restoration church." It was not long before she invited him to come up here and debate Reverend Rogers.

Never been to one of those debates, but I've really enjoyed myself. This Mr. Cornish really knows what he is saying. I've never heard anyone talk with such authority. He almost makes you want to get up and get baptized before it's too late. He says he's going home tomorrow to his wife and seven kids in Reed City. But he promised us he would be back if we will come and listen to him.

He is a platform orator. He covers lots of ground the way he prances up and down and back and forth; before, behind, and around his big gospel charts. He is an advertiser, he is always announcing his subject around town and putting up posters and talking to anyone who will talk to him on the street. I can hear him saying something now, "Don't miss it, don't miss it! You can't afford to!" Everyone comes because we want to hear what he is going to say next. It is like we are hypnotized while he fills us up with the restoration gospel. He sure knows how to keep our attention.

Even though he is short, gray haired, and almost bald, he has a snap in the way he walks and talks. He sure makes that Reverend Rogers look silly. You know I'm thinking of joining this here Reorganized Church. It's not just because I like listening to J.J. talk, and that I do like. But it's because he has shown me that I need to "obey the gospel." I should live my life for Jesus Christ and join the church. Well I better get going or I'll be late for tonight's debate. You should come along, it's the best thing that has ever happened around these parts. Come on, we better hurry before all the seats are gone. I know you will enjoy yourself. There is nothing else for you to do around here anyway.

Appendix B: Field Assignments

The following are the Joint Council of First Presidency, Twelve, and Presiding Bishopric missionary field assignments of the Reorganized Church of Jesus Christ of Latter Day Saints for J. J. Cornish from 1878–1922:[48]

1878	Michigan and Canada (self-sustaining)
1879	Michigan and Canada (self-sustaining)
1880–1883	No field assignment, living in Michigan
1884	Michigan and Canada
1885	Michigan
1886	Michigan
1887	Northern Michigan
1888	Northern Michigan
1889	Northern Michigan
1890	Michigan
1891	Northern Michigan
1892	Michigan
1893	Michigan and Northern Indiana
1894	Pittsburgh/Kirtland Districts, First Quorum of Seventy
1895	Michigan and Northern Indiana
1896	Michigan
1897	Michigan
1898	Michigan
1899	Michigan
1900	Michigan
1901	Michigan and First Quorum of Seventy
1902	Michigan and First Quorum of Seventy
1903	Michigan and First Quorum of Seventy
1904	Northern Michigan and Eastern Michigan
1905	Northern Michigan and Eastern Michigan
1906	Michigan
1907	Michigan
1908	Western Michigan
1909	Michigan
1910	Michigan
1911	Michigan
1912	Northwestern Canada
1913	Saskatchewan
1914	Saskatchewan and Alberta
1915	Saskatchewan
1916	Saskatchewan and Alberta
1917	Saskatchewan District
1918	First Presidency: Special Assignment to Washington
1919	Saskatchewan
1920	Saskatchewan
1921	Saskatchewan
1922	Superannuation and Retirement
1922–1937	Retired living in Senlac, Saskatchewan

Appendix C: Vital Statistics for J.J. Cornish and Family

Personal data about J. J. Cornish:[49]
Born: 17 October 1854, Osbourne, Huron County, Ontario, Canada
Married: Mary Jane (Jannie) Stratton in 1875
Died: 24 June 1937 in Senlac, Saskatchewan, Canada
Baptized: 22 February 1872, Camden, Kent County, Ontario, Canada
Ordained Priest: 5 April 5 1875, London, Ontario, Canada
Ordained Elder: 4 October 1875, London, Ontario, Canada
Church Appointment: April 1884
Ordained Seventy: 31 August 1891, Juniata, Michigan
Superannuated: April 1922

The following are J.J. Cornish's children (birth date):[50]
William J. (14 October 1878)
Bertha (27 October 1880)
Alma James (8 May 1885)
Rosetta (7 June 1887)
John J., Jr. (7 July 1893)
Maud Leotus (2 September 1895)
Annie (4 August 1898)

As far as can be documented, J. J. lived in these places:[51]
1870–1879: London, Ontario
1879–1885: Richmondville, Michigan
1885: Deckerville, Michigan
1886: Bay City, Michigan
1886–1897: Reed City, Michigan
1897–1910: Garfield, Michigan
1910–1937: Senlac, Saskatchewan

Appendix D: Branch Baptismal Data

The following are baptisms by J.J. Cornish. The first four branches were located within a three-mile radius of each other. Cornish baptized some individuals in more than one place on the same date. Assuming these records are accurate, it is conceivable that Cornish walked between these places and participated in the baptisms:[52]

Forester, Michigan (1878): Cornish baptized 22.
    31 July = 2; 2 August = 1; 15 August = 1; 21 August = 5; 24 August = 3;
    27 August = 1; 1 September = 3; 8 September = 5; 3 November = 1.

Lebanon, Michigan (1878): Cornish baptized 20.
    3 July = 1; 21 July = 2; 28 July = 7; 31 July = 1; 4 August = 2;
    10 August = 1; 19 August = 1; 24 August = 2; 10 September = 3.

St. Johns, Michigan (1878–1879): Cornish baptized 28.
    1878: 22 baptisms.
        31 July = 2; 4 August = 4; 21 August = 3; 27 August = 4;
        1 September = 2; 8 September = 2; 10 September = 2; 13 December = 3.
    1879: 6 baptisms.
        17 May = 1; 19 May = 1; 4 September = 2; 4 July = 1; 6 October = 1.

Bridgehampton, Michigan (1878–1879): Cornish baptized 19.
    1878: 11 baptisms.
        16 November = 3; 23 November = 1; 26 November = 2;
        30 November = 3; 2 December = 2.
    1879: 8 baptisms.
        27 April = 8.

London, Ontario (1875–1878): Cornish baptized 62.
    1875: 18 baptisms overall, Cornish baptized 11.
    1876: 85 baptisms overall, Cornish baptized 46.
    1877: 8 baptisms overall, Cornish baptized 3.
    1878: 3 baptisms overall, Cornish baptized 2.

Sand Beach, St. Thomas, Michigan (1885–1887): Cornish baptized 43.
    1885: 18 baptisms.
        24 June = 3; 13 July = 7; 10 August = 7; 14 November = 1.
    1886: 20 baptisms.
        18 January = 2; 1 February = 9; 13 March = 3; 18 March = 4; 24 May = 2.
    1887: 5 baptisms.
        12 March = 1; 30 March = 4.

Delaware (1882–1883): Cornish baptized 13.
    1882: 4 baptisms:
        13 August = 1; 17 September = 3.
    1883: 9 baptisms:
        11 February = 6; 10 April = 1; 5 August = 2.

Pigeon River, Owendale (1886–1888): Cornish baptized 10.
  1886: 1 baptism: 23 May.
  1887: 5 baptisms:
    24 March = 2; 21 August = 2; 27 December = 1;
  1888: 4 baptisms: 16 July = 3; 20 July = 1.

Grant, Michigan (1886–1888): Cornish baptized 12.
  1886: 1 baptism: 23 May.
  1887: 7 baptisms: 24 March = 2; 21 August = 1; 22 August = 3; 27 December = 1.
  1888: 4 baptisms: 5 February = 3; 16 July = 3; 20 July = 1.

Bay Port/Caseville, Michigan (1886–1888): Cornish baptized 97.
  1886: 3 baptisms: 9 December = 3.
  1887: 88 baptisms:
    6 February = 1; 18 February = 4; 27 February = 2; 3 March = 10; 6 March = 15;
    7 March = 11; 8 March = 7; 20 March = 8; 22 March = 2; 27 March = 3;
    22 May =   5; 23 May = 4; 13 July = 3; 17 July = 3; 30 October = 9;
    18 December = 1.
  1888: 6 baptisms: 4 January = 1; 12 February = 1; 11 July = 2; 13 July = 2;

South Boardman, Michigan (1892–1897): Cornish baptized 45.
  1892: 23 baptisms:
    8 May = 7; 31 July = 7; 29 November = 2; 4 December = 4; 5 December = 1;
    17 December = 1; 18 December = 1;
  1893: 1 baptism: 15 May
  1894: 7 baptisms: 1 July = 3; 8 May = 1; 22 July = 1; 20 August = 2;
  1895: 11 baptisms: 5 May = 2; 24 October = 3; 27 October = 1; 30 October = 2;
    3 November = 1; 15 December = 2;
  1896: 1 baptism: 13 November
  1897: 2 baptisms: 15 August = 1; 16 August = 1;

Artland Branch; Senlac, Saskatchewan (1912–1917): Cornish baptized 21.
  1912 = 2 baptisms.
  1913 = 10 baptisms.
  1914 = 3 baptisms.
  1915 = 1 baptism.
  1916 = 2 baptisms.
  1917 = 3 baptisms.

Appendix E: Baptisms and Ordinations

These are baptisms and ordinations by J. J. Cornish in branches that he helped organize:[53]

Forester, Michigan:

NAME	BAPTISM	ORDAINED	OFFICE	ELDER
*James Simmons	3 July 1878	29 August 1878	Priest	31 May 1879
*Hugh Campbell	4 August 1878	29 August 1878	Priest	
*Thomas Barr	15 August 1878	29 August 1878	Priest	31 May 1879
Willard J. Smith	8 September 1878	18 September 1878	Priest	1 March 1883

*Presiding priests of three newly organized missions, 29 August 1878

Bridgehampton, Michigan:

NAME	BAPTISM	ORDAINED	OFFICE
*Daniel Wilkie	16 November 1879	15 December 1879	Priest
Hugh Kidd	16 November 1879	24 December 1879	Deacon
George Sampson	2 December 1879	24 December 1879	Teacher

*Presiding priest when mission organized December 1878

Bay Port, Michigan:

NAME	BAPTISM	ORDAINED	OFFICE	ELDER
*Robert E. Grant	6 February 1887 1	9 September 1888	Priest 25	October 1891
William Dowker	6 March 1887	7 August 1887	Priest	10 June 1890
Pearl Dutcher	7 March 1887	7 August 1887	Teacher	
Charles E. Grant	7 March 1887	7 August 1887	Teacher	
Charles W. Grant	8 March 1887	13 December 1905	Priest	25 October 1914
John Bracherbery	8 March 1887	7 August 1887	Deacon	
Charles Gillingham	13 March 1887	7 August 1887	Deacon	
John Grant	13 March 1887	7 August 1887	Priest	17 October 1892
*Francis Smith	13 March 1887	20 November 1887	Priest	10 October 1892

*Ordained seventy: R. Grant: 3 March 1895; F. Smith: 7 October 1900

Harbor Beach-St. Thomas-Sand Beach, Michigan:

NAME	BAPTISM	ORDAINED	OFFICE	ELDER
Oscar Frescott	24 June 1885	2 February 1886	Priest	
Thomas Whitford	24 June 1885	2 February 1886	Priest	
Thomas Rawson	13 July 1885	23 February 1888	Priest	20 September 1899
Joseph Barass	13 July 1885	2 February 1886	Deacon	
Charles Rawson	10 August 1885	2 February 1886	Teacher	

Bay City, Michigan

NAME	BAPTISM	ORDAINED	OFFICE
William McKinzie	10 July 1887	3 April 1888	Deacon
John Busget	10 July 1887	3 April 1888	Priest
Synus Smith	12 July 1887	3 April 1888	Teacher
Cyrus Smith	12 July 1887	3 April 1888	Priest
David Petee	22 November 1888	21 June 1889	Teacher

Free Soil, Michigan:

NAME	BAPTISM	ORDAINED	OFFICE
George Smith	25 August 1889	29 November 1893	Deacon

Gilmour, Michigan:

NAME	BAPTISM	ORDAINED	OFFICE
Thomas Maguire	10 April 1893	4 September 1893	Deacon

Appendix F: Fellow Missionaries

One of J. J. Cornish's methods of missionary outreach was to use other priesthood members in his missionary efforts. The following are some of individuals associated with J. J. Cornish's missionary outreach to Michigan, Ontario, and Saskatchewan:[54]

William Davis: worked with J. J. in Michigan and Ontario.

Robert Davis: helped J. J. organize Forester, St. John's, and Lebanon, Michigan, branches 29 August 1878, and Bridgehampton Branch November 1878.

Andrew Barr: baptized and ordained by J. J. in August 1878; first pastor of Forester, Michigan; helped in several areas including: Bridgehampton, Marion, Minden City, and Black River.

Hugh Campbell: baptized and ordained by J. J. in August 1878; first pastor of St. John's, Michigan, Branch.

James Simmons: first person baptized by J. J. in Michigan; ordained priest, and first pastor of Lebanon Branch.

Robert E. Grant: baptized by J. J. in Bay Port February 1887; later ordained priest, elder, and seventy; worked throughout Michigan.

Francis C. Smith: baptized by J. J. in Bay Port March 1887; later ordained priest, elder, and seventy; worked throughout Michigan.

Willard J. Smith: baptized and ordained by J.J. in September 1878; traveled and assisted many times as singer and speaker.

F. L. Smith: baptized and ordained by J. J.; assisted J. J. in Garfield debate and many other areas of Michigan.

Levi Phelps: helped J. J. organize Cornish Branch, Michigan; later the second pastor of Farwell Branch in Michigan.

J. J. Bailey: organized Ubly, Michigan, Branch with J. J. March 1886.

J. A. Carpenter: 146 baptisms in Bay Port, Michigan, with J. J. 1887.

William J. Cornish: J.J.'s son, helped in Michigan and Canada.

John A. Grant: J. J. baptized and ordained.

John Shippy: helped J. J. organize branch in Caseville, Michigan.

Others who worked with J. J. in Michigan were:

H. J. Martindale, Leonard Scott, Edward Delong, I. J. Smith, J. L. Bear, William Dowker, F. M. Cooper, E. J. Goodenough, M. T. Short, Hiram Rathburn, G. E. Deud, Charles K. Green.

Appendix G: Debates of John J. Cornish

All locations are in Michigan.

Sources: *Into the Latter-day Light (LDL)* and *Saints' Herald (SH)*:

1   October 1878: Lexington; *SH* (15 August 1878): 269.
2. November 1878: Forester; Holt, Bullock, & Hallington; *LDL*, 71.
3. February 1880: Richmondville; James Mohan concerning the Roman Catholic-Church; *SH* (1 April 1880): 108.
4. July 1880; Jeddo; *SH* (15 July 1880): 364.
5. August 1882: Burnham; H. E. Russell; *SH* (1 September 1882).
6. Winter 1883: Leitch Schoolhouse; Walter W. Simms; *LDL*, 115.
7. November 1885: Ubly; Elder Weeks, Adventist; *LDL*, 130.
8. December 1885: Inwood; Reverend Stables, Methodist; *LDL*, 131.
9. October 1885: Forest Grove; Walter Simms; *LDL*, 120.
10. February 1886: Ubly; Reverend Chism, Disciples of Christ; *LDL*, 128.
11. November 1886: near Bad Axe at Canboro; against Reverend Lilland, Seventh Day Adventist, 3 nights; *LDL*, 134.
12. February 1887: Bay Port; *SH* (12 March 1887): 171.
13. December 1887: Canboro, Huron County; *SH* (7 January 1888): 391.
14. January 1888: Juniata; other minister did not show, J.J. preached to the people who came; *SH* (21 January 1888): 36.
15. June 1888: Lake Station; Elder Weeks; *LDL*, 147.
16. June 1888: Free Soil; Reverend Snider; *SH* (23 June 1888): 391.
17. July 1888: Bay City; *SH* (4 August 1888): 495.
18. July 1888: Brinton; Conant, Adventist; *SH* (15 September 88): 590.
19. January 1891: Burnham; E. B. Scott, Christian Adventist, Scott-Cornish Debate, pamphlet, RLDS Library-Archives.
20. October 1891: Reed City; Reverend Watson, Cornish Letter (11 November 1891), RLDS Library-Archives.
21. December 1891: Sanford; Reverend Rogers, Church of Christ; *LDL*, 155.
22. June 1894: Gilmore; Reverend M. D. Rogers; *LDL*, 159.
23. July 1901: Shabonna; R. B. Brown, Christian Church; *LDL*, 169.
24. June 1903: R. B. Brown, Christian Church; *LDL*, 172.
25. 20 May 1905: Rose City; Reverend Clark Braden; *LDL*, 174.

Bibliography

Branch Records, numerous branches, RLDS Library-Archives

Cornish Letters from Joseph Smith III, RLDS Library-Archives

Cornish Letters to E. L. Kelley, RLDS Library-Archives

Cornish Letters to Joseph Smith III, RLDS Library-Archives

Cornish Letters to Henry Stebbins, RLDS Library-Archives

Cornish Letters (Miscellaneous), RLDS Library-Archives

Cornish to R. C. Evans, Open Letter, RLDS Library-Archives

J. J. Cornish, Missionary Tracts, RLDS Library-Archives

Joint Council Minutes, RLDS Library-Archives

Rogers-Cornish Debate, RLDS Library-Archives

Scott-Cornish Debate, RLDS Library-Archives

Cornish, J.J. *Into the Latter-day Light*. Independence, Missouri: Herald House, 1929.

Cheville, Roy A. *They Made a Difference*. Independence, Missouri: Herald House, 1959.

The History of the Reorganized Church of Jesus Christ of Latter Day Saints, Volume 4. Independence, Missouri: Herald House, 1896.

Edwards, F. Henry. *The History of the Reorganized Church of Jesus Christ of Latter Day Saints*, Volume 5. Independence, Missouri: Herald House, 1969.

Edwards, F. Henry. *The History of the Reorganized Church of Jesus Christ of Latter Day Saints*, Volume 6. Independence, Missouri: Herald House, 1970.

Edwards, F. Henry. *The History of the Reorganized Church of Jesus Christ of Latter Day Saints*, Volume 7, Independence, Missouri: Herald House, 1973.

Edwards, F. Henry. *The History of the Reorganized Church of Jesus Christ of Latter Day Saints*, Volume 8., Independence, Missouri: Herald House, 1976.

J.J. Cornish, "Letters and Contributions," *Zion's Ensign* (8 June 1922).

J. J. Cornish, *Journal of History* 15 (1922).

J. J. Cornish, *Journal of History* 16 (1923).

J. J. Cornish, *Journal of History* 17 (1924).

J. J. Cornish, *Journal of History* 18 (1925).

J. J. Cornish, *Saints' Herald* 20 (15 September 1873): 581.

J. J. Cornish, *Saints' Herald* 21 (1 January 1874): 20.

J. J. Cornish, *Saints' Herald* 21 (1 October 1874): 598.

J. J. Cornish, *Saints' Herald* 22 (1 July 1875): 411.

J. J. Cornish, *Saints' Herald* 22 (15 September 1875): 567.

J. J. Cornish, *Saints' Herald* 22 (1 December 1875): 724.

J. J. Cornish, *Saints' Herald* 23 (15 January 1876): 51–53.

J. J. Cornish, *Saints' Herald* 23 (1 April 1876): 212.

J. J. Cornish, *Saints' Herald* 23 (1 September 1876): 537.

J. J. Cornish, *Saints' Herald* 23 (15 November 1876): 698.

J. J. Cornish, *Saints' Herald* 23 (1 December 1876): 730.

J. J. Cornish, *Saints' Herald* 24 (1 April 1877): 110.

J. J. Cornish, *Saints' Herald* 24 (1 May 1877): 142.

J. J. Cornish, *Saints' Herald* 24 (15 August 1877): 244.

J. J. Cornish, *Saints' Herald* 25 (1 June 1878): 189.

J. J. Cornish, *Saints' Herald* 25 (15 August 1878): 269.

J. J. Cornish, *Saints' Herald* 25 (1 October 1878): 290, 301.

J. J. Cornish, *Saints' Herald* 25 (1 December 1878): 364.

J. J. Cornish, *Saints' Herald* 26 (1 May 1879): 133.

J. J. Cornish, *Saints' Herald* 26 (1 August 1879): 236.

J. J. Cornish, *Saints' Herald* 26 (15 September 1879): 285.

J. J. Cornish, *Saints' Herald* 26 (15 October 1879): 317.

J. J. Cornish, *Saints' Herald* 27 (1 April 1880): 108.

J. J. Cornish, *Saints' Herald* 27 (15 July 1880): 224.

J. J. Cornish, *Saints' Herald* 27 (1 October 1880): 304.

J. J. Cornish, *Saints' Herald* 28 (15 September 1881): 303.

J. J. Cornish, *Saints' Herald* 29 (1 July 1882): 207.

J. J. Cornish, *Saints' Herald* 29 (1 August 1882), 237.

J. J. Cornish, *Saints' Herald* 29 (1 September 1882).

J. J. Cornish, *Saints' Herald* 29 (15 November 1892): 351.

J. J. Cornish, *Saints' Herald* 30 (15 August 1883): 540.

J. J. Cornish, *Saints' Herald* 31 (1 August 1884): 475.

J. J. Cornish, *Saints' Herald* 31 (1 December 1884): 771.

J. J. Cornish, *Saints' Herald* 32 (14 February 1885): 105–106.

J. J. Cornish, *Saints' Herald* 32 (1 May 1885): 279.

J. J. Cornish, *Saints' Herald* 32 (15 May 1885): 301.

J. J. Cornish, *Saints' Herald* 32 (27 June 1885): 416.

J. J. Cornish, *Saints' Herald* 32 (11 July 1885): 449.

J. J. Cornish, *Saints' Herald* 33 (16 January 1886): 40.

J. J. Cornish, *Saints' Herald* 33 (27 February 1886): 134.

J. J. Cornish, *Saints' Herald* 33 (11 December 1886): 777.

J. J. Cornish, *Saints' Herald* 34 (12 March 1887): 171.

J. J. Cornish, *Saints' Herald* 34 (25 June 1887): 409.

J. J. Cornish, *Saints' Herald* 34 (10 September 1807): 593.

J. J. Cornish, *Saints' Herald* 34 (17 December 1887): 818.

J. J. Cornish, *Saints' Herald* 35 (7 January 1888): 8.

J. J. Cornish, *Saints' Herald* 35 (21 January 1888): 36.

J. J. Cornish, *Saints' Herald* 35 (3 March 1888): 137.

J. J. Cornish, *Saints' Herald* 35 (7 April 1888): 214.

J. J. Cornish, *Saints' Herald* 35 (14 April 1888): 233.

J. J. Cornish, *Saints' Herald* 35 (1 May 1888): 244.

J. J. Cornish, *Saints' Herald* 35 (26 May 1888): 326.

J. J. Cornish, *Saints' Herald* 35 (23 June 1888): 391.

J. J. Cornish, *Saints' Herald* 35 (7 July 1888): 432.

J. J. Cornish, *Saints' Herald* 35 (15 July 1888).

J. J. Cornish, *Saints' Herald* 35 (4 August 1888): 495.

J. J. Cornish, *Saints' Herald* 35 (15 September 1888): 590.

J. J. Cornish, *Saints' Herald* 35 (1 October 1888).

J. J. Cornish, *Saints' Herald* 35 (17 November 1888): 735.

J. J. Cornish, *Saints' Herald* 36 (2 March 1889): 157.

J. J. Cornish, *Saints' Herald* 39 (17 December 1892): 813.

J. J. Cornish, *Saints' Herald* 40 (5 October 1893).

J. J. Cornish, *Saints' Herald* 49 (12 November 1902): 1108–1109.

J. J. Cornish, *Saints' Herald* 66 (12 March 1919): 145–148.

J. J. Cornish, *Saints' Herald* 66 (25 June 1919): 609–612.

J. J. Cornish, *Saints' Herald* 69 (29 January 1922): 120–124.

Saints' Herald 84 (17 July 1937): 901.

Lottie Clark Diggle, *Saints' Herald* 104 (18 February 1957): 156; 104 (25 February 1957): 179.

Saints' Herald 89 (25 April 1942): 20–21.

Saints' Herald 96 (26 December 1949): 7–8.

Notes

1. *Saints' Herald* 84 (17 June 1937): 901.
2. *Saints' Herald* 89 (25 April 1942): 532.
3. See Appendix D for examples of this happening.
4. See Appendix E for Willard J. Smith, Forester, Michigan.
5. See Appendix E for further insight.
6. *Saints' Herald* 96 (26 December 1949): 8.
7. John J. Cornish, *Into the Latter-day Light* (Independence, Missouri: Herald House, 1929), 102.
8. *Saints' Herald* 89 (25 April 1942): 532.
9. Cornish, *Into the Latter-day Light*, 6.
10. Ibid., 10.
11. Ibid., 14.
12. Lottie Clark Diggle, *Saints' Herald* 104 (25 February 1957): 178.
13. J. J. Cornish, *Saints' Herald* 26 (1 May 1879): 133.
14. Cornish, *Into the Latter-day Light*, 31.
15. J. J. Cornish, *Saints' Herald* 28 (1 October 1881): 303.
16. Cornish, *Into the Latter-day Light*, 101.
17. Ibid., 102.
18. See Appendix B for a list of J. J.'s field assignments.
19. See Appendix F for a partial list of ministers who worked with J. J.
20. See Appendix C for personal data on J. J. and his family.
21. Cornish letters to Joseph Smith III (April to June 1919) while on missionary trip to Washington state, RLDS Library-Archives.
22. See Appendix G for a partial list of Cornish debates.
23. Cornish, *Into the Latter-day Light*, 53.
24. Roy Cheville, *They Made a Difference* (Independence, Missouri: Herald House, 1959), 282.
25. *Saints' Herald* 96 (26 December 1949): 1232.
26. J. J. Cornish, *Saints' Herald* 20 (15 September 1873): 581.
27. Cornish, *Into the Latter-day Light*, 7.
28. *Saints' Herald* 96 (26 December 1949): 8.
29. J. J. Cornish, *Saints' Herald* 27 (15 July 1880): 224.
30. Cornish, *Into the Latter-day Light*, 42.
31. Ibid., 31.
32. Lottie Clark Diggle, *Saints' Herald* 104 (18 February 1957): 156.
33. Cornish, *Into the Latter-day Light*, 33.
34. Ibid., 30.
35. J. J. Cornish, *Saints' Herald* 35 (14 April 1888): 233.
36. *Saints' Herald* 89 (25 April 1942): 20.
37. J. J. Cornish, *Journal of History* 18: 419.
38. J. J. Cornish, *Into the Latter-day Light*, 71.
39. J. J. Cornish, *Saints' Herald* (1 July 1875): 40.
40. Cornish, *Into the Latter-day Light*, 78.
41. Cheville, 285.
42. J. J. Cornish, *Saints' Herald* 35 (7 January 1888): 8.
43. Cornish, *Into the Latter-day Light*, 78.
44. See Appendix F for some of the ministers who worked with J. J.
45. J. J. Cornish, *Saints' Herald* 21 (1 October 1874): 598.
46. J. J. Cornish, *Journal of History* 18: 419.
47. *Saints' Herald* 89 (25 April 1942): 532.
48. Minutes from Joint Council sessions, RLDS Library-Archives.
49. Branch records, Cornish, Michigan, Branch, RLDS Library-Archives.
50. Ibid.
51. Several sources including *Into the Latter-day Light*, various articles in *Saints' Herald*, and branch records from RLDS Library-Archives.
52. Branch records from RLDS Library-Archives.
53. Ibid.
54. Cornish, *Into the Latter-day Light*, numerous Cornish reports in *Saints' Herald*, and Cornish letters from RLDS Library-Archives.

Capturing the Past: G. E. Anderson's 1907 Photographic Mission to Missouri

Richard Neitzel Holzapfel and T. Jeffery Cottle

In a 1928 letter to Joseph Fielding Smith, church historian and apostle of the Church of Jesus Christ of Latter-day Saints (LDS Church), Junius F. Wells (Mormon author and amateur historian), described the nature and value of a photographic collection being offered for sale. The photographs and negatives belonged to a poor and almost forgotten Utah landscape and portrait photographer, George Edward Anderson of Springville, Utah, who had only recently died.[1]

That there are in this collection negatives of Church scenes, groups of historic gatherings, views of notable celebrations, parades and pageants, of almost inestimable interest and value to the [LDS] Historian's Office, I believe you already realize. . . . That George Ed Anderson performed a very remarkable mission while traversing the scenes of the Church History—the missions at the East and abroad, visiting hundreds of homes and neighborhoods where he bore a faithful testimony of the Truth and made countless friends for the Church, I personally know; and that he did so without adequate recompense in poverty at times to the distress of his family. The increment of his life's work should now come to them.[2]

The collection, numbering more than 30,000 negatives, was purchased by the LDS Church for $2,500 from Anderson's widow, Olive Lowry Anderson, through Wells' efforts.[3]

Photography was still considered magical at the turn of the century. Wells understood the significance of a collection of photographs taken over a period of several decades, especially for future unborn generations who could see through them people, places, and a world that was quickly being transformed beyond recognition. Anderson's photographs captured the past intact, miraculously freezing in time and space by the most ephemeral of substances—photons of reflected light. When the packet *British Queen* docked in New York City harbor following a transatlantic voyage on Friday afternoon, 20 September 1839, one of Western civilization's most astonishing and versatile discoveries arrived—photography.[4]

By the time George Edward Anderson began practicing this art form, photography had made several significant advances from the first daguerreotypes. During his professional career, Anderson was compelled to purchase new equipment to keep up with the fast-improving field. While Anderson, out of financial necessity, practiced a wide variety of photographic skills, including portraiture, he became increasingly interested in one branch of the art: documentary photography.

Anderson was not the first Utah-Saint photographer to dream of a complete photographic record of the rise of Mormonism, but he was the first professional Latter-day Saint to travel from the Rocky Mountain kingdom back East to begin the effort. Anderson wrote in his journal on 20 April 1907 as he departed for his mission to England:

Rose about six . . . bid father and mother goodby. Bro Thornburg got grips etc. from depot and Olive assisted me in packing up. Bid all good bye and left Springville on #6 about 10:15. Snow in canyon and all the way up . . . off at Price and took next section of #6 which left Price about 7:00. Dinner with Jos Jones, gave me sack of apples and $2.00.[5]

The sack of apples and the two dollars would long be gone by the time Anderson reached his final destination—England—but his appetite to capture the Mormon past through the medium of photography never subsided. At forty-six years of age, he was beginning a mission for the LDS Church.

This 1907 mission to England was not the first time Anderson had been called to lay service in his church. He had already been a Mormon bishop in Springville, Utah, for four years, serving at his own expense as he was likewise financing this mission. Dedicated to building a new chapel in Springville along with his other church duties, Anderson incurred a heavy personal debt in his own business, which took second place to his ecclesiastical assignment. His debt increased when he completed a new studio, the G. E. Anderson Art Bazaar, following his release as bishop.

In March 1907, shortly before his mission departure, another national depression caused widespread unemployment, resulting in a steady decline in Anderson's business. After all, when a family had to choose between bread and a portrait, there was no contest. Olive, his wife, had already become a major financial contributor to the family budget by working in a local cannery.[6] Now, as she gave George Edward a final embrace before he left for England, she assumed complete responsibility for feeding and clothing their three children, ages four to sixteen years.[7]

Though Anderson was bound for England, it took him almost a year to reach his destination. En route, he systematically visited Mormon historical sites in New England, New York, Pennsylvania, Ohio, Illinois, and Missouri to make a photographic record of them for a Utah-born generation of Mormons who heard the stories of the early Saints but generally were unable to visit the sites of the events. At several points he asked William C. Spence, the transportation agent for the LDS Church, to reschedule his departure date so as to have more time to continue his photographic efforts in the United States.[8] "Telegraphed W. C. Spence," he noted, "Have fine views, need more time, can steamer ticket be extended? Wire G. Ed Anderson."[9] At first, this passion was a personal calling; but two months later in Chicago, he encountered LDS Church Apostle George Albert Smith, a grandson of Joseph Smith's cousin, George A. Smith, and everything changed.[10] Smith was in Chicago on LDS Church business when Anderson recorded:

Apostle George A. Smith came into Priesthood meeting. Brother Smith told me to meet him 1:30 to 2:00 p.m. and he would look at views and give me what information he could about Palmyra [New York] and Sharon [Vermont]. I made notes of the points he gave. I asked him if I should sail on the Rebbel that sails on the 3rd. He said, "No, keep on with the work."[11]

Anderson carried his heavy 8-by-10 view camera, supplies, and personal belongings and traversed the midwestern plains, wooded forests of New York and New England, and grain-ripened fields of early Restoration country, often finding the only lodging to be under a tree with only his camera cloth for covering.[12] Seeking the most telling views of Mormon historical sites, he recorded, "Would like to get the views I can see in my mind's eye.... Could not get the effect of light and shade I wished." Later, he regretfully wrote, "Need painter's hand to fix colors to do it justice."[13] Like his photographs, Anderson's diaries contain precise historical details about these landmarks of the Restoration—details that he learned from local individuals, informed members of the LDS or Reorganized Church of Jesus Christ of Latter Day Saints (RLDS Church), and history books written about the areas he visited.

A few examples of Anderson's work first appeared in the *Boston Sunday Globe* on 10 May 1908, along with a balanced article about the LDS Church—a surprising development in light of the Reed Smoot hearing, then occurring in Washington before a senatorial subcommittee.[14] The press's gleeful and sensational treatment of Mormon polygamy, political "interference," and temple rites marked a deterioration in a public image which had never been overwhelmingly positive, to say the least. A year later, the LDS Sunday School organization published a more complete collection of Anderson photographs in *The Birth of Mormonism in Pictures: Scenes and Incidents in Early Church History*, written by LDS Church author and teacher, John Henry Evans.[15]

"I feel impressed," Anderson wrote, "with the necessity of making the views. I can see what a blessing they would be to our people in arousing an interest in this land."[16] Documenting Mormon historical sites was a master-dream, almost an obsession, and certainly a religious mission in his eyes. To it he had sacrificed his business in Utah, association with his family, personal conveniences, and even, at times, his health. He produced hundreds of photographic views of Mormon historical sites outside Utah and many other views of the people and places of his own time. He eventually returned to Springville in November 1913, nearly seven years from the time he bid his family good-bye.

George Edward Anderson's celebrated photographic pilgrimage in 1907 to Missouri was not the first nor the last visit to Mormon historical sites by interested Utahans.[17] Nor was Anderson the first individual to photograph these places of historic interest; he was obviously not alone in his quest to record the Mormon past. But his views remain among the most memorable images of these sites.

Anderson's first stop to photograph Mormon historical sites was Missouri, and the sixty-two extant views he made there are memorable and noteworthy. It is not clear how much detailed information he had about Missouri and its Mormon past, but surely he would have known the historical outline and the folk tales of mythic promises and tragic sufferings that the Saints experienced there.

The Saints' preoccupation with the land of Missouri began during a period when speculation increased among them as to the future location of "Zion," the "New Jerusalem" spoken of in their new scripture, the Book of Mormon.[18] Joseph Smith, while on a visit to the western boundary of the United States in 1831, recorded a revelation that stated he was standing upon the very land "appointed and consecrated for the gathering of the saints...the land of promise, and the place for the city of Zion."[19]

During the next few years, the Saints began to gather to Missouri, particularly to Jackson County, in anticipation of building a temple and preparing for the Second Coming of Jesus Christ. Following their expulsion from the Independence area in 1833, the Saints continued to gather in Missouri and settled in a number of counties surrounding Jackson County. Within a short time, two new counties were organized in northern Clay County, called Caldwell and Daviess. The Saints established several settlements in the two counties and remained there until they left the state under executive order by Governor Lilburn Boggs in 1838.

Even during the difficult days of persecution in Missouri, many Saints visited Jackson County following the 1833 expulsion. James and Drusilla Hendricks, recent converts, arrived in Missouri to find the majority of Saints living in Clay County, just across the river from Independence.[20] Drusilla remembered, "There were a number of Saints...that had been driven from Jackson County, and we had great times in talking of their trials in that county." After an invitation by her in-laws, she and her husband decided to visit Independence. She recalled that they decided to make the journey despite the peril involved, "to satisfy our own curiosity to see Independence where the center stake of Zion should be.... After crossing the Missouri River, we had an excellent view of the country."[21]

Joseph Smith was another early visitor to Jackson County following the Mormon exodus in 1833. He and several brethren were taken prisoners in Far West after the city capitulated to Missouri state militia units at the end of the so-called "Mormon War." The prisoners were conducted to Richmond, Missouri, in 1838 to stand trial. During their journey, they stopped at Independence before continuing on to Richmond. While in Jackson County, the prisoners were treated with much kindness and given some freedom to walk around the town. Lyman Wight, one of the prisoners, wrote, "We now found ourselves in Jackson County, from which we were driven in 1833.... We landed at Independence about three o'clock p.m."[22] On 4 November 1838, the following day, Lyman recorded in his journal, "This day we were at liberty to go where we pleased about through the town. We walked down to the temple lot."[23]

Church Apostle Parley P. Pratt wrote of this occasion, "We were soon at liberty to walk the streets without a guard...[;] we walked out of town and visited the desolate lands which belonged to our society, and the place which seven years before we had dedicated and consecrated for the building of a temple."[24]

The longing to build up "the waste places of Zion" lingered in the Mormon consciousness as part of their grief and resentment over the forced final expulsion in the winter of 1838–1839. The assassination of Joseph and Hyrum Smith and the succession crisis that followed kindled a new interest in a return to Jackson County. The Church of Christ, a small Restoration group, moved from Woodford County, Illinois, to Jackson County during the winter of 1866–1867. They are credited with being the first group to return to Independence. Albert and Maria Noble are reported to be the first members of the RLDS Church to return to Independence. They arrived in 1867 and settled near the Missouri River. Henry and Hannah Etzenhouser's family moved to the area soon thereafter.[25] E. C. Brand of Lee's Summit organized a branch meeting in Independence Courthouse on 25 May 1873.[26] Eventually, the RLDS Independence District was organized in 1878.

The RLDS Church purchased land on East Lexington for a church building in 1879 and dedicated a small brick church thereon in July 1884.[27] In 1888 they built a beautiful stone building, known as the Stone Church, just outside of the original temple lot boundary on West Lexington. The RLDS Independence Stake was organized in April 1901, just six years before Anderson arrived to photograph the "center place." One year before Anderson began his photographic mission, Joseph Smith III moved to Independence; the RLDS Church formally moved its headquarters in 1918.

Although photography was not yet invented when the Saints first gathered to Missouri (1831–1838), C. C. A. Christensen, a Danish convert to the LDS Church, attempted to create a visual record through his panorama of twenty-three scenes of Mormon history produced in Utah during the latter half of the nineteenth-century.[28] This may have been the first attempt to create a visual history of the early church. It was based on interviews he had with participants to the events but no visits to the acutally sites. Later, others used the photographic medium in effect to "freeze in time" the important historical sites associated with the rise of Mormonism and the Saints' sojourn in Missouri during the 1830s.[29]

Many leaders and missionaries from the Utah-based Latter-day Saints who followed Brigham Young and his successors came to Missouri on official business, and others traveled through on the way to some other destination during the latter half of the nineteenth-century. Nostalgia for the older members and curiosity drew many of them to the Mormon historical sites in the area. Most likely during this period, it was individuals rather than places that dominate the main concern of visitors. Orson Pratt, an original member of the Twelve Apostles and now an LDS Church leader, and Joseph F. Smith, son of Hyrum Smith, visited Missouri in September 1878 to interview David Whitmer, one of the Three Witnesses of the Book of Mormon.[30] Their letters back to Utah include this observation: "We arrived at Independence on the morning of Friday, September 6th....After breakfast we visited the 'Temple Lot,' about three-fourths of a mile west of the Court House."[31] During his visit to Richmond, Joseph F. Smith recorded in his journal,

Miss Josie Schweich, granddaughter of Father David Whitmer, a very fine young lady, came in and was introduced....They showed me some views of Liberty, among which was that of old Liberty jail, where the Prophet and his brethren were so long and brutally confined in chains, etc. I asked if it would be possible for me to get a copy, whereupon Miss Josie very kindly presented me with hers, for which I am very thankful as it is a monument to me of Missouri cruelty and barbarism.[32]

Apparently the first LDS-commissioned photographs of Missouri sites were the result of a visit by Andrew Jenson, an LDS Church historian from Utah.[33] Jenson toured Missouri and other Mormon historical sites in the East during 1888. In Liberty, Missouri, he wrote, "We secured the aid of a photographer, who took a very good negative, showing the ruins [of the Liberty jail] as they

stand at the present time."[34] Shortly after his return to Utah, Jenson sent LDS Apostle Joseph F. Smith the photograph of the jail at Liberty, Missouri. Joseph F. Smith wrote appreciatively:

I take pleasure in acknowledging the receipt of a photograph of the remains of Liberty Jail for the presentation of which I desire to thank you. It is a place I have never visited but once, and then in the arms of my mother, not long after my birth ...to take her last look and farewell, for aught she knew, of her imprisoned and manacled husband.[35]

This visit was a transition for Utah Saints who made trips to church historical sites, including those in Missouri. Edward Stevenson (member of LDS Church First Council of Seventy) had been a participant in the events, but Jenson and Black were not. They appear to have been more interested in seeking some type of religious experience from the visit, more like the traditional religious pilgrimage to holy sites, than Stevenson. By 1901, the last leader of the LDS Church to have participated in the early history of the church, Lorenzo Snow, had died. Now, his successor in the LDS Church presidency, Joseph F. Smith, began a movement to purchase historic sites throughout the United States in an effort to memorialize the events of the founding of Mormonism. The use of photography as a means to help in this process now was greatly expanded.

Another important photographer to visit Missouri was James Ricalton, a retired New Jersey teacher. Ricalton, a non-Mormon hired by the firm of Underwood & Underwood, made sets of international stereoviews for sale in the United States.[36] At the time of his visit to Missouri in 1904, Ricalton was on his way to the Far East to continue that work. His photographs of Mormon historical sites were published in a thirty-six stereo-view, entitled, "The Latter-day Saints Tour from Palmyra, New York to Salt Lake City, Utah through the Stereoscope," by Underwood & Underwood shortly thereafter. The set includes views of Mormon historical sites in Missouri. Just three years later, George Edward Anderson became the second known professional photographer to visit Missouri to photograph Mormon historical sites.

George Edward Anderson, arguably the most important photographer of Mormon historical sites, both numerically and artistically, arrived in Missouri just a few days following his departure from Springville, Utah. Anderson visited the temple lot site in Independence on 24 April 1907, a day after his arrival in the Midwest. The train arrived at the Kansas City station on 23 April, three days following his departure from Utah.

Anderson, unacquainted with the social reality of American life in a divided society outside of Utah, attempted to find lodging in the city. The hotel he chose, however, was "for colored folks" only. A "poor" black gentleman Anderson met at the place wanted to help carry his bags and heavy photographic equipment. "[He] was hungry," Anderson noted with a sense of sympathy, and "wished a nickel which I gave him."[37] Anderson was entering a new world which was not part of his previous experience—a world where the close-knit family and church ties were nowhere present, nor were the pastoral settings and homogenous society of the rural valleys of Utah. After a brief period of frustration, he sought some contact with his Utah roots and decided to leave the big midwestern city for what he hoped would be a more familiar place where he would be welcomed with open arms. He noted in his journal,

I found [LDS Central States Mission] President Samuel D. Bennion's address and phone number and concluded to go out to Independence, it was after 10:00 [p.m.] when I reached the mission headquarters at 302 S. Pleasant Street. Pres. Bennion five miles to Sister Leonora McCarthy [a local LDS member who served as the Women's Relief Society Assistant Secretary in 1907]. Fixed me a bed, as all full at the Mission Home... Sister McCarthy made me welcome. Was thankful to get out of the noise, bustle, and smoke of Kansas City.[38]

The LDS Mission headquarters had only recently moved from Kansas City to Independence. The LDS presence increased in the Independence area during this period. A church printing office was also established and produced a periodical entitled, *The Liahona*, named after the miraculous ball described in the Book of Mormon (see LDS Book of Mormon I Nephi 16:10 and RLDS Book of Mormon I Nephi 5:11–12). The first number of the *Liahona* was issued on 6 April 1907, just a short time before Anderson arrived. Anderson found a haven and a refuge among the missionaries and local members of the church. Independence also represented a kind of homecoming, a return to Zion—something every LDS member in the Rocky Mountains thought and talked about, and even prayed for.[39] Anderson was no different; it was a momentous occasion for the Utah missionary.

The following day, Anderson wrote with some sacredness, "Rose about 5:30 a.m., bathed my feet, prayer with [LDS missionary] Elder [George] Harris, he then took me on to the temple lot."[40] For Anderson, this was a solemn moment of reflection and contemplation. He notes, "I selected points that I thought would make good views and show the temple grounds so that a person from the outside [particularly the Utah Saints] could see how it was situated."[41] This attitude seems to have been his constant concern, "so a person from the outside could see how it was situated." Anderson's journal and photographs reflect his feeling for the spirit of the place. "This is a beautiful place, quiet and pleasant, agreeable to the eye. I feel it a privilege," he recorded, "to be in this land which the prophet of the Lord designated as the center stake of Zion, where the great temple of our God should be raised."[42]

Anderson took numerous views of the temple lot, even climbing out on the RLDS Stone Church roof in his quest to capture the spirit of the place he mentioned in his journal. Albert Thatcher, a local RLDS member and custodian, assisted Anderson in getting ladders and climbing "all the way to the top of the west tower of the Rock Church."[43] Anderson noted, "I secured some negatives of temple lot and Independence. Very difficult climb we had in the church tower."[44]

A local RLDS bishop lent Anderson a map so he could "copy plot of temple lot and vicinity...feel very well satisfied with the record made of the temple lot pictures."[45] RLDS members are mentioned with fondness in Anderson's journal for their help and hospitality. They are remembered in his photographs also, including a Far West RLDS Sunday school group.[46]

While visiting Independence, Anderson made other views, including the new LDS Church Mission Home on Pleasant Street; the local Independence newspaper, *The Examiner* office building (it also served thirty to forty LDS members for their Sunday school meetings in 1907); the new *Liahona* office (LDS printing facility); and the 1888 RLDS Stone Church (built just outside the original temple lot boundary).

During his visit he had one setback, however. On the day he arranged to photograph the LDS Mission Home a wind gust blew his camera equipment "over and [it was] so damaged by the wind that I could not make the picture."[47] The camera was taken to a repair shop, an added expense the mission could not afford. Anderson, however, took the opportunity to visit Kansas City on an escorted tour from one of the LDS missionaries. Later in the evening he returned to the LDS Mission Home in Independence for dinner. To help offset the cost of eating at the Mission Home he "assisted in mail, they hand out twelve sacks today."[48]

During another brief trip to Kansas City, Anderson visited several photographic supply houses, purchasing some Azo contact paper. He noted in his journal after a long taxing day, "Fixed trays and developed about sixty-five prints on Azo. Printed by gaslight. Elder [George V.] Harris assisted me in washing the prints it was after 12 nearly when we got to bed."[49]

In every location, Anderson met with the gracious hospitality of other professional photographers. While in Missouri, he noted,

[25 April] Developed...negatives (six or seven) at Mr. Evan Davies studio very kind, negs all came out good considering the dull day...[26 April] At Mr. Davis studio before 6:00 a.m. and developed negatives made last evening, felt very well satisfied with the record made.... [29 April] Mr. Davis fixed trays and develop about 65 prints.... [30 April] Mr. Evan Davis gave me key to the gallery and I moved and finished the views and delivered all except a set I took with me came out very good.[50]

This kindness allowed Anderson to earn some much needed cash to help pay for his expenses as he progressed toward his missionary field of labor. Following two full days of work that began before six in the morning, he delivered some views to B. F. Cunning who "was very pleased to get the views he ordered. I took a number more orders so late I concluded can not to go tomorrow."[51] These "orders" consisted of portraits of LDS missionaries, church groups, local residents, and scenic views. For the LDS missionaries, Anderson produced prints and post cards that could be used by them as visual aids in their proselyting or for mailing to family and friends back home.

Just as the Saints' exodus more than half a century earlier took them to the Illinois shore of the Mississippi River, Anderson left Missouri and traveled to Quincy, Illinois. He wrote that "at about 4:40 p.m. made a view of Quincy while waiting for the train. East side of Mississippi on the bluffs presents striking appearance."[52] Anderson then left Quincy and headed north to Nauvoo, the former city of the Saints where Joseph Smith established the church's headquarters following the Saints' expulsion from Missouri in 1838–1839. After visiting the most prominent places in the area and photographing these sites, Anderson received help from two LDS missionaries "in packing up negs etc" for his return trip to Zion, where he spent most of the month of May continuing his photographic work of Mormon historical sites.[53]

George Edward arose at 5:35 a.m. to begin his work in Missouri again on 9 May. He traveled some five miles to make "a view of the Big Blue."[54] The Big Blue River, Jackson County, Missouri, was the location of an early 1830s Mormon settlement near present-day Kansas City. Anderson's peaceful scene with a man leisurely reading a newspaper leaning up against one of the barren trees near the banks of the Big Blue contrasts with the mob violence perpetrated upon the Whitmer settlement nearly seventy-five years earlier on 31 October 1833. It was a "muddy and sluggish" walk to the spot, but soon Anderson was on a train as he made his way to Richmond, Clay County, Missouri.

Anderson "made negative of Richmond, from hill northwest of town. Also of the tombstone of one of the Eight Witnesses of the Book of Mormon plates, Jacob Whitmer in the old cemetery" during this first visit to Missouri.[55] His journal contains statements relating to his photographic views in an effort to make his photographs important and valuable. For example, he noted of Richmond Cemetery: "In this cemetery lies the remains of Oliver Cowdery," he wrote, "and Peter Whitmer, Sr. and wife [Mary Musselman Whitmer] in whose house the church was organized April 6th 1830 [in Fayette, New York]."[56] His concern for

documentation is noted in the same entry, "This cemetery is in the north east corner of town and just east of the road, on a little rise."[57] He also made view of "David Whitmer tomb stone," along with his entry about his photographic work, Anderson included statements he recorded as he interviewed relatives and friends of the David Whitmer, Oliver Cowdery, and Hiram Page families. In particular he was interested in hearing and preserving their knowledge about the first Mormon disciples.[58]

Again in Richmond, Anderson found room and board with a fellow photographer. "Mr. J. Encoe (photographer & Jeweler) asked me to stay over the night with them and take supper with them last evening. As I could not locate the Elders [LDS missionaries] I stopped."[59] Such visits allowed Anderson to talk to colleagues, "I had a long chat with Mr. Encoe yesterday while I was waiting for negs to dry and clear up—regarding the moral condition of the world. He believes in a man being pure and clean. His wife a fine lady and did all she could to make it pleasant for me. Told me some of his experiences in the world with men and women. The diseased condition they get us thro impure lives."[60]

Anderson expanded his own religious experience again on his Sabbath visit to Richmond. "At the Methodist S[unday] S[chool]. At services Baptist church minister, 'Let They Kingdom come."[61] During his stay at the Encoe's residence, he expressed the kindness offered him and reflected:

J. Encoe and wife have been very kind to me, asked to eat with them and I have slept there 2 nights, Saturday and Sunday. Mrs. E said had extra bed and would be pleased to have me stay. She also asked me to ask the blessing at a number of meals.[62]

While in Richmond, Anderson "made negative of place where old jail stood that Parley P. Pratt and Morris Phelps were confined in."[63] Pratt and Phelps, Mormon leaders, were imprisoned here from November 1838 through approximately May 1839, before being transferred to Columbia, Missouri, where they eventually escaped on 4 July 1839. A local resident showed him "the ashes (wood) from the fire place also the brichs etc. of the foundation. One of [the men] has a key that belonged to the jail which was demolished by the cyclone which struck Richmond June 1, 1898."[64] Later in the day he developed his negatives at Mr. Encoe's. "He did not charge for the developing I done," Anderson noted in his diary, "no charge for meals or lodging and wished me success on my journey. Mrs. Encoe said believed the Lord would bless me and I would get along all right that Providence helped those who were trying to [do] good."[65]

The warm day's sky turned dark and threatening, "just before I got to the depot commenced the rain and it just poured down, I like to have got wet there."[66] The train finally departed Richmond for Lawson about eight-thirty in the evening. The storm still raged when Anderson arrived, "too late and storming to hunt a cheaper place," so he stayed in a hotel across the street from the station which cost him fifteen cents for bed and breakfast.[67]

Anderson traveled to another important Mormon historical site "thru the fields most of the way so I would not get so muddy.... The Blue grass and brush wet," however. The next site on his itinerary was the location of the 24 October 1838 battle of Crooked River that left three Mormons dead, including David W. Patten, an apostle and leader of the Saints' militia in Caldwell County.[68]

A local resident welcomed Anderson to his home, "not far from the brook over battle ground." Mr. Besbee, the kind farmer "gave me all the information he could have," George Edward noted. Mr. Besbee's sons

"would help me out, they were close to the Lord." The gentleman and Anderson himself believed that divine assistance certainly would help them find the right location for his views.[69] The visit in Mr. Besbee's home also caused George Edward to reflect upon his own family back in Utah, especially his three-year-old son, George Lowry. "Mrs. Trouth, Mr. Besbee's daughter has a boy Clyde between 3 & 4 who reminds me more of Lowry than any should have since I left."[70]

In the evening, Anderson was able to share the history of the Saints through words and pictures to a few local inhabitants. "James F. Thompson who had said could keep me over night, his wife had a good supper for me, and I was getting dry and comfortable. Edger White and wife, neighbors came over & I showed them the views and answered their questions about the Mormons and how cruly they were driven out of the state. Read to them letters from the history of the church." The young children present on the occasion "listened to with marked attention by the older ones as well. Near 11 o'clock" when Anderson finished.[71]

On the following day, Anderson noted in his journal:

At James F. Thompson's two miles southeast of Elmira. Rose before 5:00 a.m. Cold and cloudy. Breakfast soon after 6:00 a.m. and over to J. L. Thompson's. The brothers had a team hooked up and soon had us on Crooked River Battle ground or Bogart's Battle ground. It is about half a mile north of their (Thompson brothers') home. These same two brothers took Bro[thers] Andrew Jenson, [Edward] Stevenson and [Joseph] Black [Utah visitors] on to the ground in 1888....Secured an excellent place to make the picture on the west side of Crooked River. Showing the ford, also the battle ground, which has been cleared and is now farmed. We are looking north and in the clearing which the road on the other side of ford...the battle ground which, lies just east of the river and it was on this bank where Bogart and men were camped. To the right of the center of the picture can be seen the hill down which Col. Page charged and it was behind the tree on this hill where the old field house was and where Col. Page divided his men. Tried to get some prints would show the river in several places and the battle ground, but no elevation suitable. Banks too high and too many trees which prevent us from seeing the stream."[72]

Upon his return to the Thompson home, Anderson "made neg of him, wife, and boy. Boy frightened and it was a long time before we could get him to get before the instrument."[73] After saying goodbye to the kind family, Anderson made his way "thro the field and woods almost straight west to Elmira," a village several miles away. The trip was made somewhat easier because Mr. Thompson carried "the instruments half of the time." When they reached Elmira it was near noon. Now Anderson "bade Mr. Thompson goodbye and thanked him for his kindness also his wife did not make any charge so I told him I would send him picture of the Battle ground also 1 of his family." As if to remind himself, Anderson noted again, "I must send 1 of B. Gr to J. L. Thompson as they made no charge."[74]

In the early afternoon, Anderson sent his photographic equipment ahead to the home of J. D. Whitmer, son of Book of Mormon plates witness, John Whitmer.[75] Anderson himself rode half way with the mailman and then "walked the balance and by keeping on the grass got along very well." Upon his arrival Anderson found his "instruments reached Mr. Whitmers just a few moments before" he did. The Whitmer family (husband, wife, and son) "made it very pleasant showed them the views I had along and talked about Utahs Worlds fair Chicago, our church, the Reorganized church."[76]

The Whitmers lived near the site of the Mormon settlement of Far West. The city of Far West as known by Joseph Smith and the early Saints was all but gone when Anderson reached the site on 16 May 1907. He noted that only a few of the original Mormon buildings remained standing. He also mentioned a new structure. "Just southwest and across the street from Temple Block," he

wrote, "is the Re-organized Church dedicated 18th November 1906." RLDS Church President Joseph Smith III and his son Frederick M. spoke in a meeting attended by Anderson while in Far West.[77]

Anderson's journals demonstrate his keen interest in details of church history and are surprisingly free of entries dealing with the specifics of the photographic process or the techniques he used. In Far West, Anderson took particular note on how the community looked during the Mormon period. He noted, "John Whitmer's Hotel [was] just southwest of Temple, see old barn [and] Joseph Smith's home southwest of Temple 60 rods."[78] During his stay Anderson stayed up late "washing negs" and "reading history of Caldwell" county.[79]

Anderson traveled to Kingston, some seven miles east of Far West. Here he again was welcomed by strangers. "Supper and bed a Mr. Andrew Jackson Smith, Reorganized." Anderson's purpose for this visit was to obtain views of the cemetery where John Whitmer was buried.[80] On the following day, Anderson wrote to his wife Olive as he waited for the mailman to deliver his equipment.[81] On the next day he noted, "I remain bored." Without his instruments, Anderson continued to be frustrated.[82] He eventually made the walk back to Far West and found his photographic equipment. Anderson attended an RLDS Sunday School meeting which he enjoyed. "I suggested that a picture be made," he noted, "all grouped on the north side of the building after school." In the evening Mr. Whitmer took Anderson back to Kingston to make his view of John Whitmer's tombstone.[83]

Early in the morning on Monday, Anderson arose at 5:00 a.m. "Bid goodby to Whitmers...and asked the Lord to bless them." He made his way to Cameron, "a thriving town. Largest I have seen since Richmond."[84] From there he proceeded to

Gallatin and then attempted to find a ride to the abandoned Mormon settlement of Adam-ondi-Ahman.

Counting every penny, Anderson's gratitude was real for the generosity and hospitality he encountered. As an example of his limited budget, from Gallatin, he "tried to find someone going to Adam-ondi-Ahman. Everyone wished $1.50 so concluded to walk and carry instruments." Following his arrival he "made negatives of Lyman Wight's house also the old site of Adam-ondi-Ahman." Like many other church historical sites in Missouri, Anderson noted, "Nothing now left to mark the place, but excavations and foundations."[85]

While in Gallatin, Anderson witnessed a historical event and captured the ceremony in print. "At 11 o'clock the corner stone of the court house was laid by Ex Gov. Duckery. I made several pictures of building or NE corner of its crowd and procession. 100s of buggy & people came in from the surrounding towns. The railroads brought many."[86] Again, a local photographer, Mr. Schultz "allowed me to change plates in his dark room, also sold me some 8 X 10 [inch] plates."[87] When finished, Anderson was again on his way searching for another important Mormon historical site. At the next stop, he "found supper and bed at Mr. Myers 2 or 3 blocks north of depot. Breakfast, 2 glasses of butter milk, dinner bowl soup & crackers and piece of pie. A good supper at Myers, wrote some in journal and to bed before 9 o'clock."[88]

Anderson arrived at Haun's Mill, a former Mormon settlement near Far West, the next morning on 22 May 1907. Haun's Mill was the site of the Tuesday, 30 October 1838, massacre of eighteen Mormons by a group of Missouri militia. Anderson made several "beautiful views of Haun's Mill country from [Mr. Blair's home on a rise]."[89] On the following day, he noted, "At Haun's Mill

crossed the creek and located left of the old mill, stones which we worked out of the ground and down to the edge of the creek. Made two or three negatives of it, putting an inscription on one side. Mr. Parker H. Elmer, Levi Nichols, furnished the paint and brush."[90]

With help, Anderson cleared some trees with an ax which obstructed "the view of mill, creek etc." After finishing his work at the historical site, Anderson "changed plates in Mr. H. E. Parker cellar" in the evening. The kindness of Mr. Parker included the use of the basement as a make-shift darkroom and a warm dinner with the family.[91]

As Anderson finished his work in Missouri, he encountered one last setback to his work. "I spent a miserable night," he noted in his journal on 24 May, "tossing and rolling about fever and wild dreams up a number of times." Anderson continued:

I did not eat breakfast or dinner, a few blackberries for supper. Hot water bowells kept me moving often during the day. Slept a good deal of the time, did not think it wise to try to go for I felt weak....Took hot water also a bath an felt some better, the sleep and rest done me good.[92]

George Edward Anderson overcame the obstacles he encountered as he traveled from the familiar valleys of his Utah home to his mission field in Great Britian. The arduous and difficult travel, sometimes without the funds to make the trip easier; a lack of sleep, food, shelter, and photographic supplies on occasions; sickness and weather conditions that made taking appropriate views nearly impossible, and a population so diverse from the homogenous society of Springville, Utah, were among the challenges he experienced.

Anderson's journal also demonstrates his concerns for family at home, an apprehension for getting the time to complete his work before church leaders, friends, and family members back home got too concerned about his delay in reaching his English mission assignment. Despite all the troubles and setbacks he experienced in Missouri, his personal writings also reveal the unexpected help and friendship he received from local professional photographers, old timers—once former enemies of the Saints and their children; and more significantly, the members of the RLDS faith.

At a period when LDS and RLDS relations were not as positive as they now are, Anderson found a common ground of faith, belief, and a concern for preserving the past of a common heritage. Anderson, probably in somewhat of a different situation than other LDS missionaries laboring in the Central States Mission, was almost out of necessity forced to reach out to the non-Mormon community, including families of former antagonists of the church and RLDS Church members in his efforts to document the early history of the church. As he sought them out to find information or help in identifying certain locations, they extended themselves. Not only as they offered insights to the Mormon past in Missouri but in opening their homes and hospitality to this missionary. They shared in some respects his goal of capturing the past—not only of the place but also of the spirit of a time when mistrust and misunderstanding guided the events of history. Now they, along with George Edward Anderson, were willing to go beyond past difficulties and forge new relationships based on mutual respect. It is certain that Anderson's personal feelings and ideas about Missouri and those that made it their home in 1907, shifted in many respects as he came into contact with them during the months of April and May 1907.

Anderson fervently felt that it was a miracle that photography, with its unique documentary value, originated during the same general period as Mormonism itself. He saw himself in a tradition of recorders of sacred history, carefully inscribing long entries in his journal about the historical significance of his views and detailed background information gleaned from several sources. In one exceptionally long journal entry he quoted extensively from *An Illustrated Atlas of Caldwell County, Missouri* published in 1876. As he discussed his work in Caldwell County, he included page references to particular quotes.[93] As he moved from one historical site to the next, Anderson continued to feel that he "should have more time to get views of the important points in Church History."[94] Anderson often sent copies of his historical notes and photographs to Andrew Jenson, the LDS assistant historian, who himself had traversed these sites nearly twenty years earlier.

For Anderson, the incredible capacity of this modern miracle to record the reality of life with factual precision characterized photography and separated it from all other media. Furthermore, prints from his plate negatives of Mormon historical sites in Missouri could be enlarged with fidelity and then endlessly duplicated or preserved in publications. Thus, from Joseph Smith's gold plates to his own glass plates, George Edward Anderson undoubtedly found a continuum and a focus for his 1907 photographic mission to Missouri.

The full-page pro-Mormon article, illustrated with Anderson's views and printed in the 10 May 1908 issue of the *Boston Sunday Globe*, gave this testimony concerning Anderson's pictures:

Recently a photographer from Utah spent several weeks...making pictures of scenes connected with the life of Joseph Smith to be used in a history. He had been away from home more than a year, picturing the scenes connected with the life of the prophet.... These views will make a record in photography to be handed down through generation after generation of Mormon believers, as the illuminated pictures of the pious monks were handed down in the earlier days of Christianity.[95]

George Edward Anderson died on 9 May 1928 of complications from heart disease in Arizona where he was documenting the LDS Mesa Temple dedication. Like many of the early Saints, Anderson felt an urge to record history; but unlike the diaries, letters, and reminiscences written by others, Anderson chose the unique medium of photography to record the history of the Restoration. George Edward Anderson, a village photographer from Utah, should be remembered as an important chronicler of Missouri Mormon history by the members of the LDS and RLDS traditions and those friends who do not share our common heritage.[96]

Notes

1. Joseph Fielding Smith, Jr., was born on 19 July 1876 in Salt Lake City, Utah, to Joseph F. Smith, the son of Hyrum Smith. Joseph Fielding Smith was ordained an LDS apostle on 7 April 1910 and later was ordained as the church's tenth president on 23 January 1970. Junius Wells, son of non-Mormon Nauvoo Justice of the Peace Daniel H. Wells (later joined the church), born on 1 June 1854 in Salt Lake City, Utah, and was the founder and former editor of the LDS periodical, *Contributor*, and was responsible for erecting a cottage and a thirty-eight-foot-tall granite memorial to the memory of Joseph Smith in Sharon, Vermont, in 1905. Wells died in 1930. George Edward Anderson was born on 20 October 1860 in Salt Lake City, Utah. He learned the art of photography from Charles R. Savage, one of the most famous photographers in Salt Lake City and the West during the latter half of the nineteenth century, when he obtained a job at Savage's Pioneer Art Bazaar. At the age of seventeen, Anderson began his own business as a photographer; the biographical information contained in the endnotes was obtained through several sources, including RLDS Church Membership Records, courtesy of Ronald E. Romig, RLDS archivist, Library-Archives, Reorganized Church of Jesus Christ of Latter Day Saints, Independence, Missouri; Susan Easton Black, comp. *Membership of the Church of Jesus Christ of Latter-day Saints*, 50 vols. (Provo, Utah: BYU Religious Studies Center, 1989); Andrew Jensen, *Latter-day Saint Biographical Encyclopedia*, 4 vols. (Salt Lake City, Utah: Andrew Jenson History Company, 1901–1936); Lyndon Cook, *The Revelations of the Prophet Joseph Smith: A Historical and Biographical Commentary of the Doctrine and Covenants* (Salt Lake City, Utah: Deseret Books, 1985); and the LDS Church Eastern States Mission Record, Archive Division, Church Historical Department, The Church of Jesus Christ of Latter-day Saints, Salt Lake City, Utah.

2. Junius F. Wells to Elder Joseph Fielding Smith, LDS Church historian (16 October 1928), Archives Division, Church Historical Department, The Church of Jesus Christ of Latter-day Saints, Salt Lake City, Utah; hereafter cited as LDS Church Archives. All material from LDS Church Archives is used with permission.

3. Olive Lowry Anderson was born on 1 September 1862 and married Anderson on 30 May 1888 in Manti, Utah.

4. The process of permanently fixing an image to a metal plate was perfected by French painter Louis Jacques Mandé Daguerre. Daguerre, an amateur scientist as well as an artist, had revealed the secrets of his remarkable process a month earlier in the 19 August meeting of the French Academy of Sciences.

5. Journal of George Edward Anderson (20 April 1907), LDS Church Archives; Brother Thornburg appears to be Walter W. Thornburgh born 12 November 1871 and a member of the LDS Church Springville Second Ward (congregation) in Springville, Utah. Joseph Jones appears to be the son of Elijah and Margaret Jones born on 18 May 1854 and a member of the LDS Church Price, Utah, Ward in 1907.

6. She appears to have had some partnership interest in the business with her father and another Springville gentleman. The cannery began business in 1905, but eventually proved unprofitable and closed its doors in 1919.

7. George Edward arranged for another photographer to rent his studio, the Art Bazaar, in an effort to help Olive and the family with a monthly

income, but within a year of his departure the new studio was rented out to a furniture store as the steady income never materialized. On 22 October 1908 Olive sold another property to secure badly needed funds for the family.

8. William C. Spence was born on 3 December 1851 in England and emigrated to Utah in 1864 and became the transportation agent for the church in 1881.

9. Anderson Journal (26 April 1907).

10. George Albert Smith was born on 4 April 1870. He was the son of LDS Church Apostle John Henry Smith who was the grandson of John Smith, brother of Joseph Smith, Sr. George Albert became a member of the LDS Church's Council of Twelve Apostles on 8 October 1903, later he became president of the LDS Church on 21 May 1945.

11. Anderson Journal (29 June 1907).

12. Anderson's photographic apparatus and processing methods were typical of the period. His view cameras, equipped with rapid rectilinear lenses, were various sizes up to 14 by 17 inches. At his death, a bulky collection of glass plates, of various sizes up to 14 by 17 inches, weighing between three and four tons had been accumulated. Only as recently as 1991 an old wooden crate containing dozens of Anderson's glass plates was discovered in an abandoned garage. How many views Anderson made during his lifetime will never be known.

13. Anderson Journal (13 and 17 August 1907).

14. Reed Smoot was born on 10 January 1862. He became a members of the LDS Church Council of Twelve Apostles on 8 April 1900 and was elected to the United States Senate, representing the state of Utah, in 1903. In January 1904 the Senate Committee on Privileges and Elections began a long investigation regarding Smoot's seating; eventually in 1907 he took his seat in Washington, D.C.

15. John Henry Evans, *The Birth of Mormonism in Pictures: Scenes and Incidents in Early Church History* (Salt Lake City, Utah: Deseret Sunday School Union, 1909). John Henry Evans was born on 8 April 1872 and was an instructor at the Latter-day Saints' University in Salt Lake City and also wrote several biographies on LDS leaders, including *Joseph Smith, an American Prophet* published by MacMillan and Company in 1933.

16. Anderson Journal (25 April 1907).

17. A significant interpretation of Mormon pilgrimages to former historical sites in a broader religious and American setting is Paul Anderson, "Heroic Nostalgia: Enshrining the Mormon Past," *Sunstone* 5 (July-August 1980): 47–55.

18. See the Book of Mormon (Palmyra: E. B. Grandin, 1830), 497, 501, and 566–567. The same information will be found in LDS 1981 Book of Mormon in 3 Nephi 20:22 and 21:22–25 and Ether 13:3–8; also in 1966 RLDS Book of Mormon Ether 6:3–8.

19. *Times and Seasons* (5 February 1844). This revelation is printed in LDS/RLDS Doctrine and Covenants 57; see 57:1.

20. James Hendricks was born on 23 June 1808 in Kentucky and died in Richmond, Utah, on 8 July 1870. Drusilla Dorris Hendricks was born on 8 February 1810 and married 31 May 1827 and died on 20 May 1881 in Richmond, Utah.

21. Drusilla Hendricks, "Reminiscences of Drusilla Hendricks," LDS Church Archives; a published version is Kenneth W. Godfrey, Audrey M. Godrey, and Jill Mulvay Derr, *Women's Voices: An Untold History of the Latter-day Saints, 1830–1900* (Salt Lake City, Utah: Deseret Books, 1982), 85.

22. Quoted in Leland H. Gentry, "A History of the Latter-day Saints in Northern Missouri From 1836 to 1839" (Ph.D. dissertation, Brigham Young University, 1965), 532. Lyman Wight was born on 9 May 1796 in New York. In 1841 he was chosen by Joseph Smith to be a member of the Council of Twelve Apostles, filling the vacancy caused by the death of David Patten at the battle of Crooked River in 1838. Wight later separated himself from the church and established a Mormon colony in Texas where he died on 31 March 1858. Several of his descendants later united with the RLDS Church.

23. Ibid.

24. Parley P. Pratt, *Late Persecution of the Church of Jesus Christ* (New York: J. W. Harrison, 1840), 93. Parley Parker Pratt was born on 12 April 1807 in New York and was ordained a member of the first Council of Twelve Apostles on 21 February 1835. Eventually murdered in 1857 in Arkansas.

25. Henry (1824) and Hannah (1826) were born in Germany and baptized into the RLDS Church in Hixville, Sacramento County, California, in 1864.

26. E. C. Brand letter (17 May 1873) to *Saints' Herald* 20 (15 June 1873): 394.

27. "The Beginnings of Independence," *Saints' Herald* 83 (4 August 1936): 969.

28. See Richard L. Jenson and Richard G. Oman, *C. C. A. Christensen 1831–1912: Mormon Emi-*

grant Artist (Salt Lake City, Utah: The Church of Jesus Christ of Latter-day Saints, 1984).

29. A collection of Restoration-related photographs of Missouri is Richard Neitzel Holzapfel and T. Jeffery Cottle, *Old Mormon Kirtland and Missouri: Historic Photographs and Guide* (Santa Ana, California: Fieldbrook Productions, Inc., 1991); RLDS Church member, Elbert A. Smith, was active photographing important individuals and scenes of RLDS interest at the turn of the century. Frederick M. Smith shot photographs throughout his lifetime—the earliest are during his youth at Lamoni, Iowa; RLDS Church archivist Ronald Romig to Richard Neitzel Holzapfel (22 October 1992), in authors' possession.

30. Orson Pratt, brother of Parley P. Pratt, was born on 19 September 1811 in New York. Ordained an apostle on 26 April 1835 and died on 3 October 1881 in Salt Lake City, Utah. Joseph Fielding Smith, known as Joseph F. Smith, was the grandson of Joseph Smith, Sr. He was born on 13 November 1838 in Far West, Missouri, just before the Saints' exodus. He became a member of the LDS Church Council of Twelve Apostles on 8 October 1867 and eventually became church president on 17 October 1901. David Whitmer was born on 7 January 1805 in Pennsylvania. David was an early supporter of Joseph Smith and became one of the Three Witnesses to the Book of Mormon in 1829. Following his separation from the church in 1838, he eventually settled in Richmond, Missouri, where he died in 1888.

31. *Deseret News* (16 November 1878).

32. Quoted in Joseph Fielding Smith, comp., *Life of Joseph F. Smith: Sixth President of the Church of Jesus Christ of Latter-day Saints* (Salt Lake City, Utah: The Deseret News Press, 1938), 246.

33. Andrew Jenson was born on 11 December 1850 in Denmark. Following his emigration to Utah, he became the assistant LDS Church historian in 1898. Jenson died in 1938 following the compilation and publication of various types of history relating to the LDS Church.

34. Quoted in Andrew Jenson, *Autobiography of Andrew Jenson: Assistant Historian of the Church of Jesus Christ of Latter-day Saints* (Salt Lake City, Utah: The Deseret News Press, 1938), 164. The local photographer was James T. Hicks of Liberty, Missouri.

35. Ibid., 184.

36. A recent study of Underwood and Underwood's effort to photograph Mormon historical sites is Richard Neitzel Holzapfel, "Stereographs and Stereotypes: A 1904 View of Mormonism," *Journal of Mormon History* 18 (Fall 1992): 155–176.

37. Anderson Journal (23 April 1907).

38. Ibid. (23 April 1907). Samuel O. Bennion was born on 9 June 1874, later he was ordained to the LDS Church First Council of Seventy. Bennion arrived in Kansas City, Missouri, on 12 November 1904 to begin his missionary work. In 1906 he was appointed mission president and was released nearly thirty years later in 1934.

39. As Paul Anderson pointed out so adeptly to a group of historians visiting the Palymra, New York, area during an MHA annual meeting in 1980, "Like pilgrims of all ages, we travel to a far country to feel ourselves at home....We come yearning to touch with our hands and to possess with our memories a part of our heritage and history and faith that we have already owned all our lives in our imaginations." Cited in "Historic Nostalgia," *Sunstone*, 48.

40. Anderson Journal (24 April 1907). Elder Harris appears to be Elder George V. Harris from Salem, Idaho. He arrived in the Central States Mission on Friday, 22 February 1907. He was transferred to Independence in April 1907 and was assigned to labor at the *Liahona* office. Later he served as the president of the Independence Conference (LDS Church ecclesiastical area).

41. Ibid.

42. Ibid.

43. Albert Thatcher was born on 13 July 1855 in Friedsville, Wabash, Illinois. Baptized on 6 May 1881 at Stewartsville, Missouri, and removed to the Independence Branch on 7 November 1906; "General Membership Records, Stewartsville Branch, Book E, page 244," RLDS Library-Archives. Thatcher lived at 117 Bowen Avenue at the junction of the "Rock Island," Anderson Journal (26 April 1907).

44. Ibid. (26 April 1907).

45. Ibid.

46. Anderson was interested in the RLDS movement. On several occasions he had long discussions about the RLDS Church and attended some of their meetings; see Anderson Journal (26–27 April 1907).

47. Ibid. (24 April 1907).

48. Ibid. He also helped mail out the *Liahona* on another occasion; see 25 April entry.

49. Ibid. (29 April 1907); Elder George V. Harris, from Salem, Fremont County, Idaho, was serving an LDS proselyting mission in the Central States Mission at the time.

50. Ibid. (25–26, 29–30 April 1907).

51. Ibid. (30 April 1907).
52. Ibid. (1 May 1907).
53. Ibid. (8 May 1907).
54. Ibid. (9 May 1907).
55. Jacob Whitmer was born on 27 January 1800 in Pennsylvania and became a witness to the Book of Mormon plates when he was twenty-nine years of age. He died on 21 April 1856 in Richmond, Missouri.
56. Peter Whitmer, Sr., was born on 14 April 1773 in Pennsylvania. Following the 1838 crisis, he remained in Missouri and died in Richmond, Ray County, Missouri, on 12 August 1854. Mary Musselman Whitmer was born on 27 August 1778 and died shortly after her husband in 1856.
57. Anderson Journal (10 May 1907).
58. Ibid. Anderson was fascinated with Oliver Cowdery and David Whitmer's deathbed testimonies and recorded in detail interviews he had with those present on the occasions.
59. Ibid. (12 May 1907).
60. Ibid.
61. Ibid.
62. Ibid.
63. Ibid. (13 May 1907). Morris Phelps was born on 20 December 1805 in Massachusetts and died in 1876.
64. Ibid. (13 May 1907).
65. Ibid.
66. Ibid.
67. Ibid.
68. Ibid. David W. Patten was born on 17 November 1799 in New York. A member of the original Council of Twelve Apostles, he was ordained on 15 February 1835. He died on 25 October 1838 from a mortal wound as he led Mormon militiamen at the battle of Crooked River and was buried at Far West two days later on 27 October.
69. Ibid. (14 May 1907).
70. Ibid.
71. Ibid.
72. Ibid. (15 May 1907). Edward Stevenson was born on 1 May 1830. He was a member of the LDS Church First Council of Seventy when he died in 1897. Joseph S. Black was born on 14 July 1836 in Ireland. An LDS bishop in Utah, he died on 13 August 1910.
73. Ibid.
74. Ibid.
75. Ibid. John Whitmer was born on 27 August 1802 in Pennsylvania. At twenty-six years of age he became one of the Eight Witnesses of the Book of Mormon plates. Whitmer died on 11 July 1878 at Far West, Missouri.
76. Ibid.
77. Ibid. (16 May 1907).
78. Ibid.
79. Ibid.
80. Ibid. (17 May 1907). Andrew Jackson Smith was born on 14 October 1849 in Benton Township, Missouri, and baptized on 11 June 1887 in Shobe, Bates County, Missouri—south of Independence.
81. Ibid. (18 May 1907).
82. Ibid. (19 May 1907).
83. Ibid.
84. Ibid. (20 May 1907).
85. Ibid.
86. Ibid. (21 May 1907).
87. Ibid.
88. Ibid.
89. Ibid. (22 May 1907).
90. Ibid. (23 May 1907).
91. Ibid.
92. Ibid. (23 May 1907).
93. Ibid. (16 May 1907).
94. Ibid. (26 April 1907).
95. *Boston Sunday Globe* (10 May 1908).
96. Three important published works deal with aspects of Anderson's life and work: Rell G. Francis, *The Utah Photographs of George Edward Anderson* (Lincoln, Nebraska: University of Nebraska Press, 1979); Douglas S. Tobler and Nelson B. Wadsworth, *The History of the Mormons in Photographs and Text: 1832 to the Present* (New York: St. Martin Press, 1989); and Nelson Wadsworth, *Through Camera Eyes* (Provo, Utah: Brigham Young University Press, 1975).

Appendix

While Anderson's photograph collection was divided following his death in 1928, most of the views taken during the 1907 trip to Missouri are located in the LDS Church Archives in Salt Lake City, Utah, along with many of his other LDS Church history photographs. The following represents their numbered catalog list of Anderson Missouri photographs taken during his seven-year "mission" to document Mormon historical sites (we have corrected item, description, and date information when necessary).

No.	Item and Description	Date
69	Far West (Joseph Smith Home Site)	16 May 1907
70	Caldwell County (Haun's Mill Site)	23 May 1907
71	Far West (Temple Site)	16 May 1907
72	Independence (*Examiner* Building)	25 April 1907
73	Richmond (Three Witnesses Monument)	22 November 1911
74	Richmond (Three Witnesses Monument)	22 November 1911
75	Richmond (Three Witnesses Monument)	22 November 1911
76	Crooked River Battleground	15 May 1907
77	Independence (LDS Central States Mission Home)	26 April 1907
78	Independence (Temple Lot Site)	26 April 1907
79	Independence (Temple Lot Site)	26 April 1907
80	Independence (Temple Lot Site)	26 April 1907
81	Independence (Temple Lot Site)	26 April 1907
82	Independence (Temple Lot Site)	26 April 1907
83	Independence (LDS Central States Mission Home)	unknown
84	Caldwell County (H. E. Parker Home)	unknown
85	Independence (LDS Central States Mission Home)	26 April 1907
86	Independence (South Pleasant Street)	27 April 1907
87	Independence (LDS *Liahona* Office)	27 April 1907
88	Richmond (Panoramic)	10 May 1907
89	Kingston (Farm and rural setting)	1907
90	Far West (RLDS Church Building)	19 May 1907
91	Independence (Temple Lot Site)	26 April 1907
92	Independence (Temple Lot Site)	26 April 1907
93	Big Blue River (5 miles east of Kansas City)	09 May 1907
94	Crooked River Battleground	15 May 1907
95	Adam-ondi-Ahman (Lyman Wight Home)	20 May 1907
96	Adam-ondi-Ahman (Lyman Wight Home)	20 May 1907
97	Adam-ondi-Ahman	11 May 1907
98	Richmond (Three Witnesses Monument)	1911
99	Richmond Cemetery (Whitmer/Tanner Graves)	1911
100	Richmond (Cemetery before Monument)	unknown
101	Richmond (Home where Oliver Cowdery died)	May 1907
102	Richmond (David Whitmer Home)	unknown
103	Richmond (Three Witnesses Monument)	1911
104	Richmond (Three Witnesses Monument)	1911

105	Richmond (Three Witnesses Monument)	1911
106	Independence (RLDS Stone Church)	unknown
107	Haun's Mill (Haun's Mill Marker)	23 May 1907
108	Independence (Temple Lot Site)	unknown
109	Richmond (Public Square)	1913
110	Richmond (Public Square)	1923
111	Richmond (Three Witnesses Monument)	22 November 1911
112	Barre, Vermont (Three Witnesses Monument being constructed)	10 October 1911
113	John E. Johnson (Grandson J. Whitmer)	unknown
114	Richmond (Scarf belonging to Oliver Cowdery)	unknown
115	Haun's Mill (Haun's Mill Marker)	23 May 1907
116	Richmond (Three Witnesses Monument)	1911
117	Richmond (Train with Mormon Tabernacle Choir)	22 November 1911
118	Richmond (Cemetery)	10 May 1907
119	Kingston (John Whitmer Grave Marker)	19 May 1907
120	Richmond (Cemetery)	21 November 1911
121	Independence (LDS Central States Mission Home)	unknown
122	Independence (Swope Residence on Pleasant Street)	unknown
123	Richmond (Three Witnesses Monument)	21 November 1911
124	Adam-ondi-Ahman	20 May 1907
125	Richmond (Three Witnesses Monument)	20 November 1911
126	Richmond (David Whitmer's Home)	1911
127	Richmond (David Whitmer's Grave Marker)	unknown
128	Richmond (Cemetery/Whitmer graves)	unknown
129	Richmond (Jacob Whitmer's Grave Marker)	unknown
130	Richmond (Julia W. and George Schweich)	28 November 1911

Looking northeast onto the Temple Lot (Stone Church in the background), Independence, Jackson County, Missouri. The Temple Lot was a sixty-three acre parcel purchased by Bishop Edward Partridge from Jones Flournoy for $130.00 in December 1831. George Edward Anderson (26 April 1907), Archives Division, Church Historical Department, The Church of Jesus Christ of Latter-day Saints, Salt Lake City, Utah (hereafter cited LDS Church Archives); all photographs from LDS Church Archives are used with permission.

Independence Temple Lot (from the tower of the Stone Church), Independence, Jackson County, Missouri. The Temple Lot was the focus of the hopes and dreams of the Saints, even following the Saints' expulsion from Jackson County (1833) and Missouri (1838). George Edward Anderson (26 April 1907), LDS Church Archives.

Looking southwest along Lexington from the tower of the Stone Church (partial view of the Temple Lot), Independence, Jackson County Missouri. Members of several Restoration groups began to return to Zion in 1866. George Edward Anderson (26 April 1907), LDS Church Archives.

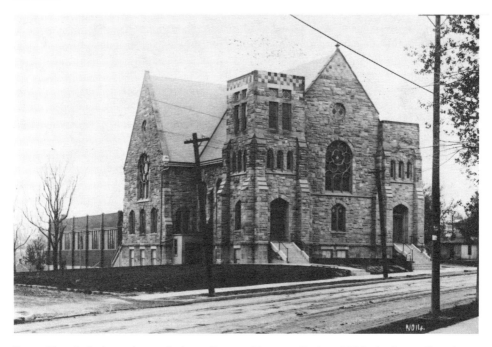

Stone Church, Independence, Jackson County, Missouri. Built in 1888, the Stone Church sits just outside the original Temple Lot. The front west tower served as the foundation for a 150-foot radio antenna which serviced the RLDS Church station KLDS from 1924 until 1937. George Edward Anderson (ca. 1907), LDS Church Archives.

The Swope Residence (400 South Pleasant Street), Independence, Jackson County, Missouri. It was an impressive structure with an elevator to service its three stories built by Logan O. Swope sometime around 1901. The RLDS Church eventually acquired the mansion for its "Independence Institute for Arts and Science." The building was eventually torn down. George Edward Anderson (ca. 1907), LDS Church Archives.

RLDS Sunday School Group, Far West, Caldwell County, Missouri. The RLDS congregation met in several locations in the Far West area from the 1870s until 1906. They have met in this white frame building (in the background) since, located near the Far West Temple site. George Edward Anderson (29 May 1907), LDS Church Archives.

Richmond Cemetery, Richmond, Ray County, Missouri. At the conclusion of the so-called "1838 Mormon War," several prominent Saints remained in the area and were buried in one of two Richmond cemeteries. George Edward Anderson (10 May 1907), LDS Church Archives.

Crooked River Battleground Site, Caldwell County, Missouri. Following several clashes between the Saints and their neighbors, Apostle David W. Patten was shot in the battle known as Crooked River and died October 1838. George Edward Anderson (15 May 1907), LDS Church Archives.

Haun's Mill Site, Caldwell County, Missouri. Jacob Haun built a grist mill on Shoal Creek in 1834. It was the second settlement founded in what would become Caldwell County. Three days after the battle of Crooked River, a renegade Missouri militia unit killed eighteen and wounded another fifteen Saints on 30 October 1838. George Edward Anderson (23 May 1907), LDS Church Archives.

Far West Temple Site, Caldwell County, Missouri. Church leaders founded the community in 1836 and within two years Far West boasted nearly 2,000 farms, 200 homes, and numerous commercial businesses but was abandoned at the conclusion of the 1838 Mormon War. George Edward Anderson (16 May 1907), LDS Church Archives.

Lyman Wight Home, Adam-ondi-Ahman, Daviess County, Missouri. Wight was an early resident of the area and an important church leader and businessman in the new settlement. Located on the Grand River, Adam-ondi-Ahman was a significant Mormon gathering place in Daviess County. George Edward Anderson (20 May 1907), LDS Church Archives.

Notes on Contributors

Andrew Bolton has a B.S. from London University, Ph.D. from the University of Wales, and M.A. in religious leadership from Park College, Parkville, Missouri. Born in England, Andrew is an adult convert to the RLDS Church. He has served as missionary, pastor, teacher, appointee minister, and religious educator for youth in a pluralism of faiths and cultures. At the present time Andrew with his wife, Jewell Holmes, and sons, Matthew and David, are living in an Anabaptist community called Darvell, in Robertsbridge, East Sussex, England.

Donald J. Breckon received his Ph.D. from Michigan State University and taught at Central Michigan University for twenty-four years. He has been serving as president of Park College, Parkville, Missouri, since 1987. Breckon has authored numerous articles and books including an adult study text, *Matters of Life and Death* (Herald House, 1987). He and his wife, Sandy, are parents of four daughters.

Anthony Chvala-Smith is a Ph.D. candidate in religious studies at Marquette University (Milwaukee). His major area of study is scripture. Tony has a B.A. in history from Central Michigan University, with an M.Div. from Princeton Theological Seminary. He also took one year of graduate study in New Testament at the Toronto School of Theology before beginning at Marquette. He and his wife, Charmaine, reside at Clare, Michigan, and are active in the Mt. Pleasant Branch of the RLDS Church.

T. Jeffery Cottle received a B.A. in anthropology from Brigham Young University and a Juris Doctor from Lewis and Clark Law School in Portland, Oregon. Jeff practices law in Orem, Utah, and is a frequent speaker on workers' compensation and so-cial security disability at professional conferences. Jeff is a Scoutmaster in an LDS Church-sponsored troop in Provo, Utah. He has shared with Richard Holzapfel in the publication of several books and articles on Restoration history.

Angela M. Crowell holds an M.A. in religious studies in biblical interpretation from Central Baptist Theological Seminary. She is a participating member of the National Association of Professors of Hebrew (NAPH) and the Society of Biblical Literature (SBL). Her research in biblical Hebrew poetry, biblical Hebrew sentence structure, and ancient Jewish midrash identified in the Book of Mormon has been presented at the regional meetings of SBL. She is the director of Qumran Quest as well as biblical Hebrew instructor and an associate with the Kansas Qumran Project.

Enid Stubbart DeBarthe, M.A., is a former English teacher and librarian who was library consultant for the thirteen-county Learning Resources Center at Red Oak, Iowa, at the time of her retirement in 1972. Her published poems, articles, children's stories, and other contributions to RLDS Church publications cover a span of sixty years. She currently serves with her husband, Joe, in a home, hospital, and nursing-home visiting program and congregational guest ministry. She has been Lamoni Stake historian since 1949. Enid has studied Latin, German, Hebrew, and Greek.

Wayne Ham is Temple Ministries administrator for the RLDS Church. Since 1980 he has served as a World Church appointee in a variety of roles at church headquarters in Independence, Missouri. His academic degrees include a B.A. in liberal arts (religion major) from Graceland College, M.A. in biblical languages from Brigham Young University, M.Div. from St. Paul School of Theology, and Ph.D. from University of Florida in early childhood education.

Richard Neitzel Holzapfel received a B.A. in social sciences from Brigham Young University and an M.A. in history from the University of California (Irvine) and is currently a Ph.D. candidate in history at UCI. Richard is employed with the LDS Church Educational System in Irvine, California, as a coordinator of weekday religious education. Richard has written several Restoration history articles and books with Jeff Cottle.

Henry K. Inouye, Jr., holds a B.A. degree in art and art history from the University of Hawaii and an M.A. in religion from the School of Theology at Claremont. He is a professional artist in both commercial and fine arts. His interest in aesthetics ranges from theory to practice, from theological studies to landscape design and beautification. He is currently involved in research and writing on aesthetics and related topics.

W. Paul Jones is professor of philosophical theology, Saint Paul School of Theology. He received his Ph.D. and M.A. from Yale University Graduate School, an M.Div. from Yale Divinity School, and a B.A. at Mount Union College. He has authored numerous articles and four books: *The Recovery of Life's Meaning: Understanding Creation and the Incarnation* (Association Press), *The Province Beyond the River* (Upper Room Press), *Theological World: Understanding the Alternative Rhythms of Christian Belief* (Abingdon Press), and *Trumpet at Full Moon: An Introduction to Christian Spirituality as Diverse Practice* (John Knox).

Piotr Klafkowski graduated from Adam Mickiewicz University (Pozna, Poland) with an M.A. in English and linguistics and a Ph.D. in linguistics and phonetics. He also studied in Delhi, India, as a government of India research fellow in Buddhist studies and was a research fellow of the Alexander von Humboldt Foundation in Bonn, Germany. In 1979 while he was teaching Tibetan studies at a university in Poland, Klafkowski was forced by Marxist pressure to leave his books, manuscripts, and family behind and escape to Norway. His wife and young son were able to join him there in a few months. Because of the political upheaval in Poland, Klafkowski has been able to return to Poland where he is chair of General and Applied Linguistics at Adam Mickiewicz University.

Roger D. Launius is chief historian for the National Aeronautics and Space Administration in Washington, D.C. His works in Mormon history include articles in several journals and five books: *Let Contention Cease: The Dynamics of Dissent in the Reorganized Church of Jesus Christ of Latter Day Saints*, ed. with Pat Spillman (Graceland/Park Press); *Father Figure: Joseph Smith III and the Creation of the Reorganized Church* (Herald House); *Joseph Smith III: Pragmatic Prophet* (University of Illinois Press); *Invisible Saints: A History of Black Americans in the Reorganized Church* (Herald House); and *Zion's Camp: Expedition to Missouri* (Herald House).

Rita Lester graduated with a B.A. in philosophy and religion from Graceland College and an M.T.S. from Garrett-Evangelical Theological Seminary. Her education focused on process theology, feminist ethics and theology, and French feminism. She is currently involved in Middle East studies. Originally from the Chicago area, Rita works and resides in Lamoni, Iowa.

Keith Norman earned a B.A. in history from Brigham Young University, an M.T.S. from Harvard Divinity School in church history and biblical studies, and a Ph.D. from Duke University in early Christian studies. He has published articles and book reviews in Sunstone, *Dialogue, BYU Studies*, and the *John Whitmer Historical Association Journal*. He and his wife, Kerry, live with their four children in Solon, Ohio, where they are active in the Kirtland LDS Stake.

Gregory Prymak is an appointee minister of the RLDS Church. His current assignment is campus pastor, visiting assistant professor of pre-law, and pre-law advisor at Park College. Before accepting ministerial appointment in 1986, he served as an executive minister and had practiced law in New Hampshire and Massachusetts. He holds a B.A. from the University of Alabama in Birmingham; a J.D. from Boston University; and an M.T.S. from Harvard University.

Ron Romig is church archivist at the RLDS Library-Archives, Independence, Missouri. He holds B.A. and M.A. degrees in elementary education from Graceland College, Lamoni, Iowa, and the University of Akron, Ohio, with special emphasis on social sciences and administration. He was also formerly employed in the field of electronic documentation and has received credit for participation in the National Archives Modern Archives Institute. Ron has authored several articles on early Restoration history. He lives with his wife, Anne, and two children in the Harvest Hills community in Independence.

Rick Sarre is a senior lecturer in law and head of the School of Law at the University of South Australia. He has also taught criminal justice and health care law for Graceland College. He holds an M.A. degree in criminology from the University of Toronto. He serves on the Advisory Council for the Temple Peace Center and the Earth Stewardship Committee.

John H. Siebert holds a B.S.E. in social studies, an M.S.E. in geography, and an Ed.Sp. in higher education. He has an avid interest in church history, especially that occurring in Jackson County, Missouri, and has co-authored several articles on this subject. John is presently manager of video communications, working as an industrial video writer/producer for Black and Veatch Engineering Firm in Kansas City, Missouri.

Kenneth Walker graduated from Central Michigan University with a B.S. in mathematics and an M.A. in economics. He has served the church as executive minister and appointee and presently teaches mathematics at the Indiana Boys' School. He lives just outside Indianapolis with his wife, Valerie, and two children, Laura and Nathan. His family was introduced to the RLDS Church in the early 1900s as a result of the ministry of J. J. Cornish.

Ruth Ann Wood is currently coordinator of the editorial office of the Temple School Center. She was graduated from Graceland College with a B.A. in education, majoring in English. After teaching English and French in public schools, Ruth Ann spent several years doing volunteer work in the community, schools, and church before working at RLDS Church Headquarters.